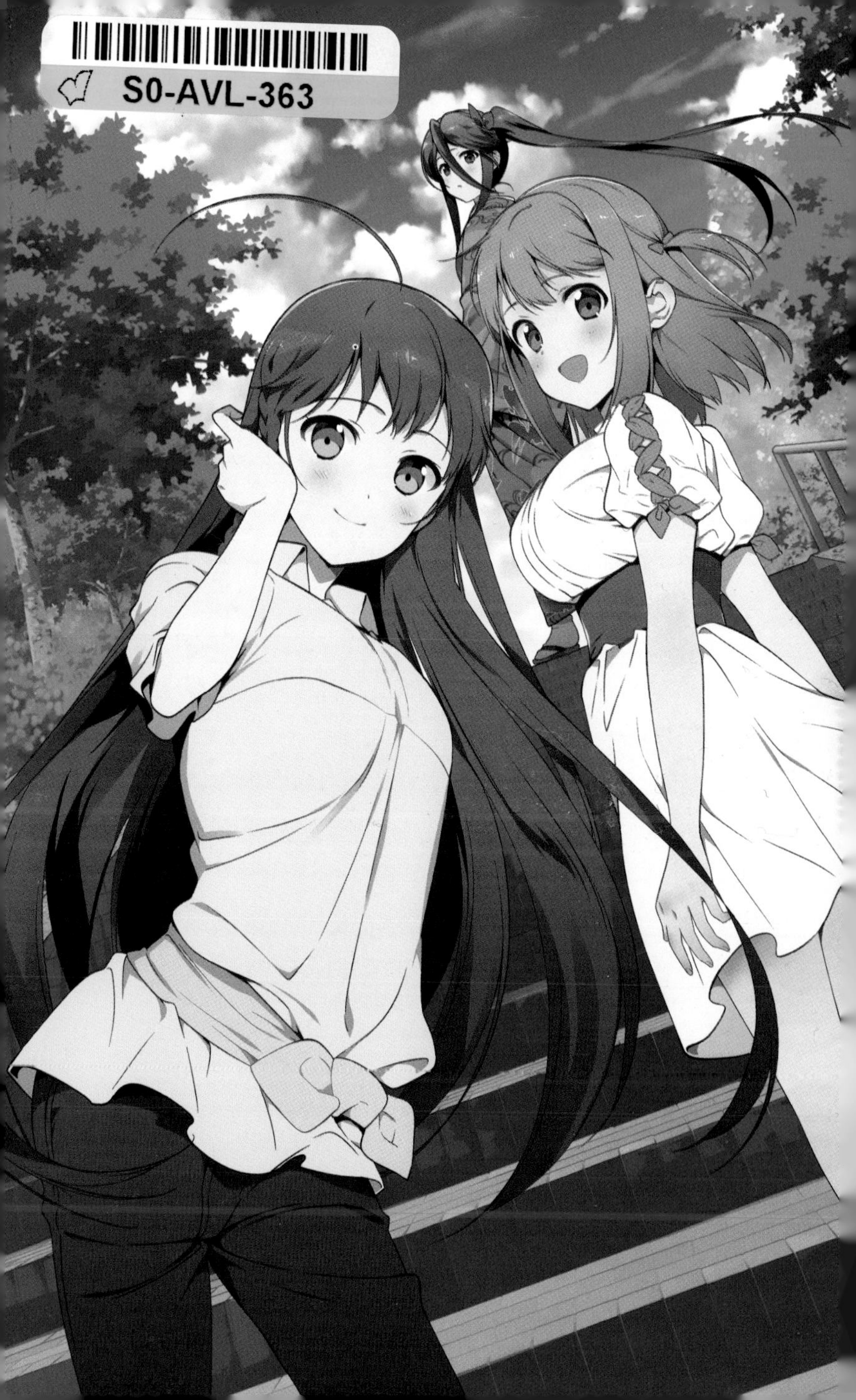

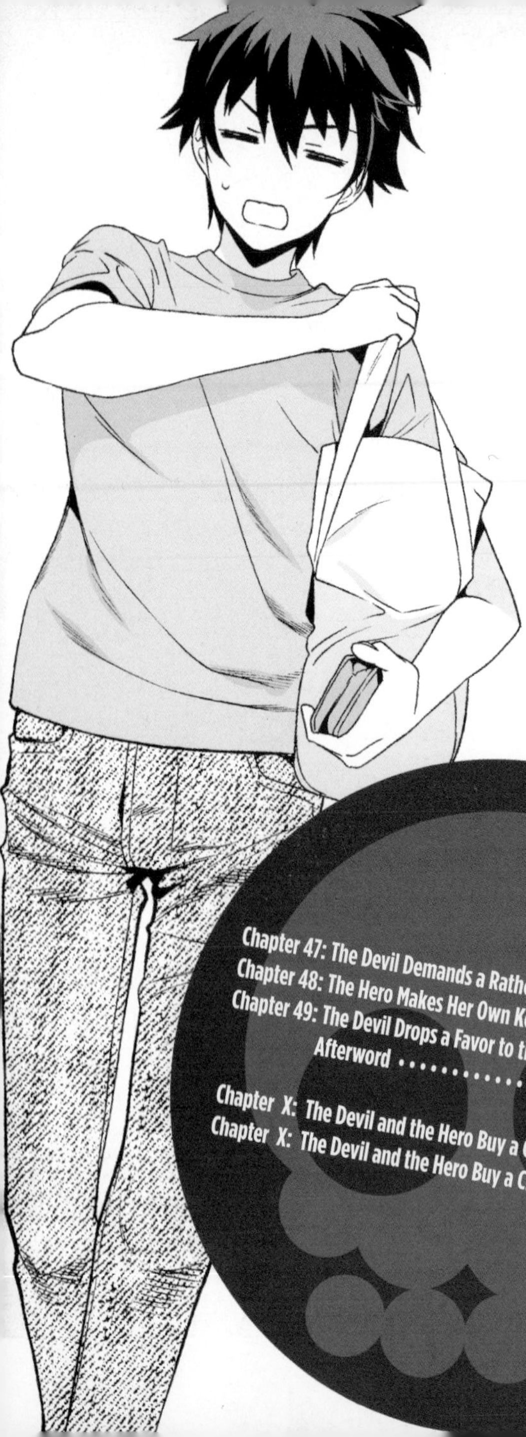

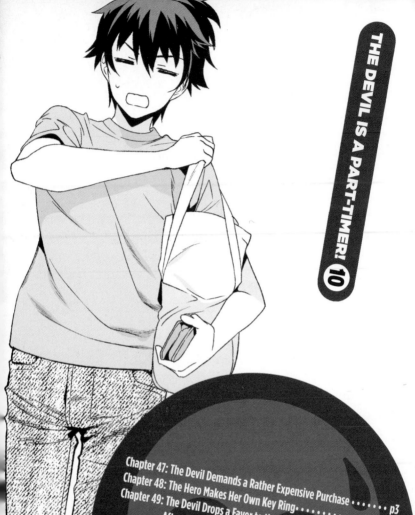

THE DEVIL IS A PART-TIMER! 10

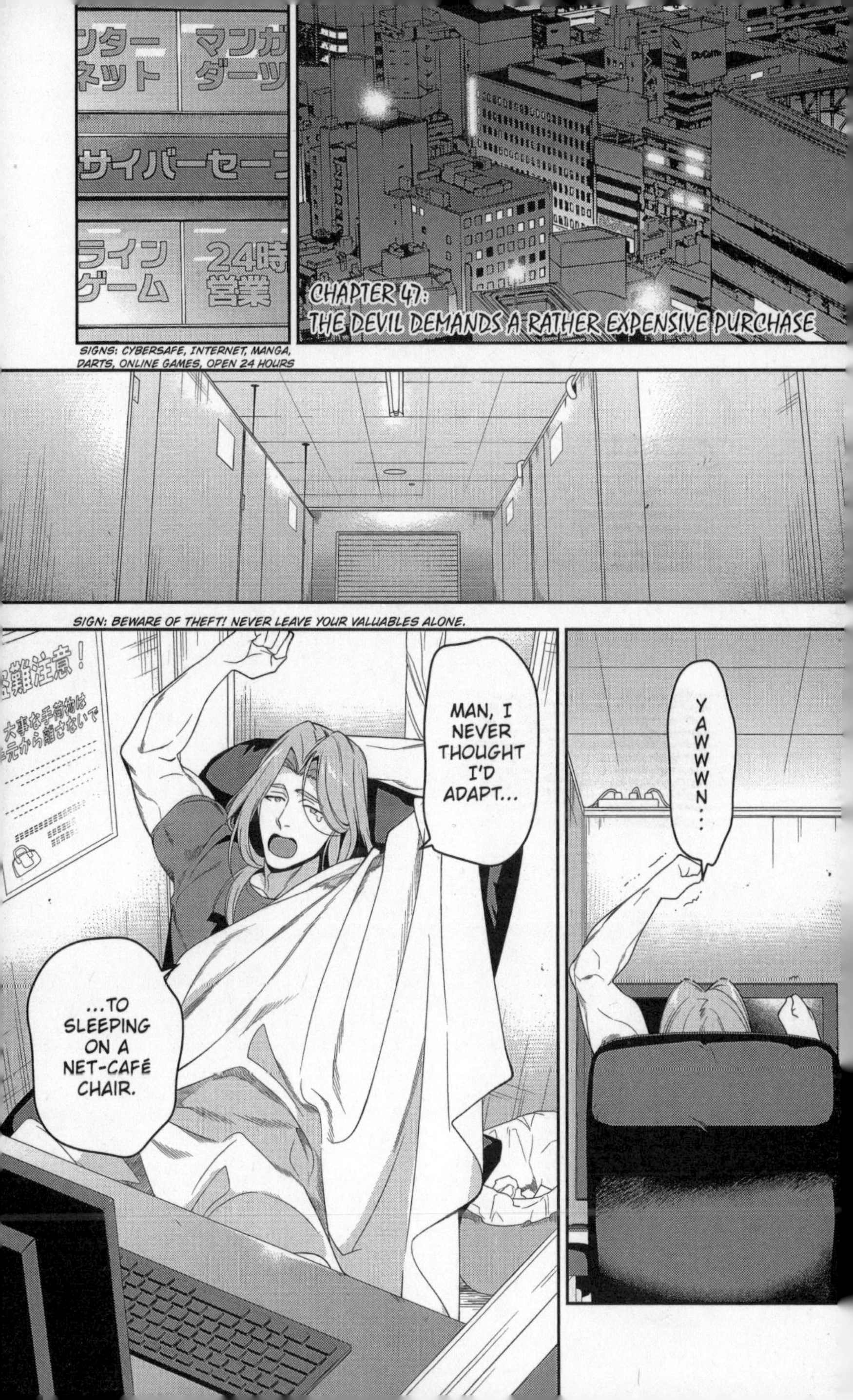
CHAPTER 47:
THE DEVIL DEMANDS A RATHER EXPENSIVE PURCHASE
ンター
ネット
マンガ
ダーツ
サイバーセー
ライン
ゲーム
24時
営業
SIGNS: CYBERSAFE, INTERNET, MANGA, DARTS, ONLINE GAMES, OPEN 24 HOURS
SIGN: BEWARE OF THEFT! NEVER LEAVE YOUR VALUABLES ALONE.
YAWWWN...
難注意！
大事な手荷物は
元から離さないで
MAN, I NEVER THOUGHT I'D ADAPT...
...TO SLEEPING ON A NET-CAFÉ CHAIR.

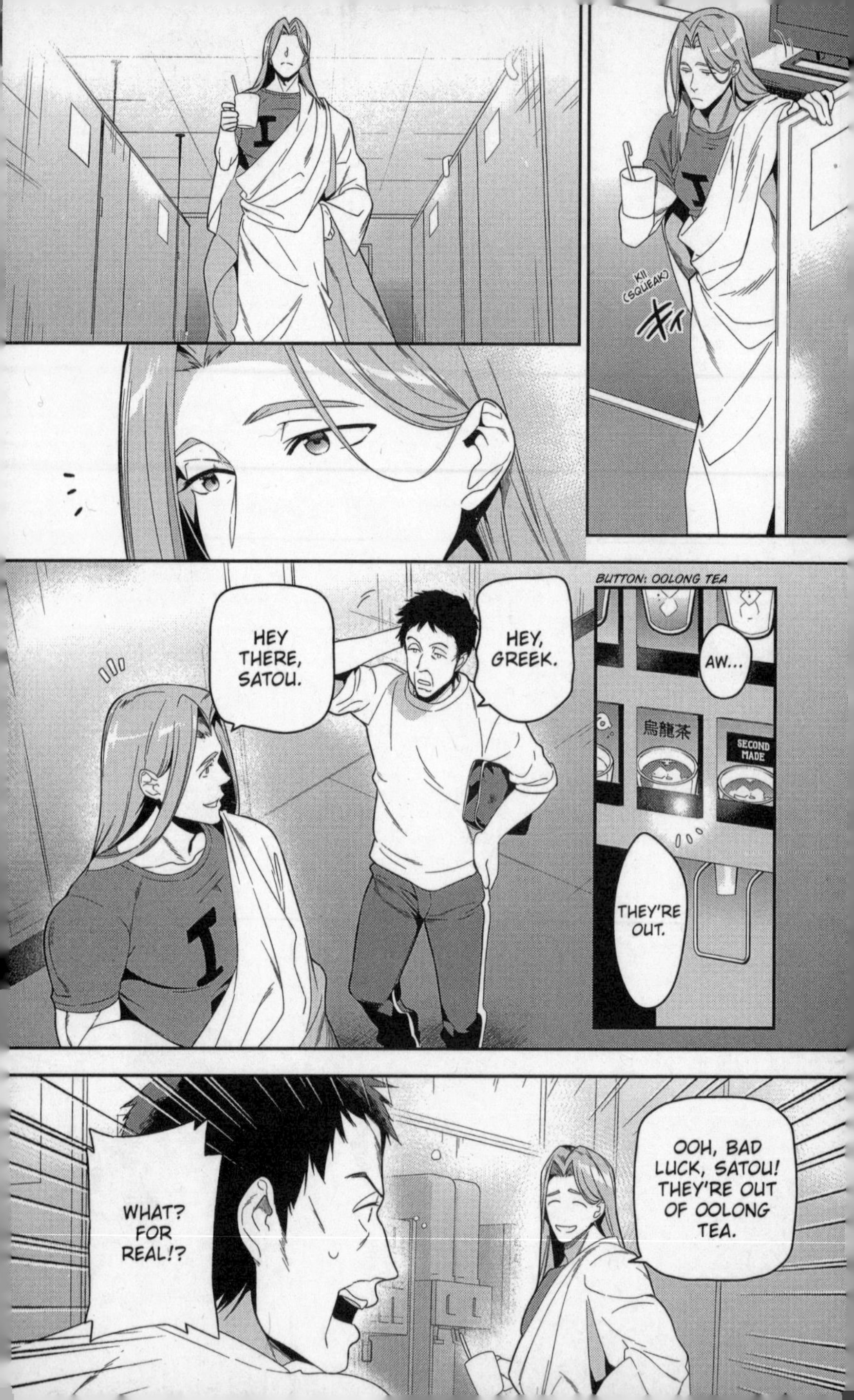
KII (SQUEAK)
キィ
BUTTON: OOLONG TEA
AW...
烏龍茶
SECOND MADE
THEY'RE OUT.
HEY, GREEK.
HEY THERE, SATOU.
OOH, BAD LUCK, SATOU! THEY'RE OUT OF OOLONG TEA.
WHAT? FOR REAL!?

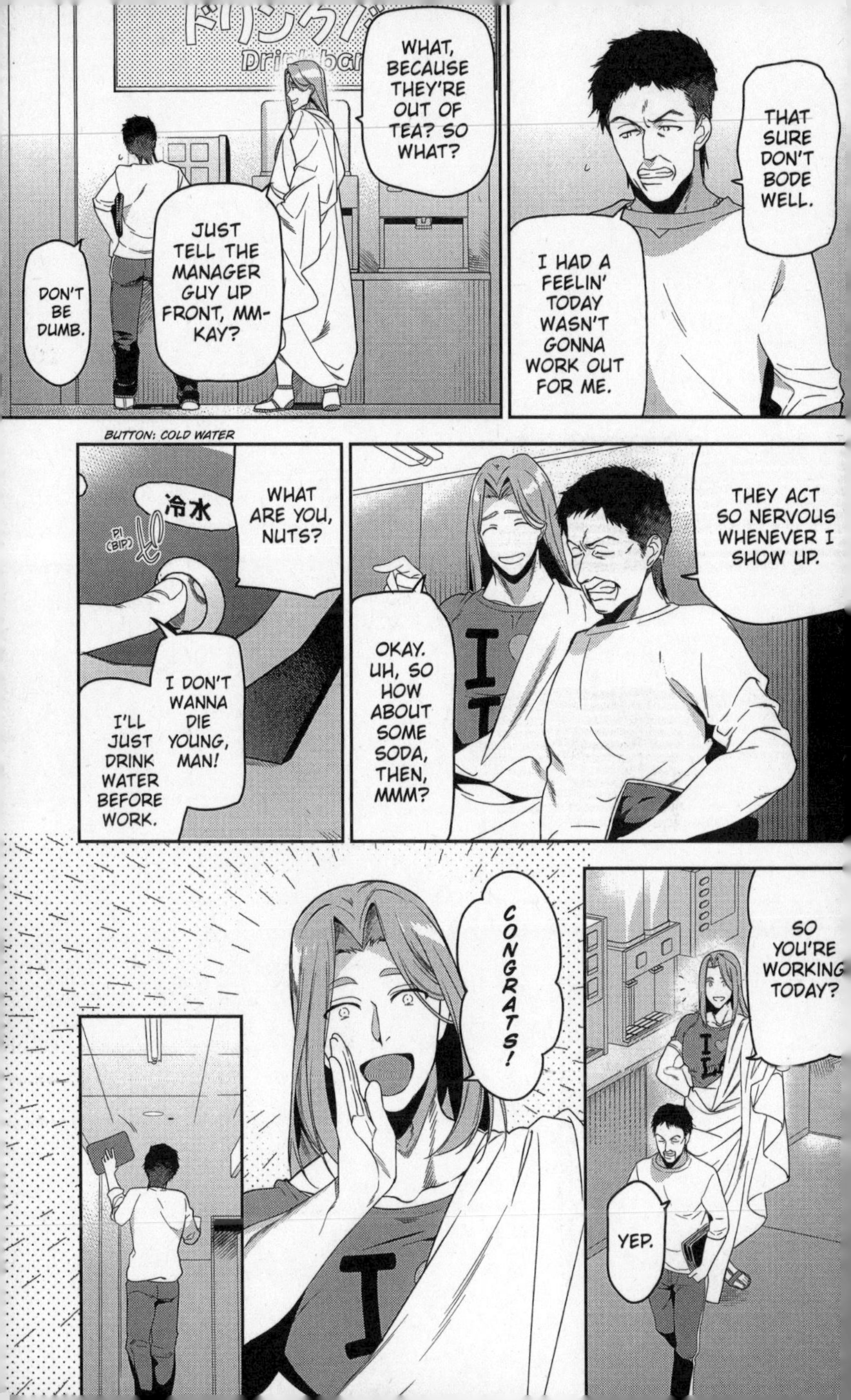

THAT SURE DON'T BODE WELL.
I HAD A FEELIN' TODAY WASN'T GONNA WORK OUT FOR ME.
WHAT, BECAUSE THEY'RE OUT OF TEA? SO WHAT?
JUST TELL THE MANAGER GUY UP FRONT, MM-KAY?
DON'T BE DUMB.
BUTTON: COLD WATER
THEY ACT SO NERVOUS WHENEVER I SHOW UP.
OKAY. UH, SO HOW ABOUT SOME SODA, THEN, MMM?
WHAT ARE YOU, NUTS?
冷水
PI (BIP)
I DON'T WANNA DIE YOUNG, MAN!
I'LL JUST DRINK WATER BEFORE WORK.
SO YOU'RE WORKING TODAY?
YEP.
CONGRATS!

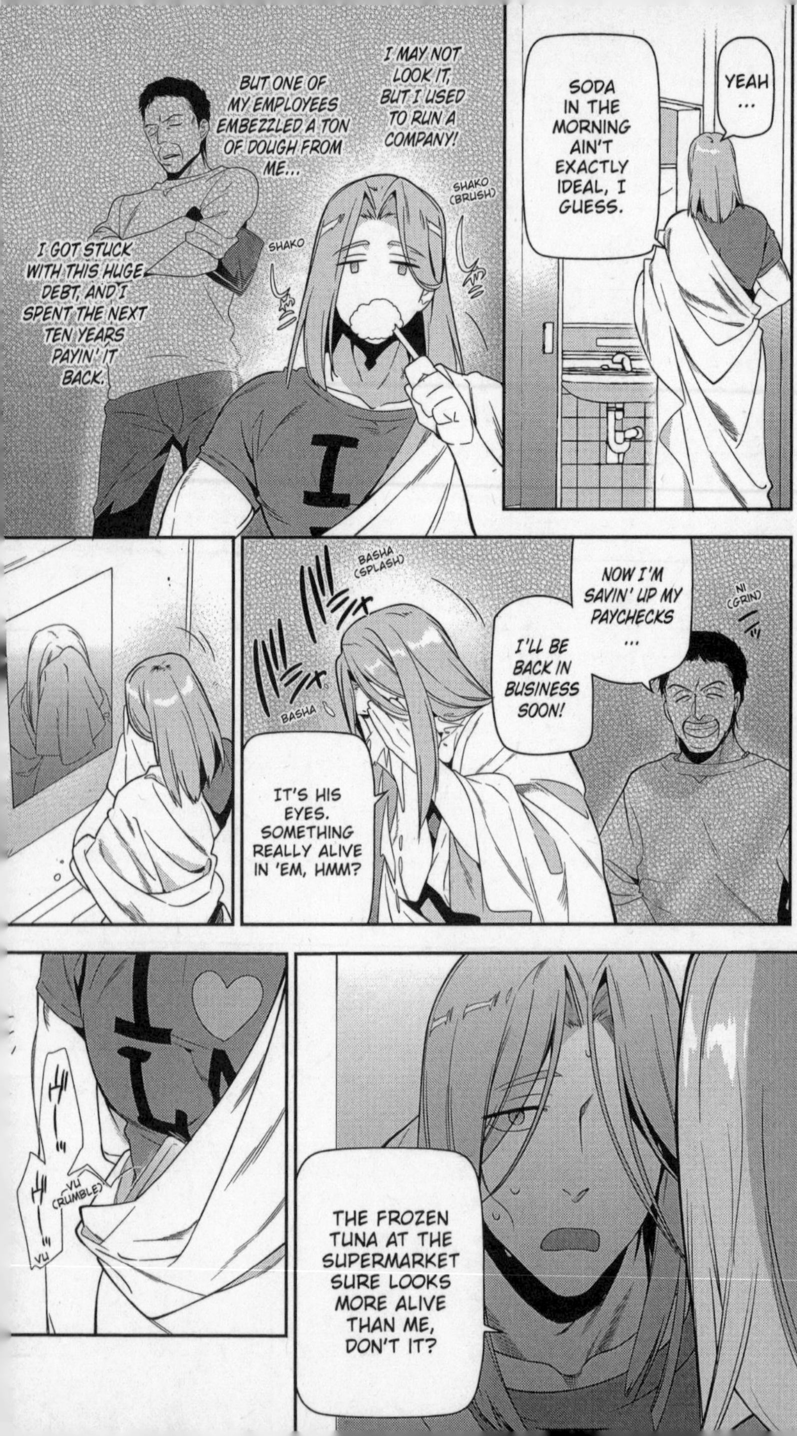
YEAH ...
SODA IN THE MORNING AIN'T EXACTLY IDEAL, I GUESS.
I MAY NOT LOOK IT, BUT I USED TO RUN A COMPANY!
BUT ONE OF MY EMPLOYEES EMBEZZLED A TON OF DOUGH FROM ME...
SHAKO (BRUSH)
SHAKO
I GOT STUCK WITH THIS HUGE DEBT, AND I SPENT THE NEXT TEN YEARS PAYIN' IT BACK.
NI (GRIN)
NOW I'M SAVIN' UP MY PAYCHECKS ...
I'LL BE BACK IN BUSINESS SOON!
BASHA (SPLASH)
BASHA
IT'S HIS EYES. SOMETHING REALLY ALIVE IN 'EM, HMM?
THE FROZEN TUNA AT THE SUPERMARKET SURE LOOKS MORE ALIVE THAN ME, DON'T IT?
YU (RUMBLE)
YU

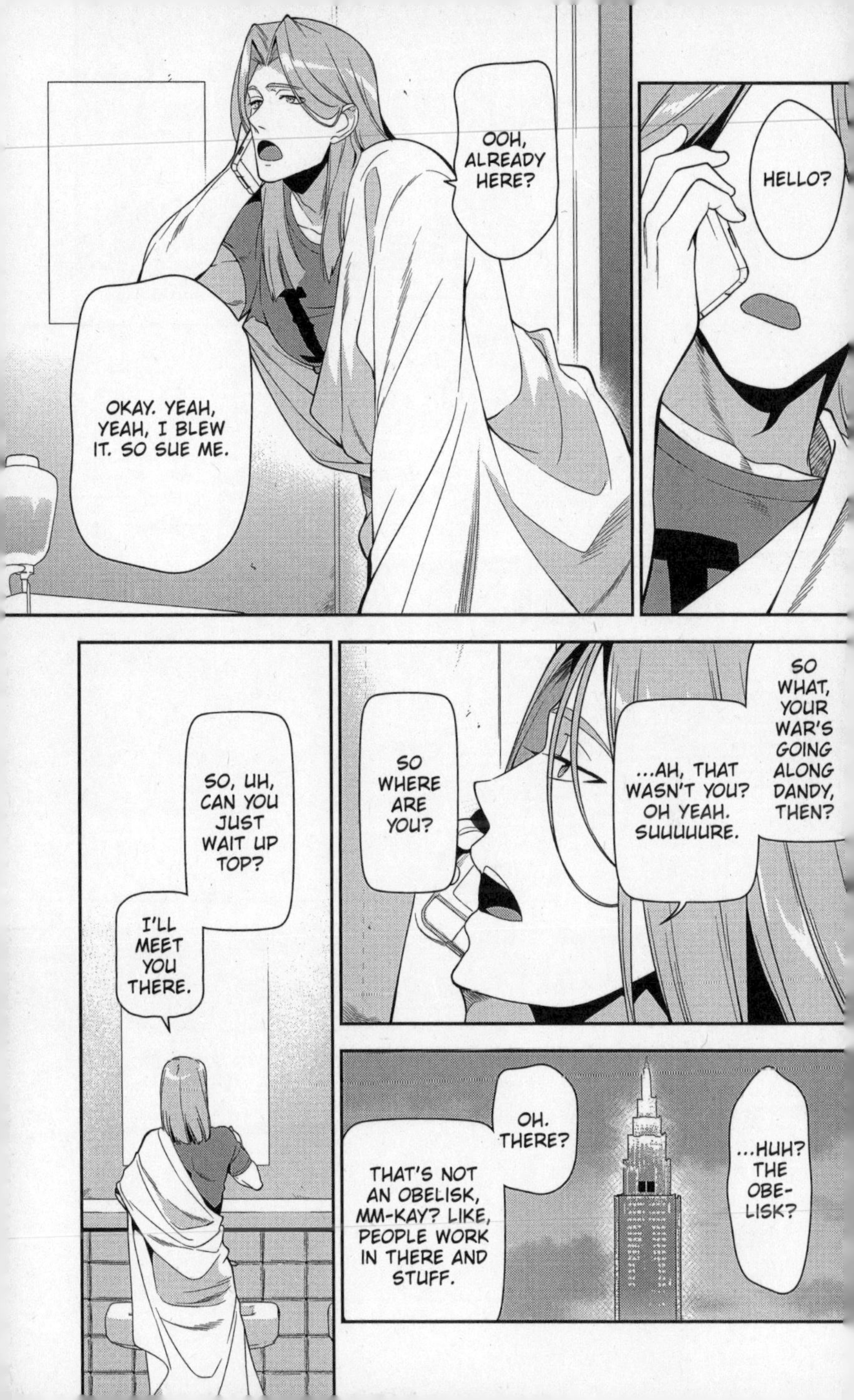
HELLO?
OOH, ALREADY HERE?
OKAY. YEAH, YEAH, I BLEW IT. SO SUE ME.
SO WHAT, YOUR WAR'S GOING ALONG DANDY, THEN?
...AH, THAT WASN'T YOU? OH YEAH. SUUUUURE.
SO WHERE ARE YOU?
...HUH? THE OBE-LISK?
OH. THERE?
THAT'S NOT AN OBELISK, MM-KAY? LIKE, PEOPLE WORK IN THERE AND STUFF.
SO, UH, CAN YOU JUST WAIT UP TOP?
I'LL MEET YOU THERE.

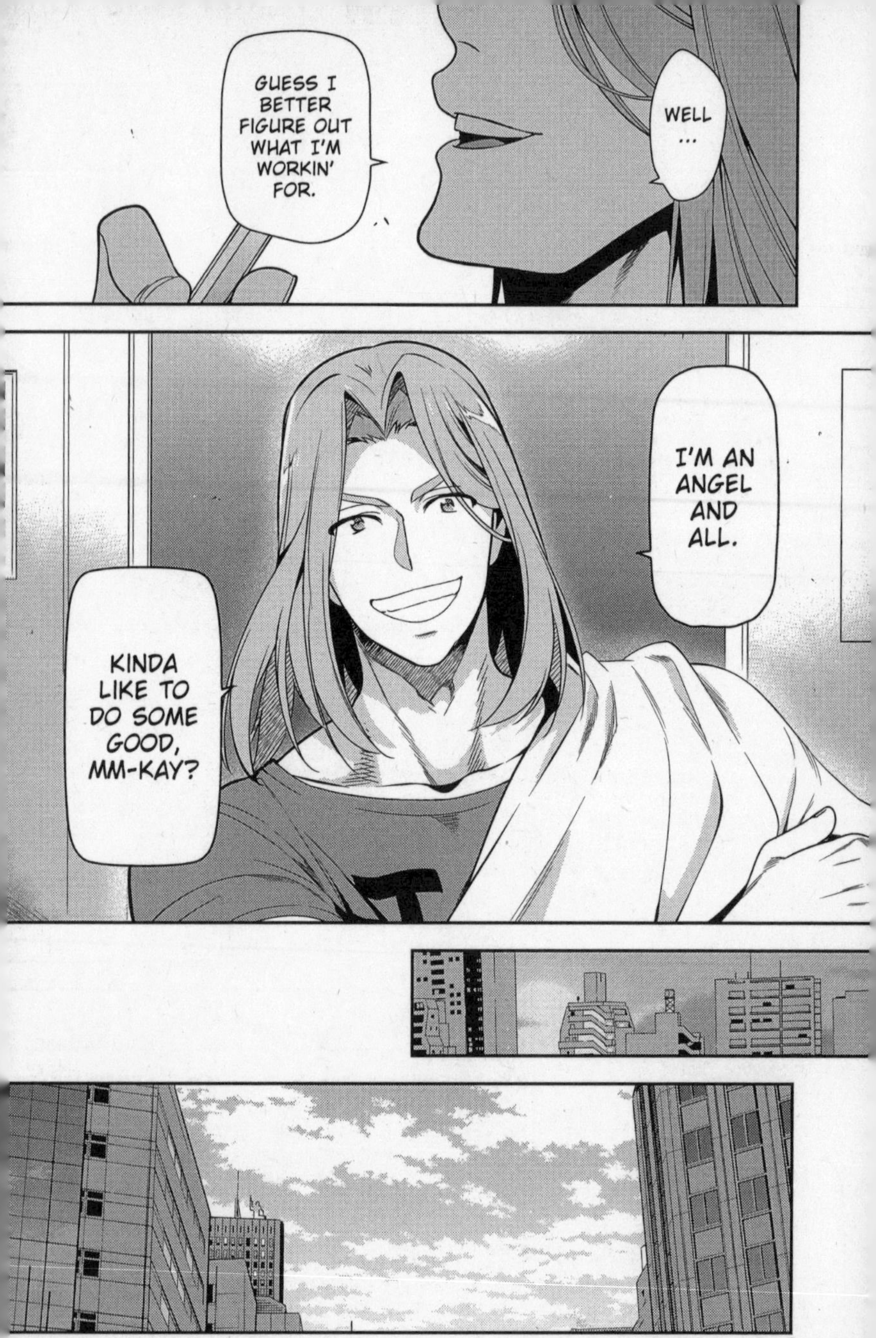
WELL ...
GUESS I BETTER FIGURE OUT WHAT I'M WORKIN' FOR.
I'M AN ANGEL AND ALL.
KINDA LIKE TO DO SOME GOOD, MM-KAY?

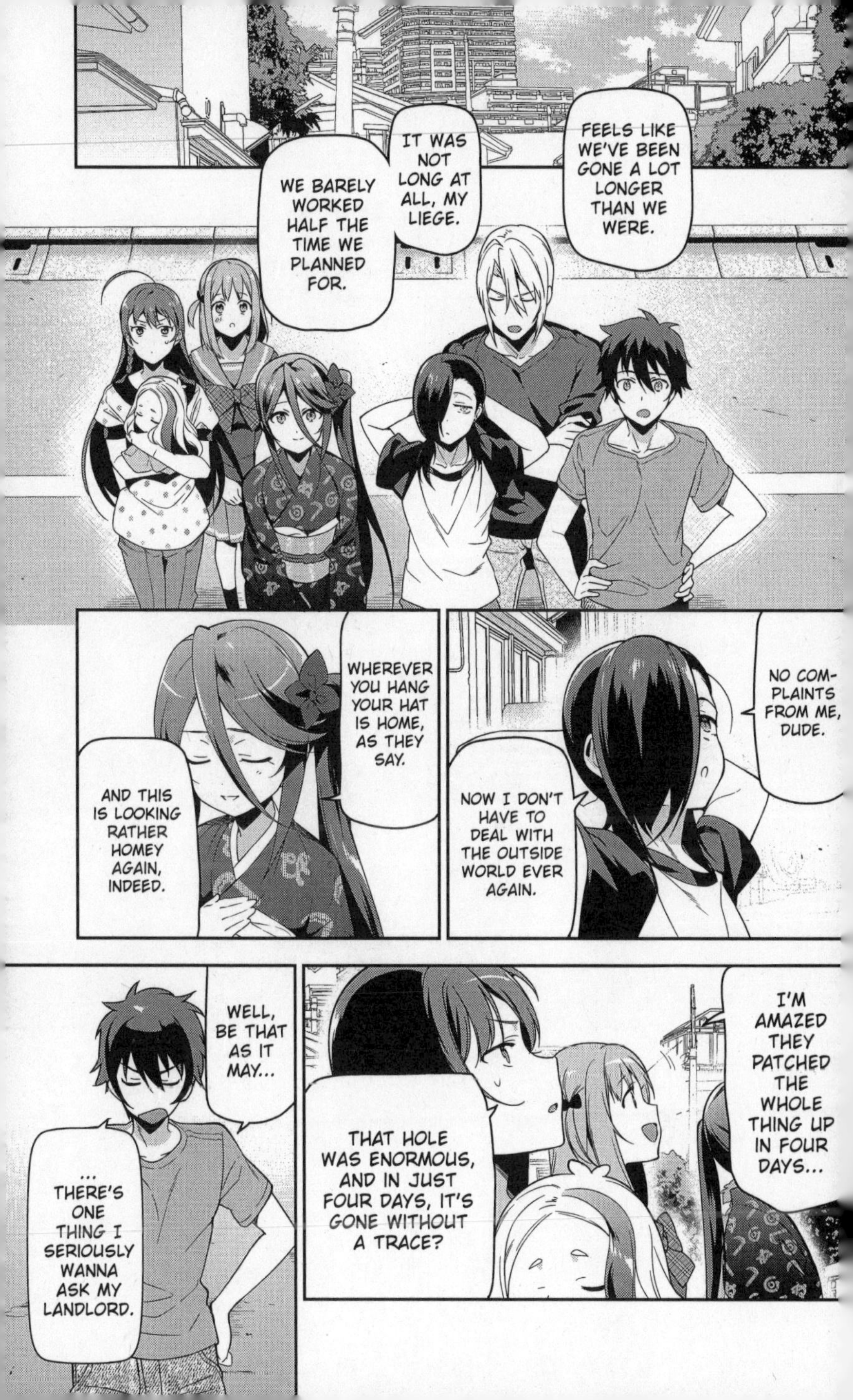
FEELS LIKE WE'VE BEEN GONE A LOT LONGER THAN WE WERE.
IT WAS NOT LONG AT ALL, MY LIEGE.
WE BARELY WORKED HALF THE TIME WE PLANNED FOR.
NO COMPLAINTS FROM ME, DUDE.
NOW I DON'T HAVE TO DEAL WITH THE OUTSIDE WORLD EVER AGAIN.
WHEREVER YOU HANG YOUR HAT IS HOME, AS THEY SAY.
AND THIS IS LOOKING RATHER HOMEY AGAIN, INDEED.
I'M AMAZED THEY PATCHED THE WHOLE THING UP IN FOUR DAYS...
THAT HOLE WAS ENORMOUS, AND IN JUST FOUR DAYS, IT'S GONE WITHOUT A TRACE?
WELL, BE THAT AS IT MAY...
...THERE'S ONE THING I SERIOUSLY WANNA ASK MY LANDLORD.

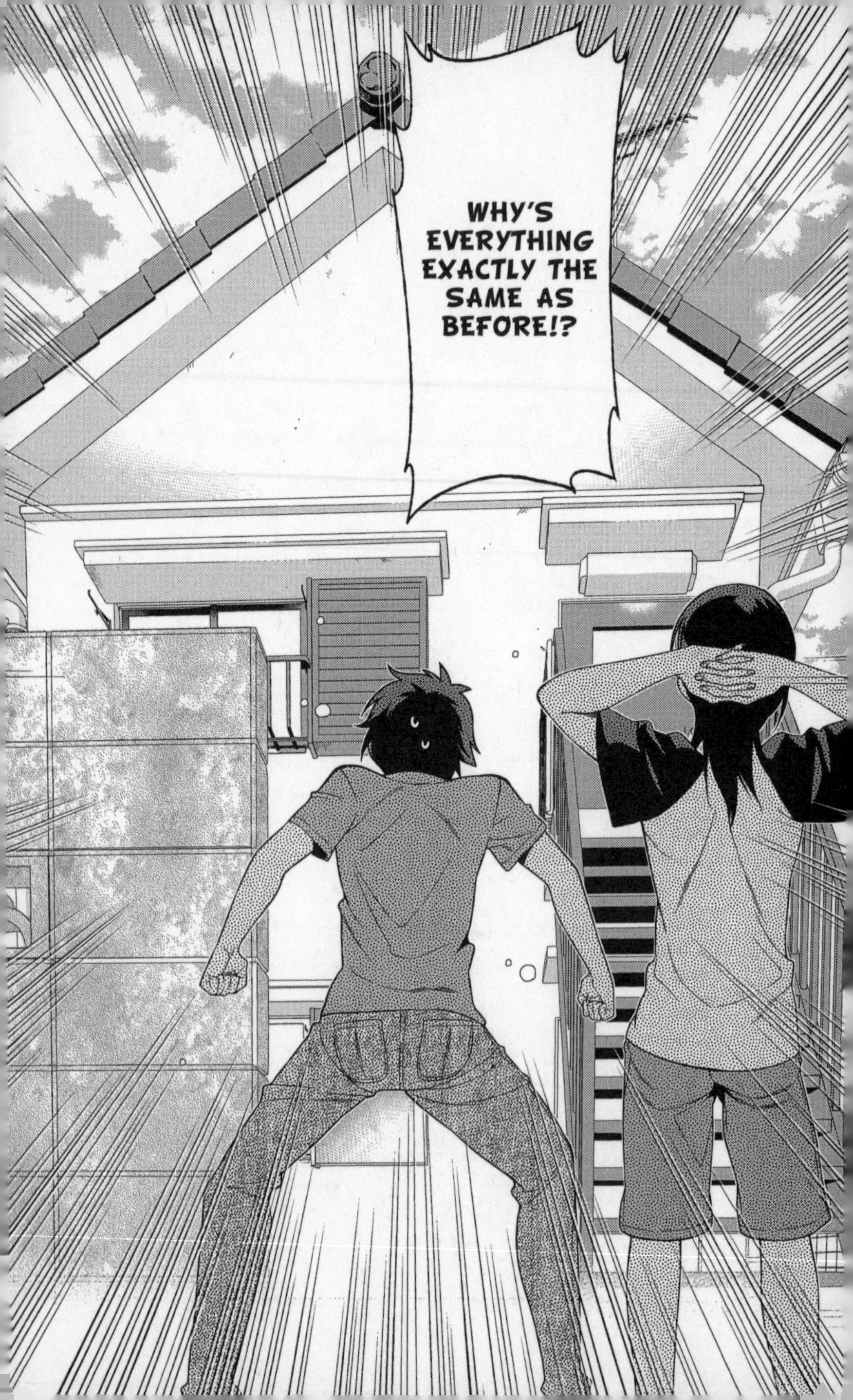
WHY'S EVERYTHING EXACTLY THE SAME AS BEFORE!?

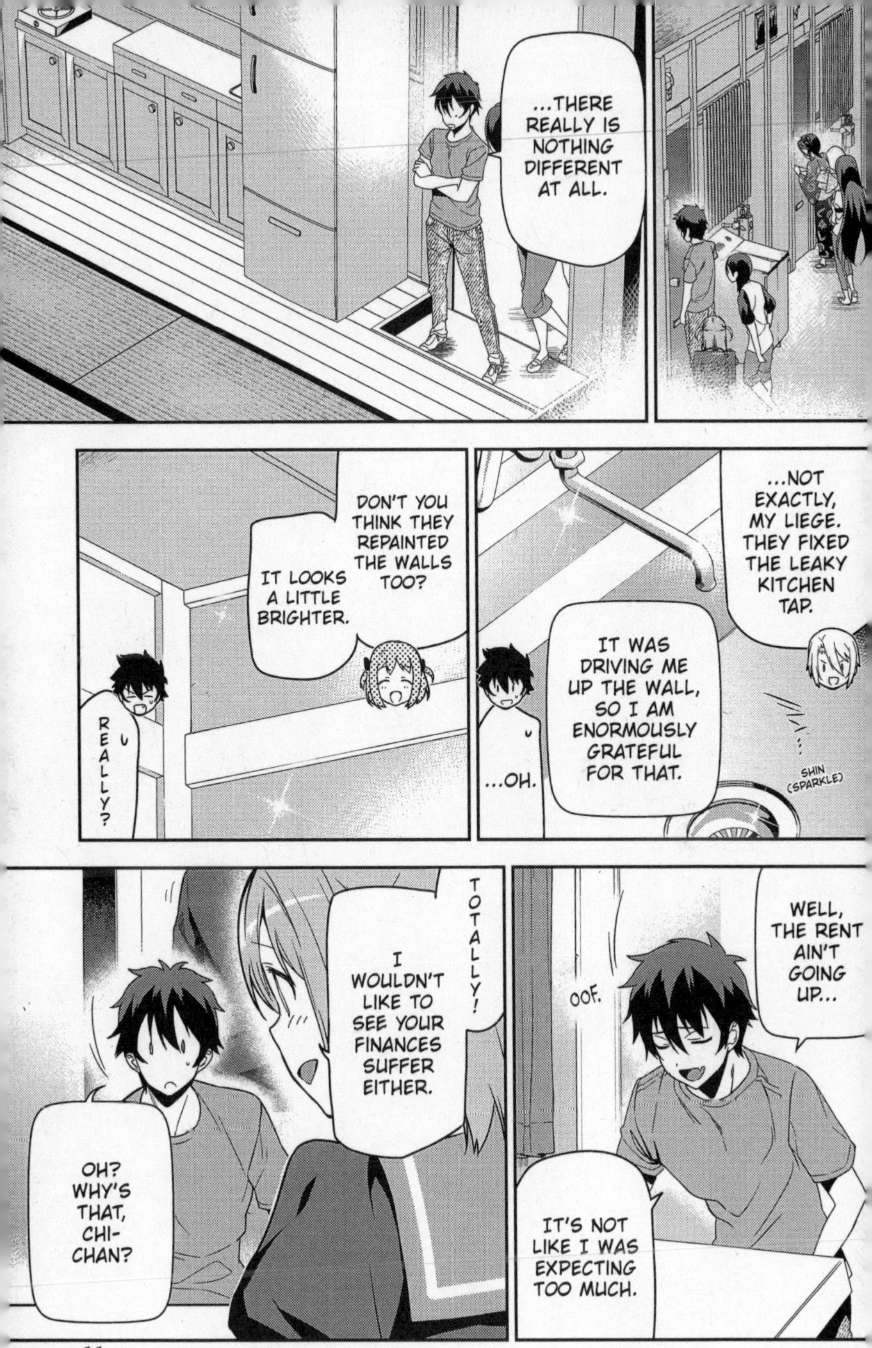
...THERE REALLY IS NOTHING DIFFERENT AT ALL.
...NOT EXACTLY, MY LIEGE. THEY FIXED THE LEAKY KITCHEN TAP.
IT WAS DRIVING ME UP THE WALL, SO I AM ENORMOUSLY GRATEFUL FOR THAT.
SHIN (SPARKLE)
...OH.
DON'T YOU THINK THEY REPAINTED THE WALLS TOO?
IT LOOKS A LITTLE BRIGHTER.
REALLY?
WELL, THE RENT AIN'T GOING UP...
OOF.
IT'S NOT LIKE I WAS EXPECTING TOO MUCH.
TOTALLY!
I WOULDN'T LIKE TO SEE YOUR FINANCES SUFFER EITHER.
OH? WHY'S THAT, CHI-CHAN?

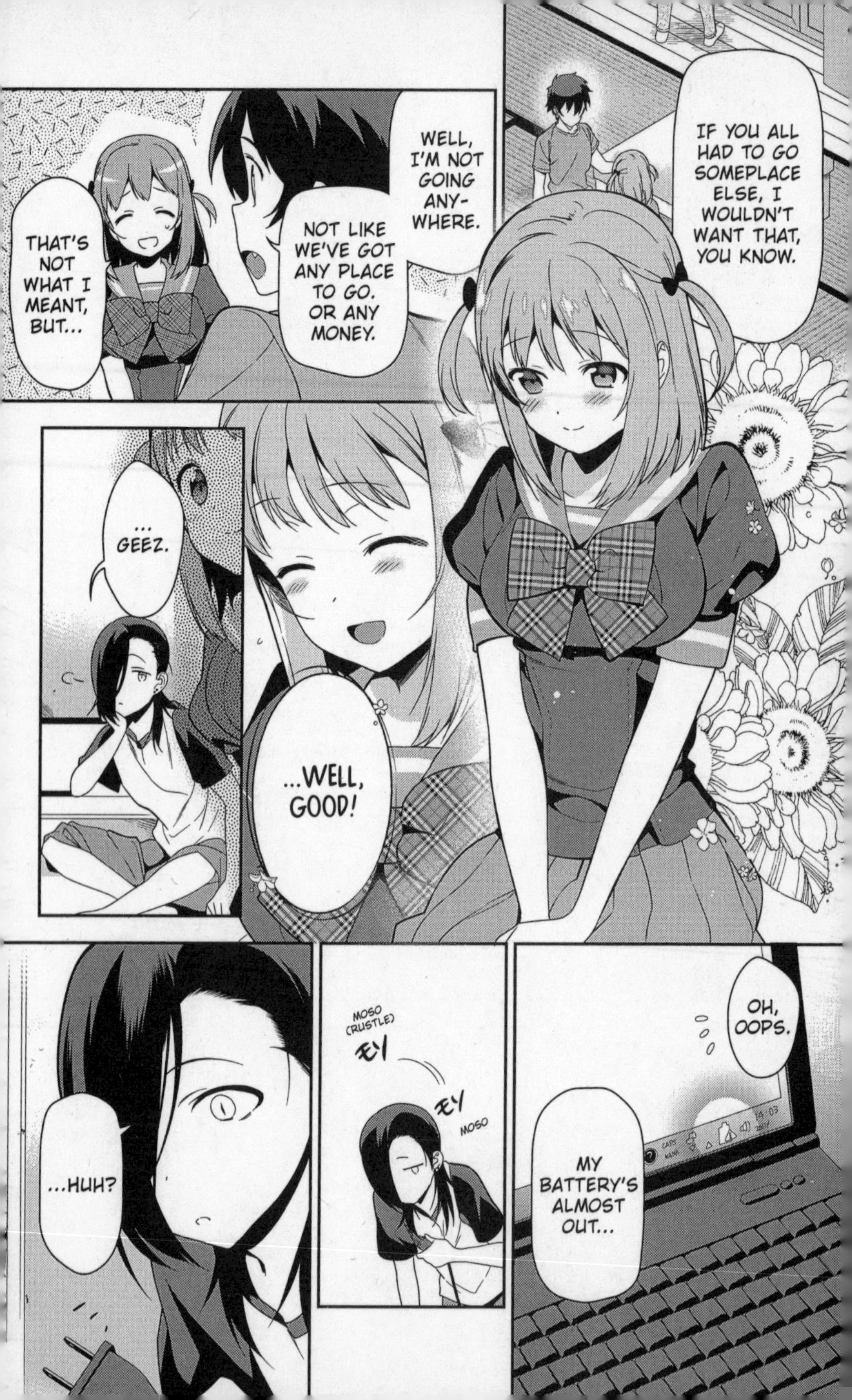
IF YOU ALL HAD TO GO SOMEPLACE ELSE, I WOULDN'T WANT THAT, YOU KNOW.
WELL, I'M NOT GOING ANY-WHERE.
NOT LIKE WE'VE GOT ANY PLACE TO GO. OR ANY MONEY.
THAT'S NOT WHAT I MEANT, BUT...
...WELL, GOOD!
... GEEZ.
OH, OOPS.
MY BATTERY'S ALMOST OUT...
MOSO (RUSTLE)
モソ
モソ
MOSO
...HUH?

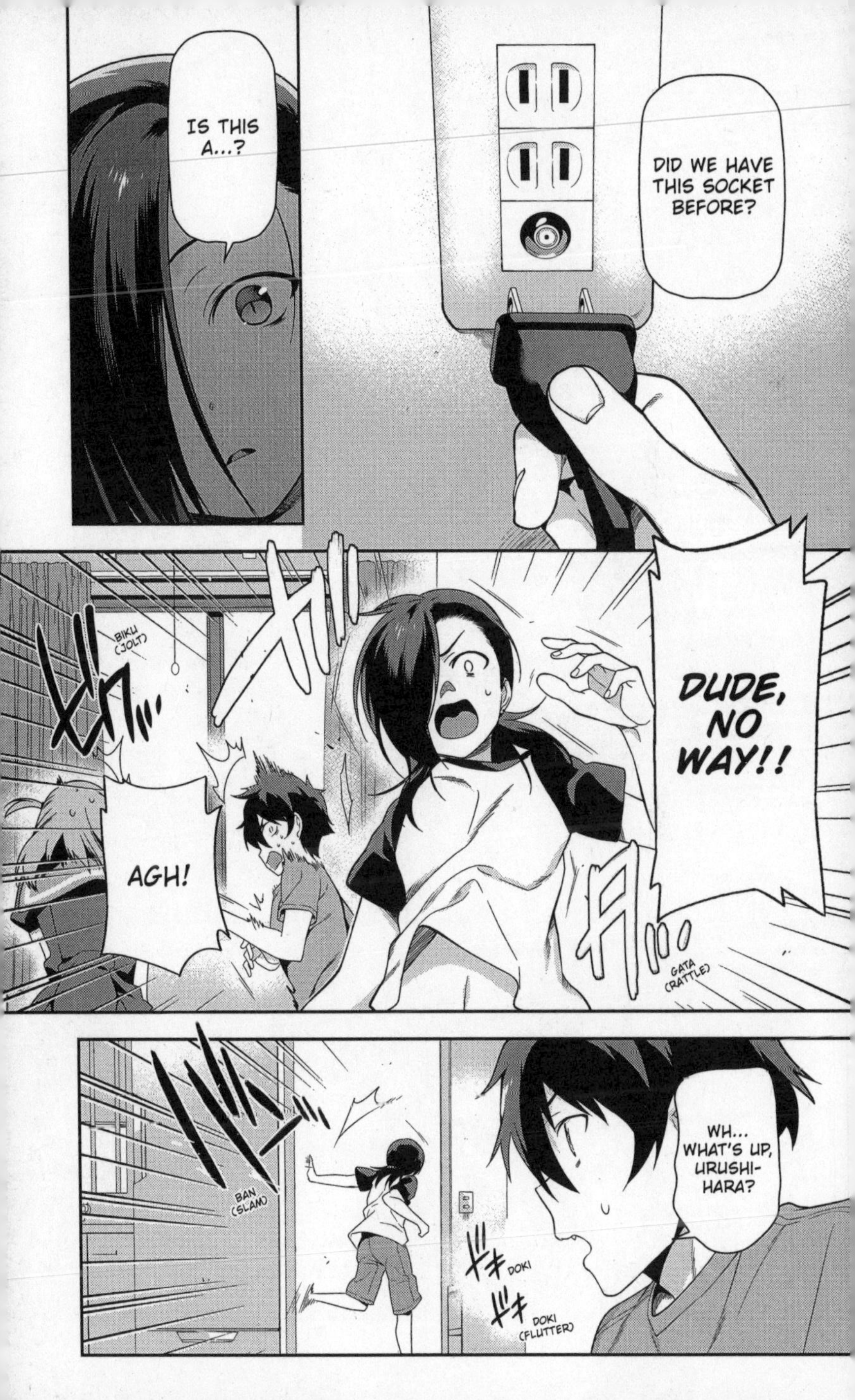
DID WE HAVE THIS SOCKET BEFORE?
IS THIS A...?
DUDE, NO WAY!!
GATA (RATTLE)
BIKU (JOLT)
AGH!
WH... WHAT'S UP, URUSHI-HARA?
DOKI
DOKI (FLUTTER)
BAN (SLAM)

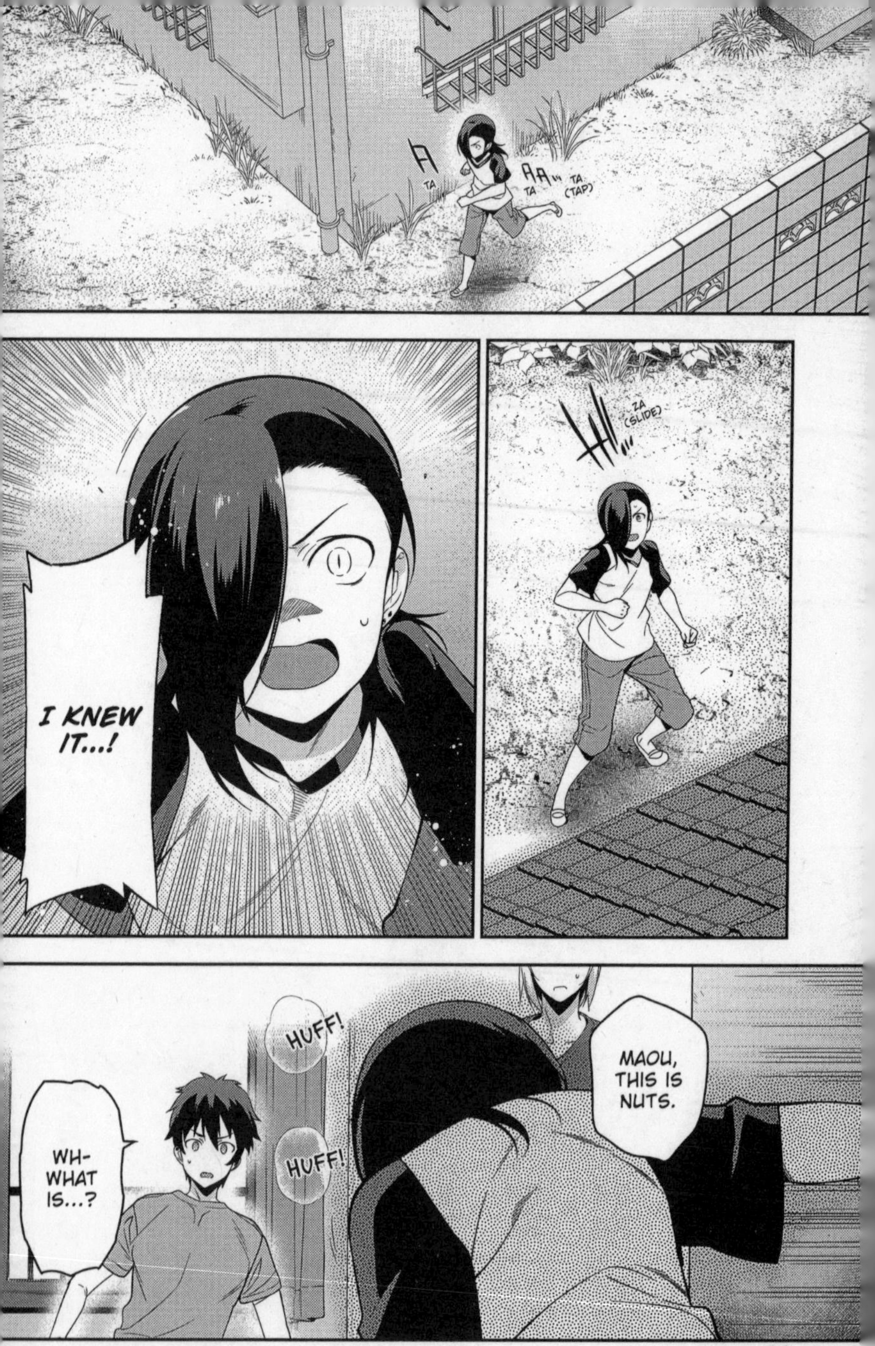
TA (TAP)
TA
TA
ZA (SLIDE)
I KNEW IT...!
MAOU, THIS IS NUTS.
HUFF!
HUFF!
WH- WHAT IS...?

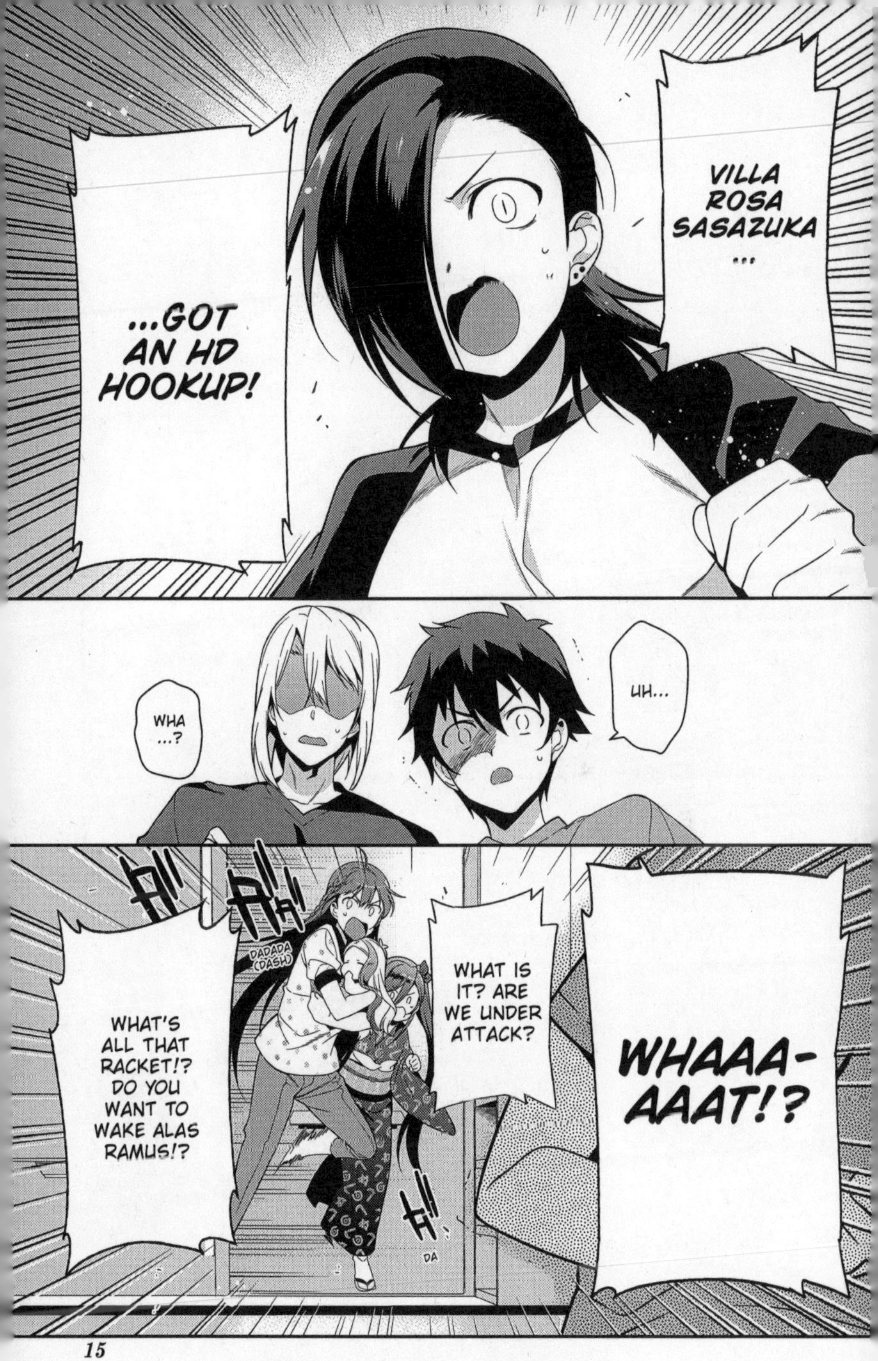

VILLA ROSA SASAZUKA...
...GOT AN HD HOOKUP!
UH...
WHA...?
WHAAAAAAT!?
WHAT IS IT? ARE WE UNDER ATTACK?
DADADA (DASH)
WHAT'S ALL THAT RACKET!? DO YOU WANT TO WAKE ALAS RAMUS!?
DA

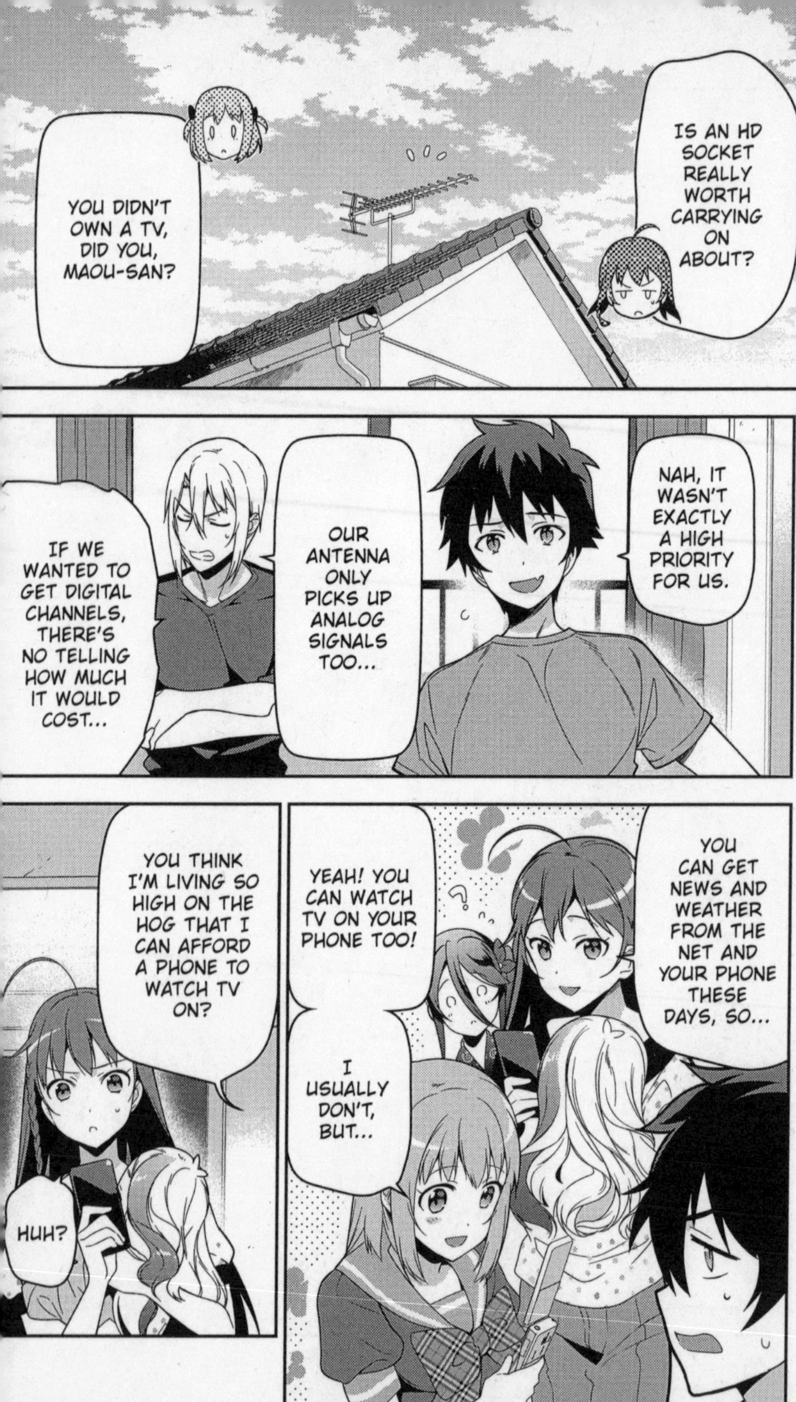
IS AN HD SOCKET REALLY WORTH CARRYING ON ABOUT?
YOU DIDN'T OWN A TV, DID YOU, MAOU-SAN?
NAH, IT WASN'T EXACTLY A HIGH PRIORITY FOR US.
OUR ANTENNA ONLY PICKS UP ANALOG SIGNALS TOO...
IF WE WANTED TO GET DIGITAL CHANNELS, THERE'S NO TELLING HOW MUCH IT WOULD COST...
YOU CAN GET NEWS AND WEATHER FROM THE NET AND YOUR PHONE THESE DAYS, SO...
YEAH! YOU CAN WATCH TV ON YOUR PHONE TOO!
I USUALLY DON'T, BUT...
YOU THINK I'M LIVING SO HIGH ON THE HOG THAT I CAN AFFORD A PHONE TO WATCH TV ON?
HUH?

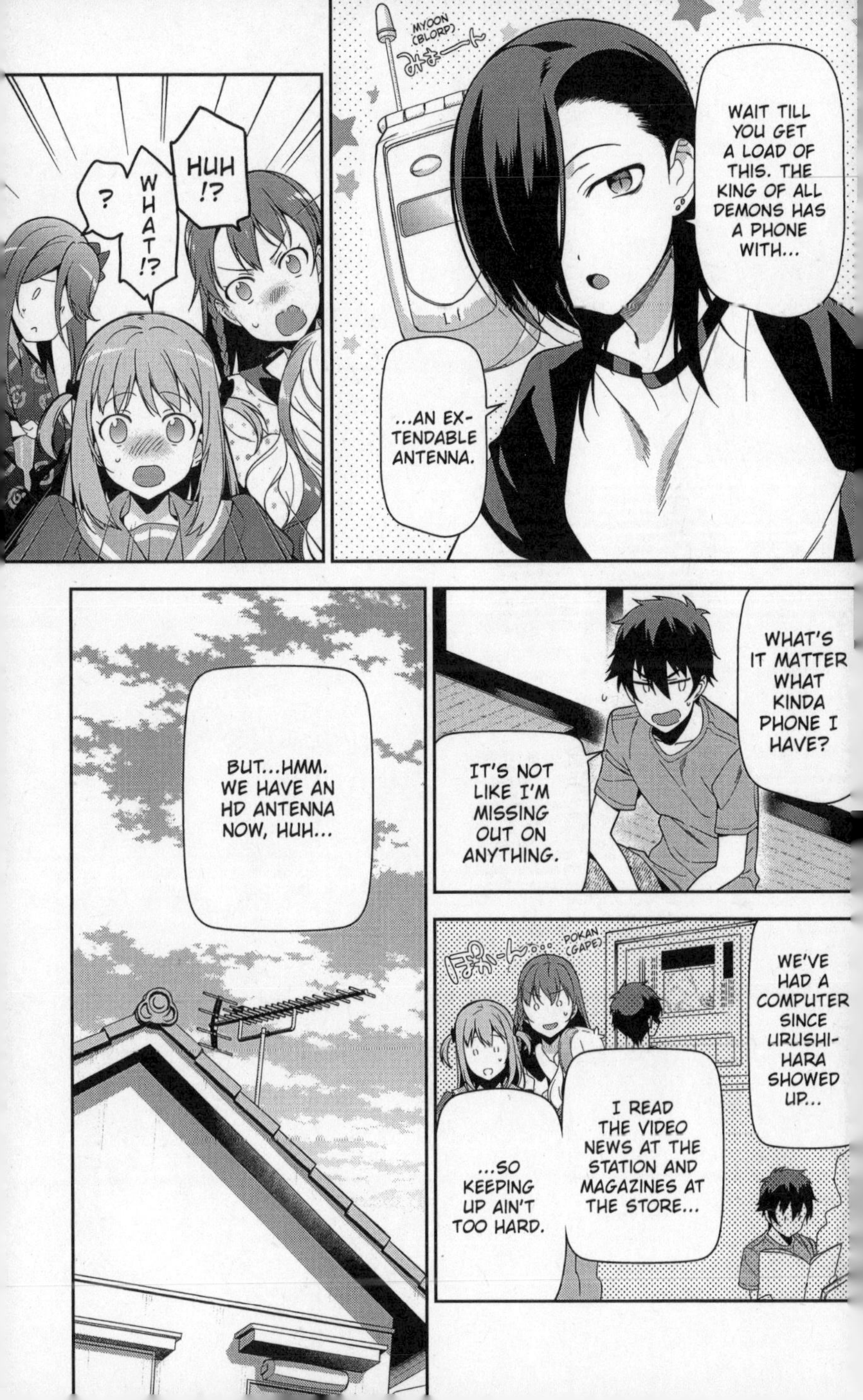
MYOON (BLORP)
WAIT TILL YOU GET A LOAD OF THIS. THE KING OF ALL DEMONS HAS A PHONE WITH...
...AN EXTENDABLE ANTENNA.
HUH!?
WHAT!?
?
WHAT'S IT MATTER WHAT KINDA PHONE I HAVE?
IT'S NOT LIKE I'M MISSING OUT ON ANYTHING.
POKAN (GAPE)
WE'VE HAD A COMPUTER SINCE URUSHIHARA SHOWED UP...
I READ THE VIDEO NEWS AT THE STATION AND MAGAZINES AT THE STORE...
...SO KEEPING UP AIN'T TOO HARD.
BUT...HMM. WE HAVE AN HD ANTENNA NOW, HUH...

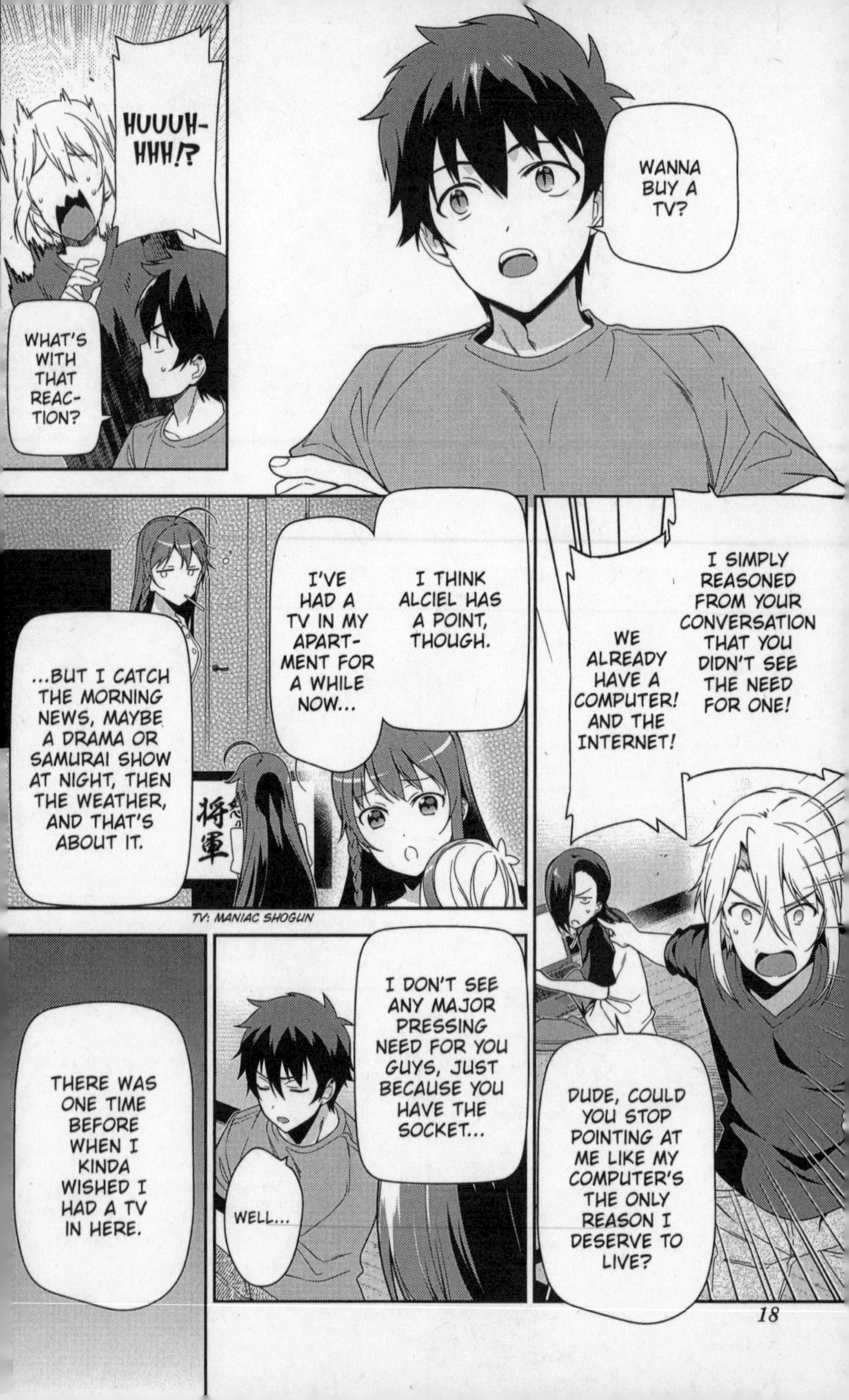
WANNA BUY A TV?
HUUUH-HHH!?
WHAT'S WITH THAT REAC-TION?
I SIMPLY REASONED FROM YOUR CONVERSATION THAT YOU DIDN'T SEE THE NEED FOR ONE!
WE ALREADY HAVE A COMPUTER! AND THE INTERNET!
DUDE, COULD YOU STOP POINTING AT ME LIKE MY COMPUTER'S THE ONLY REASON I DESERVE TO LIVE?
I THINK ALCIEL HAS A POINT, THOUGH.
I'VE HAD A TV IN MY APART-MENT FOR A WHILE NOW...
...BUT I CATCH THE MORNING NEWS, MAYBE A DRAMA OR SAMURAI SHOW AT NIGHT, THEN THE WEATHER, AND THAT'S ABOUT IT.
将軍
TV: MANIAC SHOGUN
I DON'T SEE ANY MAJOR PRESSING NEED FOR YOU GUYS, JUST BECAUSE YOU HAVE THE SOCKET...
WELL...
THERE WAS ONE TIME BEFORE WHEN I KINDA WISHED I HAD A TV IN HERE.

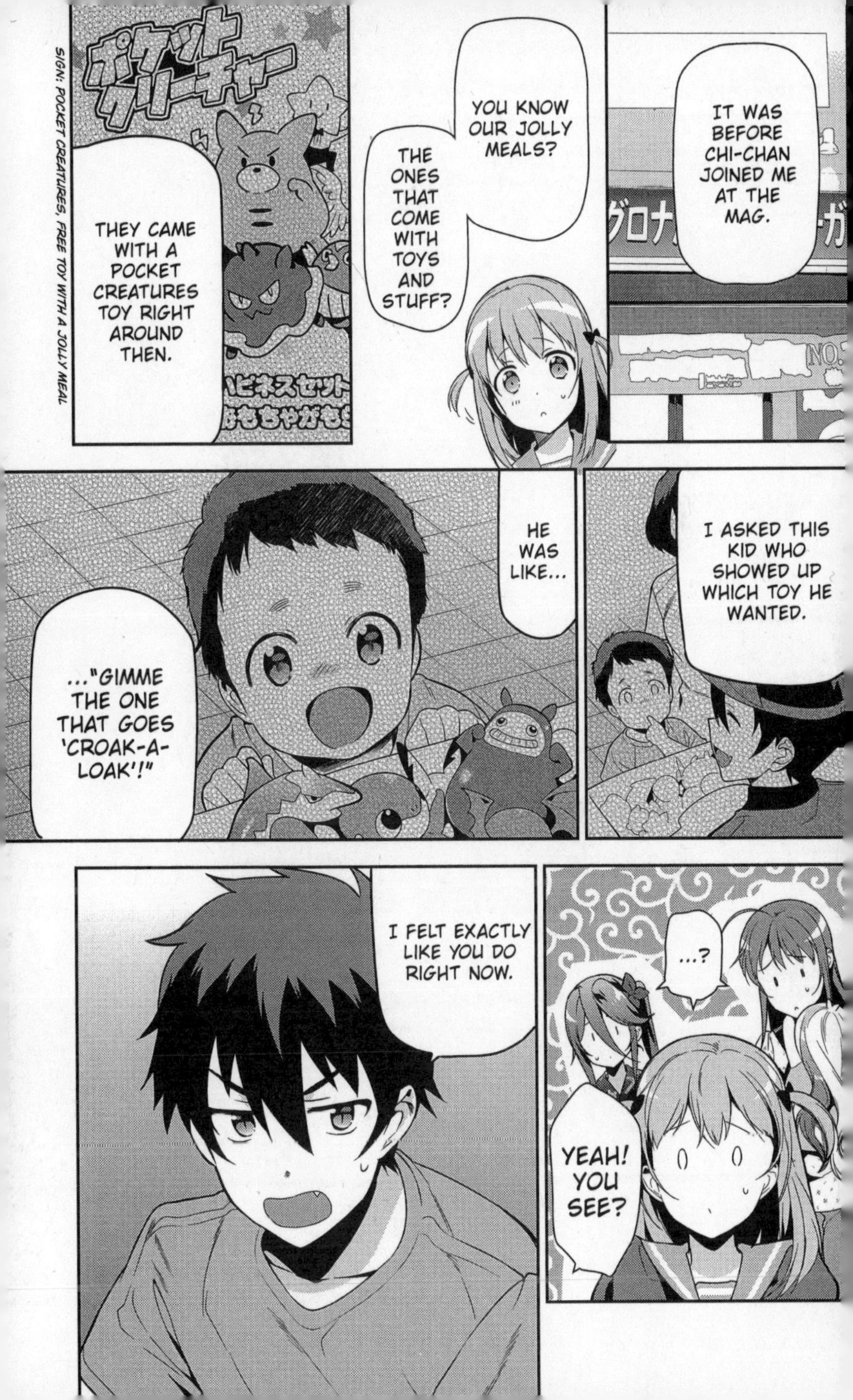
IT WAS BEFORE CHI-CHAN JOINED ME AT THE MAG.
YOU KNOW OUR JOLLY MEALS?
THE ONES THAT COME WITH TOYS AND STUFF?
ポケットクリーチャー
THEY CAME WITH A POCKET CREATURES TOY RIGHT AROUND THEN.
SIGN: POCKET CREATURES, FREE TOY WITH A JOLLY MEAL
I ASKED THIS KID WHO SHOWED UP WHICH TOY HE WANTED.
HE WAS LIKE...
..."GIMME THE ONE THAT GOES 'CROAK-A-LOAK'!"
...?
YEAH! YOU SEE?
I FELT EXACTLY LIKE YOU DO RIGHT NOW.

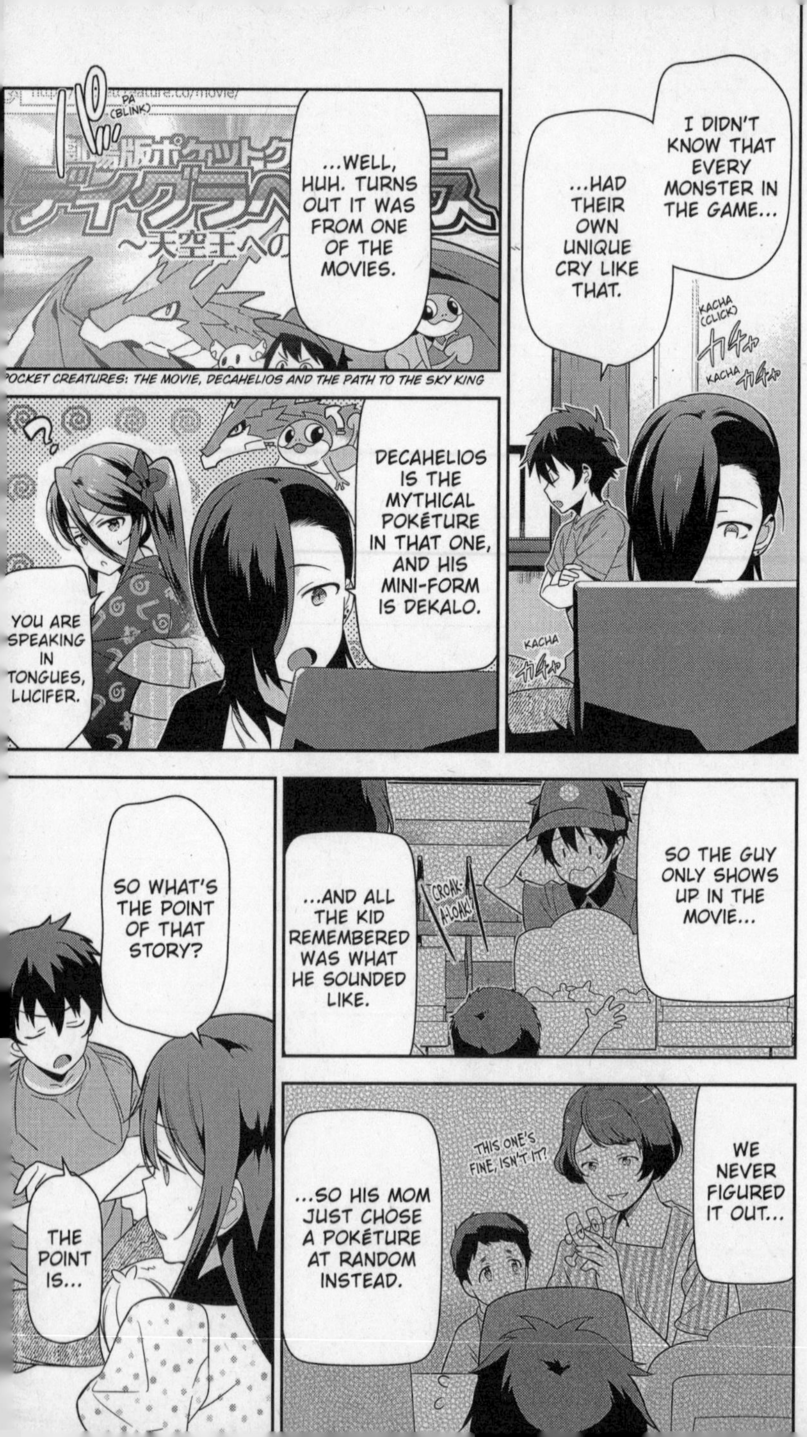
I DIDN'T KNOW THAT EVERY MONSTER IN THE GAME...
...HAD THEIR OWN UNIQUE CRY LIKE THAT.
KACHA (CLICK)
KACHA
KACHA
PA (BLINK)
...WELL, HUH. TURNS OUT IT WAS FROM ONE OF THE MOVIES.
POCKET CREATURES: THE MOVIE, DECAHELIOS AND THE PATH TO THE SKY KING
DECAHELIOS IS THE MYTHICAL POKÉTURE IN THAT ONE, AND HIS MINI-FORM IS DEKALO.
YOU ARE SPEAKING IN TONGUES, LUCIFER.
SO THE GUY ONLY SHOWS UP IN THE MOVIE...
...AND ALL THE KID REMEMBERED WAS WHAT HE SOUNDED LIKE.
CROAK-A-LOAK!
WE NEVER FIGURED IT OUT...
THIS ONE'S FINE, ISN'T IT?
...SO HIS MOM JUST CHOSE A POKÉTURE AT RANDOM INSTEAD.
SO WHAT'S THE POINT OF THAT STORY?
THE POINT IS...

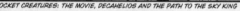

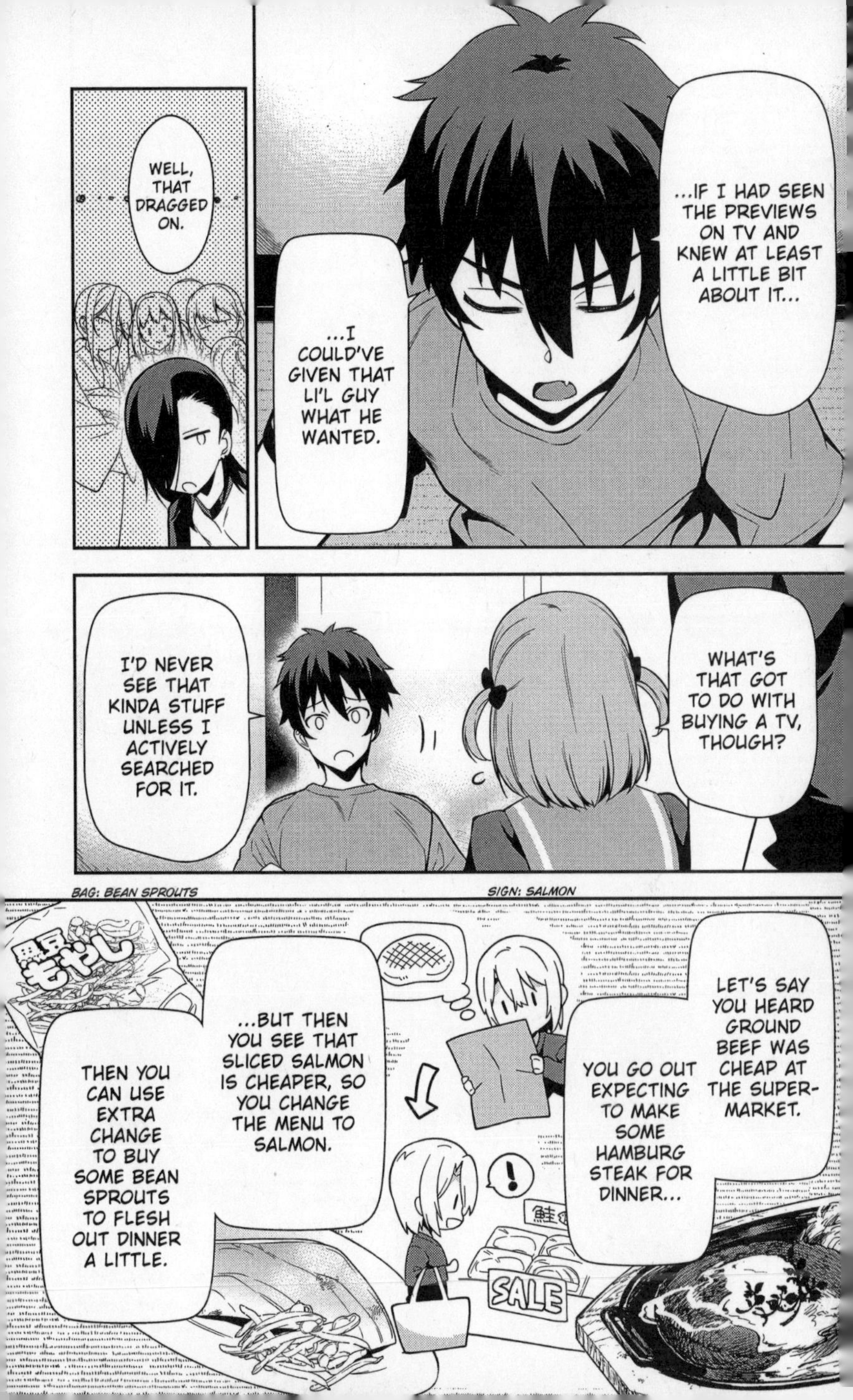
...IF I HAD SEEN THE PREVIEWS ON TV AND KNEW AT LEAST A LITTLE BIT ABOUT IT...
...I COULD'VE GIVEN THAT LI'L GUY WHAT HE WANTED.
WELL, THAT DRAGGED ON.
WHAT'S THAT GOT TO DO WITH BUYING A TV, THOUGH?
I'D NEVER SEE THAT KINDA STUFF UNLESS I ACTIVELY SEARCHED FOR IT.
SIGN: SALMON
BAG: BEAN SPROUTS
LET'S SAY YOU HEARD GROUND BEEF WAS CHEAP AT THE SUPER-MARKET.
YOU GO OUT EXPECTING TO MAKE SOME HAMBURG STEAK FOR DINNER...
...BUT THEN YOU SEE THAT SLICED SALMON IS CHEAPER, SO YOU CHANGE THE MENU TO SALMON.
SALE
THEN YOU CAN USE EXTRA CHANGE TO BUY SOME BEAN SPROUTS TO FLESH OUT DINNER A LITTLE.

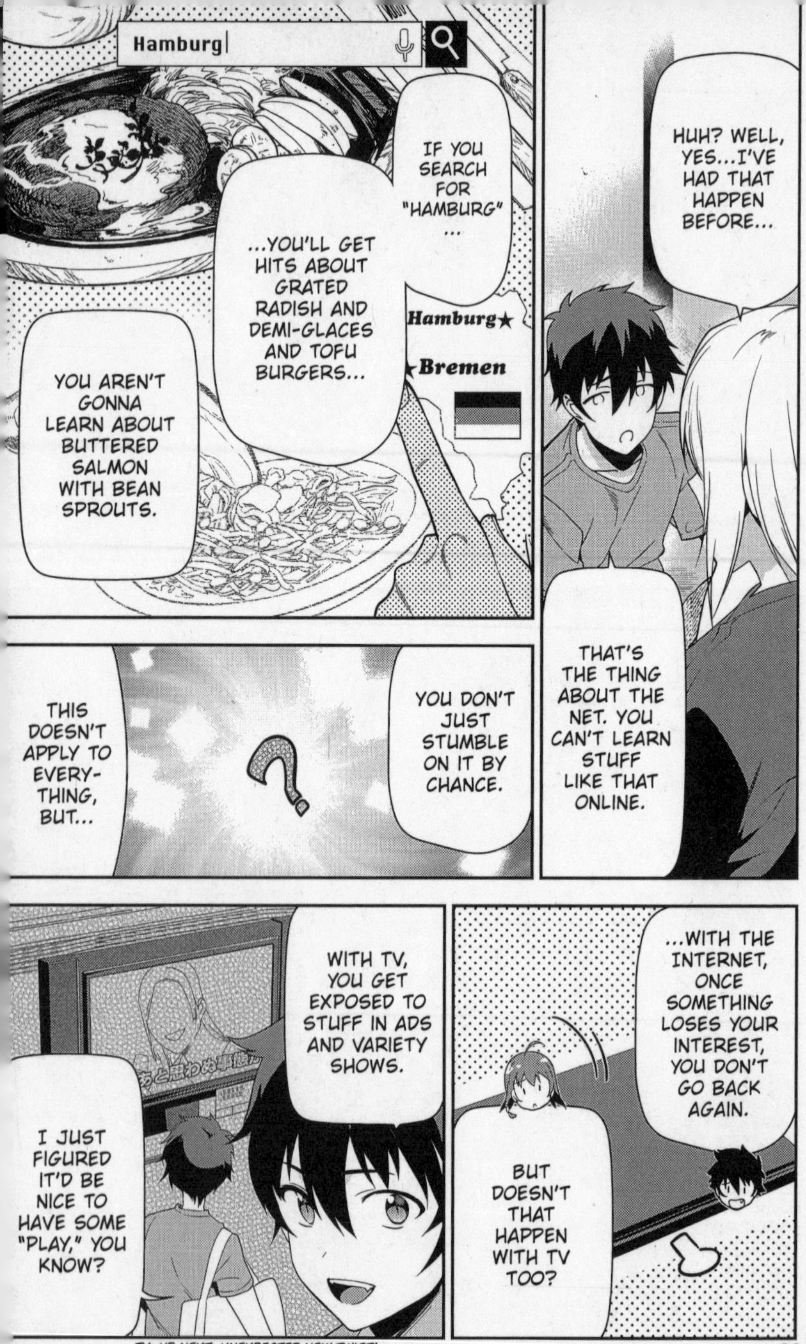
HUH? WELL, YES...I'VE HAD THAT HAPPEN BEFORE...
THAT'S THE THING ABOUT THE NET. YOU CAN'T LEARN STUFF LIKE THAT ONLINE.
Hamburg
IF YOU SEARCH FOR "HAMBURG"...
...YOU'LL GET HITS ABOUT GRATED RADISH AND DEMI-GLACES AND TOFU BURGERS...
Hamburg★
★Bremen
YOU AREN'T GONNA LEARN ABOUT BUTTERED SALMON WITH BEAN SPROUTS.
YOU DON'T JUST STUMBLE ON IT BY CHANCE.
THIS DOESN'T APPLY TO EVERY-THING, BUT...
...WITH THE INTERNET, ONCE SOMETHING LOSES YOUR INTEREST, YOU DON'T GO BACK AGAIN.
BUT DOESN'T THAT HAPPEN WITH TV TOO?
WITH TV, YOU GET EXPOSED TO STUFF IN ADS AND VARIETY SHOWS.
I JUST FIGURED IT'D BE NICE TO HAVE SOME "PLAY," YOU KNOW?

TV: UP NEXT: UNEXPECTED NEW TWIST!

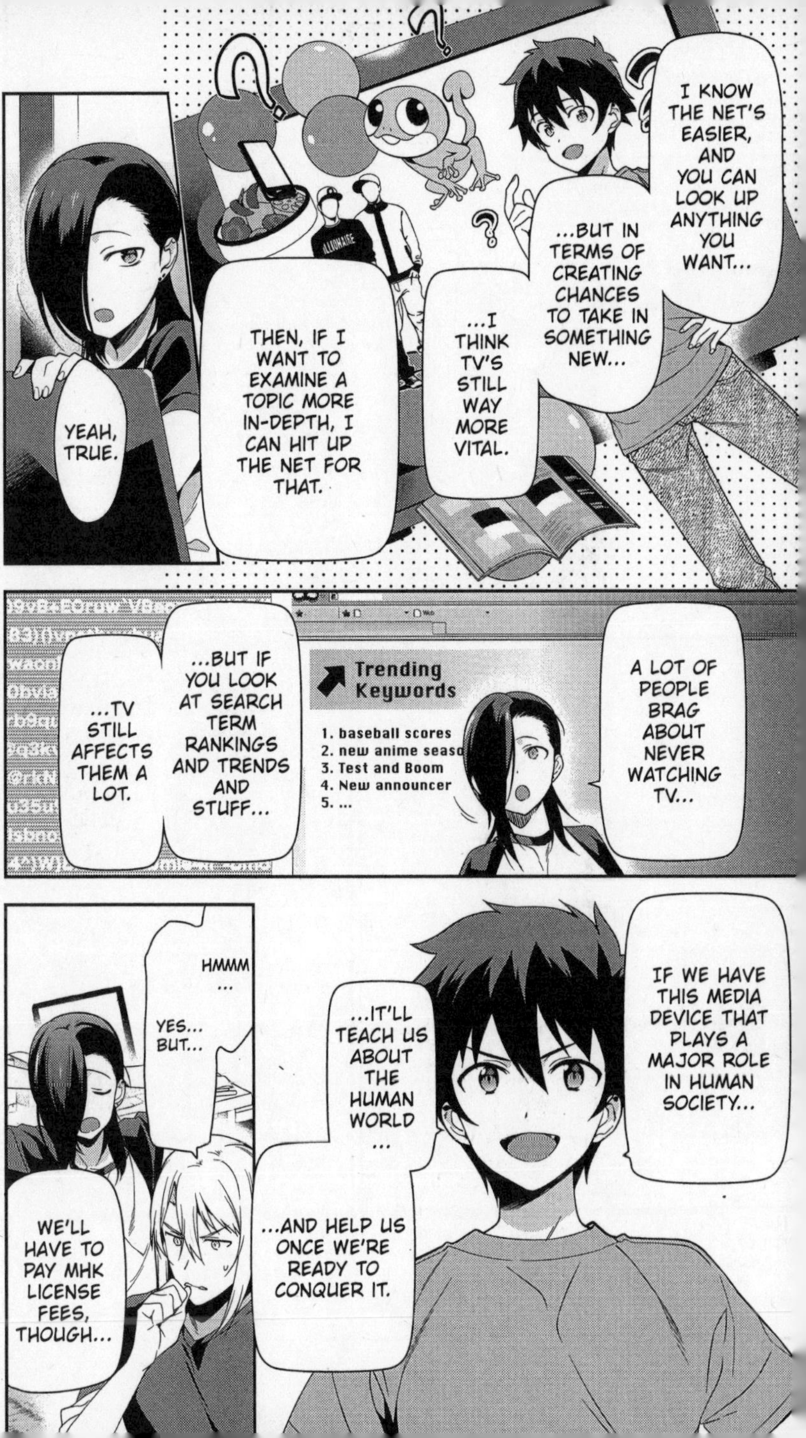
I KNOW THE NET'S EASIER, AND YOU CAN LOOK UP ANYTHING YOU WANT...
...BUT IN TERMS OF CREATING CHANCES TO TAKE IN SOMETHING NEW...
...I THINK TV'S STILL WAY MORE VITAL.
THEN, IF I WANT TO EXAMINE A TOPIC MORE IN-DEPTH, I CAN HIT UP THE NET FOR THAT.
YEAH, TRUE.
A LOT OF PEOPLE BRAG ABOUT NEVER WATCHING TV...
Trending Keywords
1. baseball scores
2. new anime seaso
3. Test and Boom
4. New announcer
5. ...
...BUT IF YOU LOOK AT SEARCH TERM RANKINGS AND TRENDS AND STUFF...
...TV STILL AFFECTS THEM A LOT.
IF WE HAVE THIS MEDIA DEVICE THAT PLAYS A MAJOR ROLE IN HUMAN SOCIETY...
...IT'LL TEACH US ABOUT THE HUMAN WORLD...
...AND HELP US ONCE WE'RE READY TO CONQUER IT.
HMMM...
YES... BUT...
WE'LL HAVE TO PAY MHK LICENSE FEES, THOUGH...

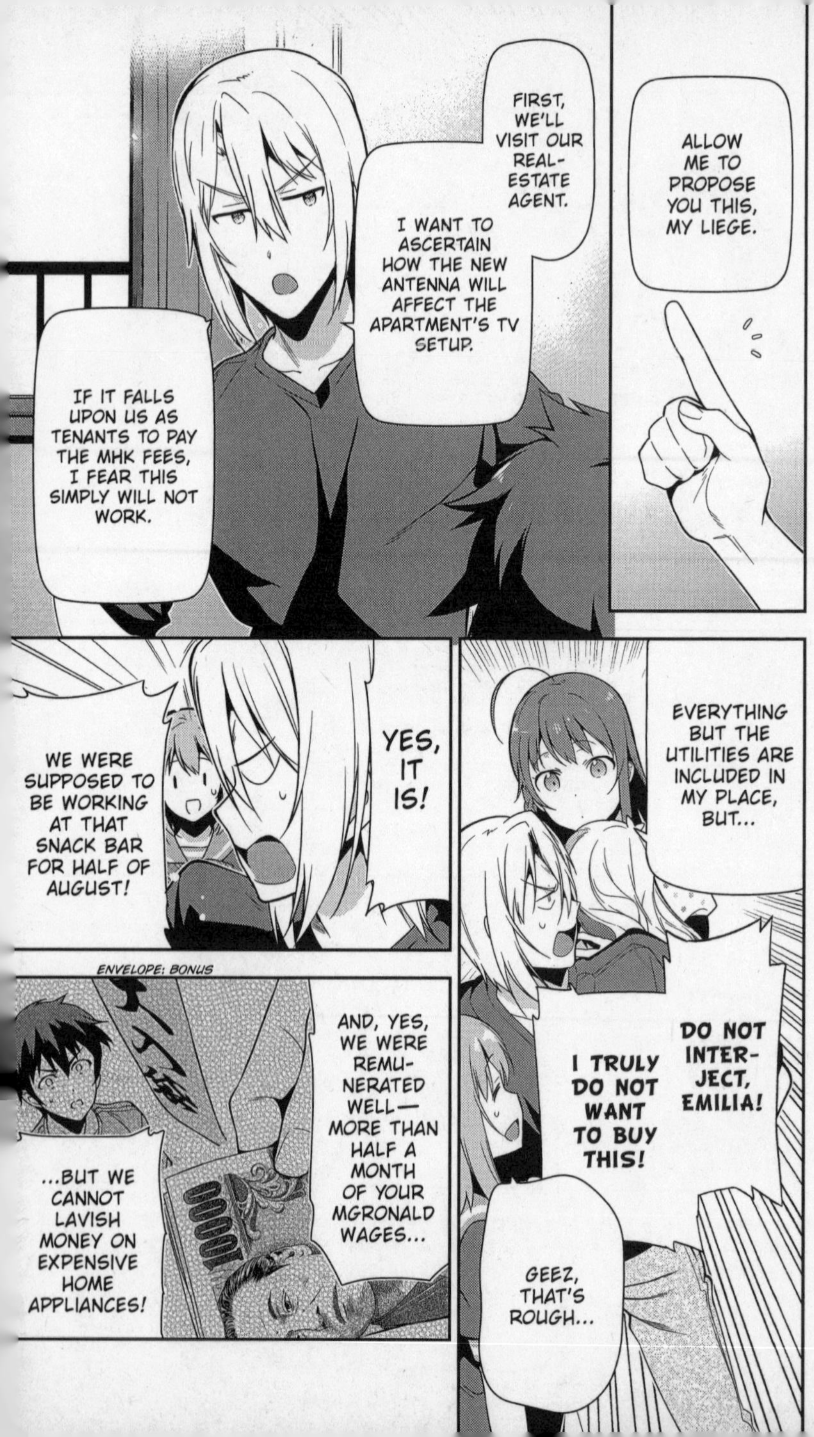
ALLOW ME TO PROPOSE YOU THIS, MY LIEGE.
FIRST, WE'LL VISIT OUR REAL-ESTATE AGENT.
I WANT TO ASCERTAIN HOW THE NEW ANTENNA WILL AFFECT THE APARTMENT'S TV SETUP.
IF IT FALLS UPON US AS TENANTS TO PAY THE MHK FEES, I FEAR THIS SIMPLY WILL NOT WORK.
EVERYTHING BUT THE UTILITIES ARE INCLUDED IN MY PLACE, BUT...
DO NOT INTER-JECT, EMILIA!
I TRULY DO NOT WANT TO BUY THIS!
GEEZ, THAT'S ROUGH...
YES, IT IS!
WE WERE SUPPOSED TO BE WORKING AT THAT SNACK BAR FOR HALF OF AUGUST!
ENVELOPE: BONUS
AND, YES, WE WERE REMU-NERATED WELL— MORE THAN HALF A MONTH OF YOUR MGRONALD WAGES...
...BUT WE CANNOT LAVISH MONEY ON EXPENSIVE HOME APPLIANCES!

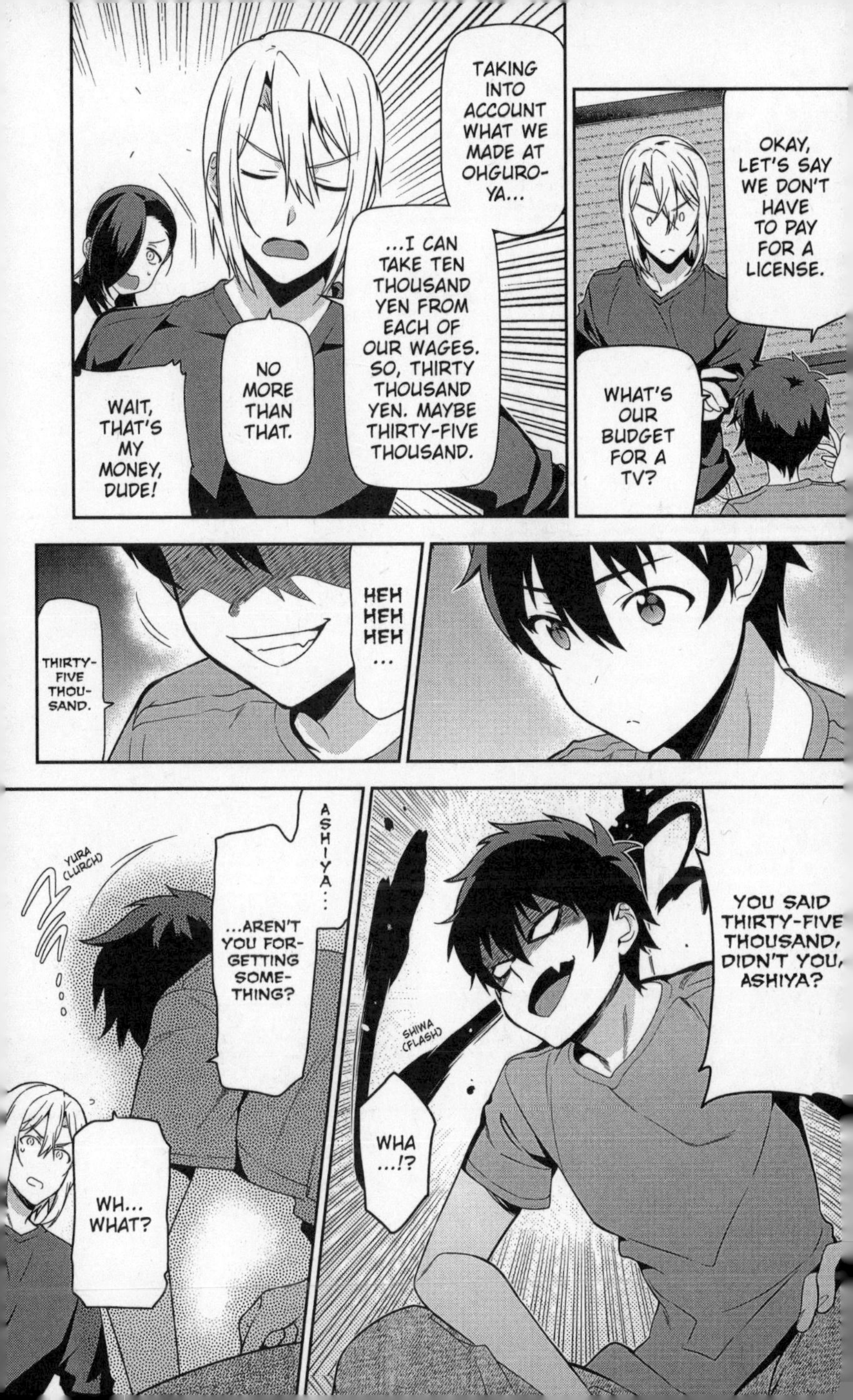
OKAY, LET'S SAY WE DON'T HAVE TO PAY FOR A LICENSE.
WHAT'S OUR BUDGET FOR A TV?
TAKING INTO ACCOUNT WHAT WE MADE AT OHGURO-YA...
...I CAN TAKE TEN THOUSAND YEN FROM EACH OF OUR WAGES. SO, THIRTY THOUSAND YEN. MAYBE THIRTY-FIVE THOUSAND.
NO MORE THAN THAT.
WAIT, THAT'S MY MONEY, DUDE!
HEH HEH HEH...
THIRTY-FIVE THOU-SAND.
YOU SAID THIRTY-FIVE THOUSAND, DIDN'T YOU, ASHIYA?
SHIWA (FLASH)
WHA...!?
ASHIYA...
...AREN'T YOU FOR-GETTING SOME-THING?
YURA (LURCH)
WH... WHAT?

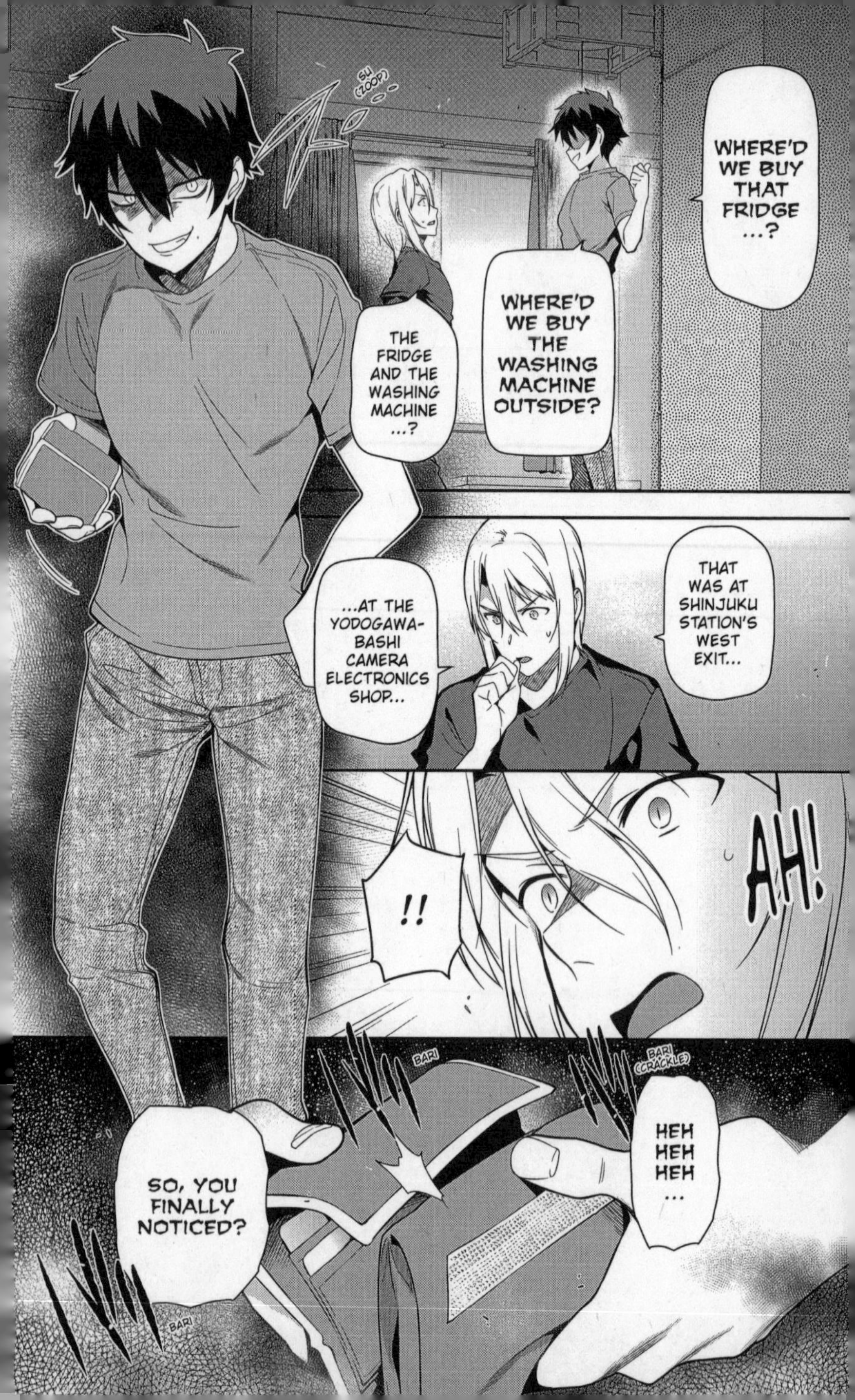
WHERE'D WE BUY THAT FRIDGE ...?
WHERE'D WE BUY THE WASHING MACHINE OUTSIDE?
THE FRIDGE AND THE WASHING MACHINE ...?
THAT WAS AT SHINJUKU STATION'S WEST EXIT...
...AT THE YODOGAWA-BASHI CAMERA ELECTRONICS SHOP...
AH!
!!
BARI (CRACKLE)
HEH HEH HEH ...
BARI
BARI
SO, YOU FINALLY NOTICED?
SU (ZOOP)

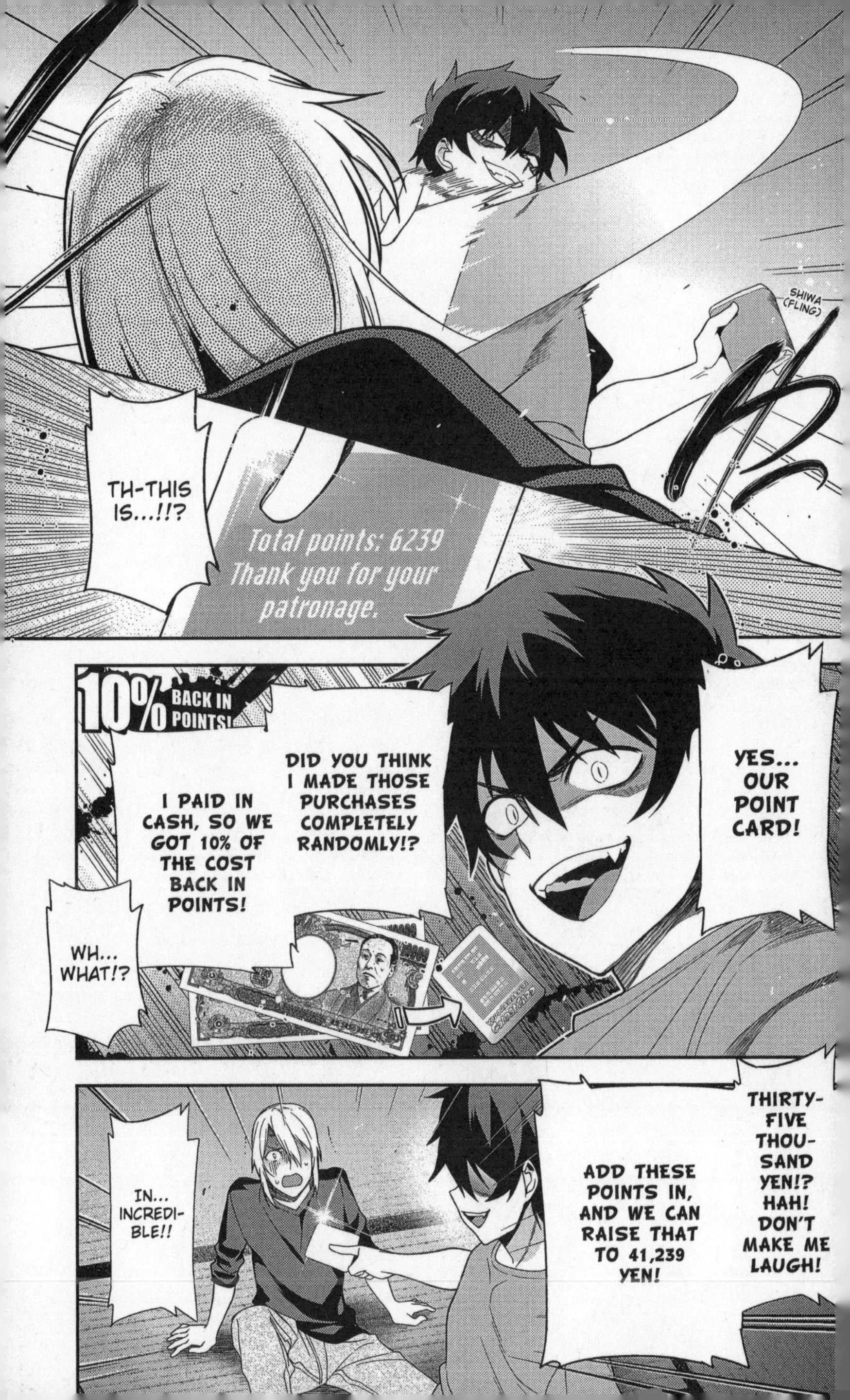
SHIWA (FLING)
Total points: 6239 Thank you for your patronage.
TH-THIS IS...!!?
YES... OUR POINT CARD!
DID YOU THINK I MADE THOSE PURCHASES COMPLETELY RANDOMLY!?
10% BACK IN POINTS!
I PAID IN CASH, SO WE GOT 10% OF THE COST BACK IN POINTS!
WH... WHAT!?
THIRTY-FIVE THOUSAND YEN!? HAH! DON'T MAKE ME LAUGH!
ADD THESE POINTS IN, AND WE CAN RAISE THAT TO 41,239 YEN!
IN... INCREDIBLE!!

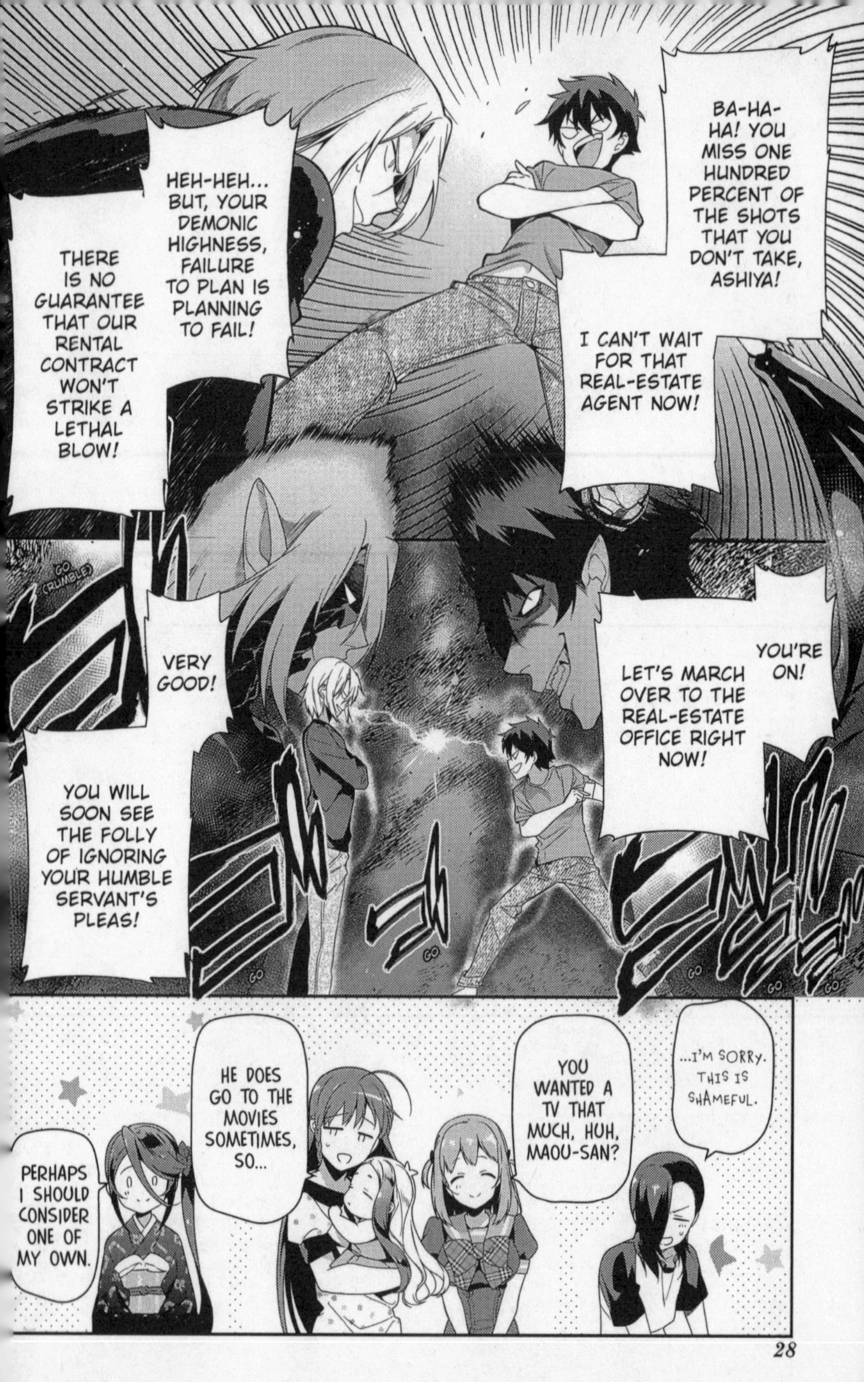
BA-HA-HA! YOU MISS ONE HUNDRED PERCENT OF THE SHOTS THAT YOU DON'T TAKE, ASHIYA!
I CAN'T WAIT FOR THAT REAL-ESTATE AGENT NOW!
HEH-HEH... BUT, YOUR DEMONIC HIGHNESS, FAILURE TO PLAN IS PLANNING TO FAIL!
THERE IS NO GUARANTEE THAT OUR RENTAL CONTRACT WON'T STRIKE A LETHAL BLOW!
YOU'RE ON!
LET'S MARCH OVER TO THE REAL-ESTATE OFFICE RIGHT NOW!
GO (RUMBLE)
VERY GOOD!
YOU WILL SOON SEE THE FOLLY OF IGNORING YOUR HUMBLE SERVANT'S PLEAS!
GO
GO
GO
GO
GO
...I'M SORRY. THIS IS SHAMEFUL.
YOU WANTED A TV THAT MUCH, HUH, MAOU-SAN?
HE DOES GO TO THE MOVIES SOMETIMES, SO...
PERHAPS I SHOULD CONSIDER ONE OF MY OWN.

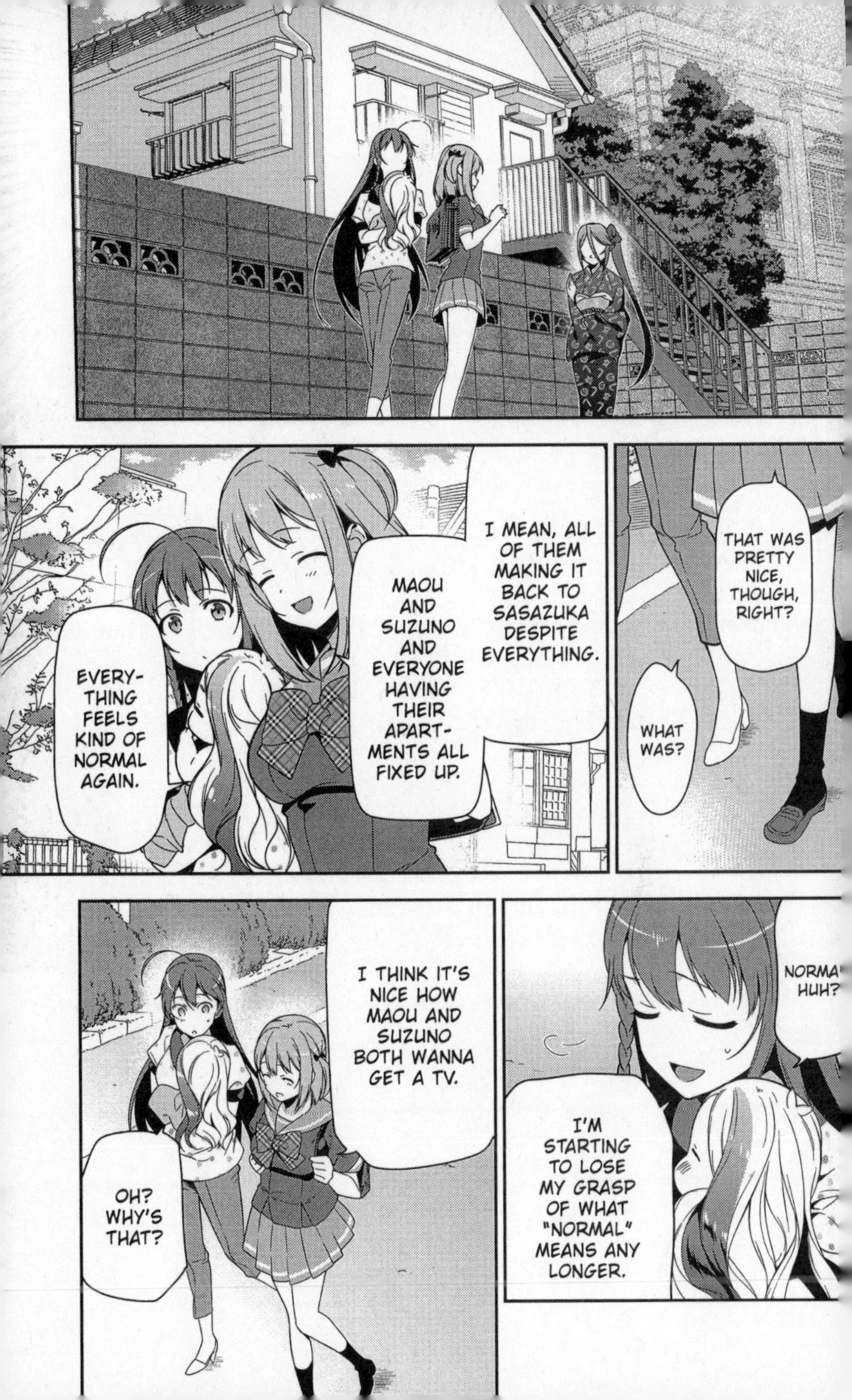
THAT WAS PRETTY NICE, THOUGH, RIGHT?
WHAT WAS?
I MEAN, ALL OF THEM MAKING IT BACK TO SASAZUKA DESPITE EVERYTHING.
MAOU AND SUZUNO AND EVERYONE HAVING THEIR APARTMENTS ALL FIXED UP.
EVERYTHING FEELS KIND OF NORMAL AGAIN.
NORMA HUH?
I'M STARTING TO LOSE MY GRASP OF WHAT "NORMAL" MEANS ANY LONGER.
I THINK IT'S NICE HOW MAOU AND SUZUNO BOTH WANNA GET A TV.
OH? WHY'S THAT?

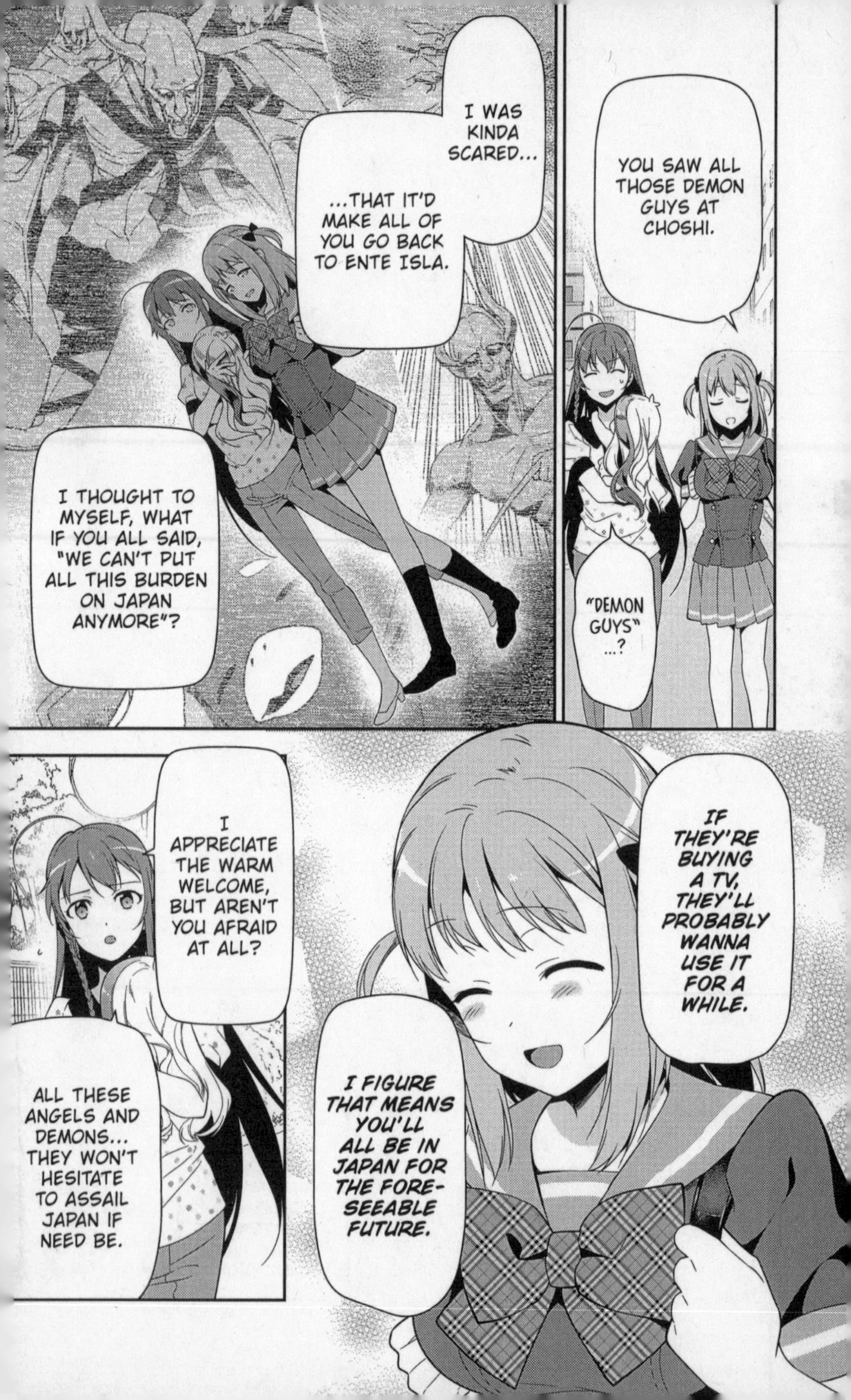
YOU SAW ALL THOSE DEMON GUYS AT CHOSHI.
"DEMON GUYS" ...?
I WAS KINDA SCARED...
...THAT IT'D MAKE ALL OF YOU GO BACK TO ENTE ISLA.
I THOUGHT TO MYSELF, WHAT IF YOU ALL SAID, "WE CAN'T PUT ALL THIS BURDEN ON JAPAN ANYMORE"?
IF THEY'RE BUYING A TV, THEY'LL PROBABLY WANNA USE IT FOR A WHILE.
I FIGURE THAT MEANS YOU'LL ALL BE IN JAPAN FOR THE FORE-SEEABLE FUTURE.
I APPRECIATE THE WARM WELCOME, BUT AREN'T YOU AFRAID AT ALL?
ALL THESE ANGELS AND DEMONS... THEY WON'T HESITATE TO ASSAIL JAPAN IF NEED BE.

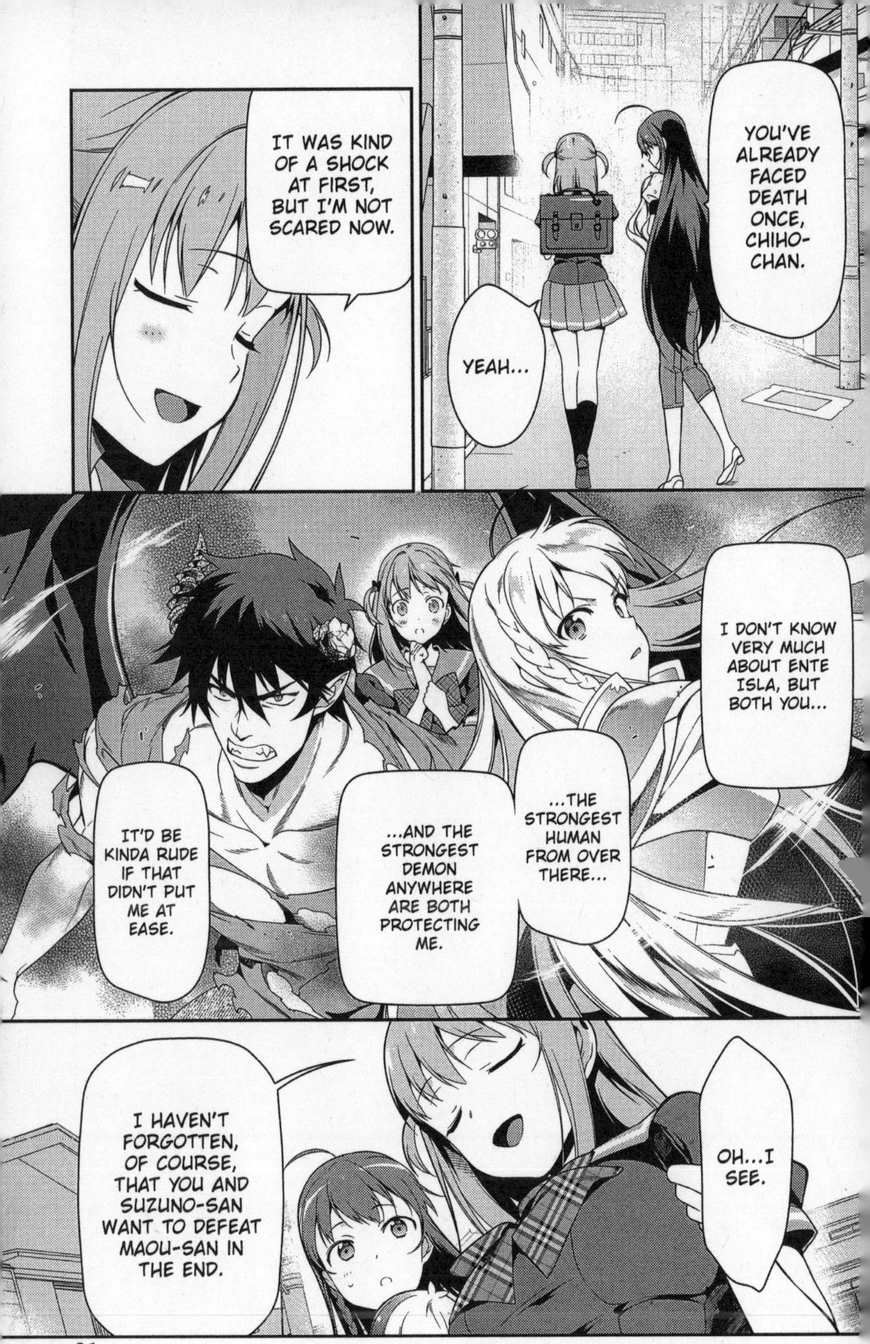
YOU'VE ALREADY FACED DEATH ONCE, CHIHO-CHAN.
YEAH...
IT WAS KIND OF A SHOCK AT FIRST, BUT I'M NOT SCARED NOW.
I DON'T KNOW VERY MUCH ABOUT ENTE ISLA, BUT BOTH YOU...
...THE STRONGEST HUMAN FROM OVER THERE...
...AND THE STRONGEST DEMON ANYWHERE ARE BOTH PROTECTING ME.
IT'D BE KINDA RUDE IF THAT DIDN'T PUT ME AT EASE.
OH...I SEE.
I HAVEN'T FORGOTTEN, OF COURSE, THAT YOU AND SUZUNO-SAN WANT TO DEFEAT MAOU-SAN IN THE END.

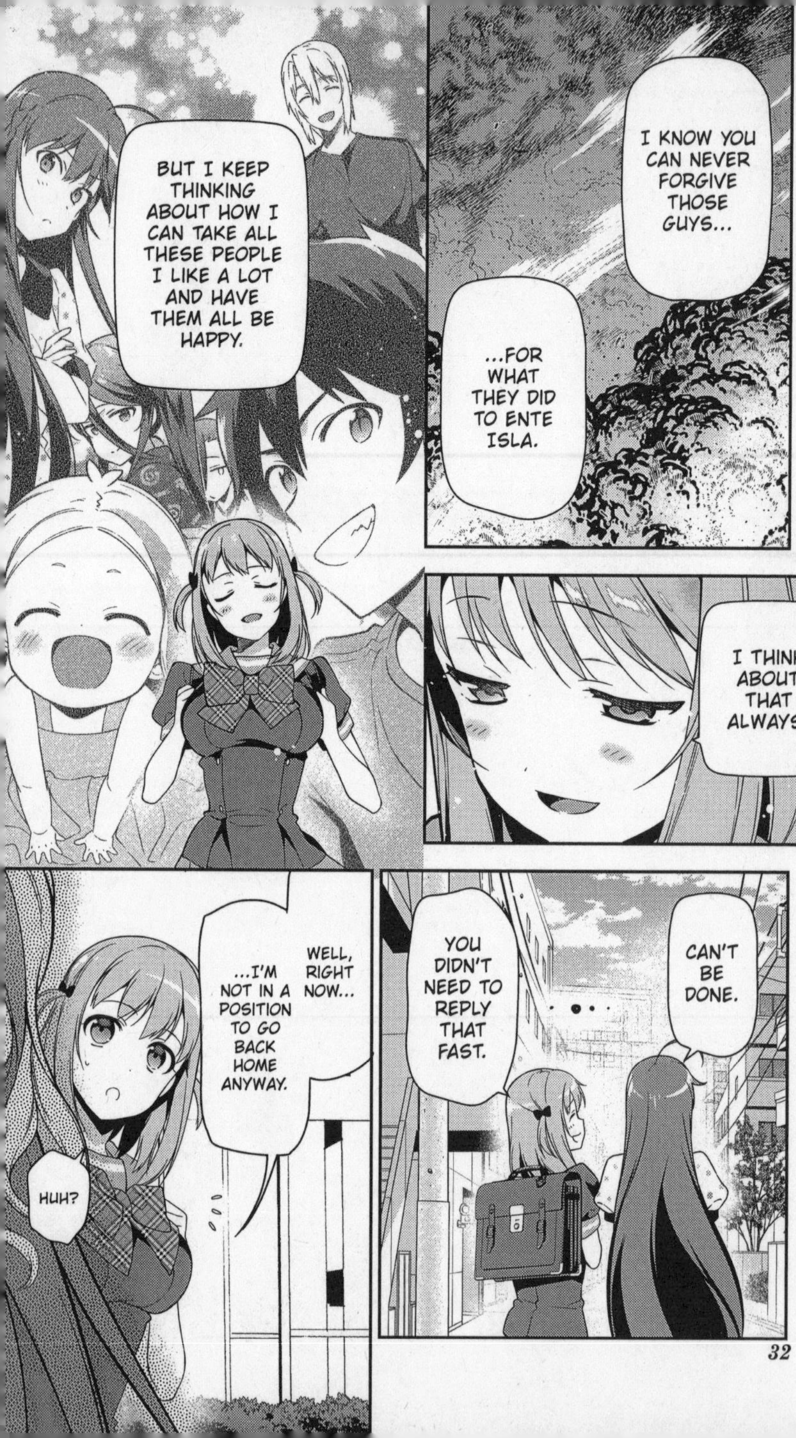
I KNOW YOU CAN NEVER FORGIVE THOSE GUYS...
...FOR WHAT THEY DID TO ENTE ISLA.
I THINK ABOUT THAT ALWAYS.
BUT I KEEP THINKING ABOUT HOW I CAN TAKE ALL THESE PEOPLE I LIKE A LOT AND HAVE THEM ALL BE HAPPY.
CAN'T BE DONE.
...
YOU DIDN'T NEED TO REPLY THAT FAST.
WELL, RIGHT NOW...
...I'M NOT IN A POSITION TO GO BACK HOME ANYWAY.
HUH?

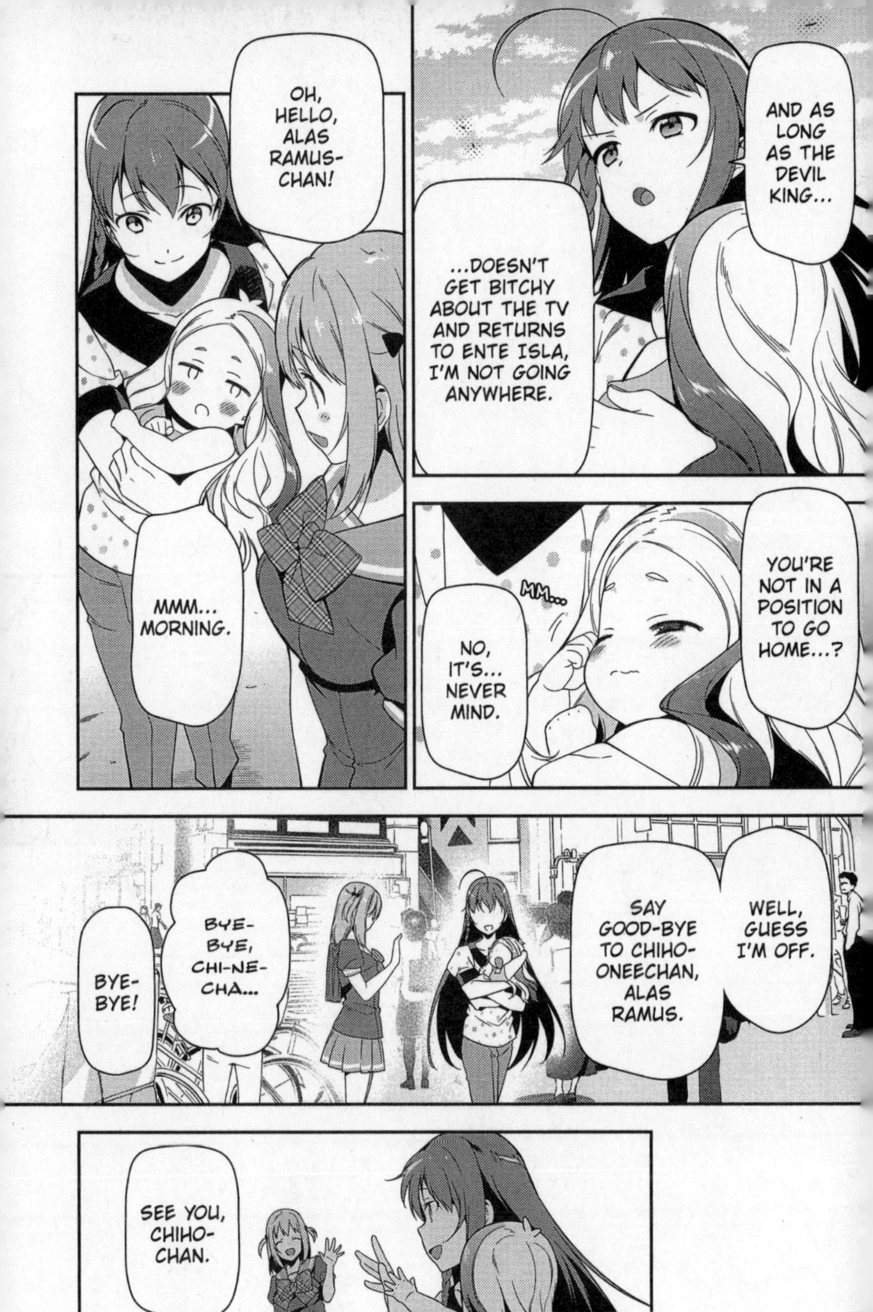
AND AS LONG AS THE DEVIL KING...
...DOESN'T GET BITCHY ABOUT THE TV AND RETURNS TO ENTE ISLA, I'M NOT GOING ANYWHERE.
YOU'RE NOT IN A POSITION TO GO HOME...?
MM...
NO, IT'S... NEVER MIND.
OH, HELLO, ALAS RAMUS-CHAN!
MMM... MORNING.
WELL, GUESS I'M OFF.
SAY GOOD-BYE TO CHIHO-ONEECHAN, ALAS RAMUS.
BYE-BYE, CHI-NE-CHA...
BYE-BYE!
SEE YOU, CHIHO-CHAN.

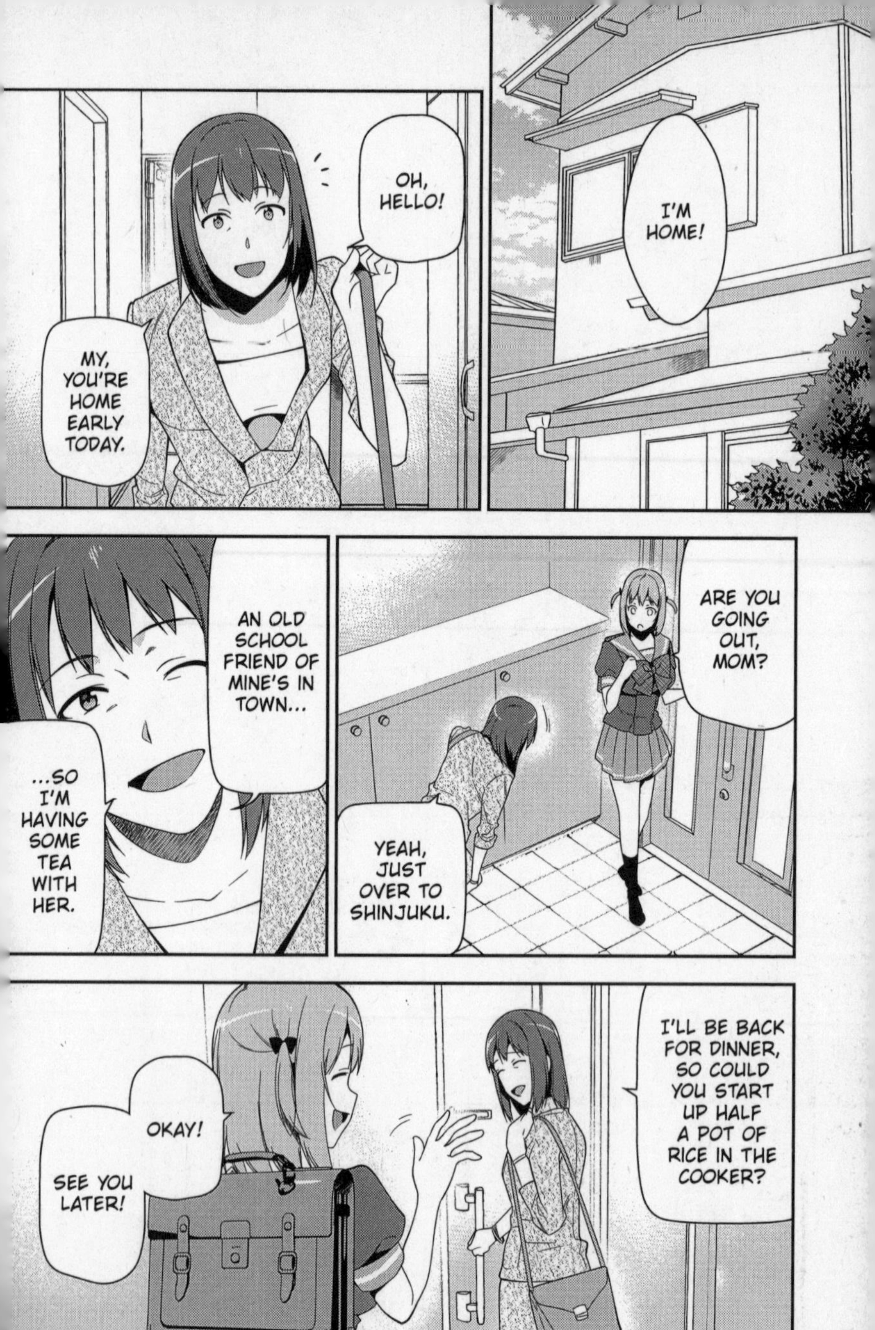
I'M HOME!
OH, HELLO!
MY, YOU'RE HOME EARLY TODAY.
ARE YOU GOING OUT, MOM?
YEAH, JUST OVER TO SHINJUKU.
AN OLD SCHOOL FRIEND OF MINE'S IN TOWN...
...SO I'M HAVING SOME TEA WITH HER.
I'LL BE BACK FOR DINNER, SO COULD YOU START UP HALF A POT OF RICE IN THE COOKER?
OKAY!
SEE YOU LATER!

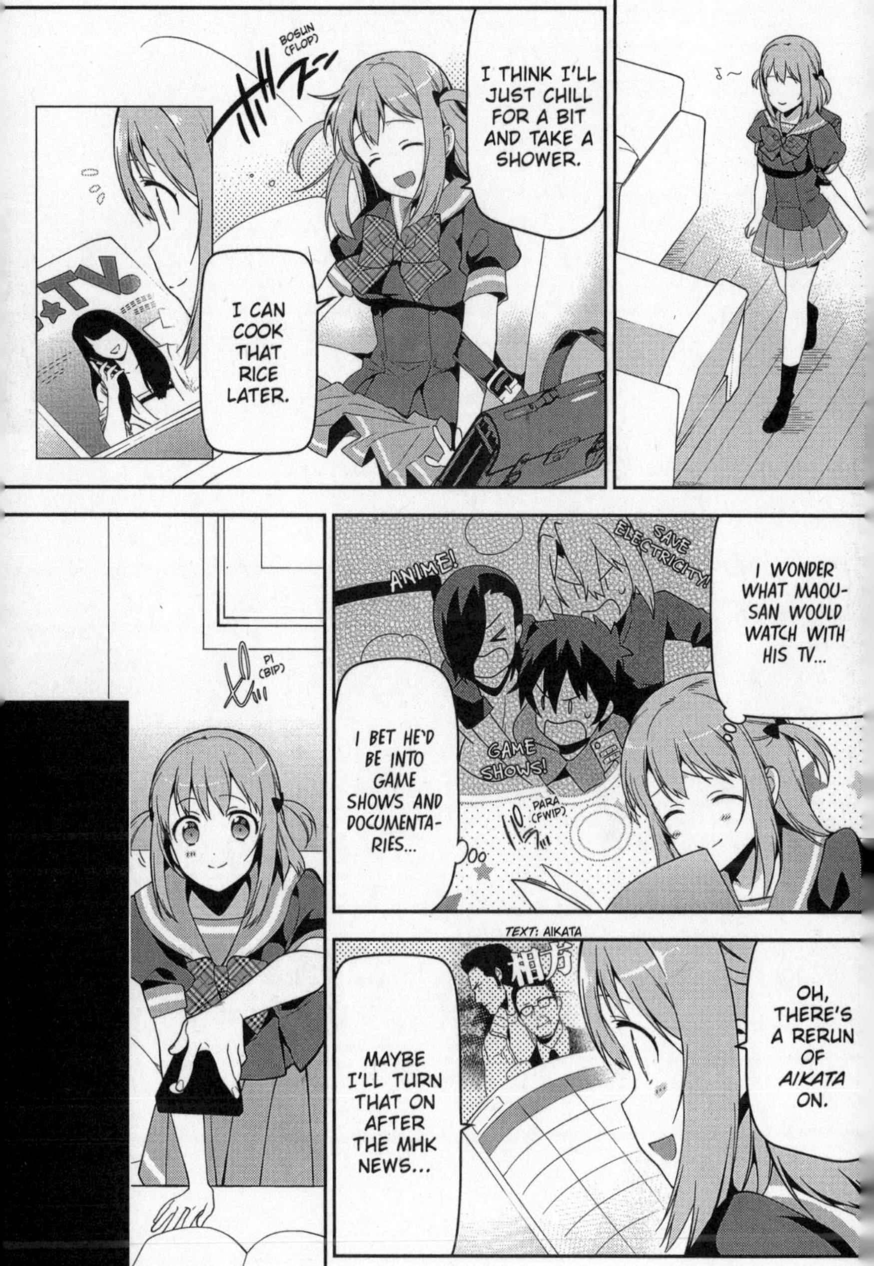

♪~
BOSUN (FLOP)
I THINK I'LL JUST CHILL FOR A BIT AND TAKE A SHOWER.
I CAN COOK THAT RICE LATER.
I WONDER WHAT MAOU-SAN WOULD WATCH WITH HIS TV...
SAVE ELECTRICITY!
ANIME!
GAME SHOWS!
I BET HE'D BE INTO GAME SHOWS AND DOCUMENTA-RIES...
PARA (FWIP)
TEXT: AIKATA
OH, THERE'S A RERUN OF *AIKATA* ON.
MAYBE I'LL TURN THAT ON AFTER THE MHK NEWS...
PI (BIP)

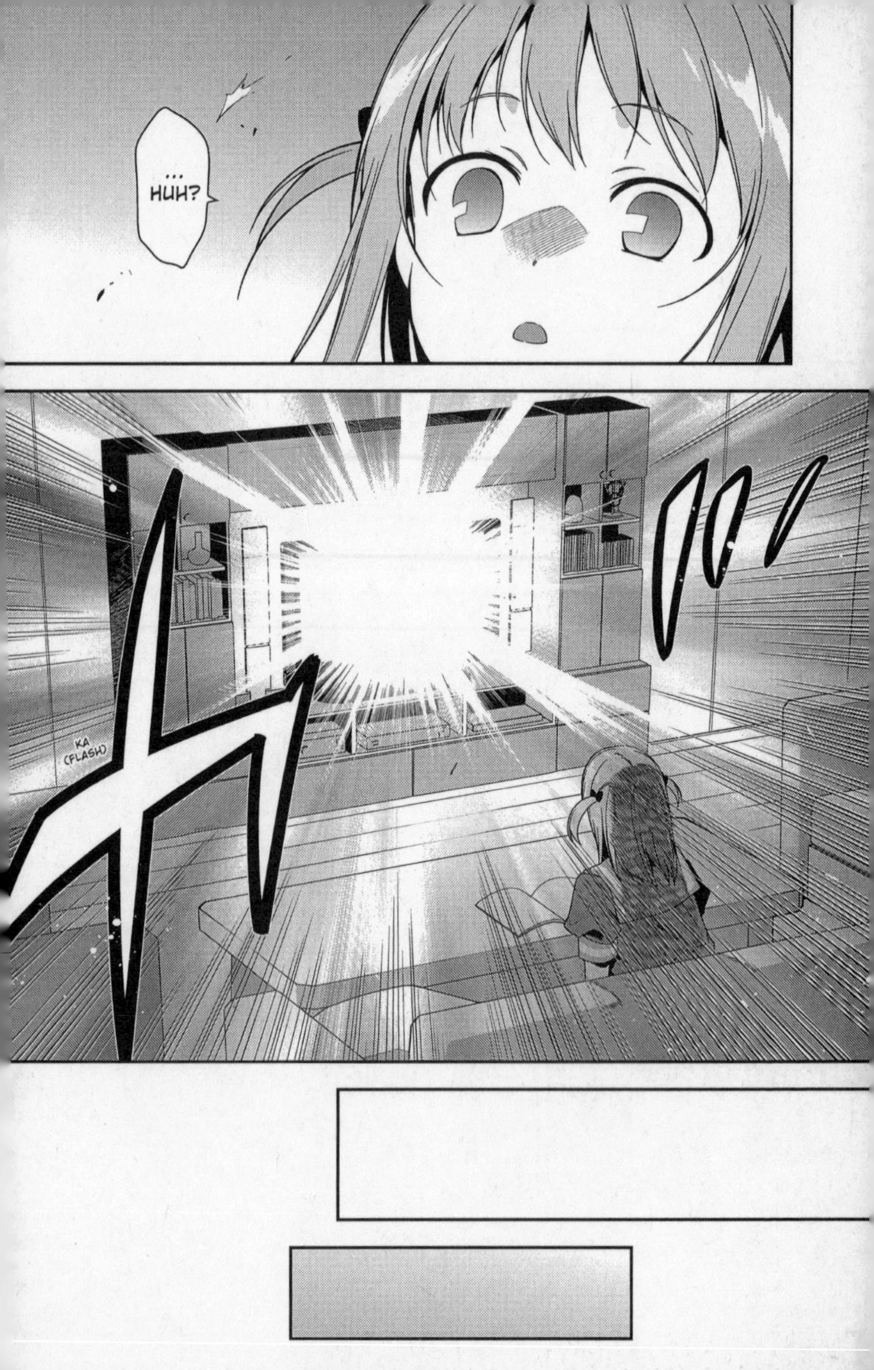
...HUH?
KA (FLASH)

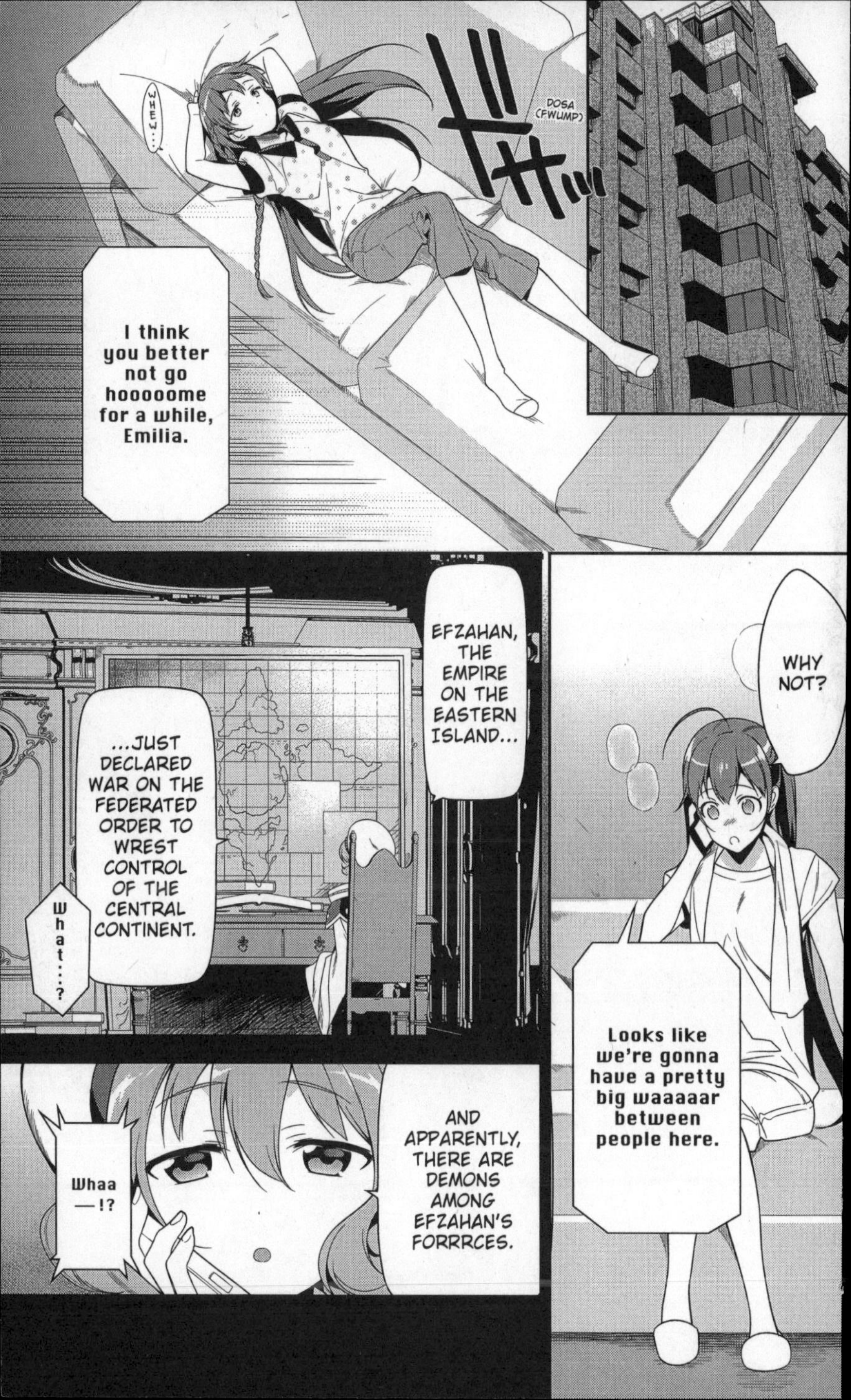
DOSA (FWUMP)
WHEW...
I think you better not go hooooome for a while, Emilia.
WHY NOT?
Looks like we're gonna have a pretty big waaaaar between people here.
EFZAHAN, THE EMPIRE ON THE EASTERN ISLAND...
...JUST DECLARED WAR ON THE FEDERATED ORDER TO WREST CONTROL OF THE CENTRAL CONTINENT.
What...?
AND APPARENTLY, THERE ARE DEMONS AMONG EFZAHAN'S FORRRCES.
Whaa—!?

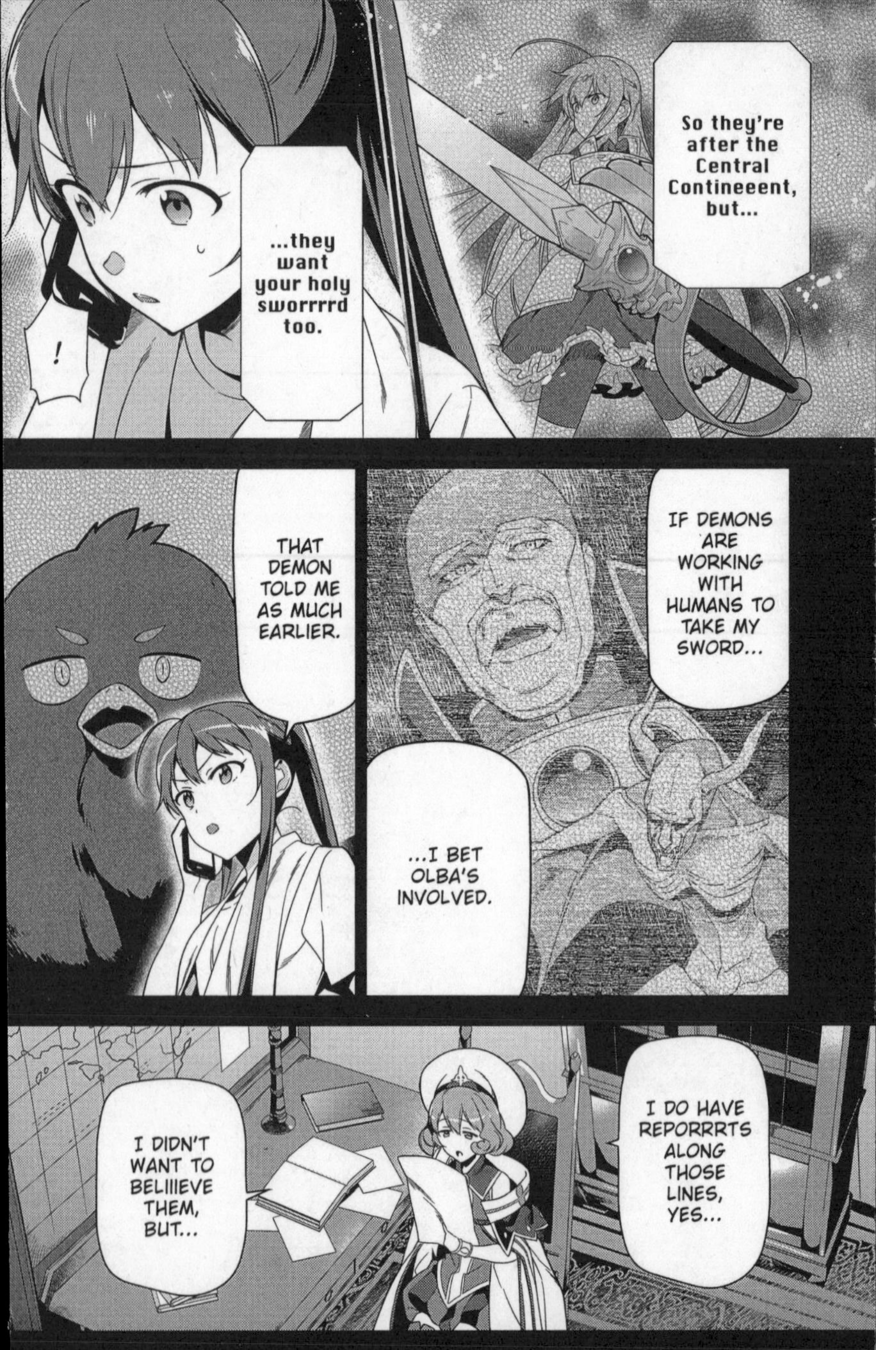
So they're after the Central Contineeent, but...
...they want your holy sworrrrd too.
!
IF DEMONS ARE WORKING WITH HUMANS TO TAKE MY SWORD...
...I BET OLBA'S INVOLVED.
THAT DEMON TOLD ME AS MUCH EARLIER.
I DO HAVE REPORRRTS ALONG THOSE LINES, YES...
I DIDN'T WANT TO BELIIIEVE THEM, BUT...

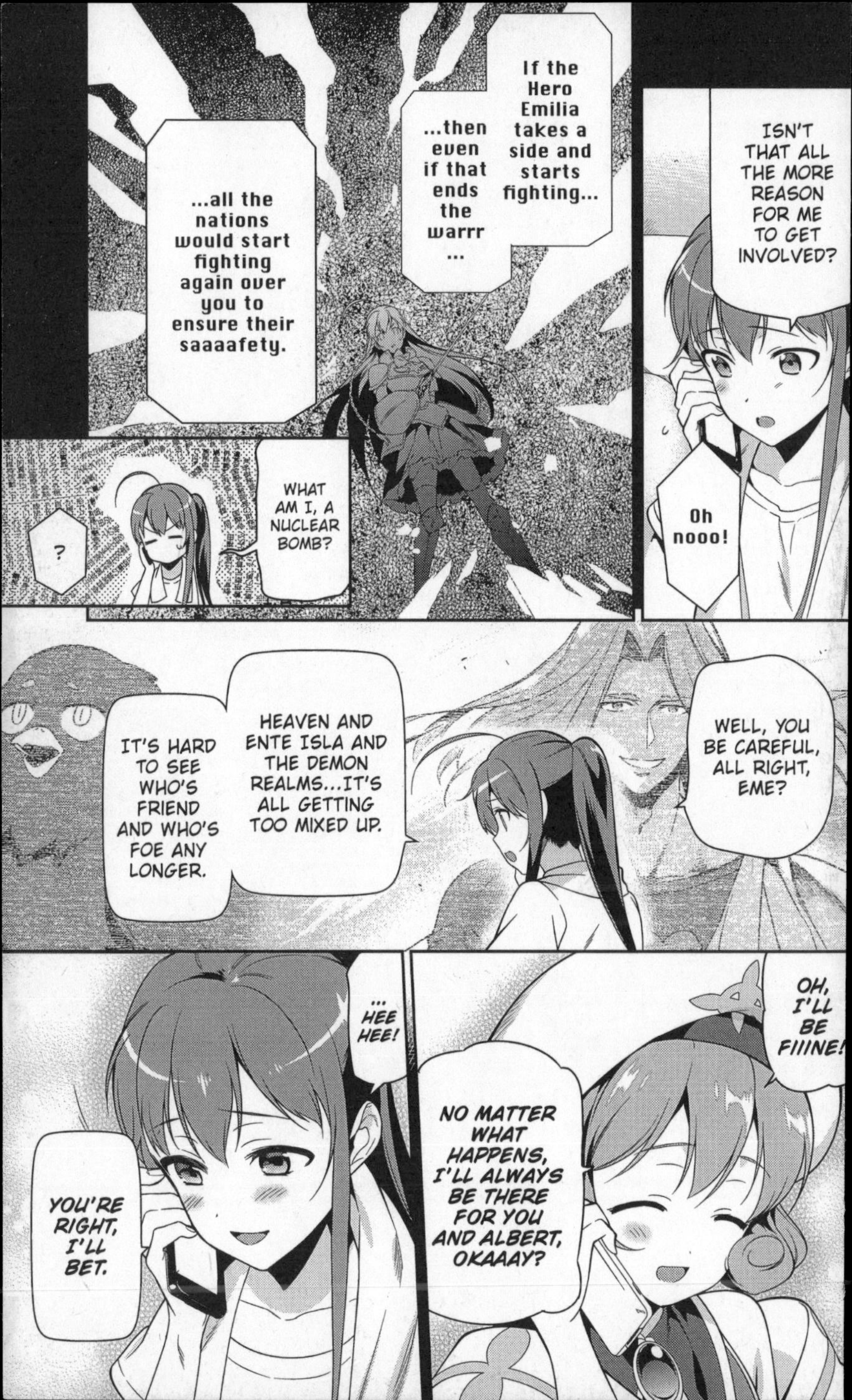
ISN'T THAT ALL THE MORE REASON FOR ME TO GET INVOLVED?
Oh nooo!
If the Hero Emilia takes a side and starts fighting...
...then even if that ends the warrr...
...all the nations would start fighting again over you to ensure their saaaafety.
WHAT AM I, A NUCLEAR BOMB?
?
WELL, YOU BE CAREFUL, ALL RIGHT, EME?
HEAVEN AND ENTE ISLA AND THE DEMON REALMS...IT'S ALL GETTING TOO MIXED UP.
IT'S HARD TO SEE WHO'S FRIEND AND WHO'S FOE ANY LONGER.
OH, I'LL BE FIIINE!
NO MATTER WHAT HAPPENS, I'LL ALWAYS BE THERE FOR YOU AND ALBERT, OKAAAY?
...HEE HEE!
YOU'RE RIGHT, I'LL BET.

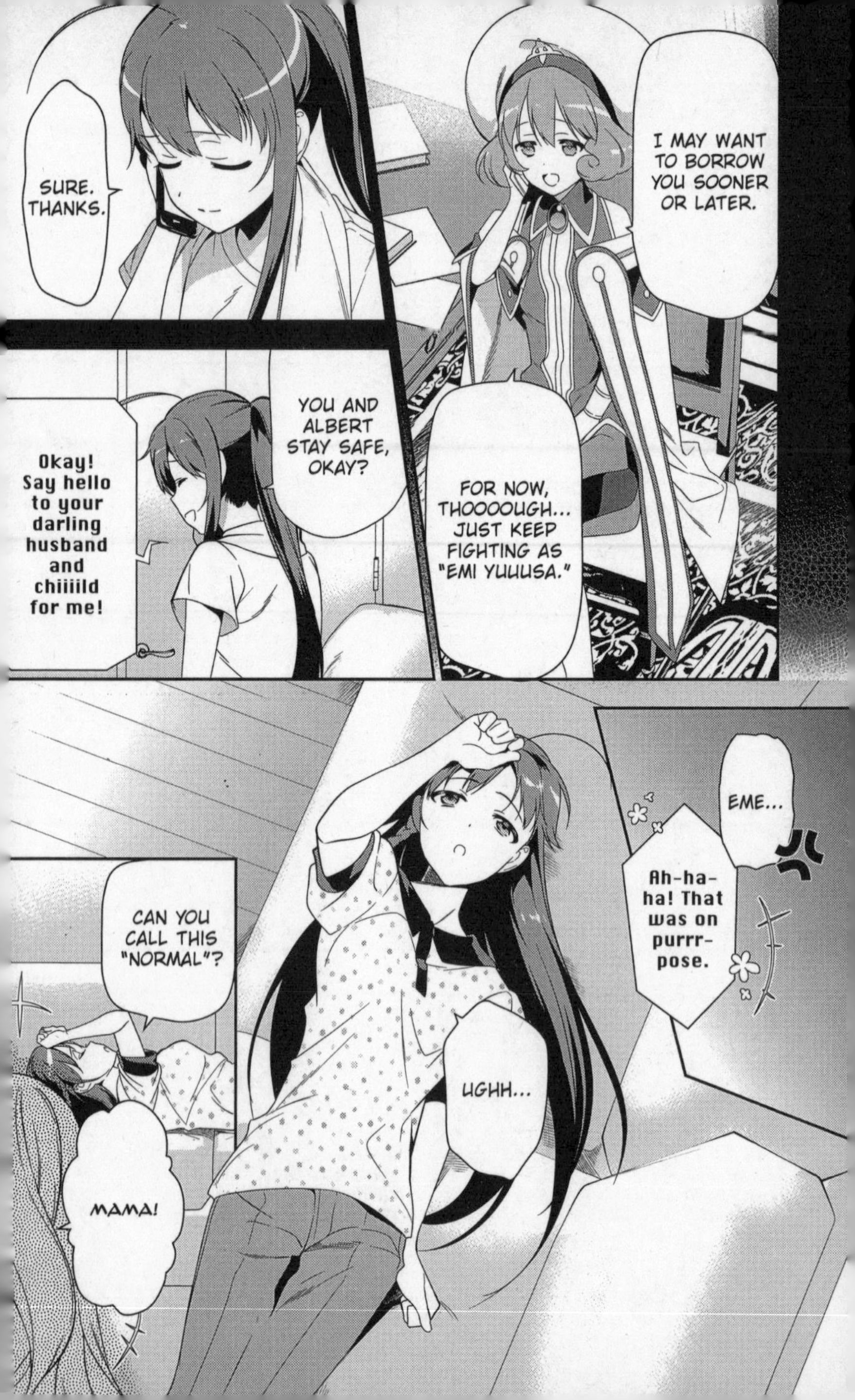
I MAY WANT TO BORROW YOU SOONER OR LATER.
FOR NOW, THOOOOUGH... JUST KEEP FIGHTING AS "EMI YUUUSA."
SURE. THANKS.
YOU AND ALBERT STAY SAFE, OKAY?
Okay! Say hello to your darling husband and chiiiild for me!
EME...
Ah-ha-ha! That was on purrr-pose.
UGHH...
CAN YOU CALL THIS "NORMAL"?
MAMA!

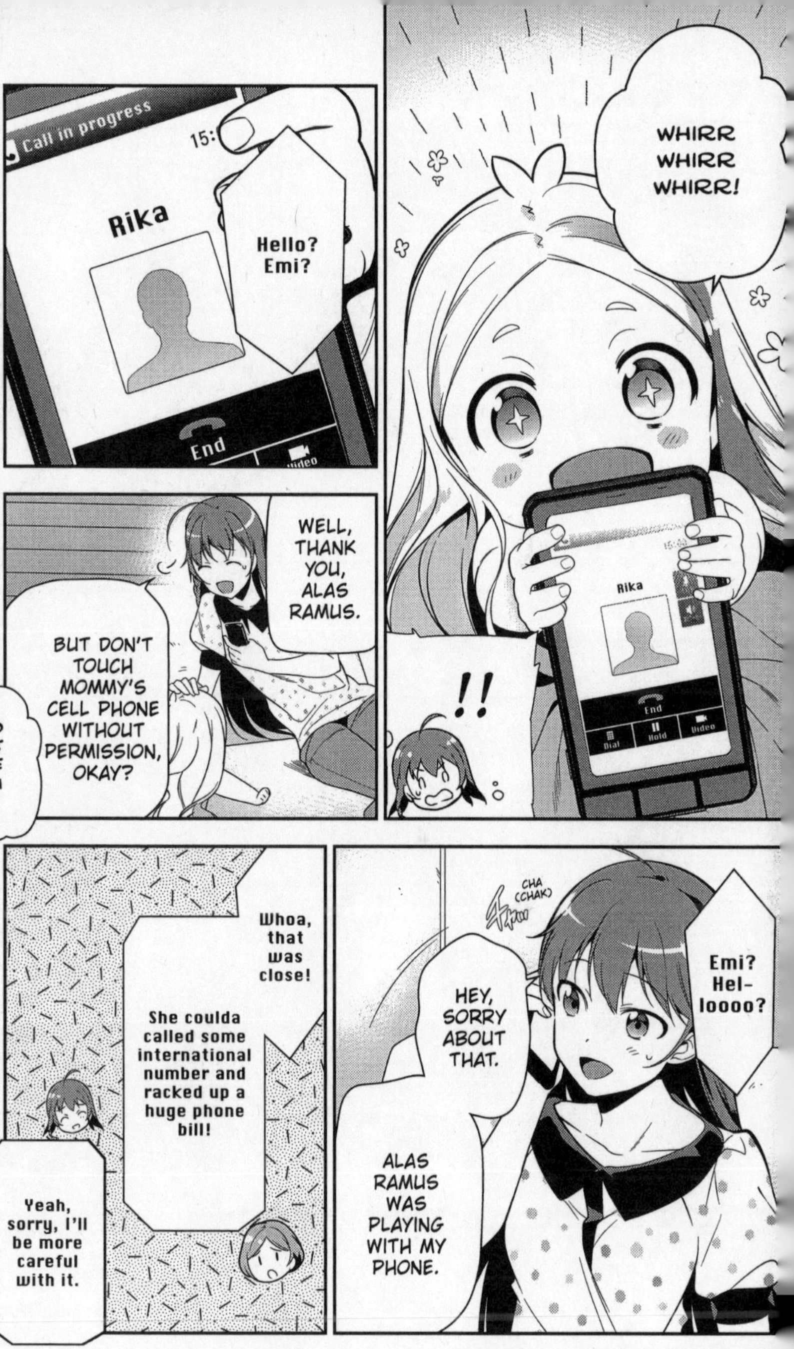
WHIRR
WHIRR
WHIRR!
Rika
End
Dial
Hold
Video
!!
Call in progress
15:
Rika
Hello? Emi?
End
Video
WELL, THANK YOU, ALAS RAMUS.
BUT DON'T TOUCH MOMMY'S CELL PHONE WITHOUT PERMISSION, OKAY?
OKEH!
CHA (CHAK)
Emi? Hel-loooo?
HEY, SORRY ABOUT THAT.
ALAS RAMUS WAS PLAYING WITH MY PHONE.
Whoa, that was close!
She coulda called some international number and racked up a huge phone bill!
Yeah, sorry, I'll be more careful with it.

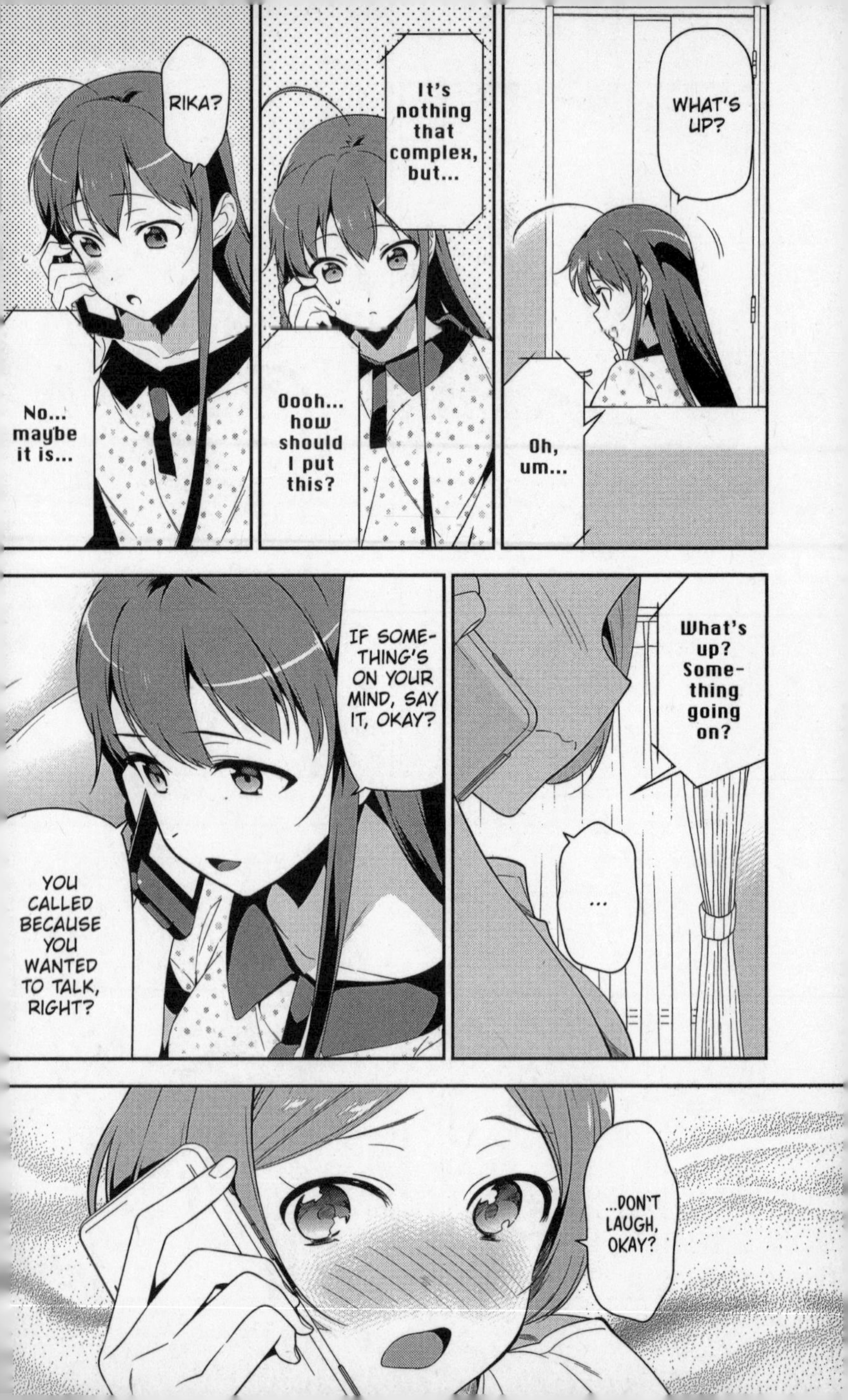
WHAT'S UP?
Oh, um...
It's nothing that complex, but...
Oooh... how should I put this?
RIKA?
No... maybe it is...
What's up? Some-thing going on?
...
IF SOME-THING'S ON YOUR MIND, SAY IT, OKAY?
YOU CALLED BECAUSE YOU WANTED TO TALK, RIGHT?
...DON'T LAUGH, OKAY?

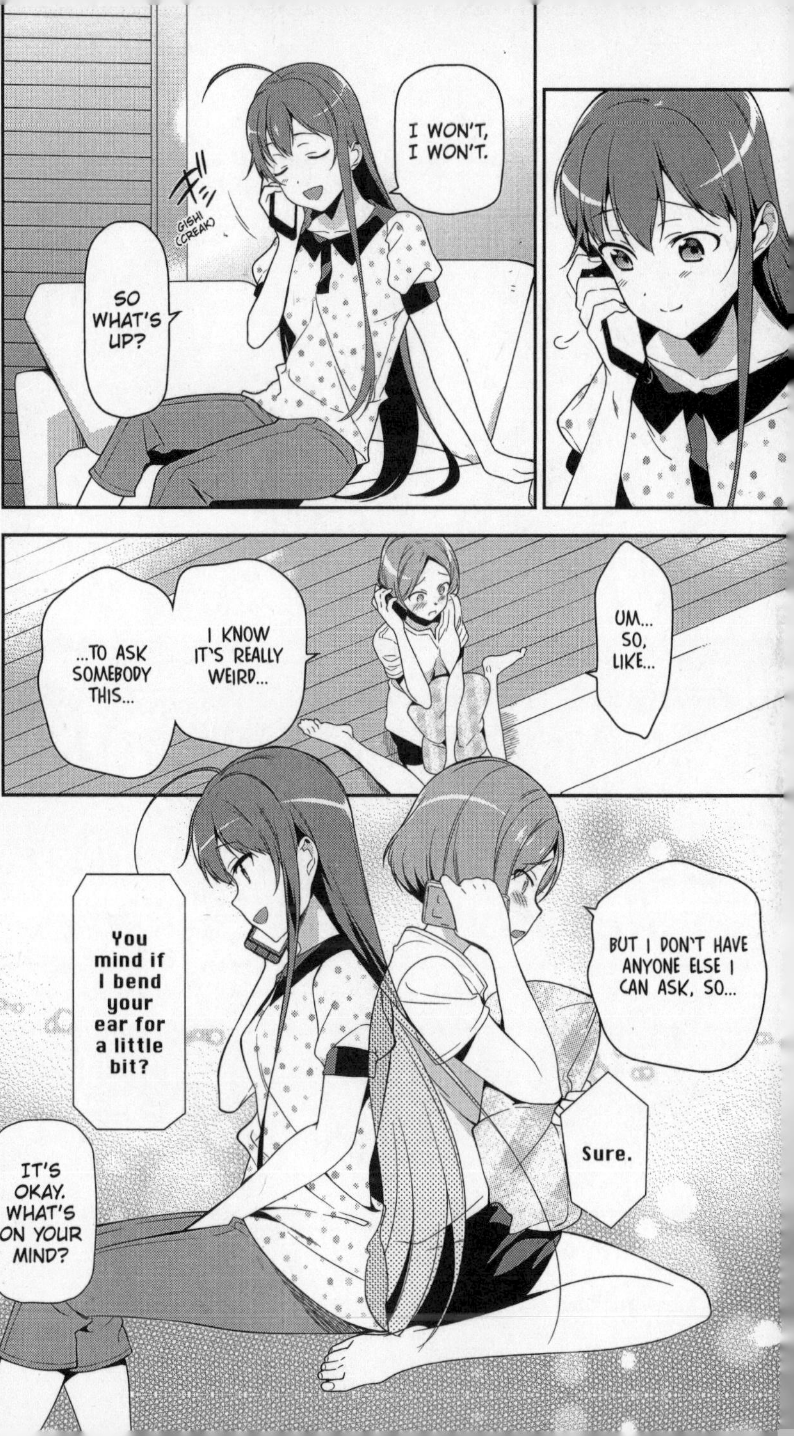
I WON'T, I WON'T.
GISHI (CREAK)
SO WHAT'S UP?
UM... SO, LIKE...
I KNOW IT'S REALLY WEIRD...
...TO ASK SOMEBODY THIS...
BUT I DON'T HAVE ANYONE ELSE I CAN ASK, SO...
You mind if I bend your ear for a little bit?
Sure.
IT'S OKAY. WHAT'S ON YOUR MIND?

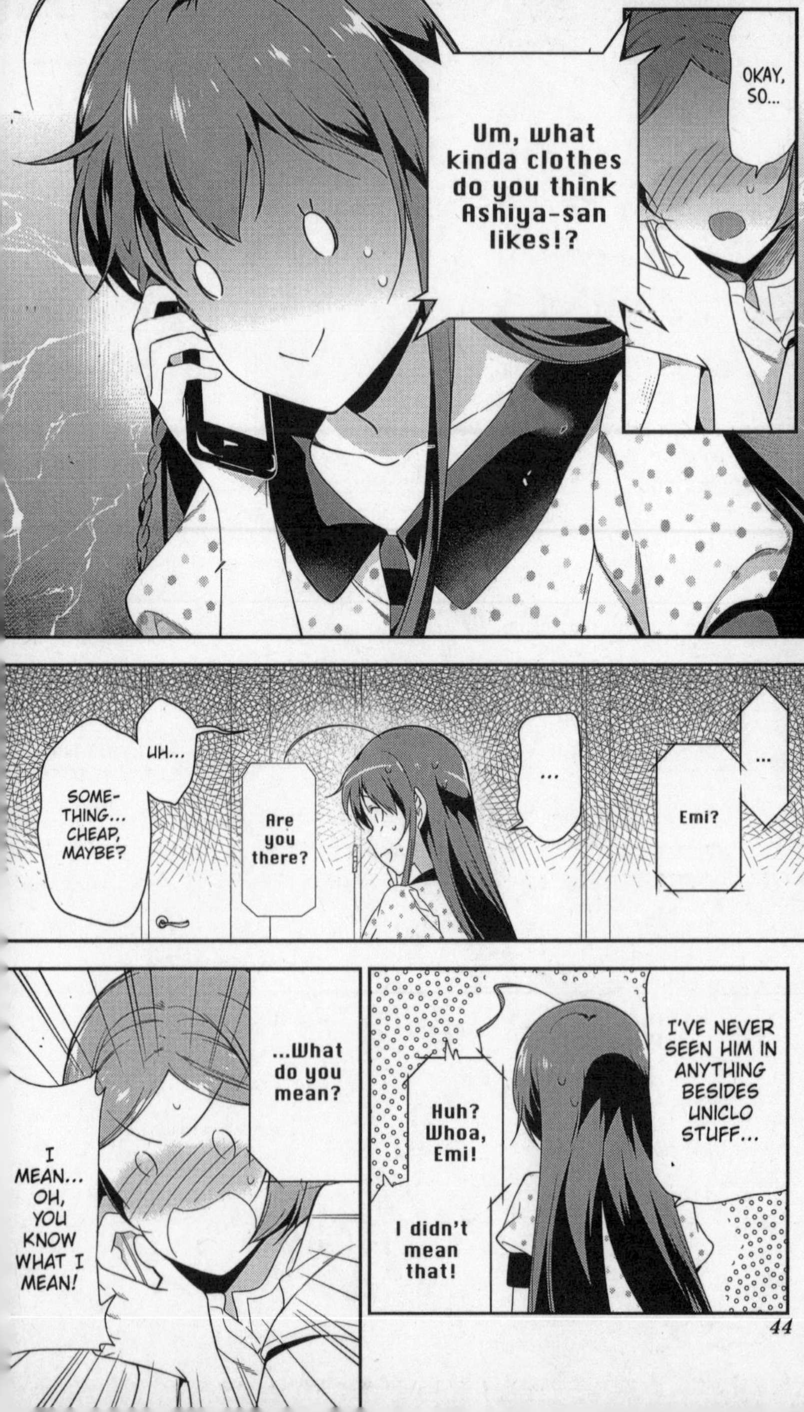
OKAY, SO...
Um, what kinda clothes do you think Ashiya-san likes!?
...
Emi?
...
Are you there?
UH...
SOMETHING... CHEAP, MAYBE?
I'VE NEVER SEEN HIM IN ANYTHING BESIDES UNICLO STUFF...
Huh? Whoa, Emi!
I didn't mean that!
...What do you mean?
I MEAN... OH, YOU KNOW WHAT I MEAN!

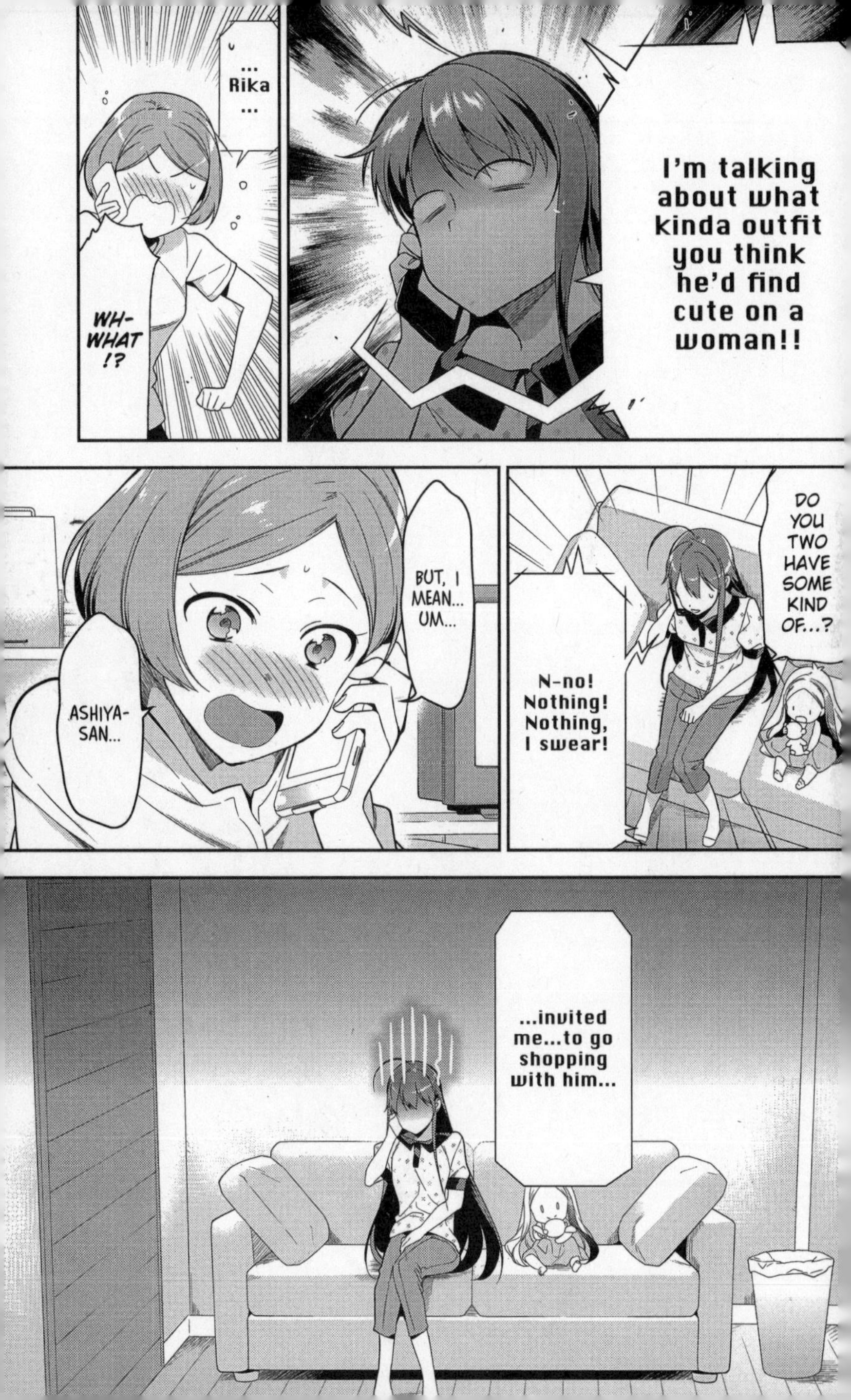
I'm talking about what kinda outfit you think he'd find cute on a woman!!
... Rika ...
WH-WHAT!?
DO YOU TWO HAVE SOME KIND OF...?
N-no! Nothing! Nothing, I swear!
BUT, I MEAN... UM...
ASHIYA-SAN...
...invited me...to go shopping with him...

THE DEVIL IS A PART-TIMER!

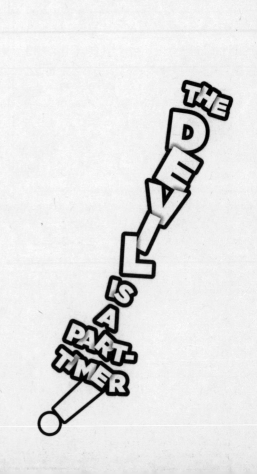

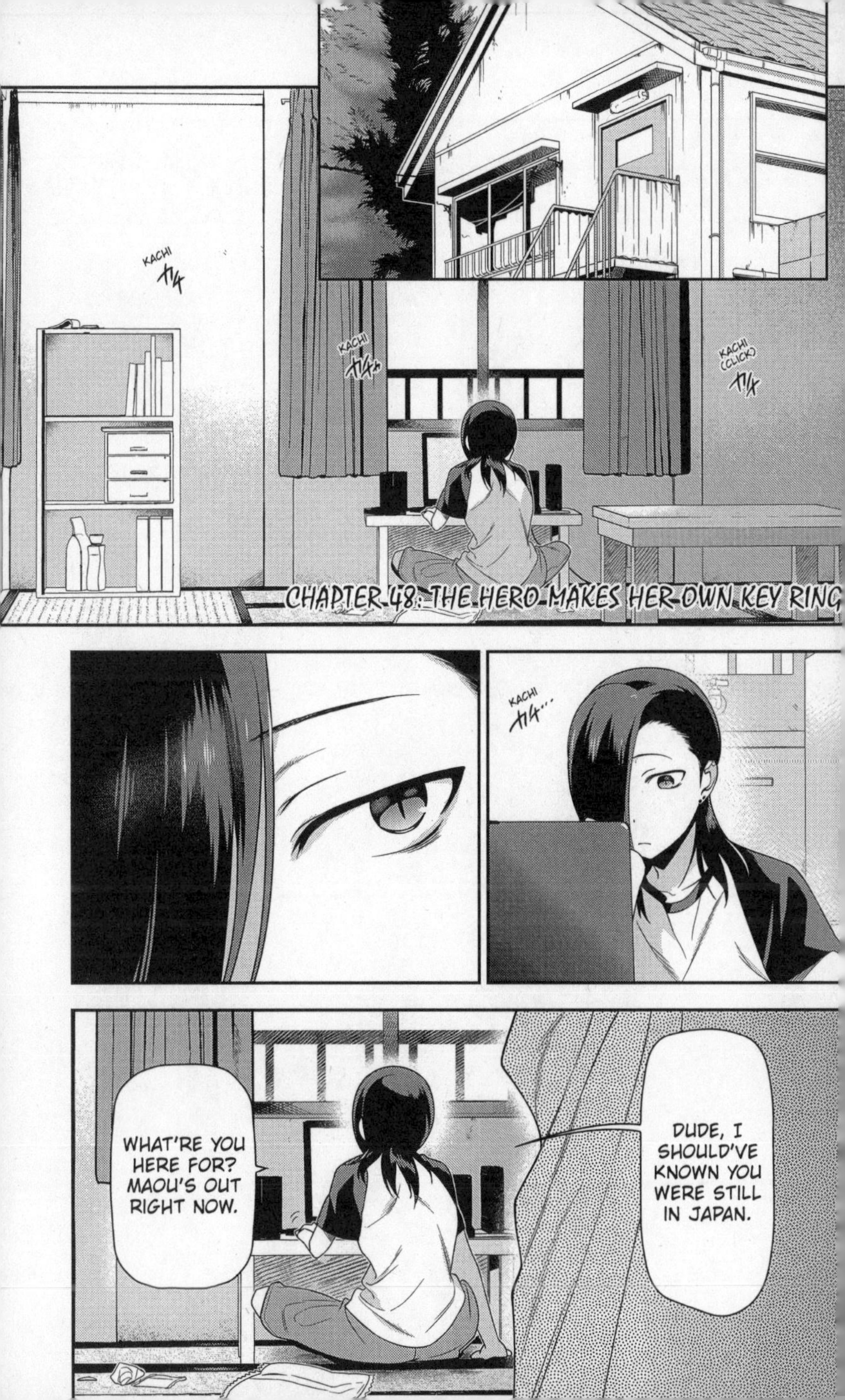
KACHI (CLICK)
カチ
KACHI
カチッ
KACHI
カチ
CHAPTER 48: THE HERO MAKES HER OWN KEY RING
KACHI
カチ…
DUDE, I SHOULD'VE KNOWN YOU WERE STILL IN JAPAN.
WHAT'RE YOU HERE FOR? MAOU'S OUT RIGHT NOW.

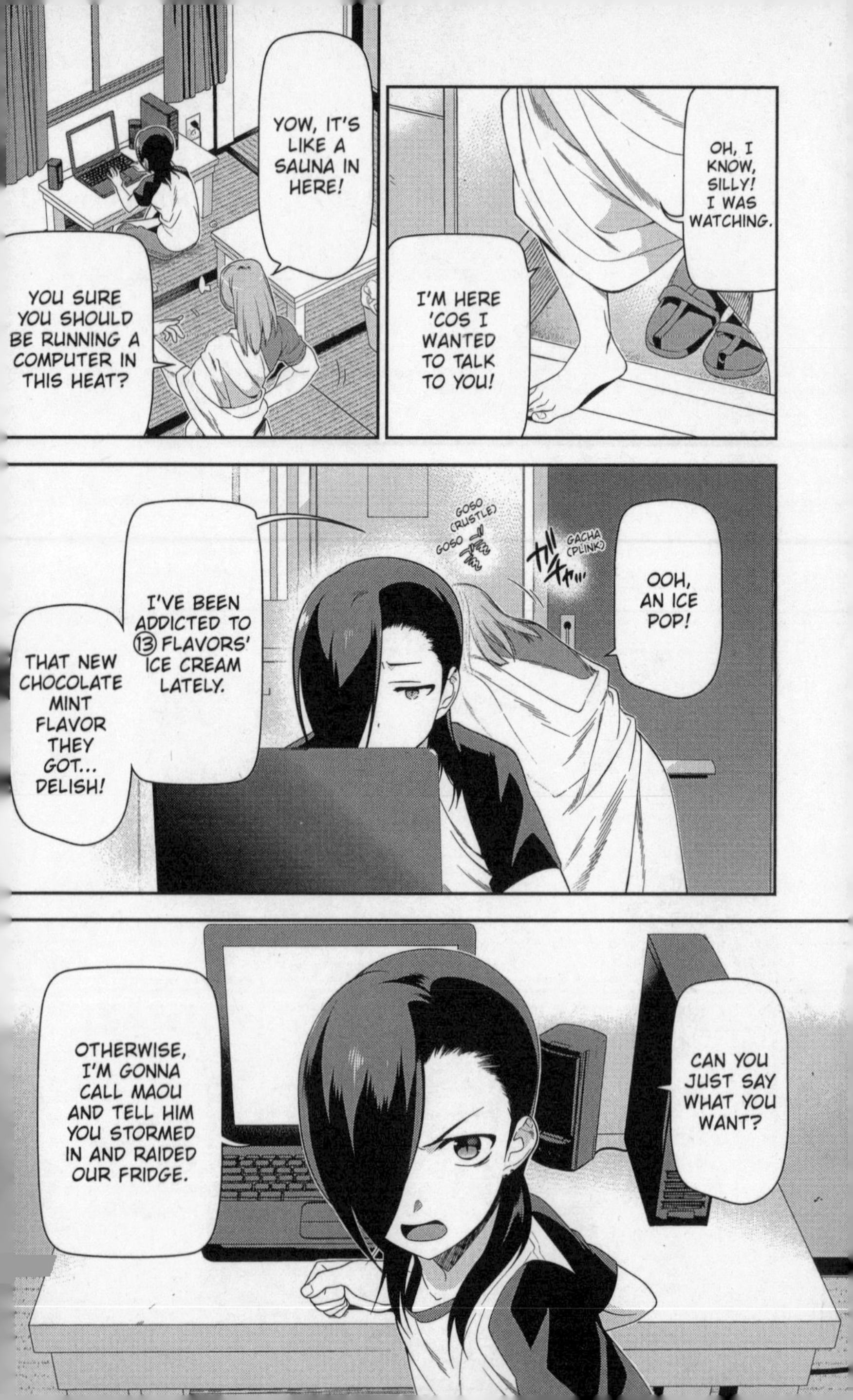
OH, I KNOW, SILLY! I WAS WATCHING.
I'M HERE 'COS I WANTED TO TALK TO YOU!
YOW, IT'S LIKE A SAUNA IN HERE!
YOU SURE YOU SHOULD BE RUNNING A COMPUTER IN THIS HEAT?
GACHA (PLINK)
OOH, AN ICE POP!
GOSO GOSO (RUSTLE)
I'VE BEEN ADDICTED TO ⑬ FLAVORS' ICE CREAM LATELY.
THAT NEW CHOCOLATE MINT FLAVOR THEY GOT... DELISH!
CAN YOU JUST SAY WHAT YOU WANT?
OTHERWISE, I'M GONNA CALL MAOU AND TELL HIM YOU STORMED IN AND RAIDED OUR FRIDGE.

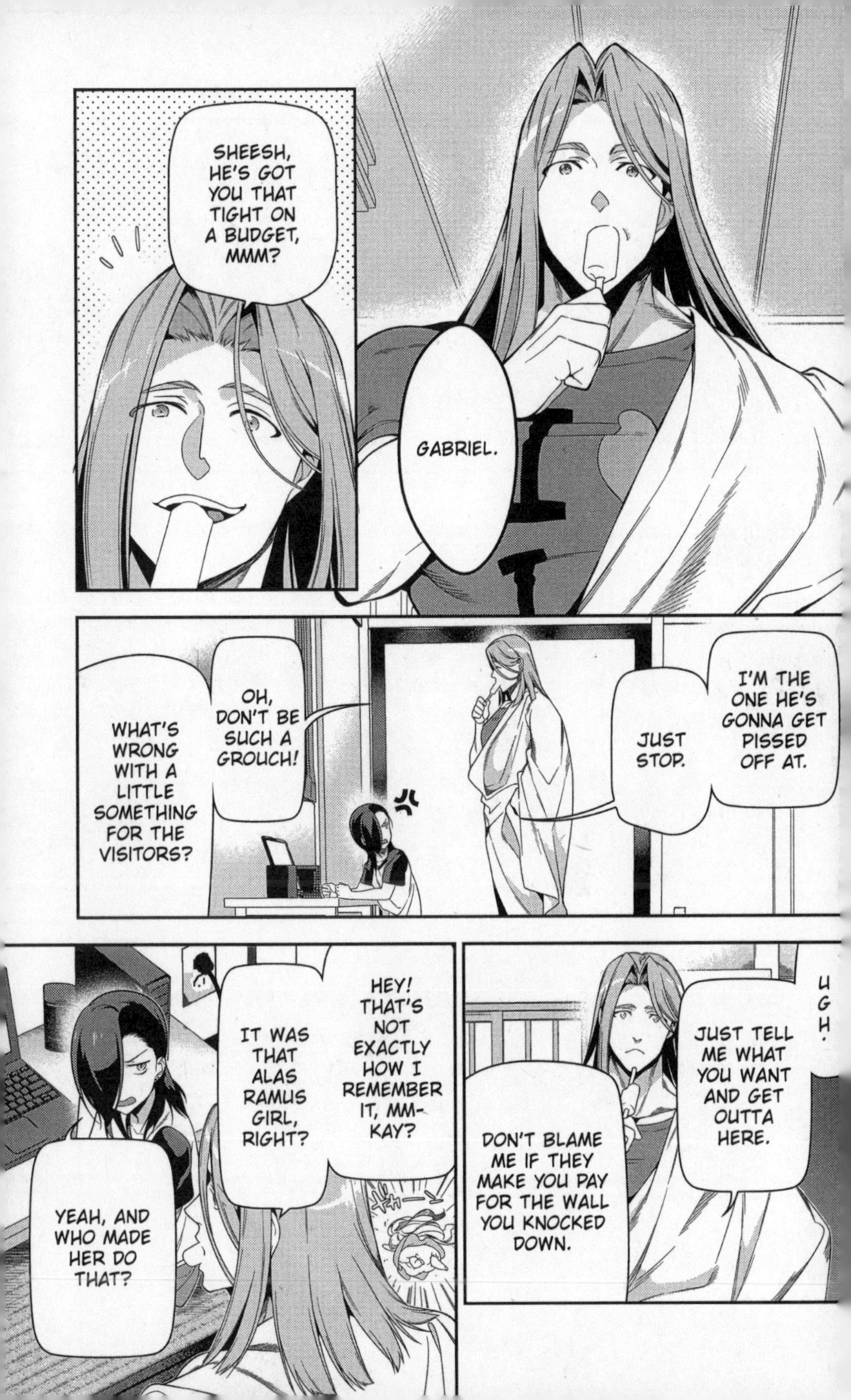
GABRIEL.
SHEESH, HE'S GOT YOU THAT TIGHT ON A BUDGET, MMM?
I'M THE ONE HE'S GONNA GET PISSED OFF AT.
JUST STOP.
OH, DON'T BE SUCH A GROUCH!
WHAT'S WRONG WITH A LITTLE SOMETHING FOR THE VISITORS?
UGH.
JUST TELL ME WHAT YOU WANT AND GET OUTTA HERE.
DON'T BLAME ME IF THEY MAKE YOU PAY FOR THE WALL YOU KNOCKED DOWN.
HEY! THAT'S NOT EXACTLY HOW I REMEMBER IT, MM-KAY?
IT WAS THAT ALAS RAMUS GIRL, RIGHT?
YEAH, AND WHO MADE HER DO THAT?

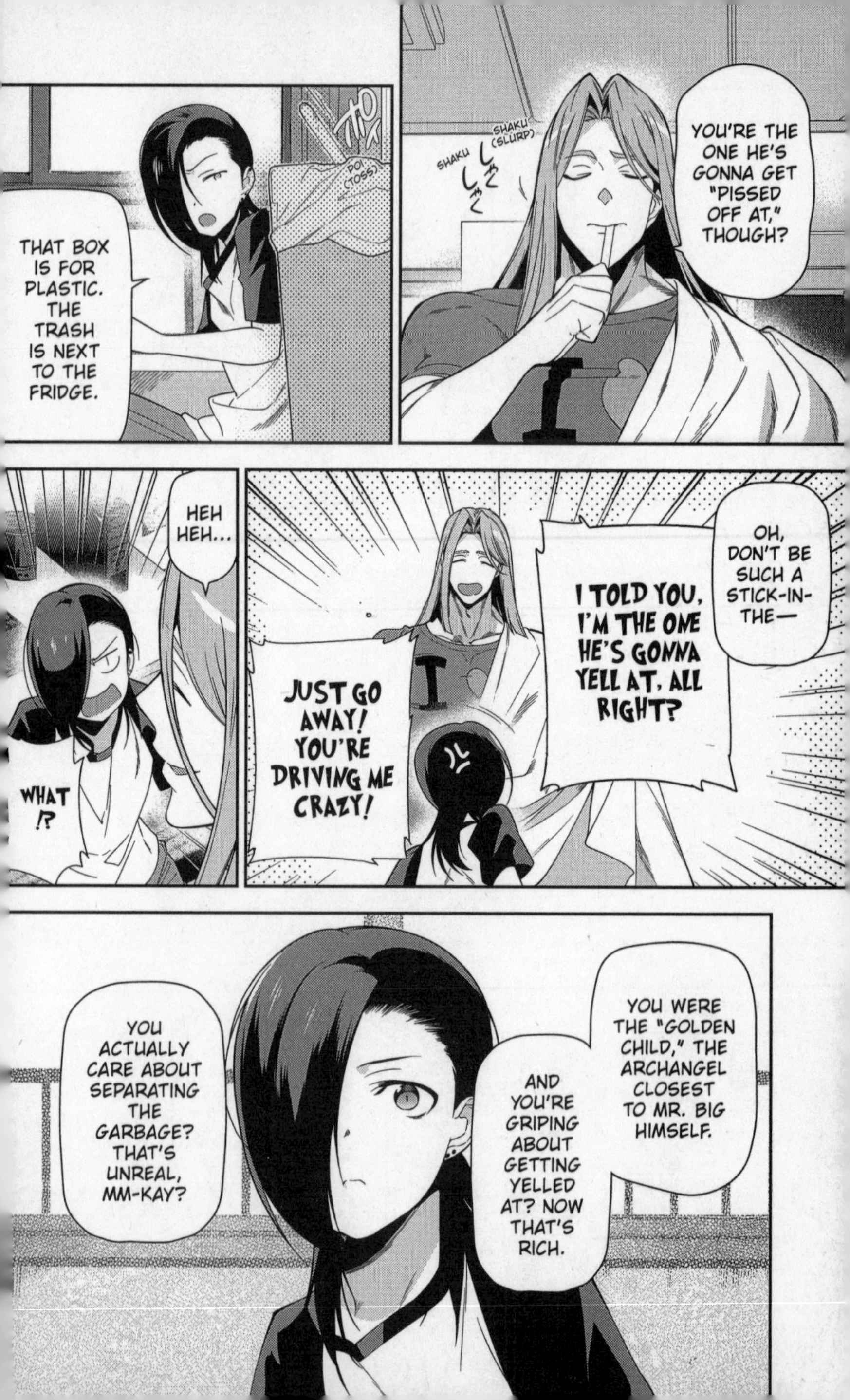

SHAKU (SLURP)
SHAKU
YOU'RE THE ONE HE'S GONNA GET "PISSED OFF AT," THOUGH?
POI (TOSS)
THAT BOX IS FOR PLASTIC. THE TRASH IS NEXT TO THE FRIDGE.
OH, DON'T BE SUCH A STICK-IN-THE—
I TOLD YOU, I'M THE ONE HE'S GONNA YELL AT, ALL RIGHT?
JUST GO AWAY! YOU'RE DRIVING ME CRAZY!
HEH HEH...
WHAT !?
YOU WERE THE "GOLDEN CHILD," THE ARCHANGEL CLOSEST TO MR. BIG HIMSELF.
AND YOU'RE GRIPING ABOUT GETTING YELLED AT? NOW THAT'S RICH.
YOU ACTUALLY CARE ABOUT SEPARATING THE GARBAGE? THAT'S UNREAL, MM-KAY?

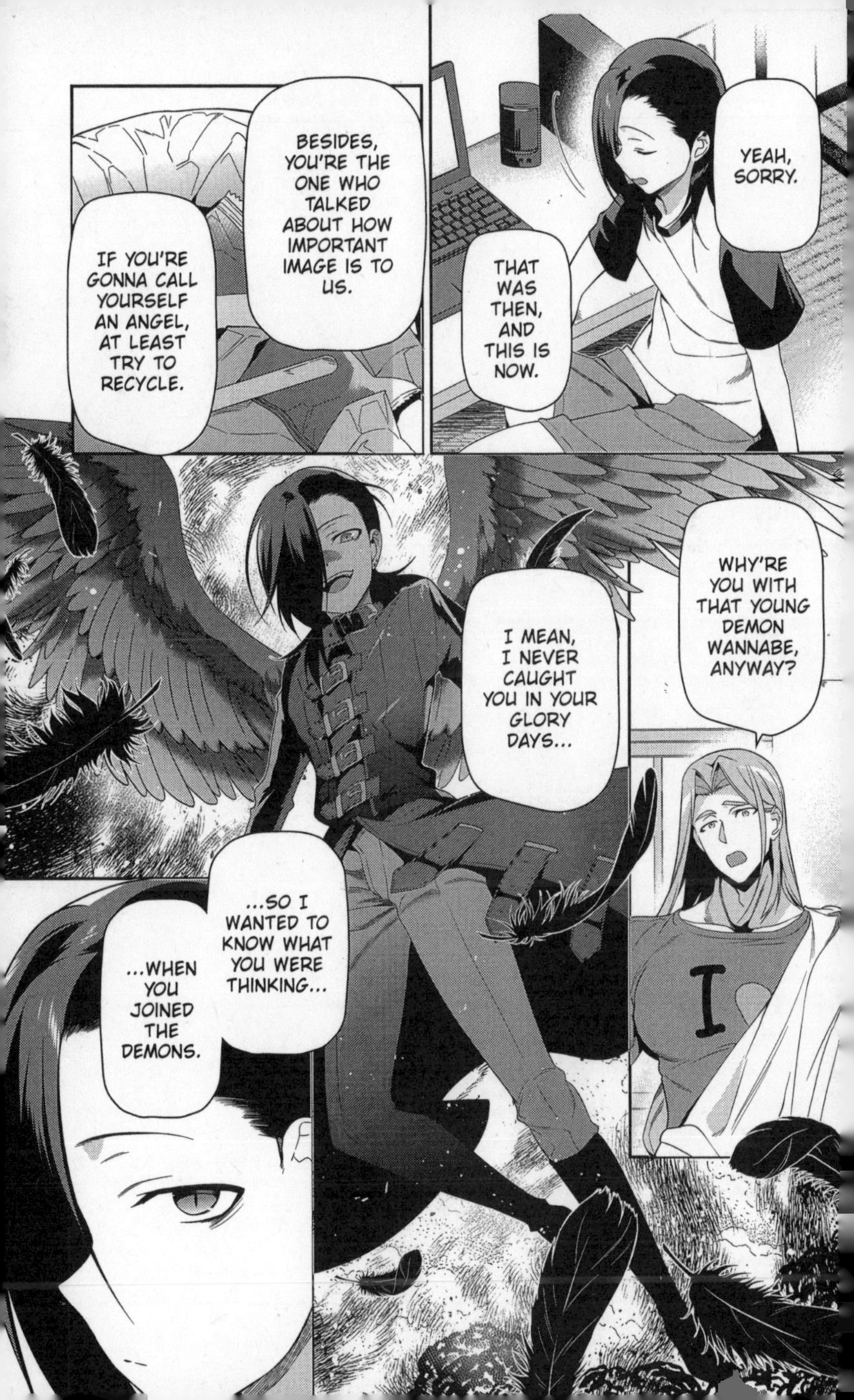
YEAH, SORRY.
THAT WAS THEN, AND THIS IS NOW.
BESIDES, YOU'RE THE ONE WHO TALKED ABOUT HOW IMPORTANT IMAGE IS TO US.
IF YOU'RE GONNA CALL YOURSELF AN ANGEL, AT LEAST TRY TO RECYCLE.
WHY'RE YOU WITH THAT YOUNG DEMON WANNABE, ANYWAY?
I MEAN, I NEVER CAUGHT YOU IN YOUR GLORY DAYS...
...SO I WANTED TO KNOW WHAT YOU WERE THINKING...
...WHEN YOU JOINED THE DEMONS.

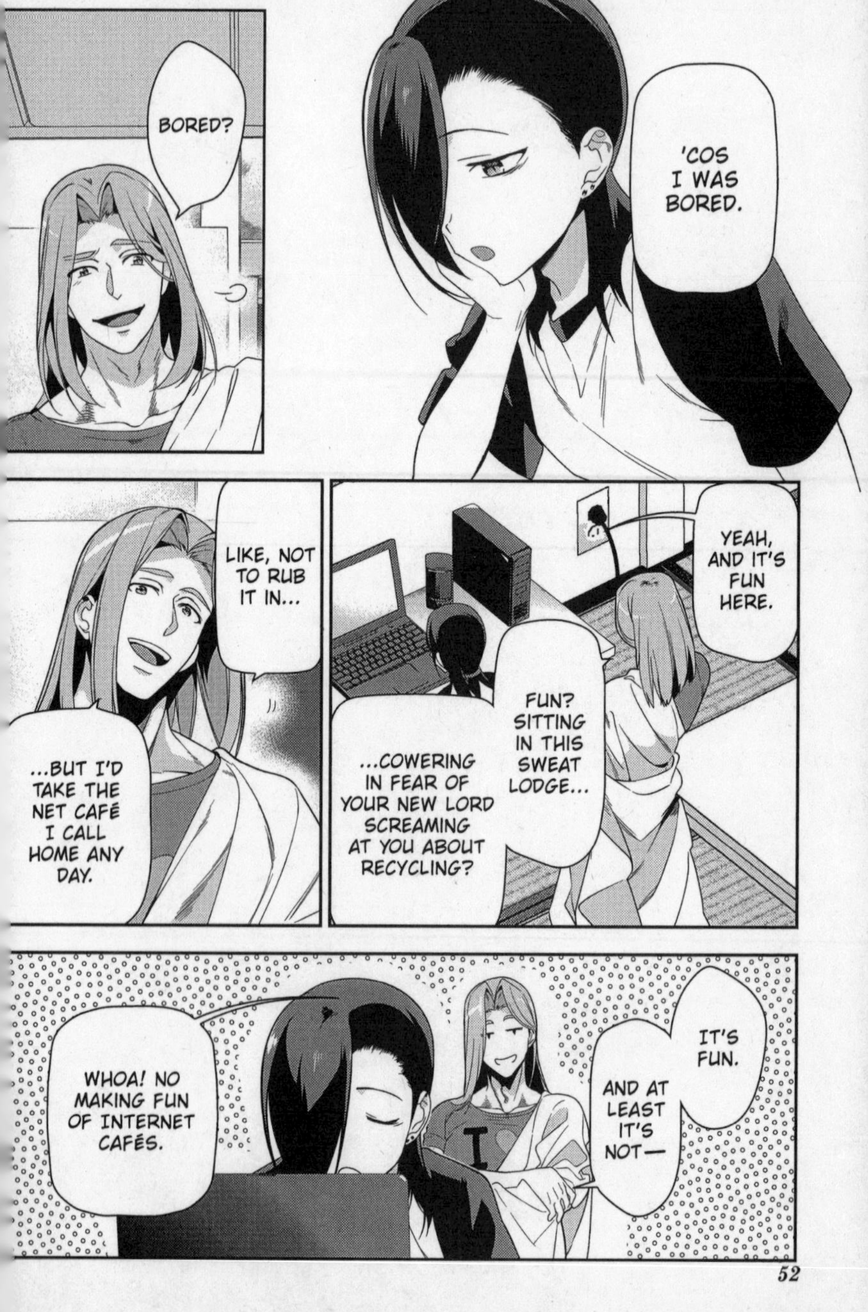
'COS I WAS BORED.
BORED?
YEAH, AND IT'S FUN HERE.
FUN? SITTING IN THIS SWEAT LODGE...
...COWERING IN FEAR OF YOUR NEW LORD SCREAMING AT YOU ABOUT RECYCLING?
LIKE, NOT TO RUB IT IN...
...BUT I'D TAKE THE NET CAFÉ I CALL HOME ANY DAY.
IT'S FUN.
AND AT LEAST IT'S NOT—
WHOA! NO MAKING FUN OF INTERNET CAFÉS.

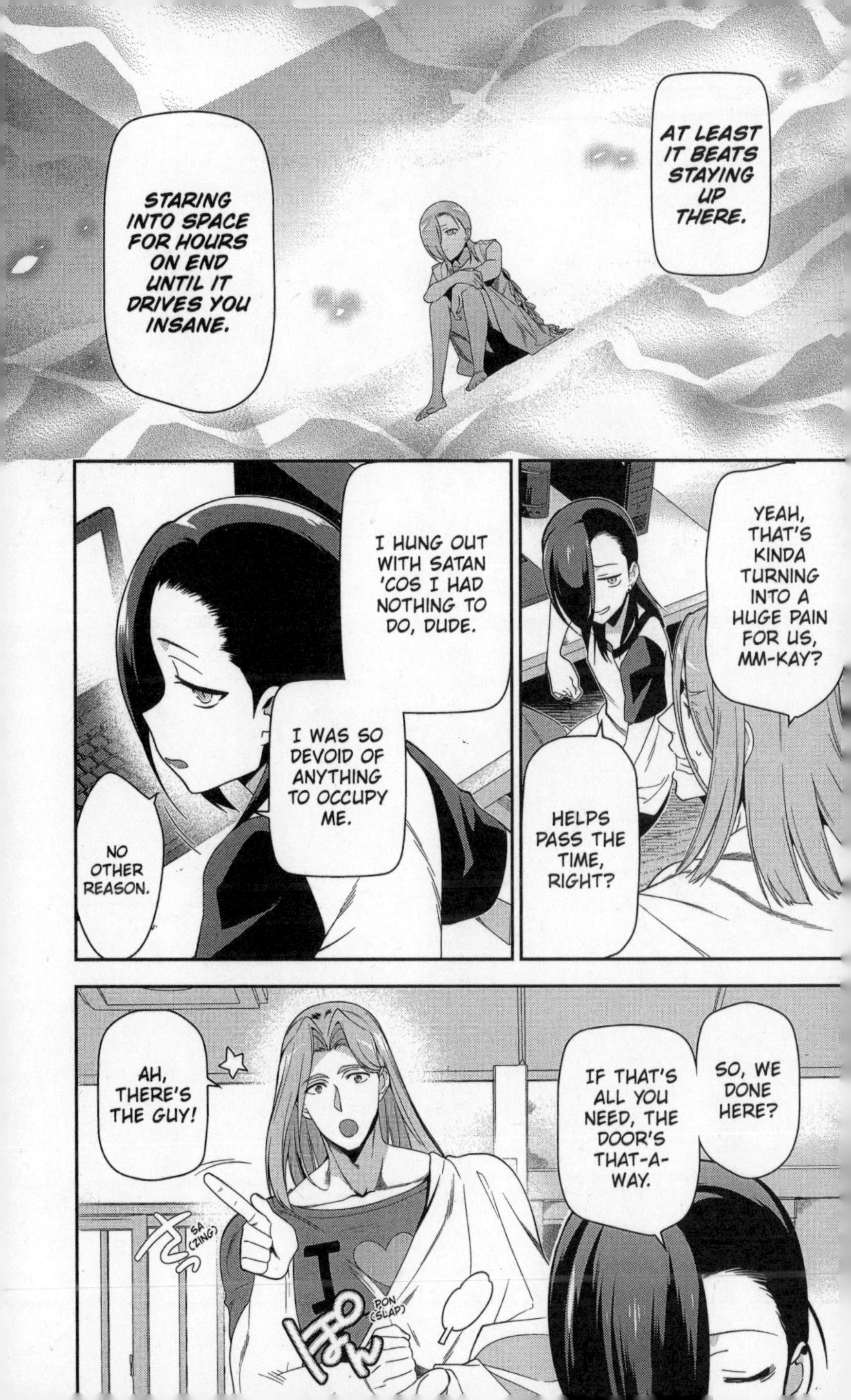
AT LEAST IT BEATS STAYING UP THERE.
STARING INTO SPACE FOR HOURS ON END UNTIL IT DRIVES YOU INSANE.
YEAH, THAT'S KINDA TURNING INTO A HUGE PAIN FOR US, MM-KAY?
HELPS PASS THE TIME, RIGHT?
I HUNG OUT WITH SATAN 'COS I HAD NOTHING TO DO, DUDE.
I WAS SO DEVOID OF ANYTHING TO OCCUPY ME.
NO OTHER REASON.
SO, WE DONE HERE?
IF THAT'S ALL YOU NEED, THE DOOR'S THAT-A-WAY.
AH, THERE'S THE GUY!
SA (ZING)
PON (SLAP)

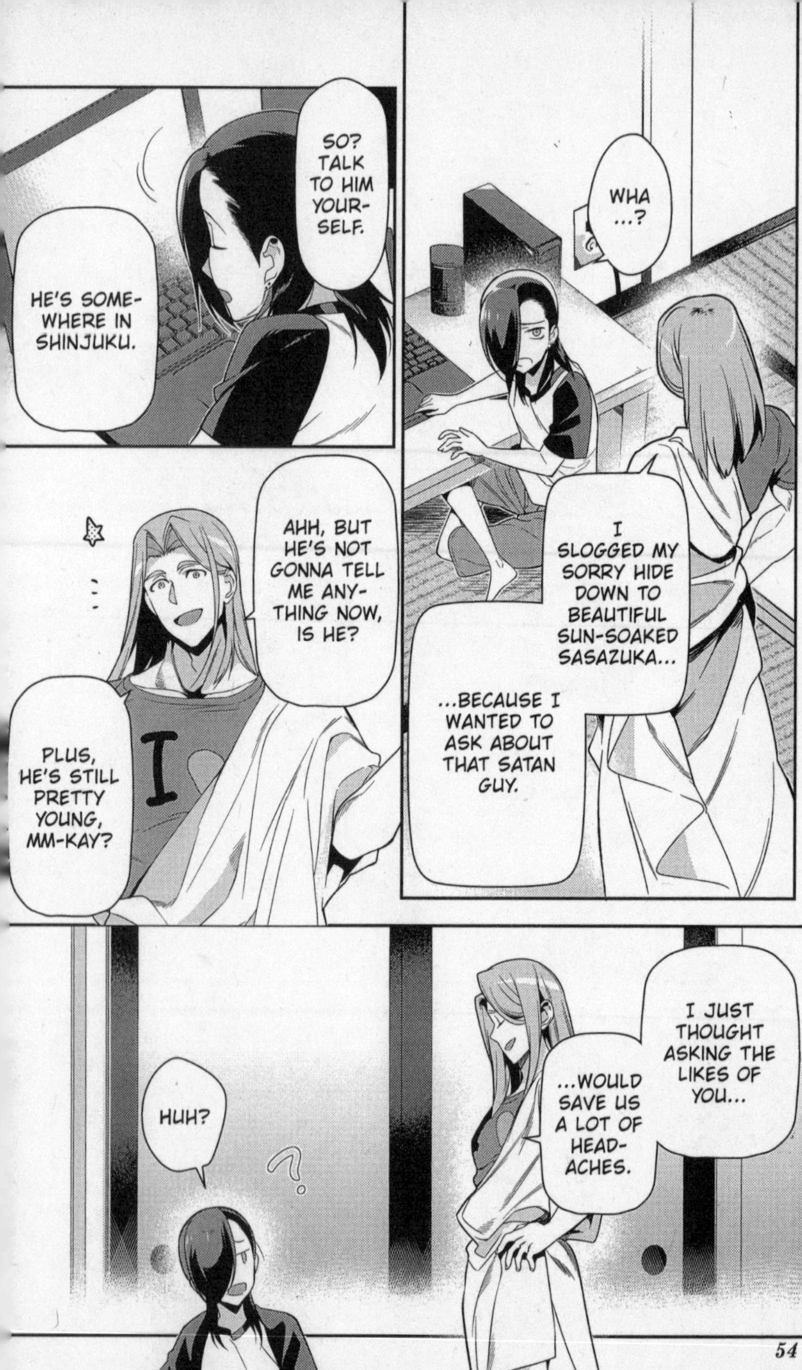
WHA ...?
I SLOGGED MY SORRY HIDE DOWN TO BEAUTIFUL SUN-SOAKED SASAZUKA...
...BECAUSE I WANTED TO ASK ABOUT THAT SATAN GUY.
SO? TALK TO HIM YOUR-SELF.
HE'S SOME-WHERE IN SHINJUKU.
AHH, BUT HE'S NOT GONNA TELL ME ANY-THING NOW, IS HE?
PLUS, HE'S STILL PRETTY YOUNG, MM-KAY?
I JUST THOUGHT ASKING THE LIKES OF YOU...
...WOULD SAVE US A LOT OF HEAD-ACHES.
HUH?

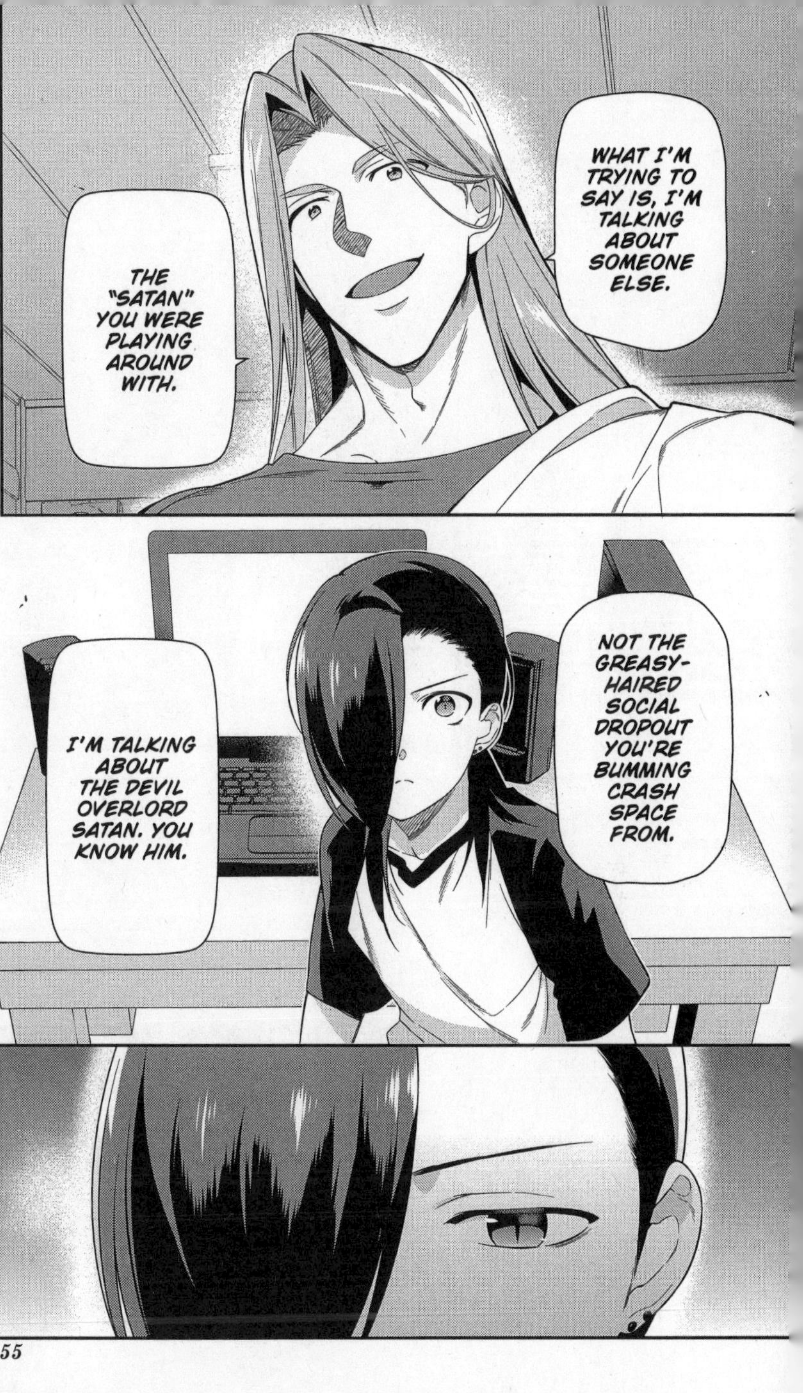
WHAT I'M TRYING TO SAY IS, I'M TALKING ABOUT SOMEONE ELSE.
THE "SATAN" YOU WERE PLAYING AROUND WITH.
NOT THE GREASY-HAIRED SOCIAL DROPOUT YOU'RE BUMMING CRASH SPACE FROM.
I'M TALKING ABOUT THE DEVIL OVERLORD SATAN. YOU KNOW HIM.

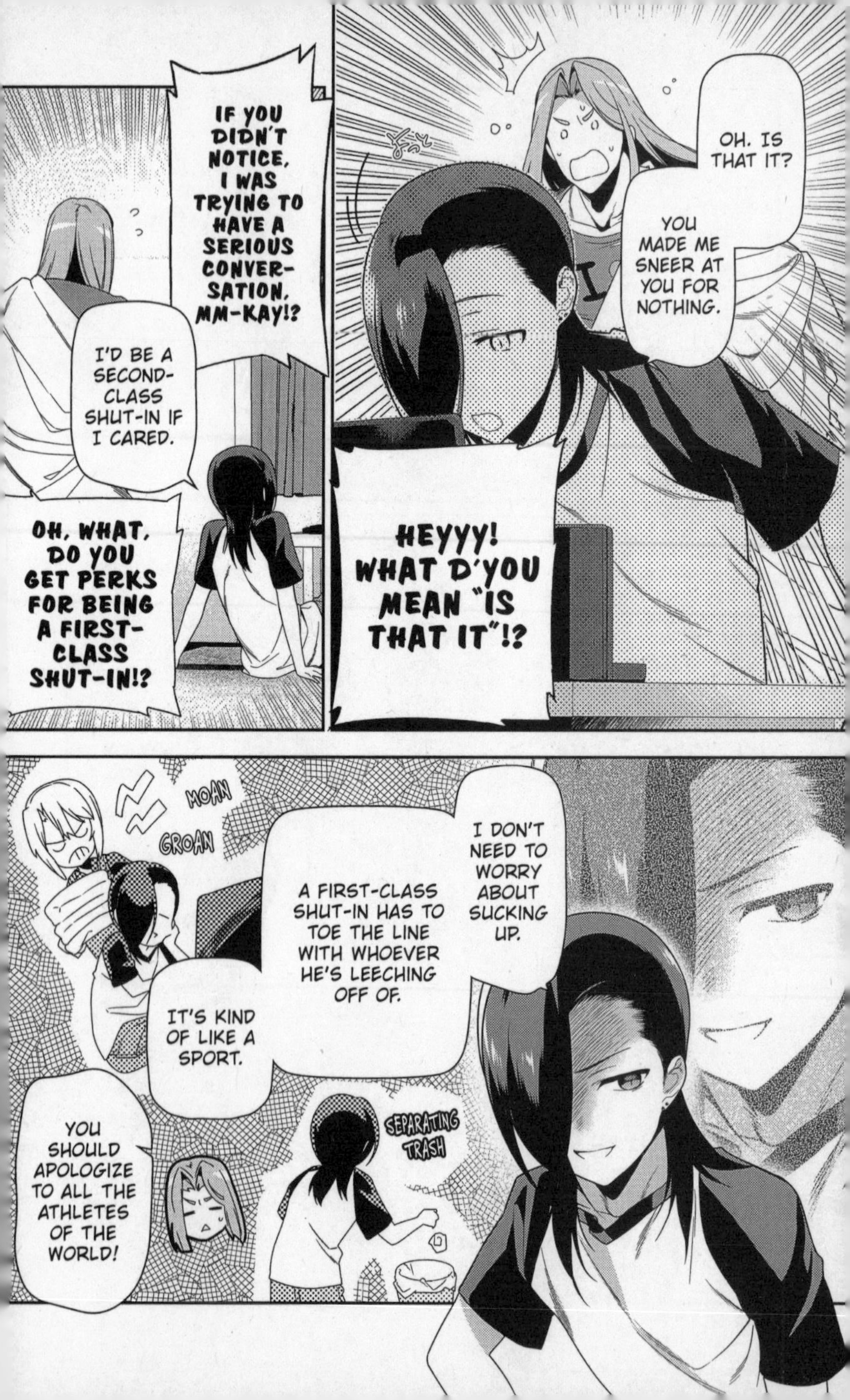

OH. IS THAT IT?
YOU MADE ME SNEER AT YOU FOR NOTHING.
HEYYY! WHAT D'YOU MEAN "IS THAT IT"!?
IF YOU DIDN'T NOTICE, I WAS TRYING TO HAVE A SERIOUS CONVERSATION, MM-KAY!?
I'D BE A SECOND-CLASS SHUT-IN IF I CARED.
OH, WHAT, DO YOU GET PERKS FOR BEING A FIRST-CLASS SHUT-IN!?
I DON'T NEED TO WORRY ABOUT SUCKING UP.
A FIRST-CLASS SHUT-IN HAS TO TOE THE LINE WITH WHOEVER HE'S LEECHING OFF OF.
MOAN
GROAN
IT'S KIND OF LIKE A SPORT.
SEPARATING TRASH
YOU SHOULD APOLOGIZE TO ALL THE ATHLETES OF THE WORLD!

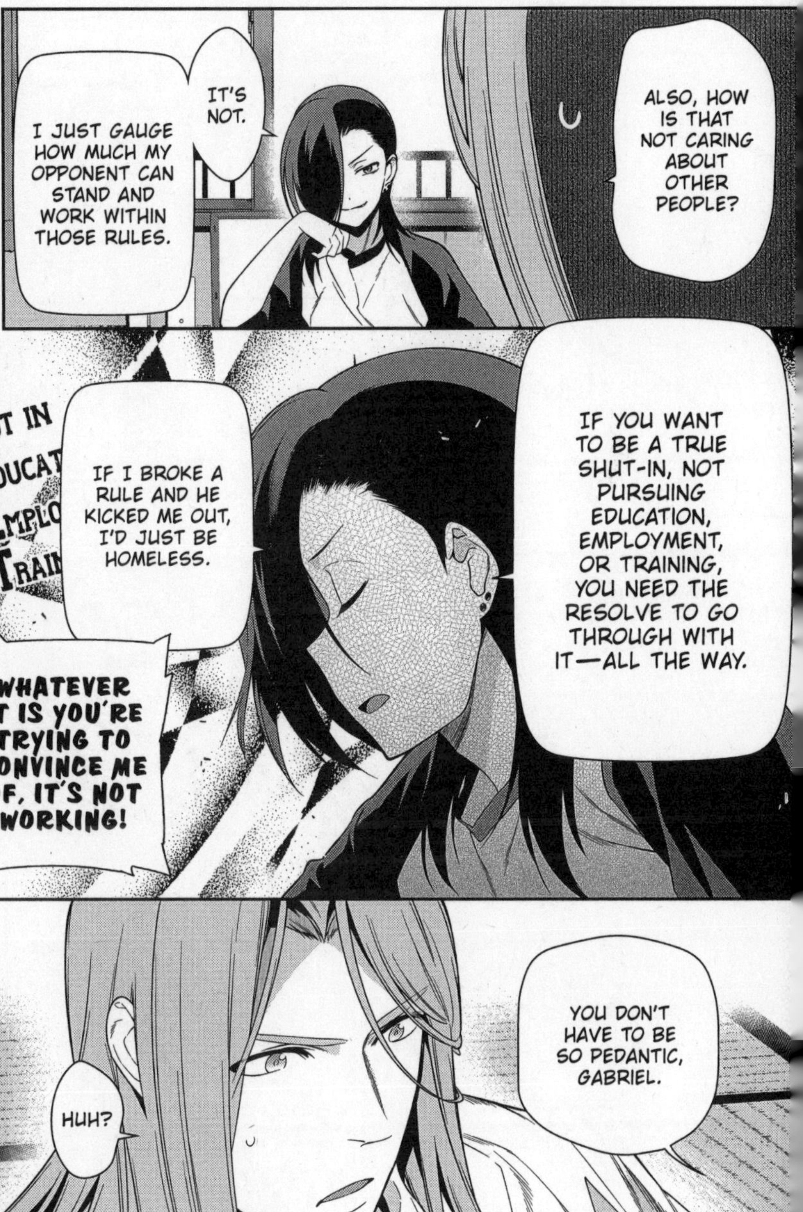
ALSO, HOW IS THAT NOT CARING ABOUT OTHER PEOPLE?
IT'S NOT.
I JUST GAUGE HOW MUCH MY OPPONENT CAN STAND AND WORK WITHIN THOSE RULES.
IF YOU WANT TO BE A TRUE SHUT-IN, NOT PURSUING EDUCATION, EMPLOYMENT, OR TRAINING, YOU NEED THE RESOLVE TO GO THROUGH WITH IT—ALL THE WAY.
IF I BROKE A RULE AND HE KICKED ME OUT, I'D JUST BE HOMELESS.
WHATEVER IT IS YOU'RE TRYING TO CONVINCE ME OF, IT'S NOT WORKING!
YOU DON'T HAVE TO BE SO PEDANTIC, GABRIEL.
HUH?

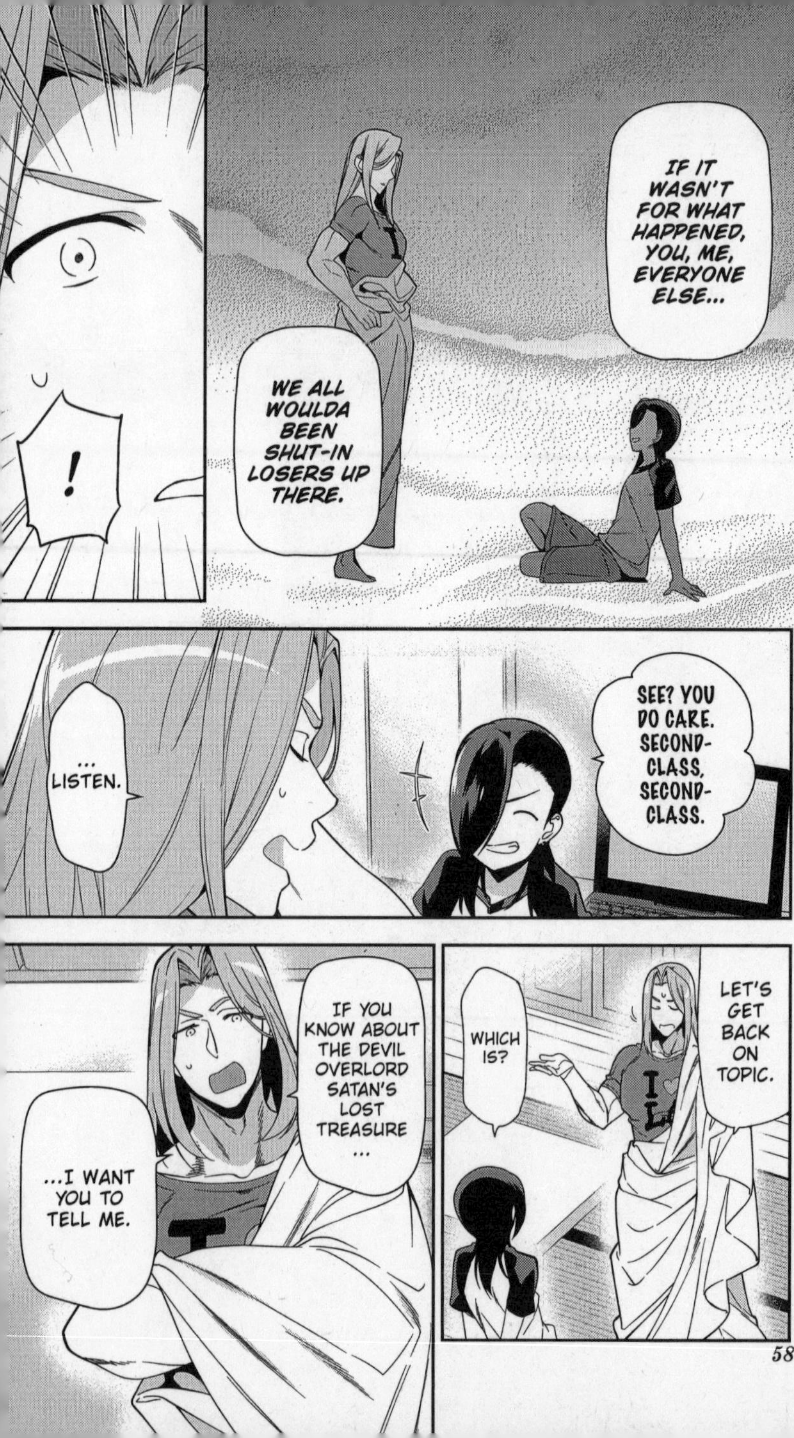
IF IT WASN'T FOR WHAT HAPPENED, YOU, ME, EVERYONE ELSE...
WE ALL WOULDA BEEN SHUT-IN LOSERS UP THERE.
!
SEE? YOU DO CARE. SECOND-CLASS, SECOND-CLASS.
... LISTEN.
LET'S GET BACK ON TOPIC.
WHICH IS?
IF YOU KNOW ABOUT THE DEVIL OVERLORD SATAN'S LOST TREASURE ...
...I WANT YOU TO TELL ME.

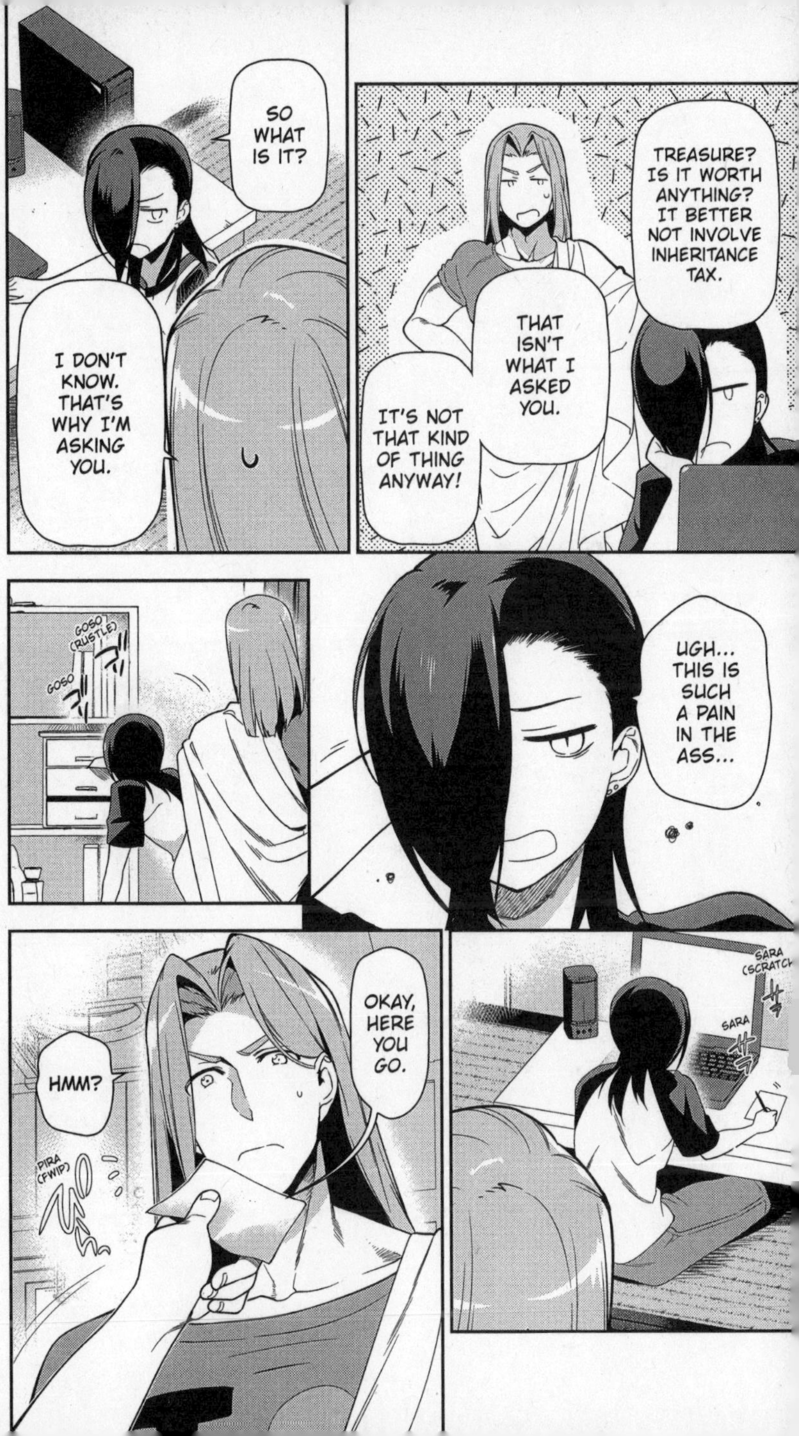
TREASURE? IS IT WORTH ANYTHING? IT BETTER NOT INVOLVE INHERITANCE TAX.
THAT ISN'T WHAT I ASKED YOU.
IT'S NOT THAT KIND OF THING ANYWAY!
SO WHAT IS IT?
I DON'T KNOW. THAT'S WHY I'M ASKING YOU.
UGH... THIS IS SUCH A PAIN IN THE ASS...
GOSO (RUSTLE)
GOSO
SARA (SCRATCH
SARA
OKAY, HERE YOU GO.
HMM?
PIRA (FWIP)

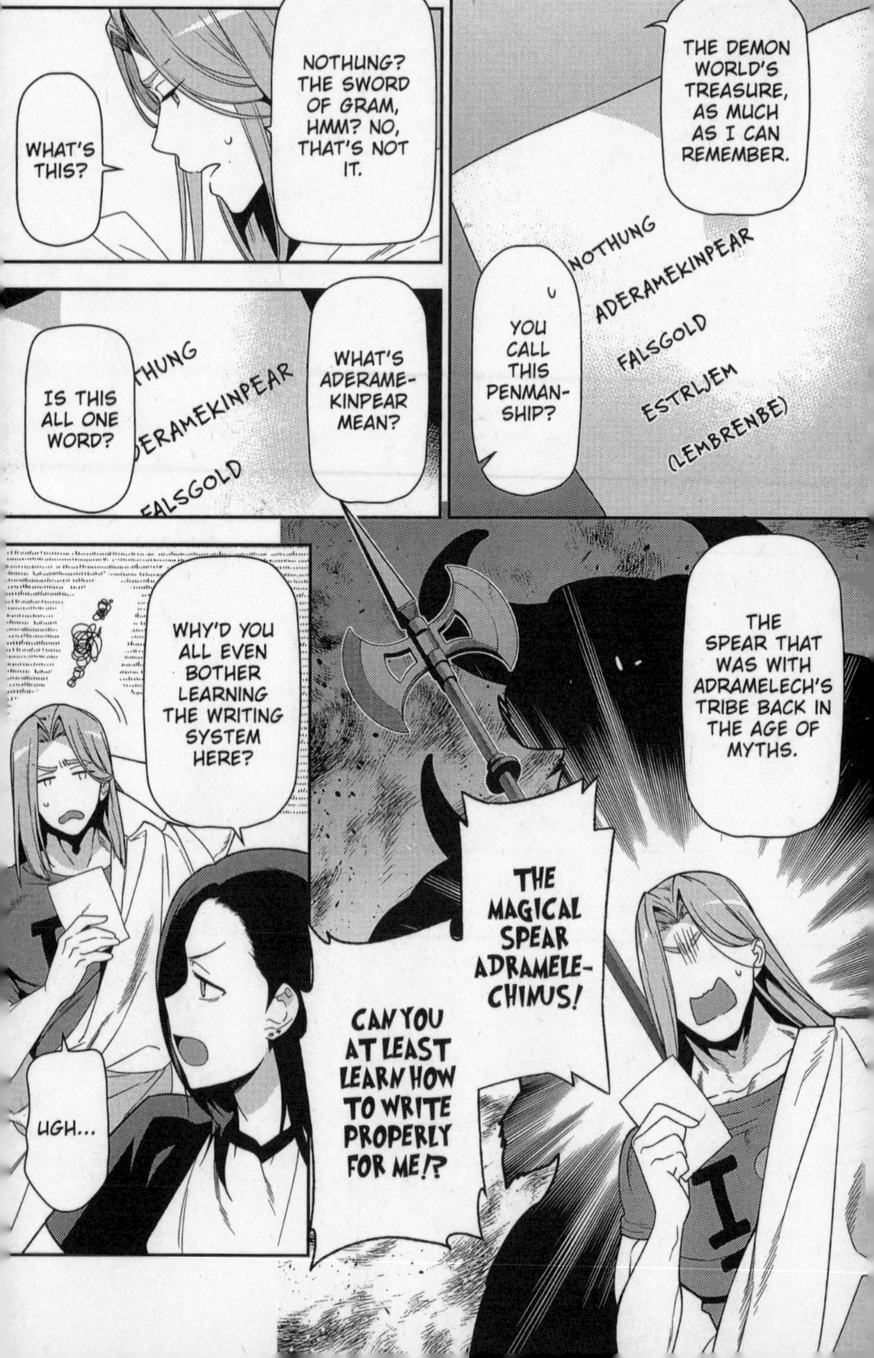
THE DEMON WORLD'S TREASURE, AS MUCH AS I CAN REMEMBER.
NOTHUNG? THE SWORD OF GRAM, HMM? NO, THAT'S NOT IT.
WHAT'S THIS?
YOU CALL THIS PENMANSHIP?
NOTHUNG
ADERAMEKINPEAR
FALSGOLD
ESTRLJEM
(LEMBRENBE)
WHAT'S ADERAME-KINPEAR MEAN?
IS THIS ALL ONE WORD?
FALSGOLD
THE SPEAR THAT WAS WITH ADRAMELECH'S TRIBE BACK IN THE AGE OF MYTHS.
THE MAGICAL SPEAR ADRAMELE-CHINUS!
WHY'D YOU ALL EVEN BOTHER LEARNING THE WRITING SYSTEM HERE?
CAN YOU AT LEAST LEARN HOW TO WRITE PROPERLY FOR ME!?
UGH...

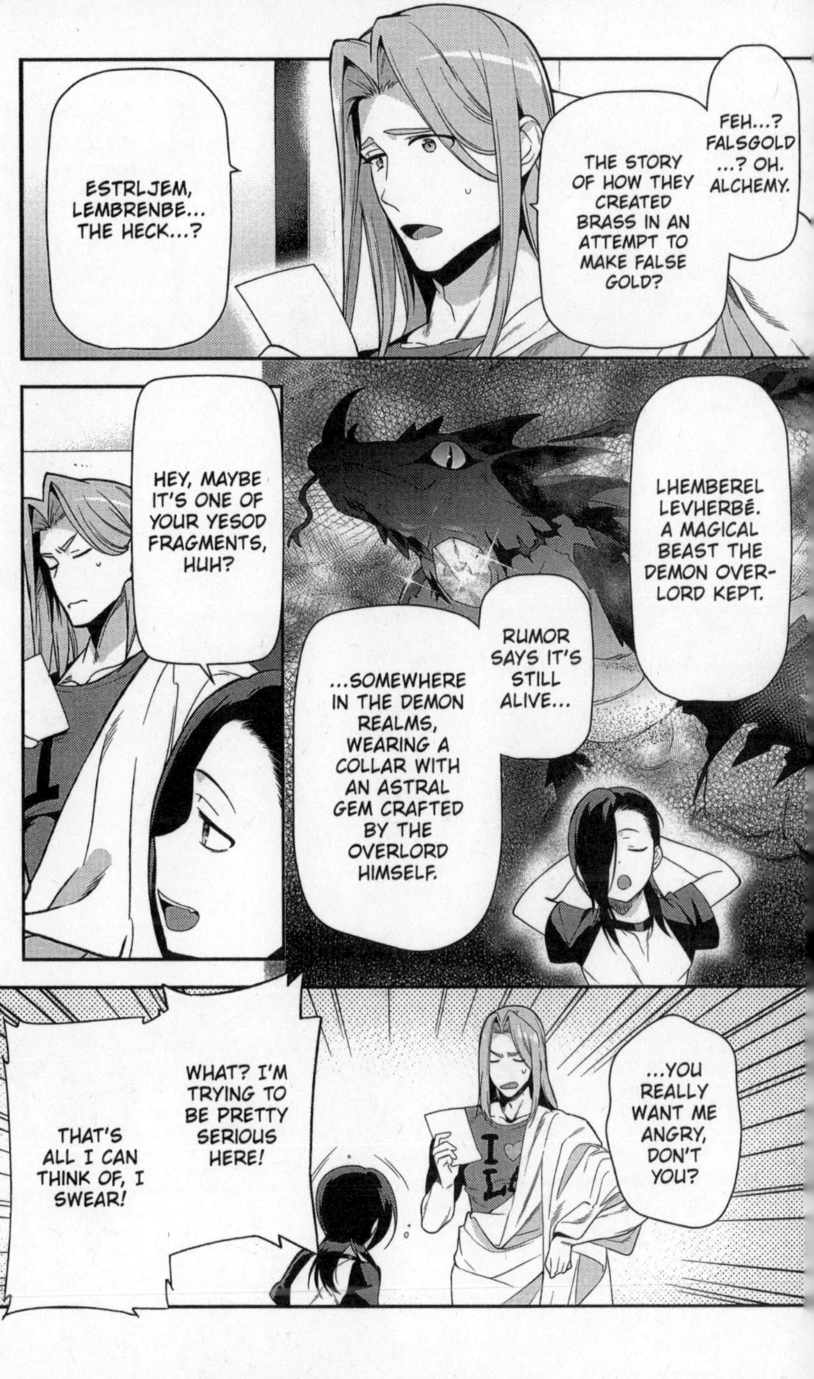
FEH...? FALSGOLD ...? OH. ALCHEMY.
THE STORY OF HOW THEY CREATED BRASS IN AN ATTEMPT TO MAKE FALSE GOLD?
ESTRLJEM, LEMBRENBE... THE HECK...?
LHEMBEREL LEVHERBÉ. A MAGICAL BEAST THE DEMON OVER-LORD KEPT.
RUMOR SAYS IT'S STILL ALIVE...
...SOMEWHERE IN THE DEMON REALMS, WEARING A COLLAR WITH AN ASTRAL GEM CRAFTED BY THE OVERLORD HIMSELF.
...
HEY, MAYBE IT'S ONE OF YOUR YESOD FRAGMENTS, HUH?
...YOU REALLY WANT ME ANGRY, DON'T YOU?
WHAT? I'M TRYING TO BE PRETTY SERIOUS HERE!
THAT'S ALL I CAN THINK OF, I SWEAR!

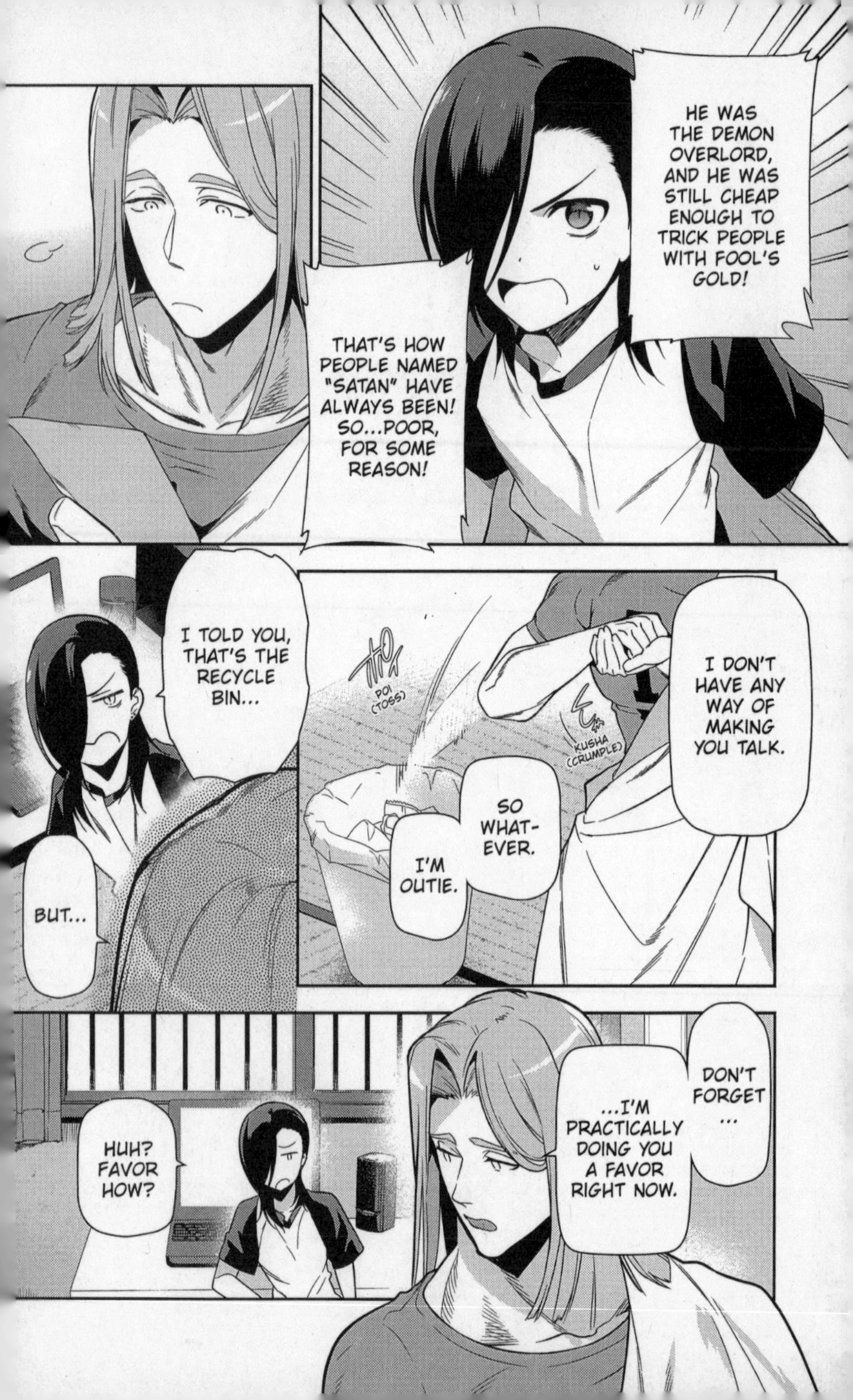
HE WAS THE DEMON OVERLORD, AND HE WAS STILL CHEAP ENOUGH TO TRICK PEOPLE WITH FOOL'S GOLD!
THAT'S HOW PEOPLE NAMED "SATAN" HAVE ALWAYS BEEN! SO...POOR, FOR SOME REASON!
I DON'T HAVE ANY WAY OF MAKING YOU TALK.
KUSHA (CRUMPLE)
SO WHATEVER.
POI (TOSS)
I'M OUTIE.
I TOLD YOU, THAT'S THE RECYCLE BIN...
BUT...
DON'T FORGET...
...I'M PRACTICALLY DOING YOU A FAVOR RIGHT NOW.
HUH? FAVOR HOW?

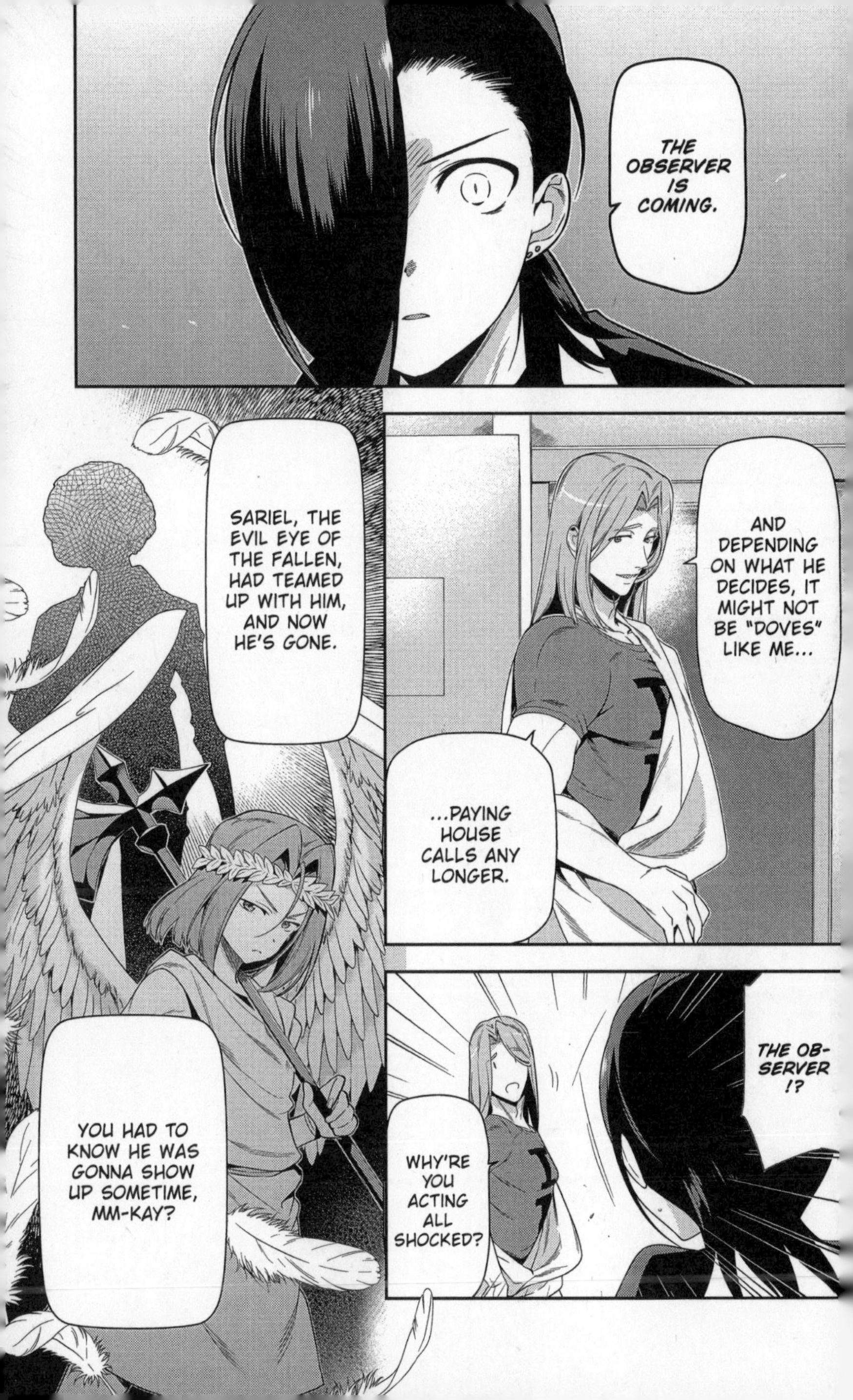
THE OBSERVER IS COMING.
AND DEPENDING ON WHAT HE DECIDES, IT MIGHT NOT BE "DOVES" LIKE ME...
...PAYING HOUSE CALLS ANY LONGER.
THE OB-SERVER!?
WHY'RE YOU ACTING ALL SHOCKED?
SARIEL, THE EVIL EYE OF THE FALLEN, HAD TEAMED UP WITH HIM, AND NOW HE'S GONE.
YOU HAD TO KNOW HE WAS GONNA SHOW UP SOMETIME, MM-KAY?

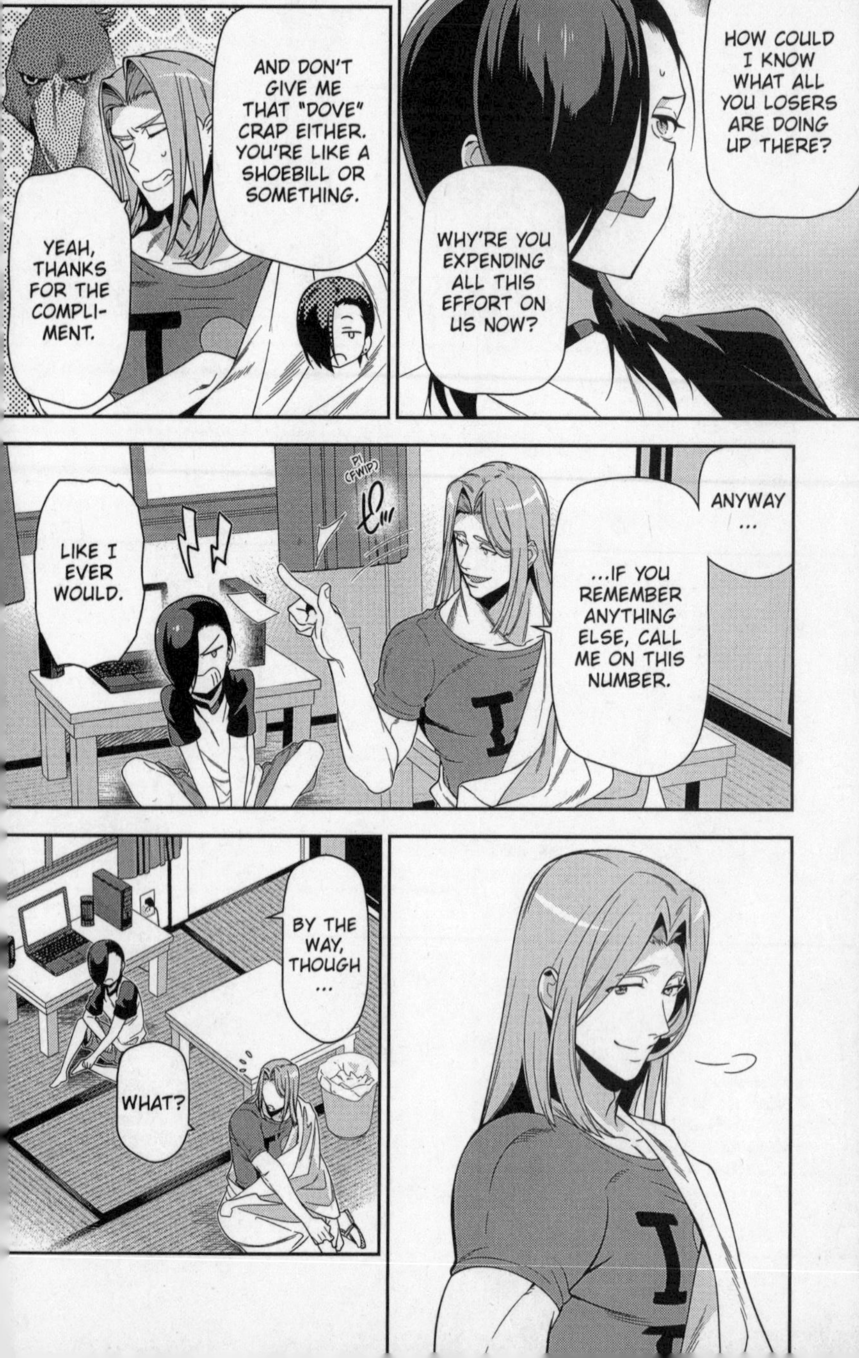

HOW COULD I KNOW WHAT ALL YOU LOSERS ARE DOING UP THERE?
WHY'RE YOU EXPENDING ALL THIS EFFORT ON US NOW?
AND DON'T GIVE ME THAT "DOVE" CRAP EITHER. YOU'RE LIKE A SHOEBILL OR SOMETHING.
YEAH, THANKS FOR THE COMPLIMENT.
ANYWAY ...
...IF YOU REMEMBER ANYTHING ELSE, CALL ME ON THIS NUMBER.
PI (FWIP)
LIKE I EVER WOULD.
BY THE WAY, THOUGH ...
WHAT?

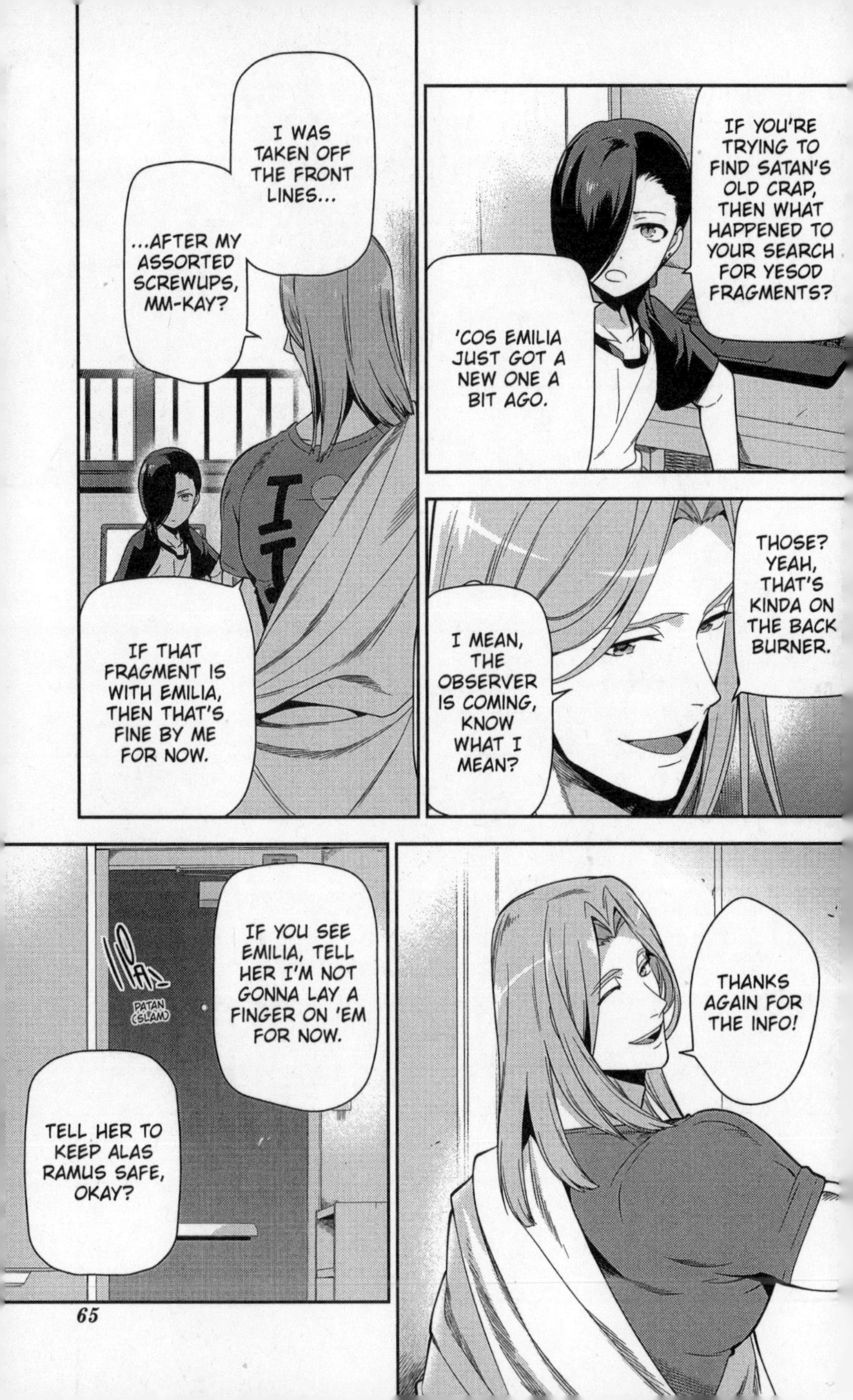
IF YOU'RE TRYING TO FIND SATAN'S OLD CRAP, THEN WHAT HAPPENED TO YOUR SEARCH FOR YESOD FRAGMENTS?
'COS EMILIA JUST GOT A NEW ONE A BIT AGO.
THOSE? YEAH, THAT'S KINDA ON THE BACK BURNER.
I MEAN, THE OBSERVER IS COMING, KNOW WHAT I MEAN?
I WAS TAKEN OFF THE FRONT LINES...
...AFTER MY ASSORTED SCREWUPS, MM-KAY?
IF THAT FRAGMENT IS WITH EMILIA, THEN THAT'S FINE BY ME FOR NOW.
THANKS AGAIN FOR THE INFO!
IF YOU SEE EMILIA, TELL HER I'M NOT GONNA LAY A FINGER ON 'EM FOR NOW.
PATAN (SLAM)
TELL HER TO KEEP ALAS RAMUS SAFE, OKAY?

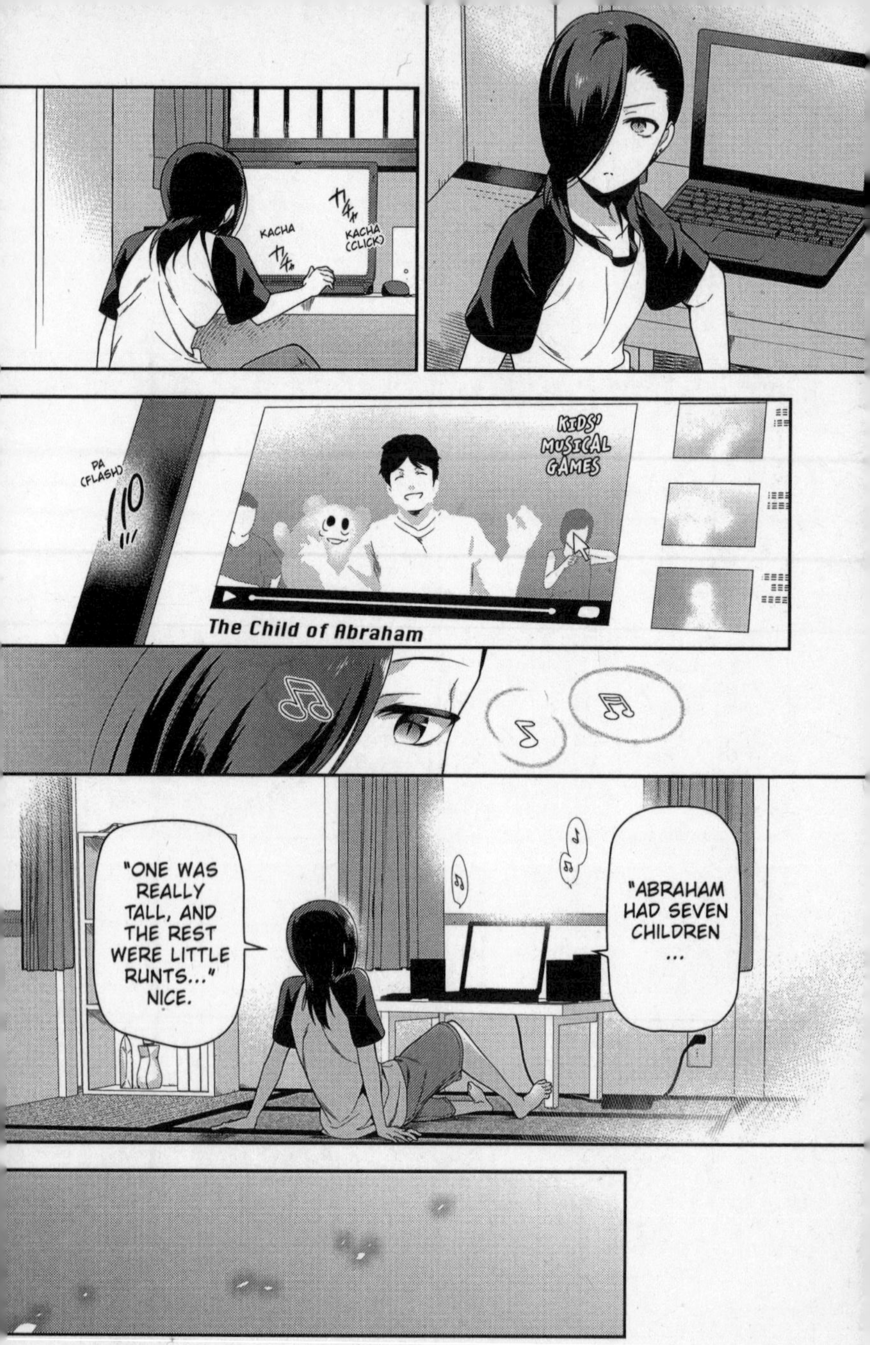
KACHA (CLICK)
KACHA
KIDS' MUSICAL GAMES
PA (FLASH)
The Child of Abraham
"ABRAHAM HAD SEVEN CHILDREN ...
"ONE WAS REALLY TALL, AND THE REST WERE LITTLE RUNTS..." NICE.

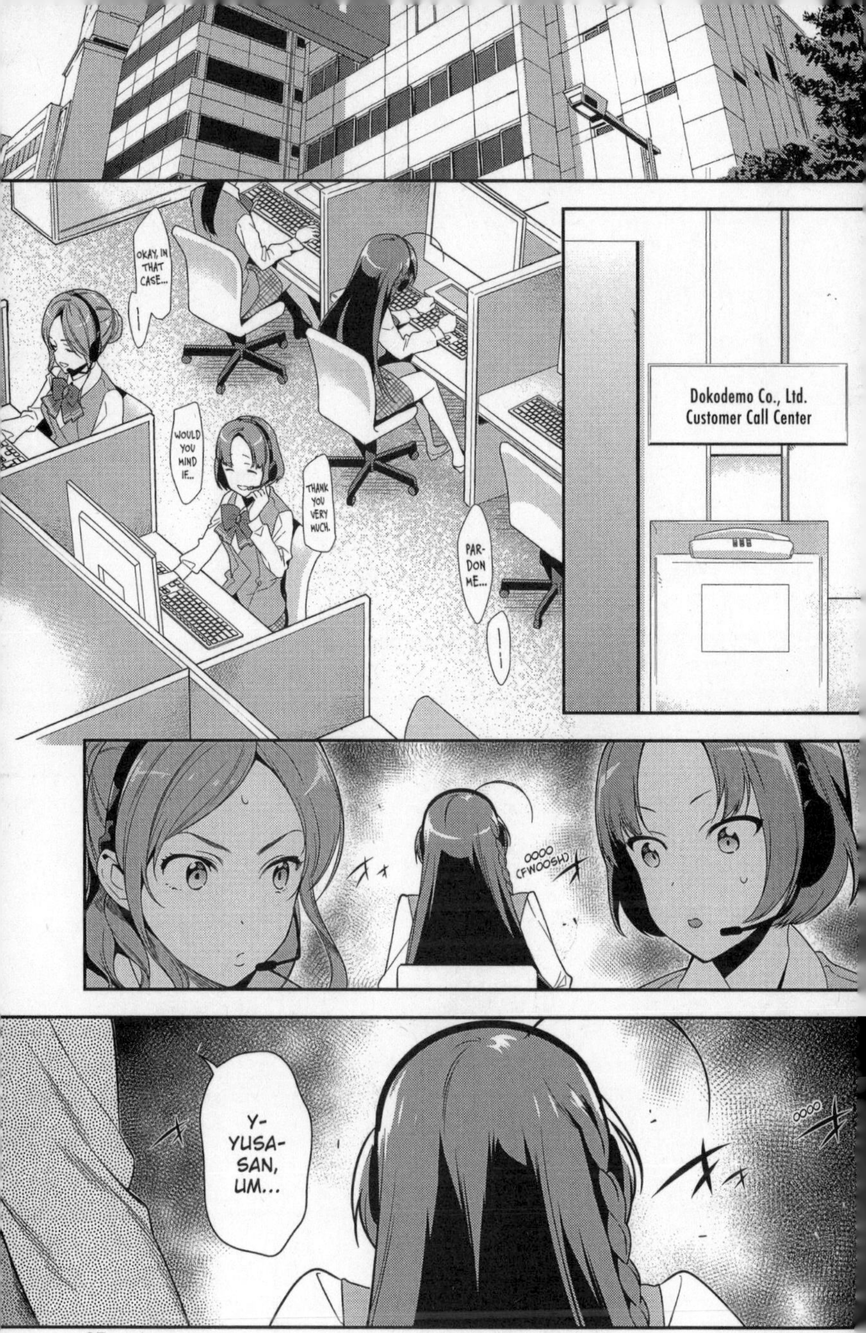
Dokodemo Co., Ltd.
Customer Call Center
OKAY, IN THAT CASE...
!
PAR-DON ME...
THANK YOU VERY MUCH.
WOULD YOU MIND IF...
!
OOOO (FWOOSH)
OOOO
Y-YUSA-SAN, UM...

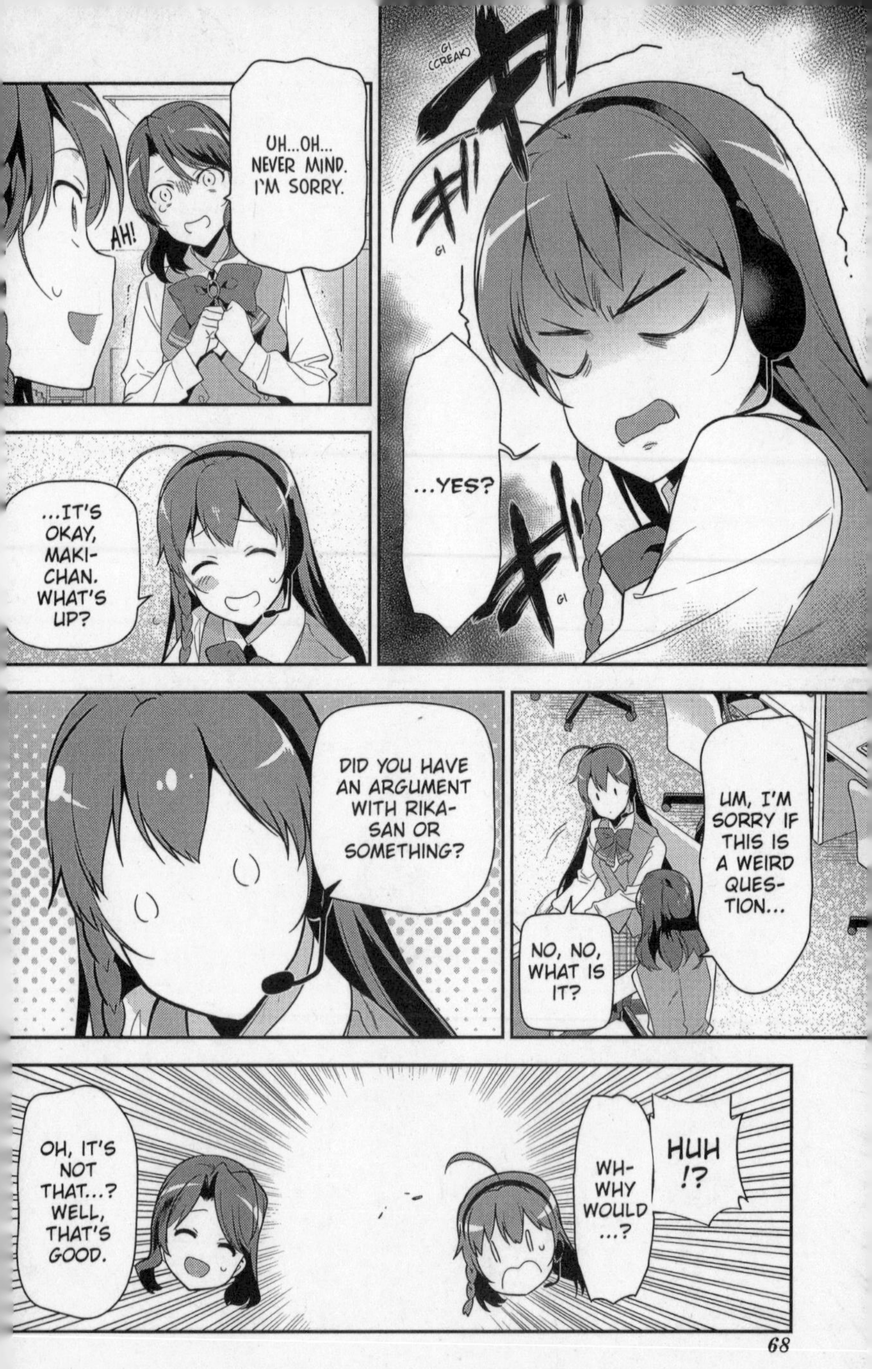
GI (CREAK)
GI
GI
...YES?
UH...OH... NEVER MIND. I'M SORRY.
AH!
...IT'S OKAY, MAKI-CHAN. WHAT'S UP?
UM, I'M SORRY IF THIS IS A WEIRD QUESTION...
NO, NO, WHAT IS IT?
DID YOU HAVE AN ARGUMENT WITH RIKA-SAN OR SOMETHING?
HUH!?
WH-WHY WOULD...?
OH, IT'S NOT THAT...? WELL, THAT'S GOOD.

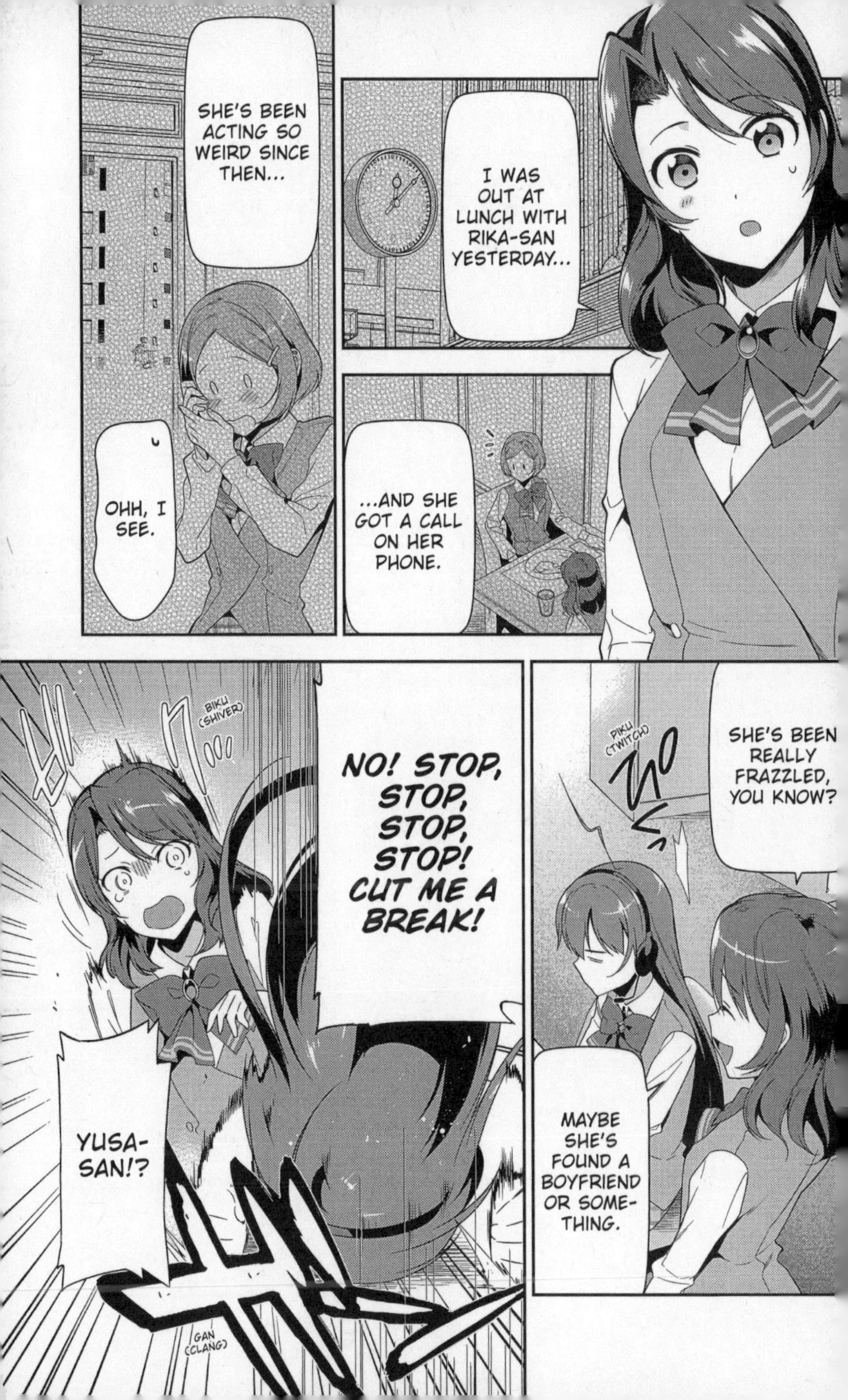
I WAS OUT AT LUNCH WITH RIKA-SAN YESTERDAY...
...AND SHE GOT A CALL ON HER PHONE.
SHE'S BEEN ACTING SO WEIRD SINCE THEN...
OHH, I SEE.
SHE'S BEEN REALLY FRAZZLED, YOU KNOW?
PIKU (TWITCH)
MAYBE SHE'S FOUND A BOYFRIEND OR SOME-THING.
NO! STOP, STOP, STOP, STOP! CUT ME A BREAK!
BIKU (SHIVER)
YUSA-SAN!?
GAN (CLANG)

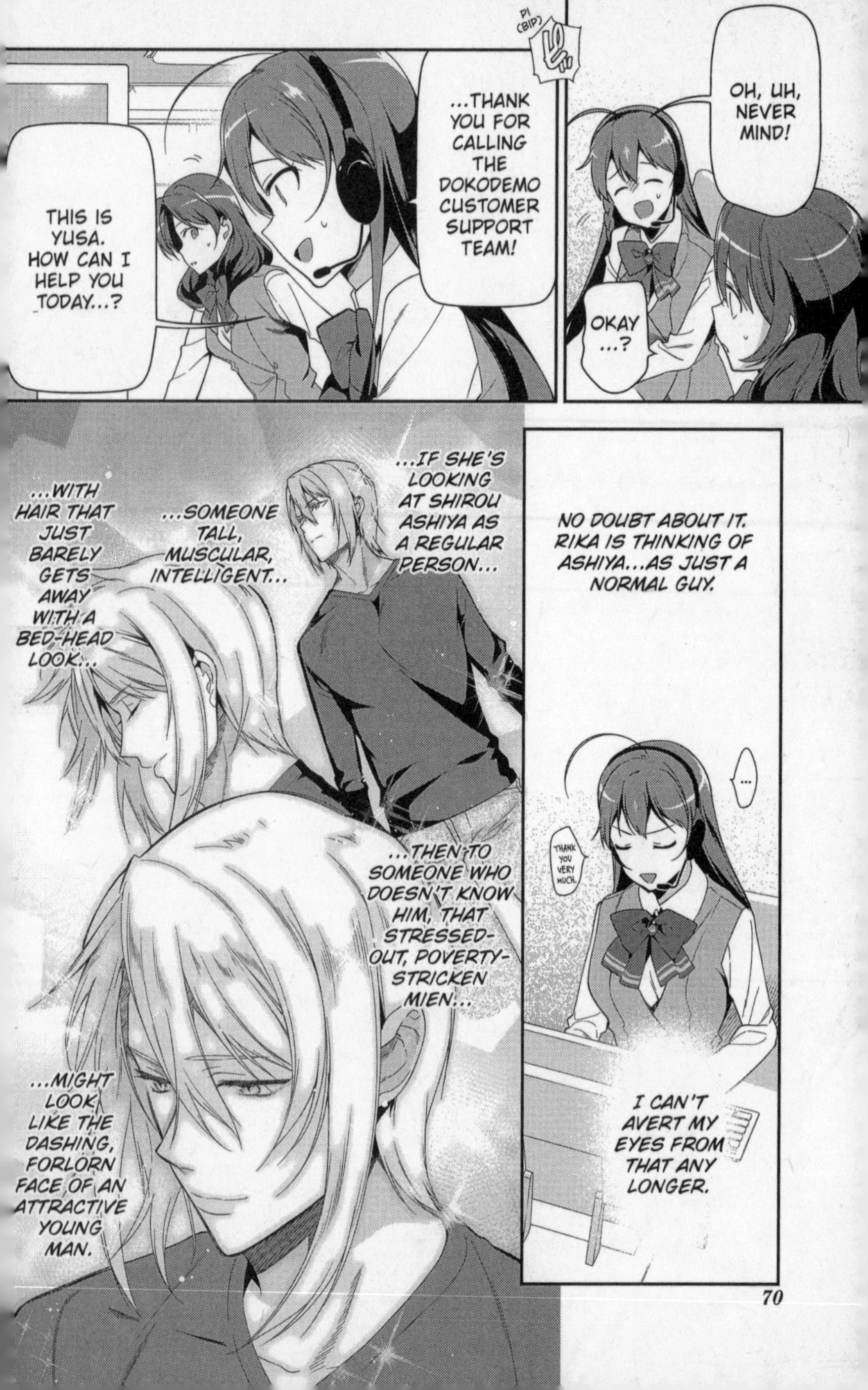
OH, UH, NEVER MIND!
OKAY ...?
PI (BIP)
...THANK YOU FOR CALLING THE DOKODEMO CUSTOMER SUPPORT TEAM!
THIS IS YUSA. HOW CAN I HELP YOU TODAY...?
NO DOUBT ABOUT IT. RIKA IS THINKING OF ASHIYA...AS JUST A NORMAL GUY.
...
THANK YOU VERY MUCH.
I CAN'T AVERT MY EYES FROM THAT ANY LONGER.
...IF SHE'S LOOKING AT SHIROU ASHIYA AS A REGULAR PERSON...
...SOMEONE TALL, MUSCULAR, INTELLIGENT...
...WITH HAIR THAT JUST BARELY GETS AWAY WITH A BED-HEAD LOOK...
...THEN TO SOMEONE WHO DOESN'T KNOW HIM, THAT STRESSED-OUT, POVERTY-STRICKEN MIEN...
...MIGHT LOOK LIKE THE DASHING, FORLORN FACE OF AN ATTRACTIVE YOUNG MAN.

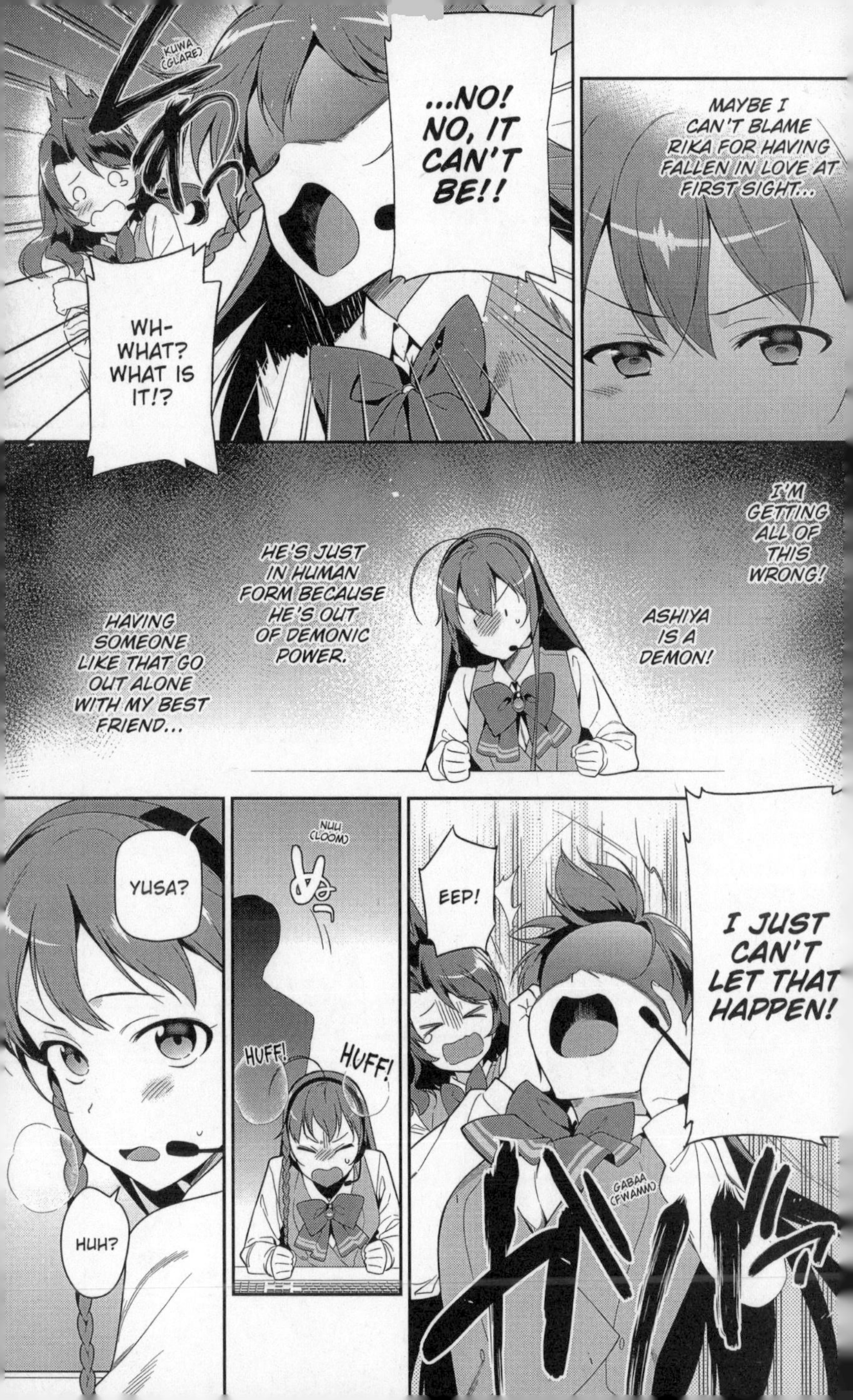
MAYBE I CAN'T BLAME RIKA FOR HAVING FALLEN IN LOVE AT FIRST SIGHT...
...NO! NO, IT CAN'T BE!!
KUWA (GLARE)
WH- WHAT? WHAT IS IT!?
I'M GETTING ALL OF THIS WRONG!
ASHIYA IS A DEMON!
HE'S JUST IN HUMAN FORM BECAUSE HE'S OUT OF DEMONIC POWER.
HAVING SOMEONE LIKE THAT GO OUT ALONE WITH MY BEST FRIEND...
I JUST CAN'T LET THAT HAPPEN!
EEP!
GABAA (FWAMM)
NUU (LOOM)
HUFF!
HUFF!
YUSA?
HUH?

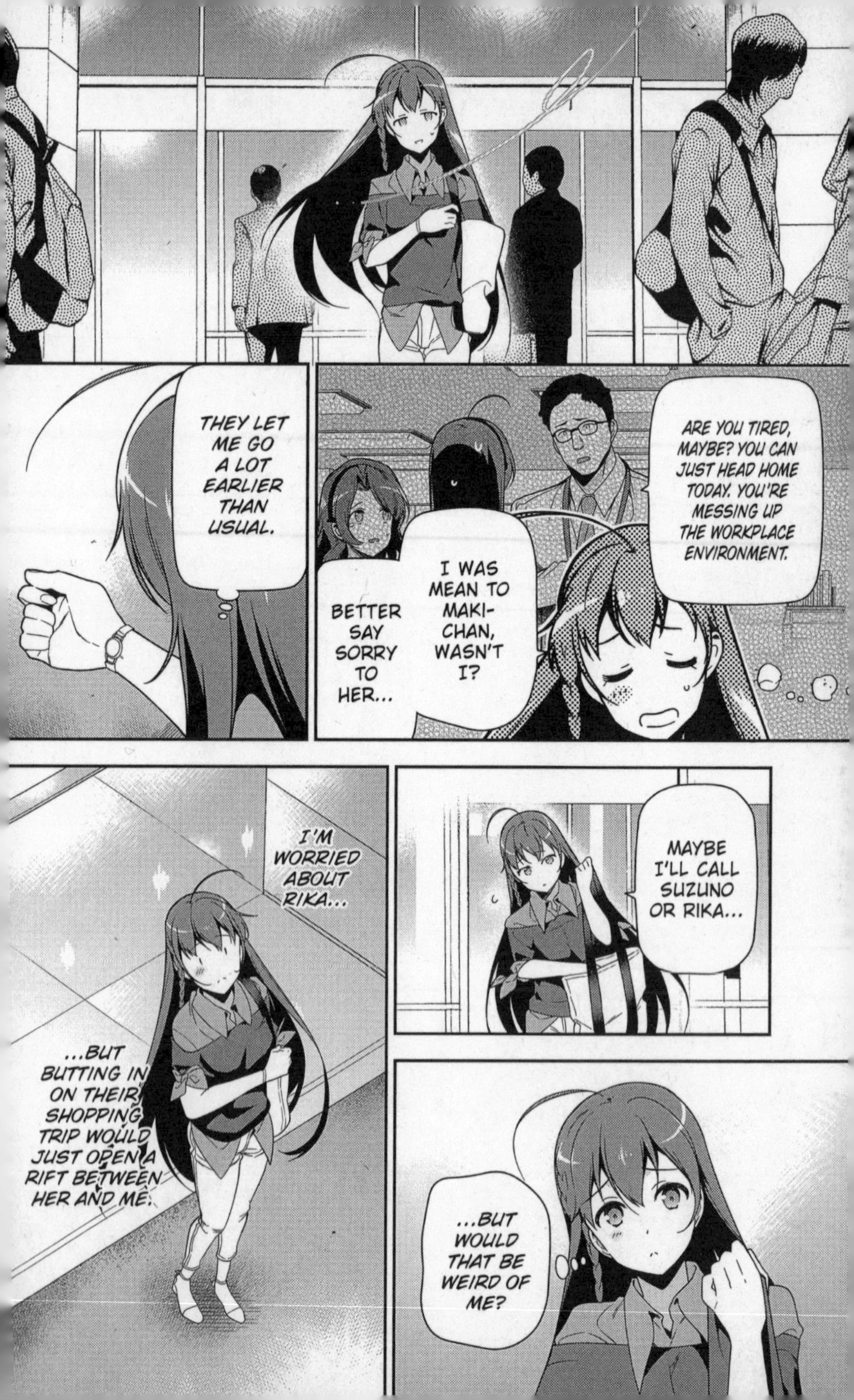
ARE YOU TIRED, MAYBE? YOU CAN JUST HEAD HOME TODAY. YOU'RE MESSING UP THE WORKPLACE ENVIRONMENT.
I WAS MEAN TO MAKI-CHAN, WASN'T I?
BETTER SAY SORRY TO HER...
THEY LET ME GO A LOT EARLIER THAN USUAL.
MAYBE I'LL CALL SUZUNO OR RIKA...
...BUT WOULD THAT BE WEIRD OF ME?
I'M WORRIED ABOUT RIKA...
...BUT BUTTING IN ON THEIR SHOPPING TRIP WOULD JUST OPEN A RIFT BETWEEN HER AND ME.

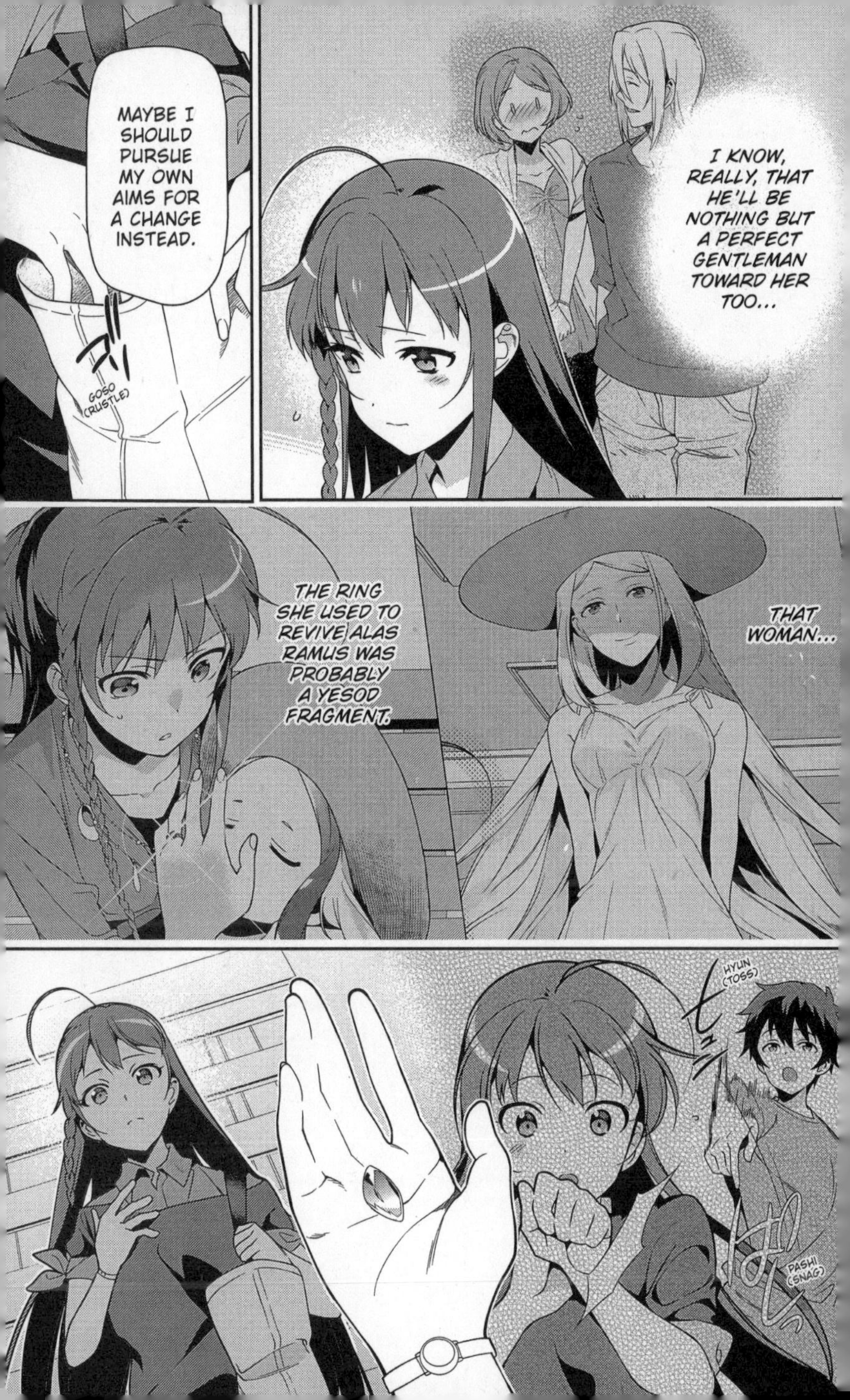
I KNOW, REALLY, THAT HE'LL BE NOTHING BUT A PERFECT GENTLEMAN TOWARD HER TOO...
MAYBE I SHOULD PURSUE MY OWN AIMS FOR A CHANGE INSTEAD.
GOSO (RUSTLE)
THAT WOMAN...
THE RING SHE USED TO REVIVE ALAS RAMUS WAS PROBABLY A YESOD FRAGMENT.
HYUN (TOSS)
PASHI (SNAG)

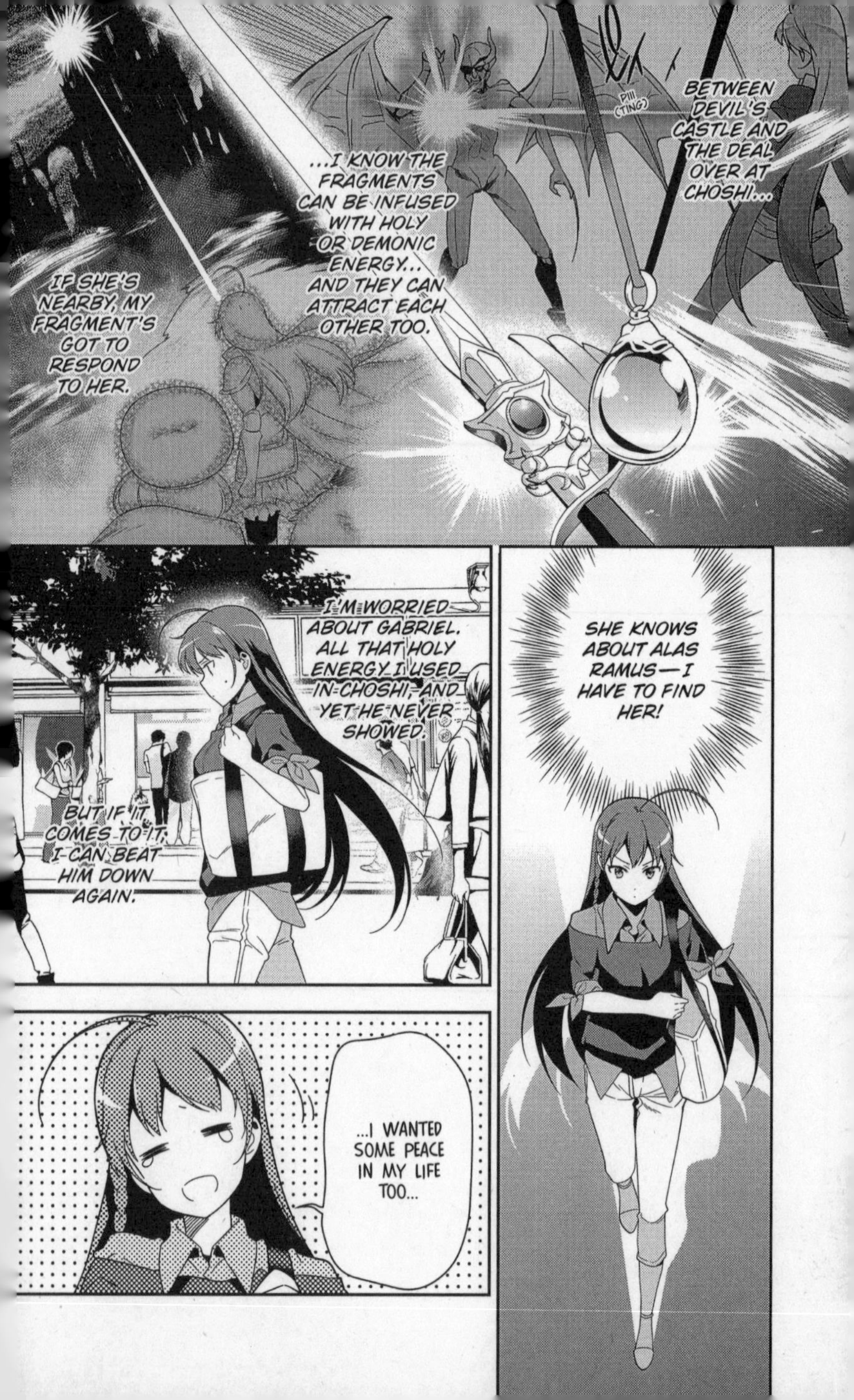

BETWEEN DEVIL'S CASTLE AND THE DEAL OVER AT CHOSHI...
PIII (TING)
...I KNOW THE FRAGMENTS CAN BE INFUSED WITH HOLY OR DEMONIC ENERGY... AND THEY CAN ATTRACT EACH OTHER TOO.
IF SHE'S NEARBY, MY FRAGMENT'S GOT TO RESPOND TO HER.
SHE KNOWS ABOUT ALAS RAMUS—I HAVE TO FIND HER!
I'M WORRIED ABOUT GABRIEL. ALL THAT HOLY ENERGY I USED IN CHOSHI, AND YET HE NEVER SHOWED.
BUT IF IT COMES TO IT, I CAN BEAT HIM DOWN AGAIN.
...I WANTED SOME PEACE IN MY LIFE TOO...

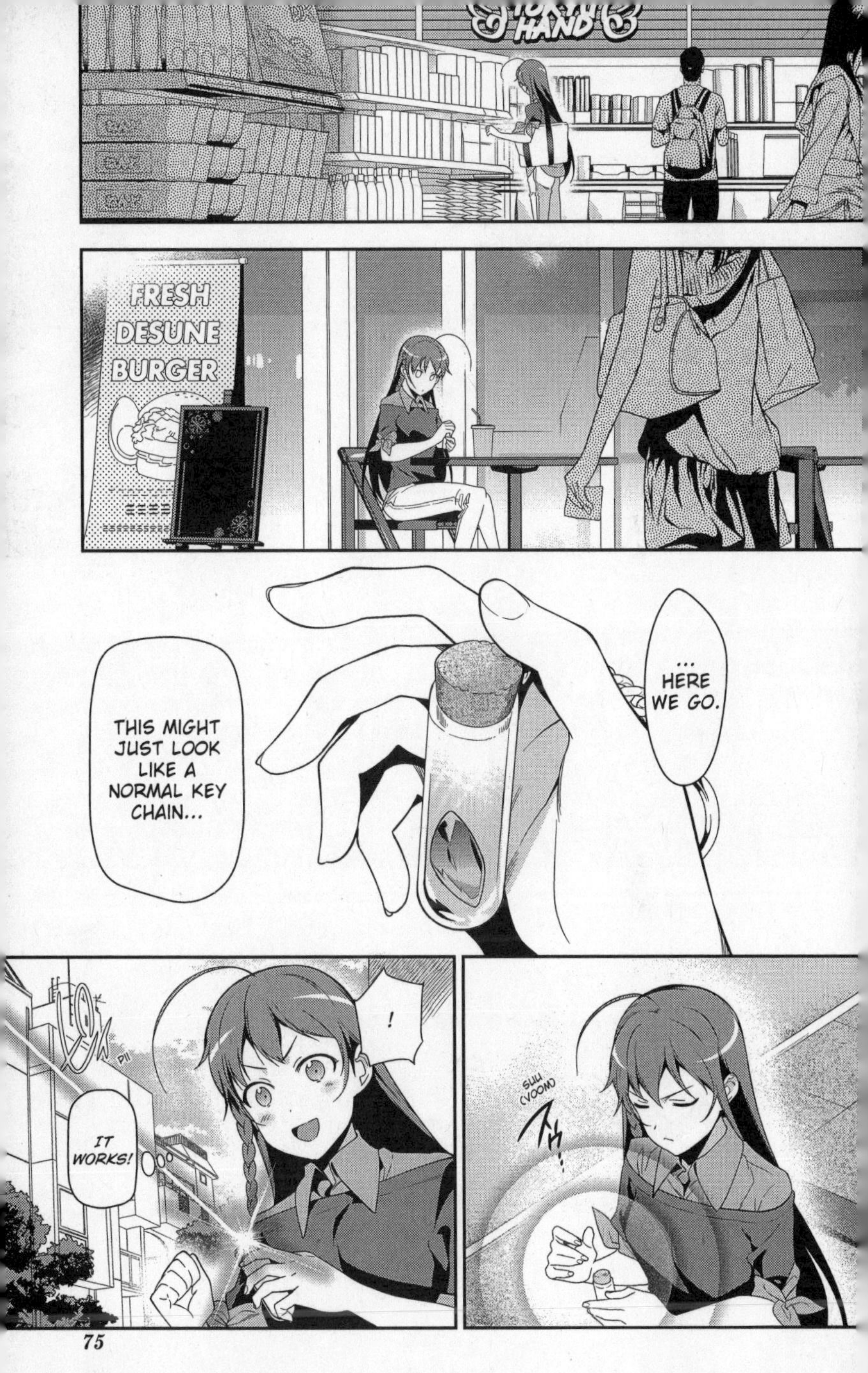
HAND
FRESH DESUNE BURGER
... HERE WE GO.
THIS MIGHT JUST LOOK LIKE A NORMAL KEY CHAIN...
SUU (VOOM)
!
PII
IT WORKS!

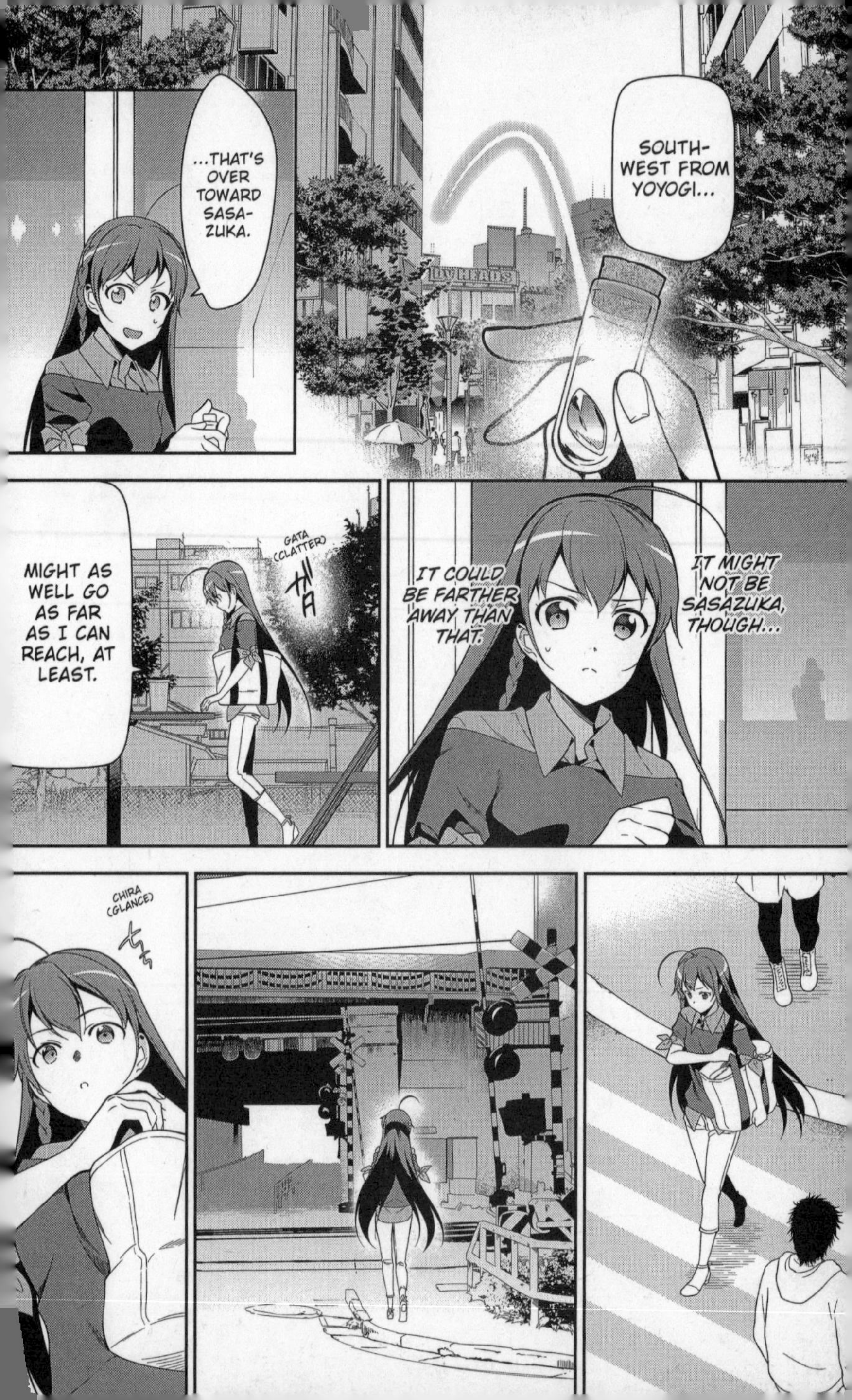
SOUTH-WEST FROM YOYOGI...
...THAT'S OVER TOWARD SASAZUKA.
IT MIGHT NOT BE SASAZUKA, THOUGH...
IT COULD BE FARTHER AWAY THAN THAT.
GATA (CLATTER)
MIGHT AS WELL GO AS FAR AS I CAN REACH, AT LEAST.
CHIRA (GLANCE)

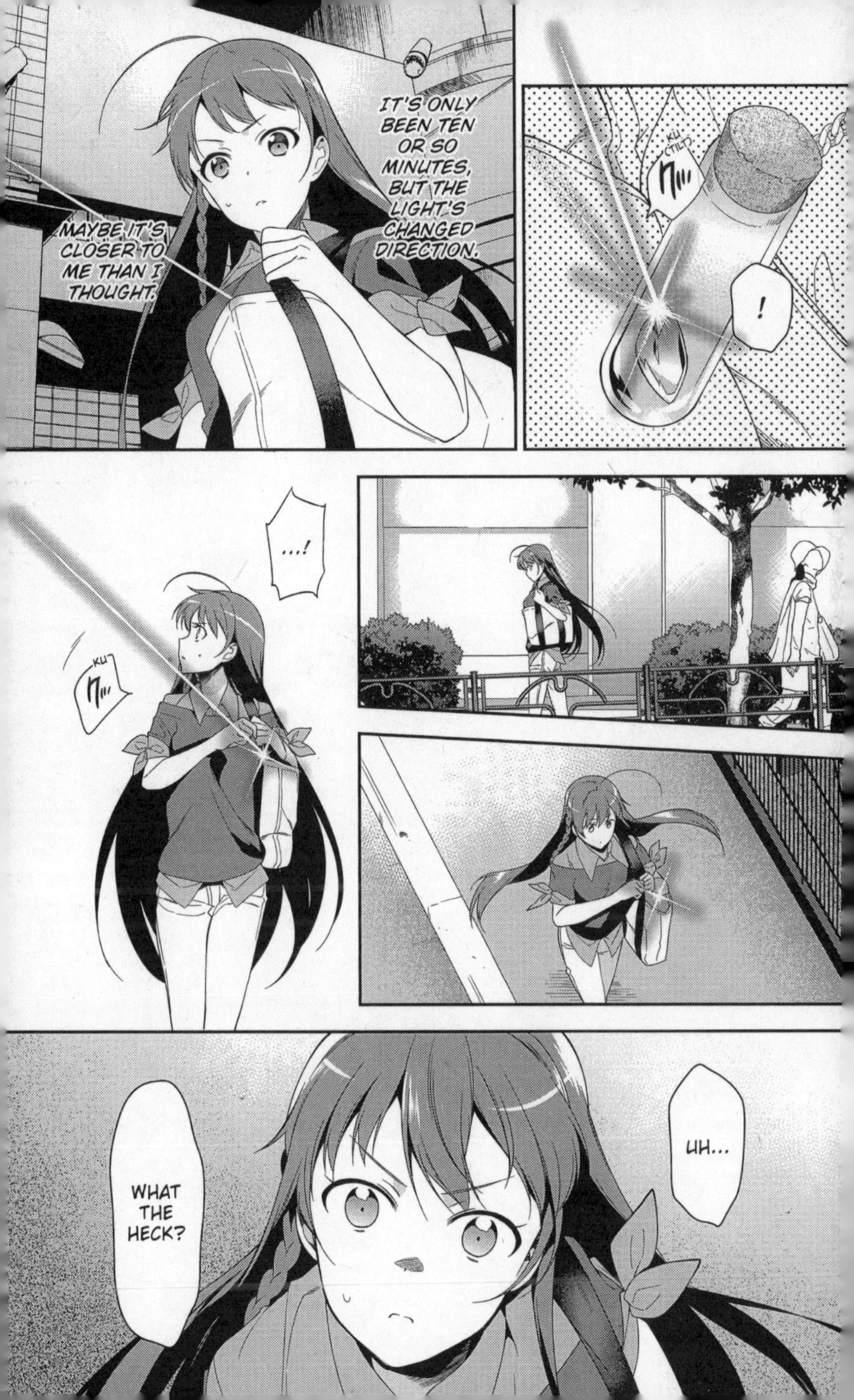
KU (TILT)
!
IT'S ONLY BEEN TEN OR SO MINUTES, BUT THE LIGHT'S CHANGED DIRECTION.
MAYBE IT'S CLOSER TO ME THAN I THOUGHT.
...!
KU
UH...
WHAT THE HECK?

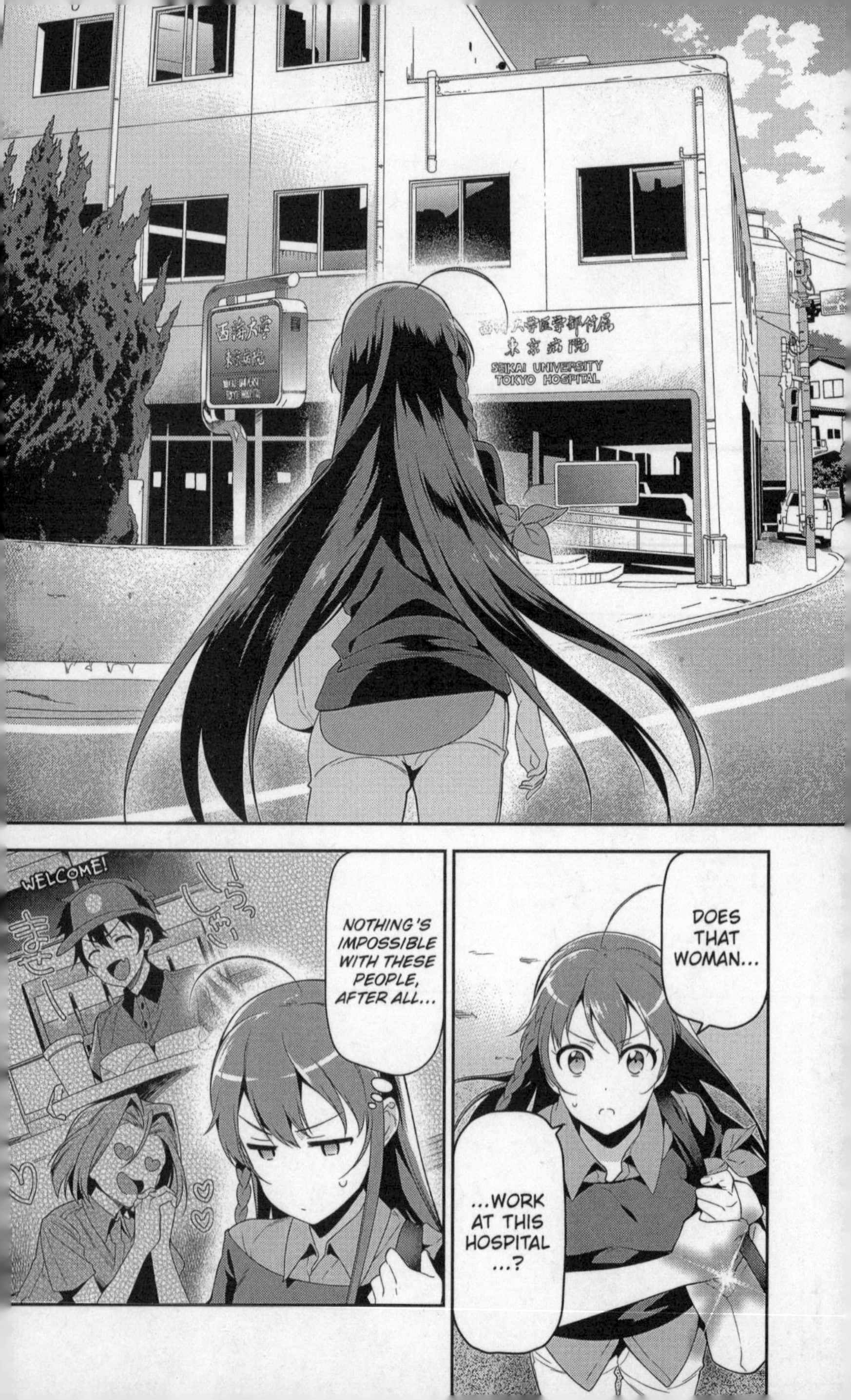
SEIKAI UNIVERSITY
TOKYO HOSPITAL
DOES THAT WOMAN...
...WORK AT THIS HOSPITAL ...?
NOTHING'S IMPOSSIBLE WITH THESE PEOPLE, AFTER ALL...
WELCOME!

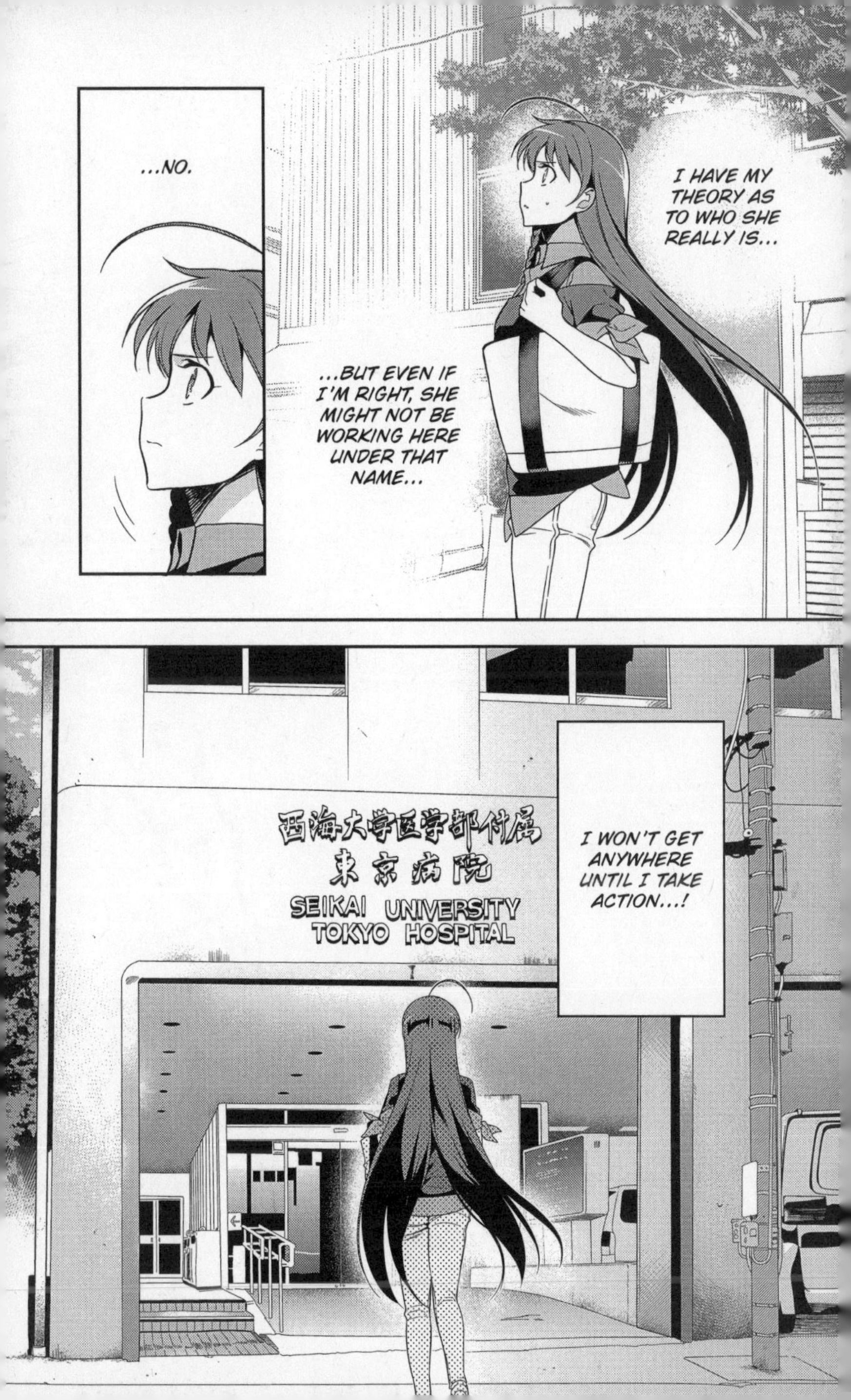
I HAVE MY THEORY AS TO WHO SHE REALLY IS...
...BUT EVEN IF I'M RIGHT, SHE MIGHT NOT BE WORKING HERE UNDER THAT NAME...
...NO.
I WON'T GET ANYWHERE UNTIL I TAKE ACTION...!
西海大学医学部付属
東京病院
SEIKAI UNIVERSITY TOKYO HOSPITAL

THE DEVIL IS A PART-TIMER!

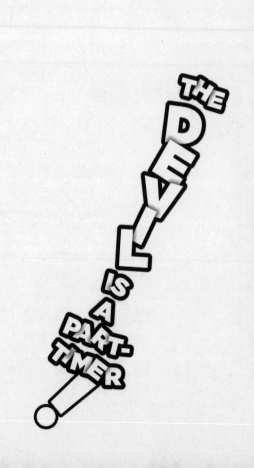

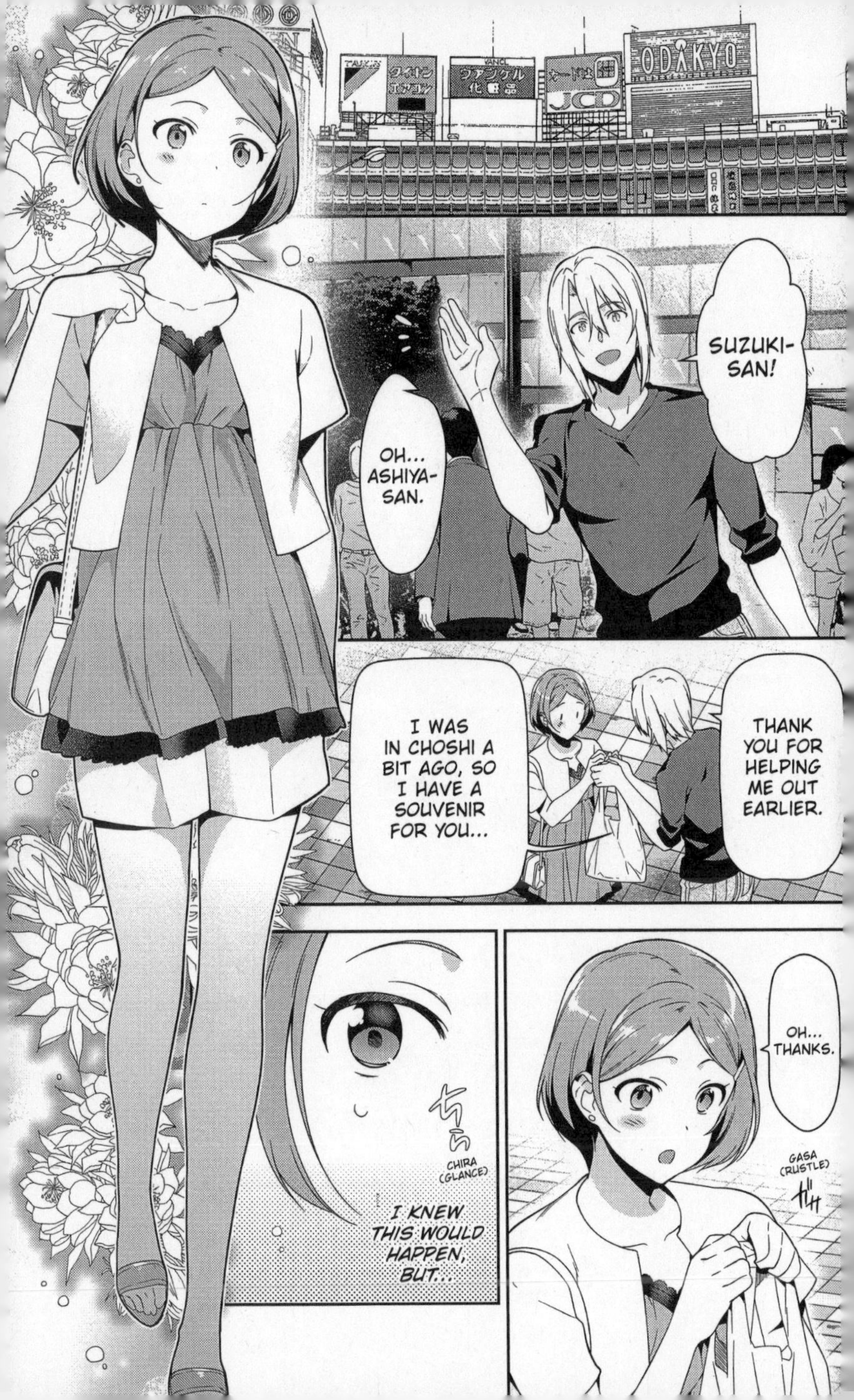

ODAKYU
JCD
SUZUKI-SAN!
OH... ASHIYA-SAN.
THANK YOU FOR HELPING ME OUT EARLIER.
I WAS IN CHOSHI A BIT AGO, SO I HAVE A SOUVENIR FOR YOU...
OH... THANKS.
GASA (RUSTLE)
CHIRA (GLANCE)
I KNEW THIS WOULD HAPPEN, BUT...

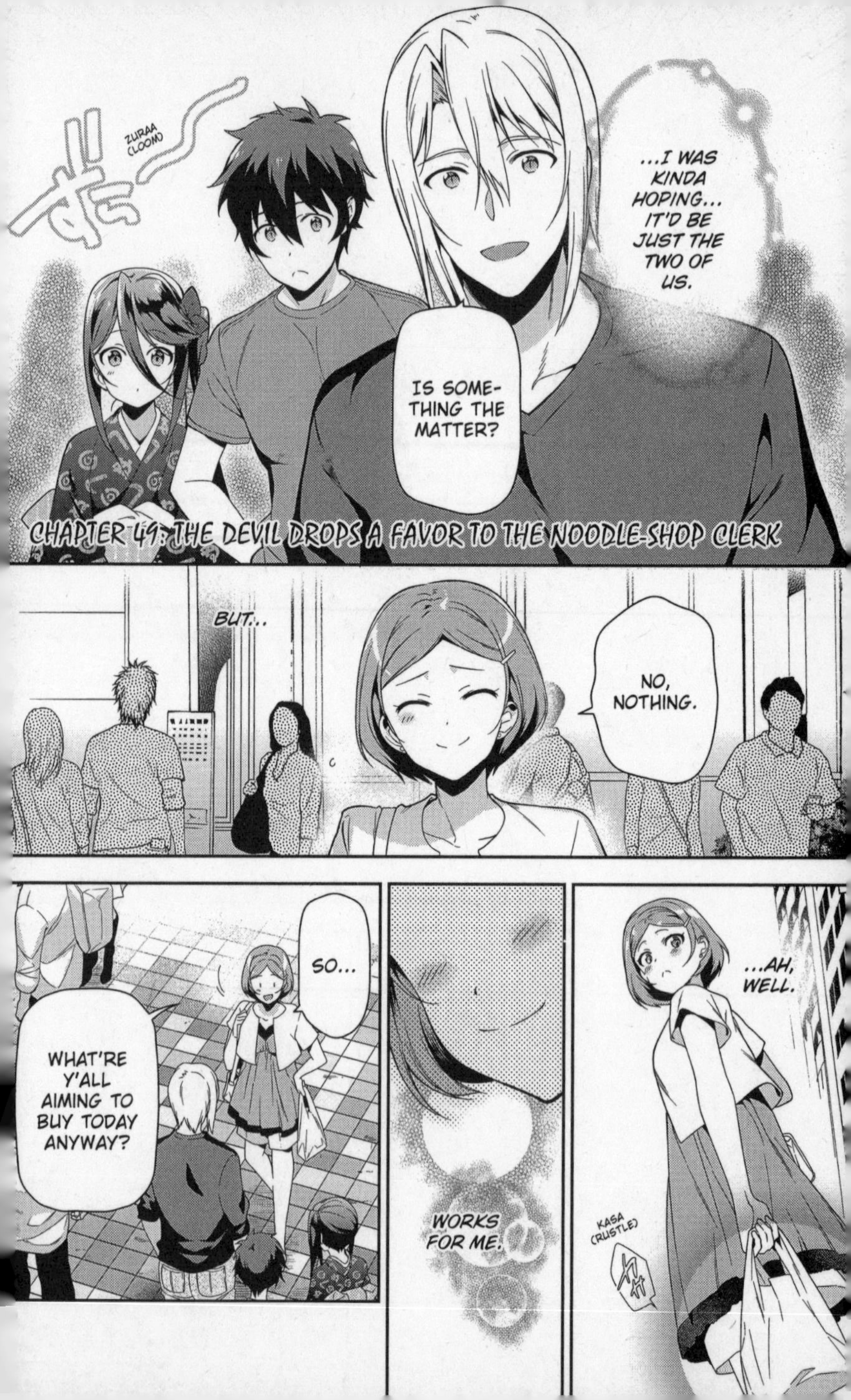
...I WAS KINDA HOPING... IT'D BE JUST THE TWO OF US.
IS SOME-THING THE MATTER?
ZURAA (LOOM)
CHAPTER 49: THE DEVIL DROPS A FAVOR TO THE NOODLE-SHOP CLERK
NO, NOTHING.
BUT...
...AH, WELL.
KASA (RUSTLE)
WORKS FOR ME.
SO...
WHAT'RE Y'ALL AIMING TO BUY TODAY ANYWAY?

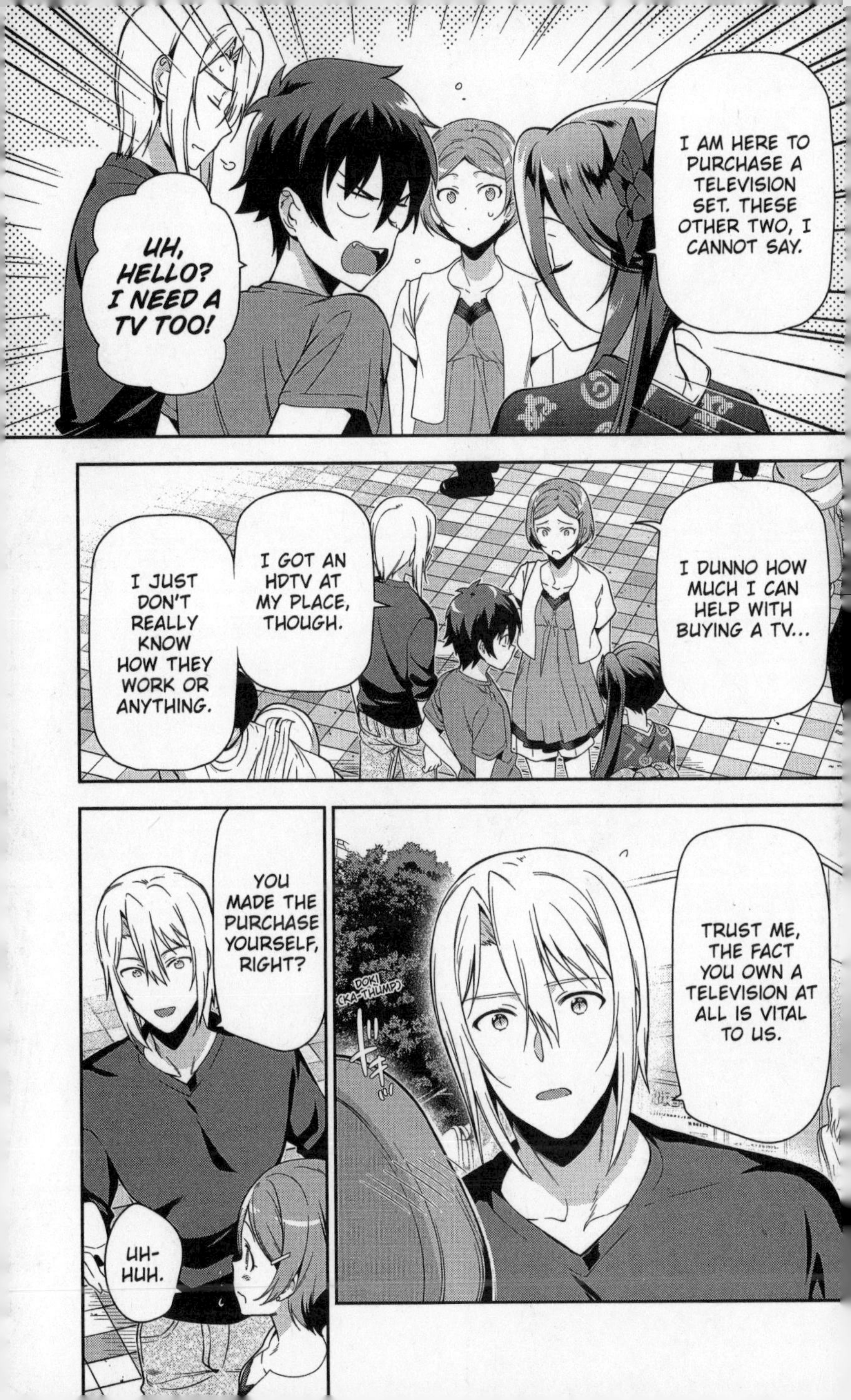
I AM HERE TO PURCHASE A TELEVISION SET. THESE OTHER TWO, I CANNOT SAY.
UH, HELLO? I NEED A TV TOO!
I DUNNO HOW MUCH I CAN HELP WITH BUYING A TV...
I GOT AN HDTV AT MY PLACE, THOUGH.
I JUST DON'T REALLY KNOW HOW THEY WORK OR ANYTHING.
TRUST ME, THE FACT YOU OWN A TELEVISION AT ALL IS VITAL TO US.
DOKI (KA-THUMP)
YOU MADE THE PURCHASE YOURSELF, RIGHT?
UH-HUH.

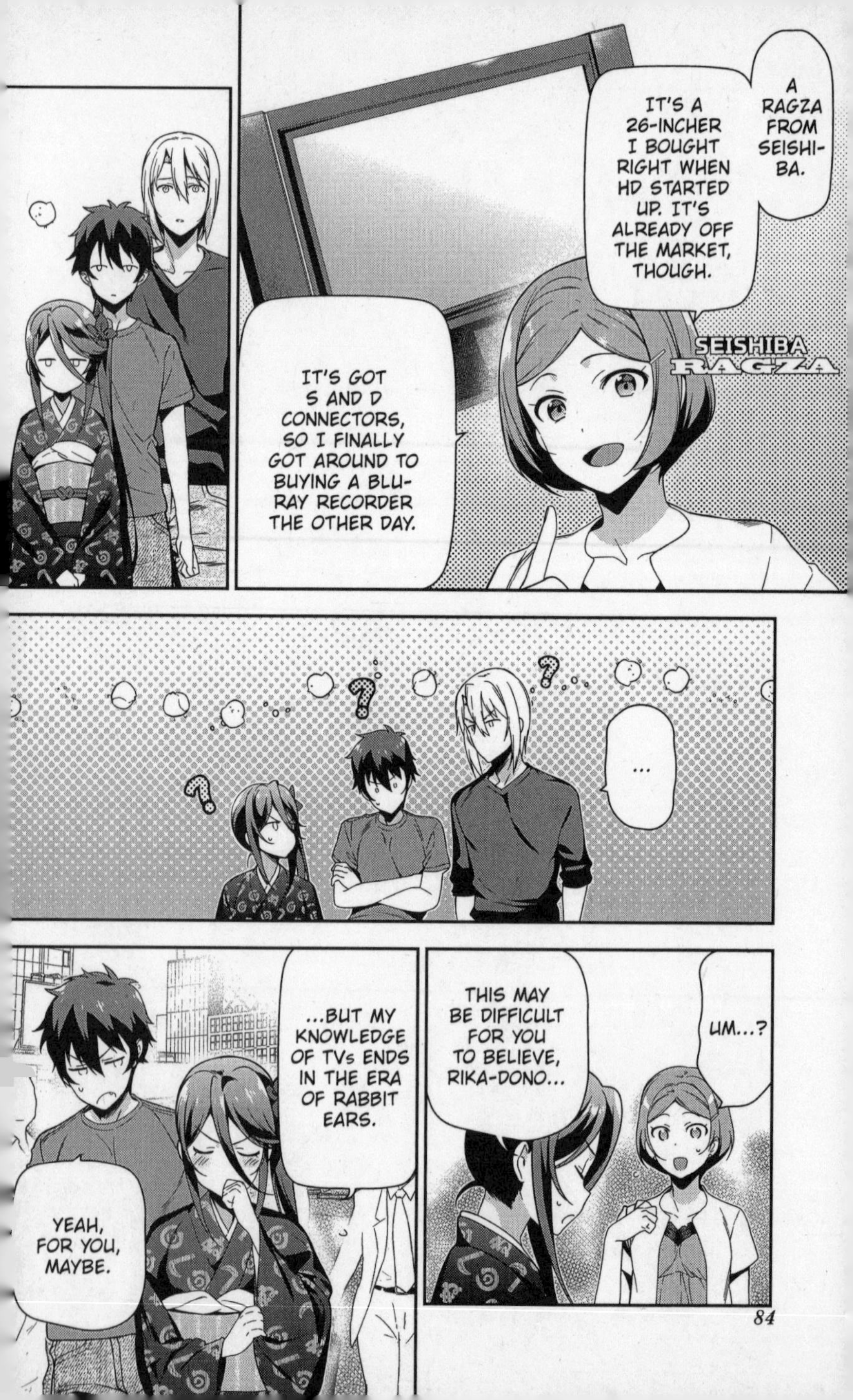
A RAGZA FROM SEISHIBA.
IT'S A 26-INCHER I BOUGHT RIGHT WHEN HD STARTED UP. IT'S ALREADY OFF THE MARKET, THOUGH.
SEISHIBA RAGZA
IT'S GOT S AND D CONNECTORS, SO I FINALLY GOT AROUND TO BUYING A BLU-RAY RECORDER THE OTHER DAY.
...
UM...?
THIS MAY BE DIFFICULT FOR YOU TO BELIEVE, RIKA-DONO...
...BUT MY KNOWLEDGE OF TVs ENDS IN THE ERA OF RABBIT EARS.
YEAH, FOR YOU, MAYBE.

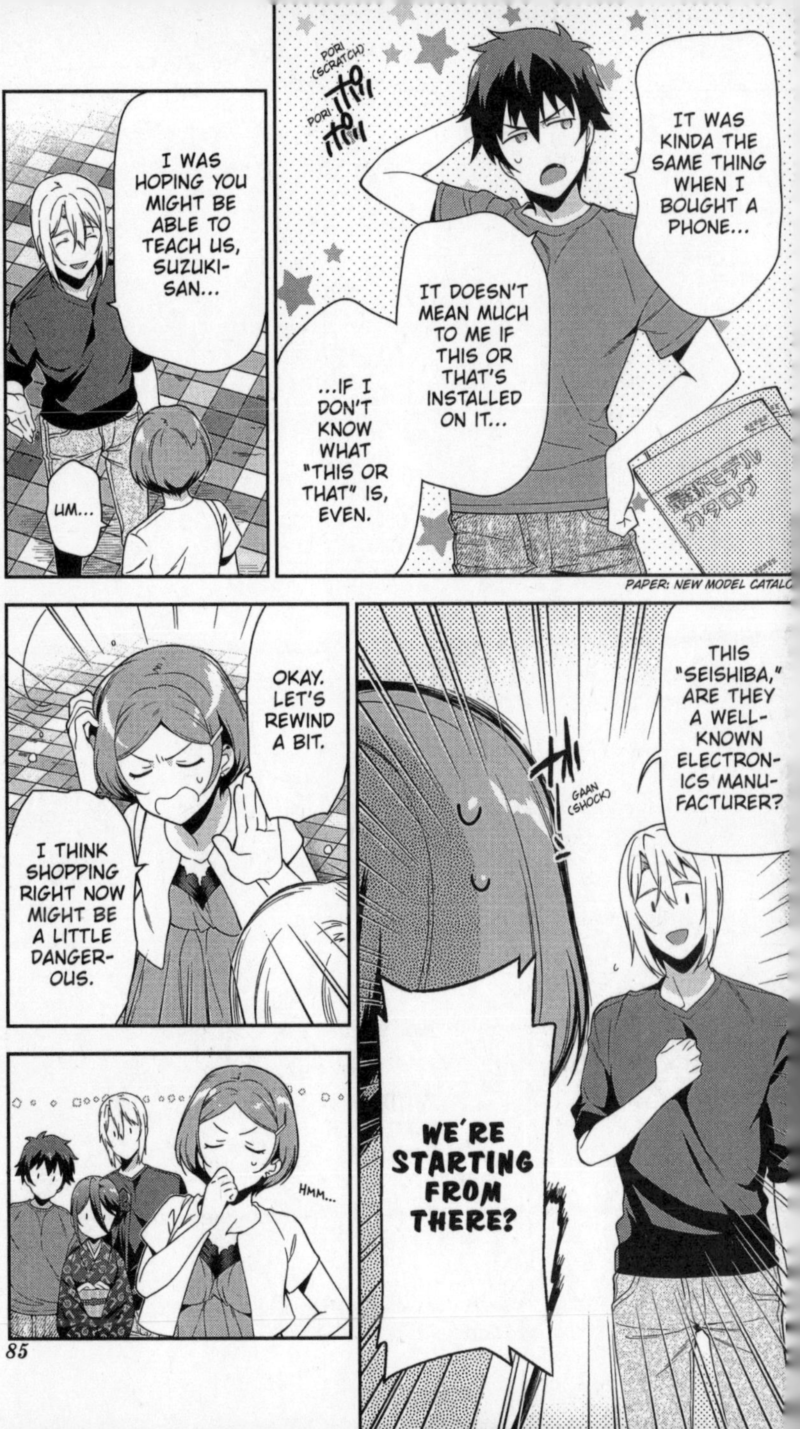
PORI (SCRATCH) PORI
IT WAS KINDA THE SAME THING WHEN I BOUGHT A PHONE...
IT DOESN'T MEAN MUCH TO ME IF THIS OR THAT'S INSTALLED ON IT...
...IF I DON'T KNOW WHAT "THIS OR THAT" IS, EVEN.
PAPER: NEW MODEL CATALO
I WAS HOPING YOU MIGHT BE ABLE TO TEACH US, SUZUKI-SAN...
UM...
THIS "SEISHIBA," ARE THEY A WELL-KNOWN ELECTRONICS MANUFACTURER?
GAAN (SHOCK)
WE'RE STARTING FROM THERE?
OKAY. LET'S REWIND A BIT.
I THINK SHOPPING RIGHT NOW MIGHT BE A LITTLE DANGEROUS.
HMM...

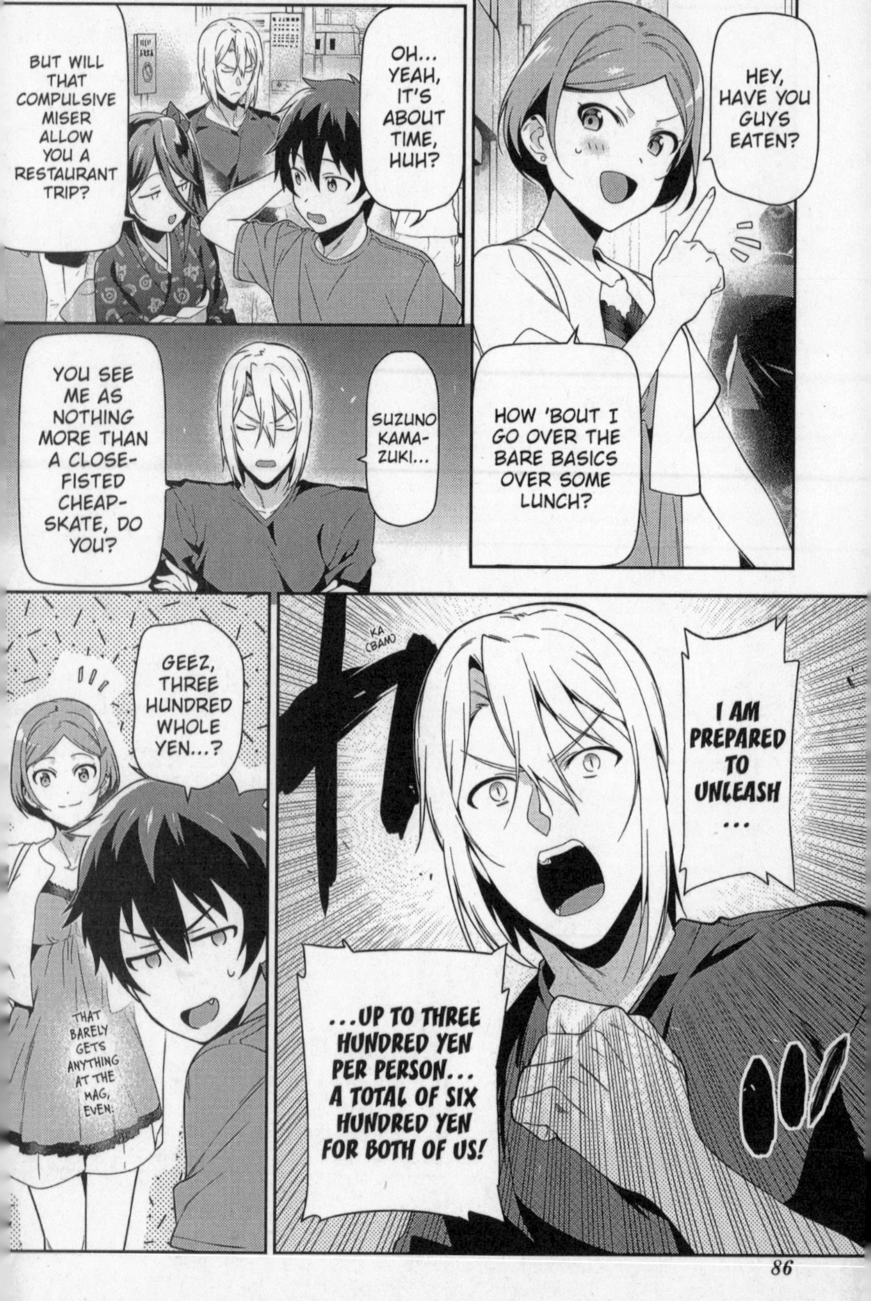
HEY, HAVE YOU GUYS EATEN?
HOW 'BOUT I GO OVER THE BARE BASICS OVER SOME LUNCH?
OH... YEAH, IT'S ABOUT TIME, HUH?
BUT WILL THAT COMPULSIVE MISER ALLOW YOU A RESTAURANT TRIP?
SUZUNO KAMA-ZUKI...
YOU SEE ME AS NOTHING MORE THAN A CLOSE-FISTED CHEAP-SKATE, DO YOU?
KA (BAM)
I AM PREPARED TO UNLEASH...
...UP TO THREE HUNDRED YEN PER PERSON... A TOTAL OF SIX HUNDRED YEN FOR BOTH OF US!
GEEZ, THREE HUNDRED WHOLE YEN...?
THAT BARELY GETS ANYTHING AT THE MAG, EVEN.

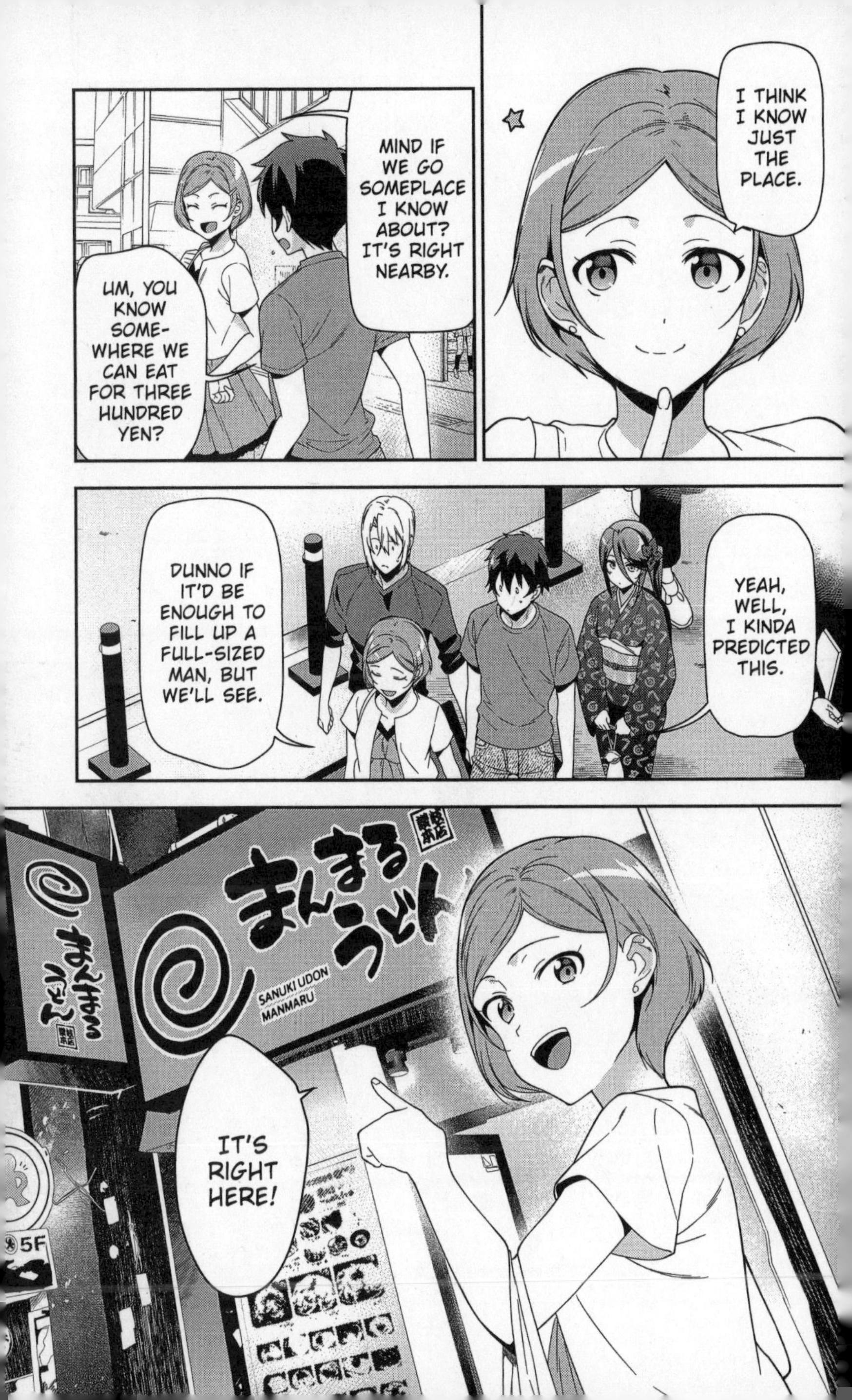
I THINK I KNOW JUST THE PLACE.
MIND IF WE GO SOMEPLACE I KNOW ABOUT? IT'S RIGHT NEARBY.
UM, YOU KNOW SOME-WHERE WE CAN EAT FOR THREE HUNDRED YEN?
YEAH, WELL, I KINDA PREDICTED THIS.
DUNNO IF IT'D BE ENOUGH TO FILL UP A FULL-SIZED MAN, BUT WE'LL SEE.
まんまるうどん
SANUKI UDON MANMARU
まんまるうどん
5F
IT'S RIGHT HERE!

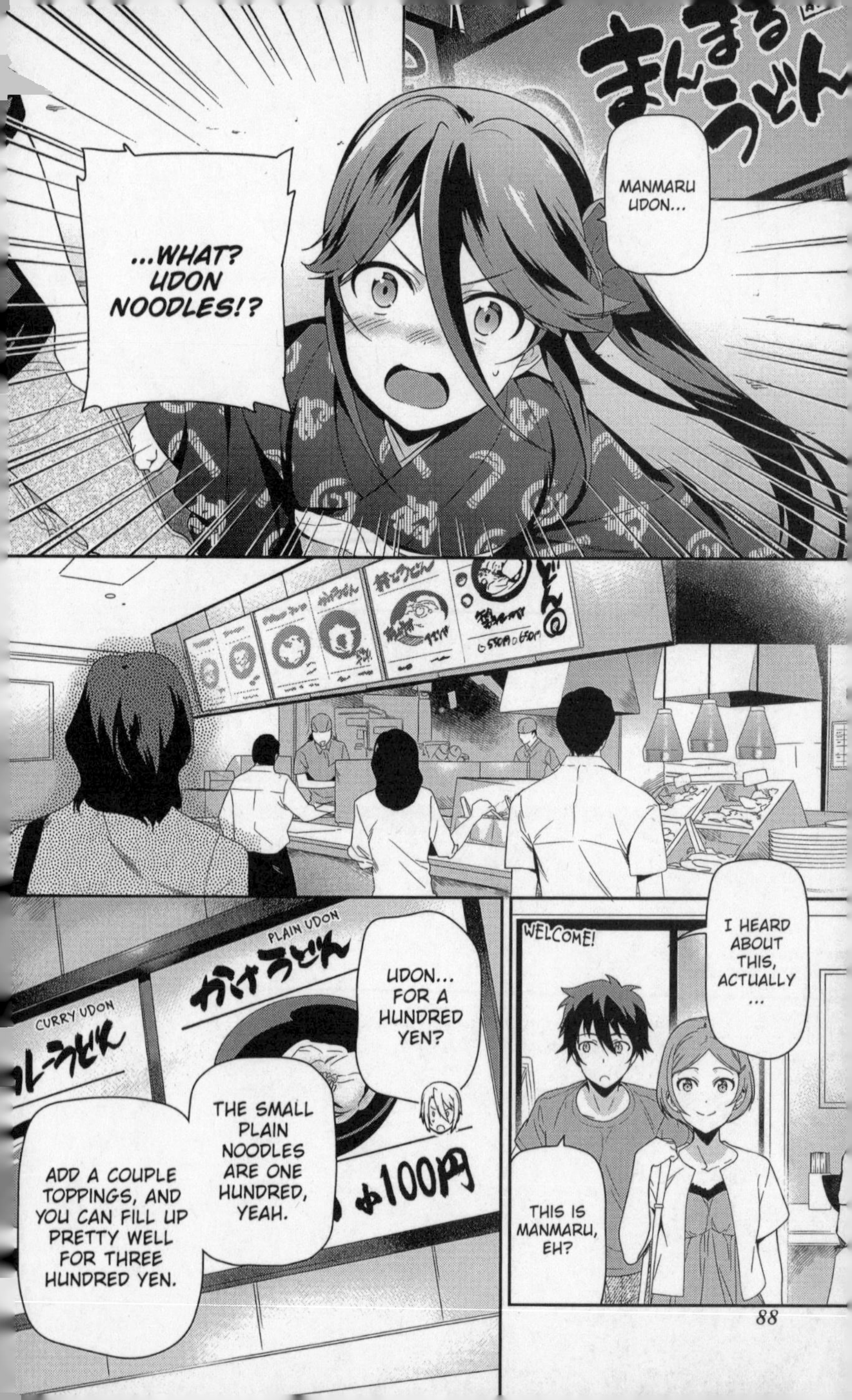
まんまるうどん
MANMARU UDON...
...WHAT? UDON NOODLES!?
I HEARD ABOUT THIS, ACTUALLY ...
WELCOME!
THIS IS MANMARU, EH?
UDON... FOR A HUNDRED YEN?
PLAIN UDON
かけうどん
CURRY UDON
THE SMALL PLAIN NOODLES ARE ONE HUNDRED, YEAH.
100円
ADD A COUPLE TOPPINGS, AND YOU CAN FILL UP PRETTY WELL FOR THREE HUNDRED YEN.

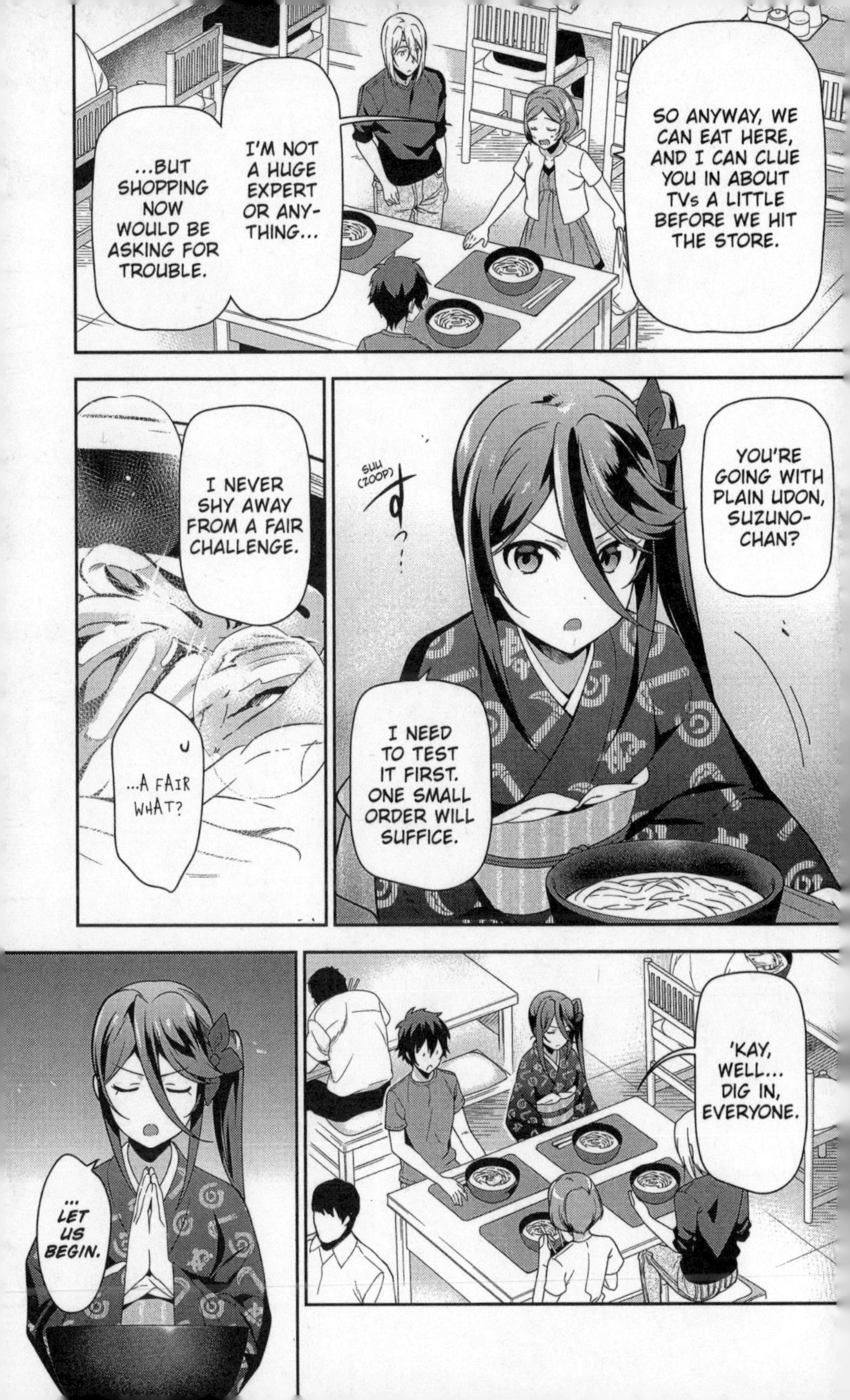
SO ANYWAY, WE CAN EAT HERE, AND I CAN CLUE YOU IN ABOUT TVs A LITTLE BEFORE WE HIT THE STORE.
I'M NOT A HUGE EXPERT OR ANY-THING...
...BUT SHOPPING NOW WOULD BE ASKING FOR TROUBLE.
YOU'RE GOING WITH PLAIN UDON, SUZUNO-CHAN?
SUU (ZOOP)
I NEED TO TEST IT FIRST. ONE SMALL ORDER WILL SUFFICE.
I NEVER SHY AWAY FROM A FAIR CHALLENGE.
...A FAIR WHAT?
'KAY, WELL... DIG IN, EVERYONE.
...LET US BEGIN.

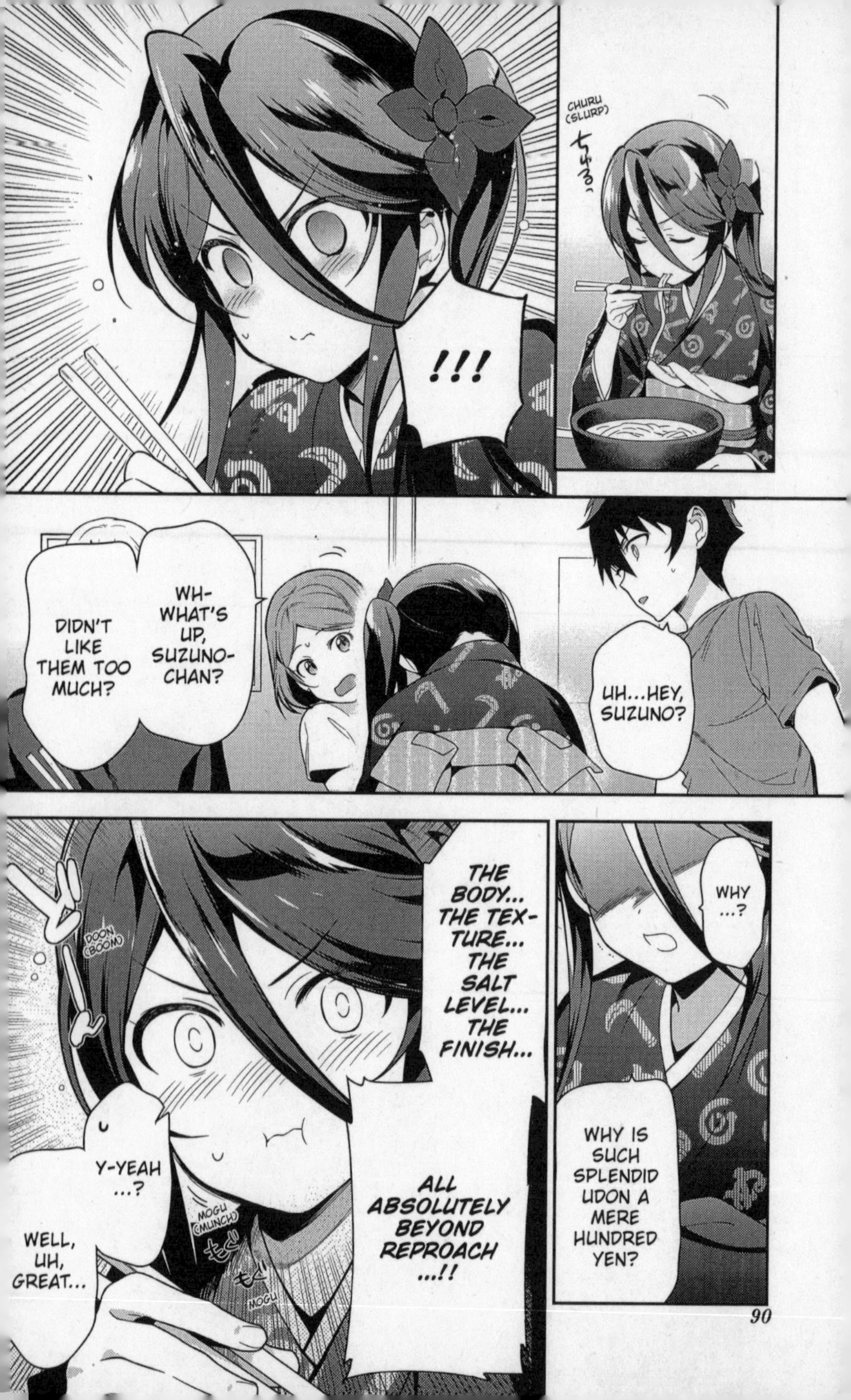

CHURU (SLURP)
ちゅるっ
!!!
UH...HEY, SUZUNO?
WH-WHAT'S UP, SUZUNO-CHAN?
DIDN'T LIKE THEM TOO MUCH?
WHY ...?
WHY IS SUCH SPLENDID UDON A MERE HUNDRED YEN?
THE BODY... THE TEXTURE... THE SALT LEVEL... THE FINISH...
ALL ABSOLUTELY BEYOND REPROACH ...!!
DOON (BOOM)
Y-YEAH ...?
WELL, UH, GREAT...
MOGU (MUNCH)
もぐ
もぐ
MOGU

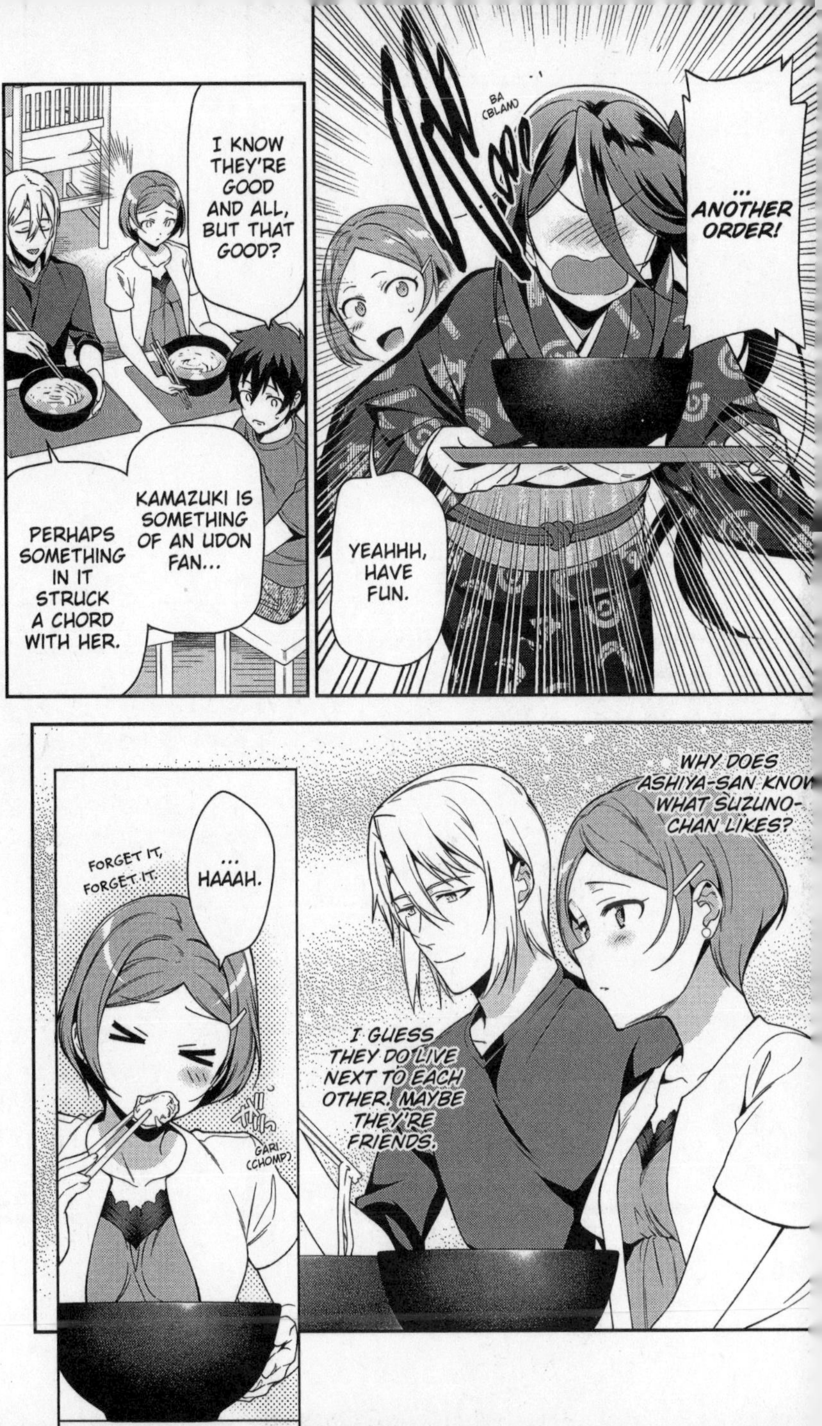
BA (BLAM)
... ANOTHER ORDER!
YEAHHH, HAVE FUN.
I KNOW THEY'RE GOOD AND ALL, BUT THAT GOOD?
KAMAZUKI IS SOMETHING OF AN UDON FAN...
PERHAPS SOMETHING IN IT STRUCK A CHORD WITH HER.
WHY DOES ASHIYA-SAN KNOW WHAT SUZUNO-CHAN LIKES?
I GUESS THEY DO LIVE NEXT TO EACH OTHER. MAYBE THEY'RE FRIENDS.
... HAAAH.
FORGET IT, FORGET IT.
GARI (CHOMP)

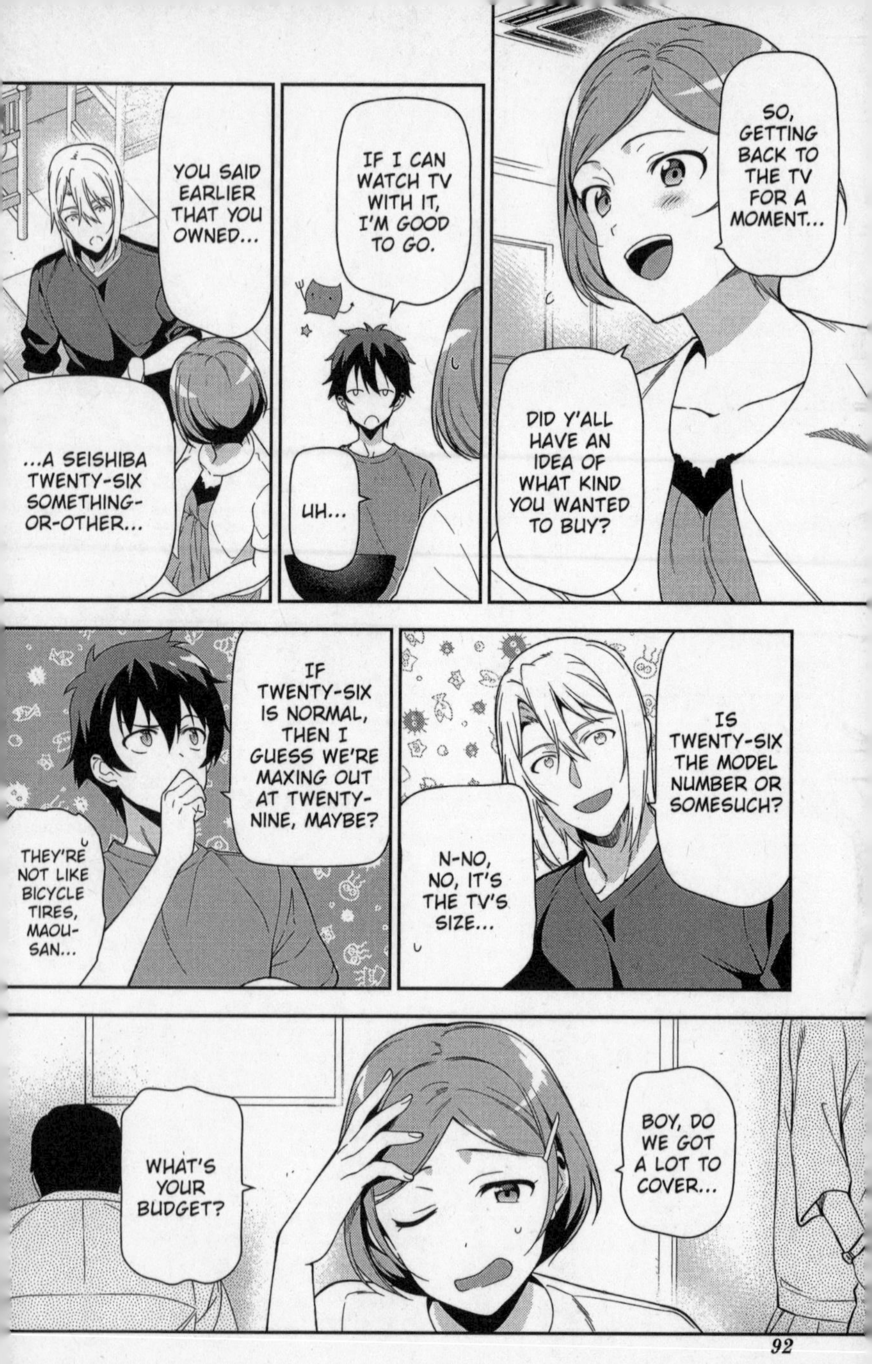
SO, GETTING BACK TO THE TV FOR A MOMENT...
DID Y'ALL HAVE AN IDEA OF WHAT KIND YOU WANTED TO BUY?
IF I CAN WATCH TV WITH IT, I'M GOOD TO GO.
UH...
YOU SAID EARLIER THAT YOU OWNED...
...A SEISHIBA TWENTY-SIX SOMETHING-OR-OTHER...
IS TWENTY-SIX THE MODEL NUMBER OR SOMESUCH?
N-NO, NO, IT'S THE TV'S SIZE...
IF TWENTY-SIX IS NORMAL, THEN I GUESS WE'RE MAXING OUT AT TWENTY-NINE, MAYBE?
THEY'RE NOT LIKE BICYCLE TIRES, MAOU-SAN...
BOY, DO WE GOT A LOT TO COVER...
WHAT'S YOUR BUDGET?

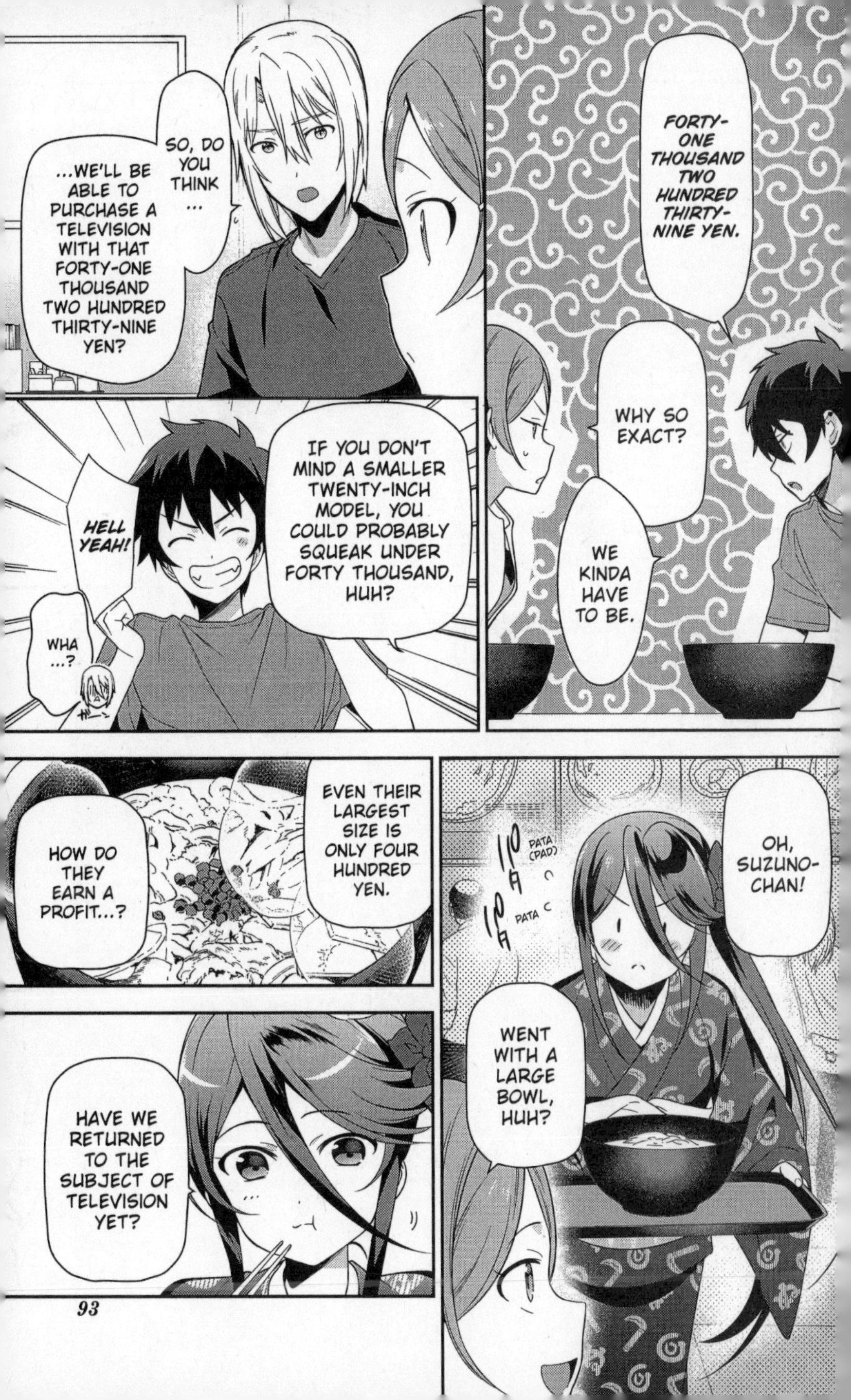
FORTY-ONE THOUSAND TWO HUNDRED THIRTY-NINE YEN.
WHY SO EXACT?
WE KINDA HAVE TO BE.
SO, DO YOU THINK...
...WE'LL BE ABLE TO PURCHASE A TELEVISION WITH THAT FORTY-ONE THOUSAND TWO HUNDRED THIRTY-NINE YEN?
IF YOU DON'T MIND A SMALLER TWENTY-INCH MODEL, YOU COULD PROBABLY SQUEAK UNDER FORTY THOUSAND, HUH?
HELL YEAH!
WHA...?
OH, SUZUNO-CHAN!
PATA (PAD)
PATA
WENT WITH A LARGE BOWL, HUH?
EVEN THEIR LARGEST SIZE IS ONLY FOUR HUNDRED YEN.
HOW DO THEY EARN A PROFIT...?
HAVE WE RETURNED TO THE SUBJECT OF TELEVISION YET?

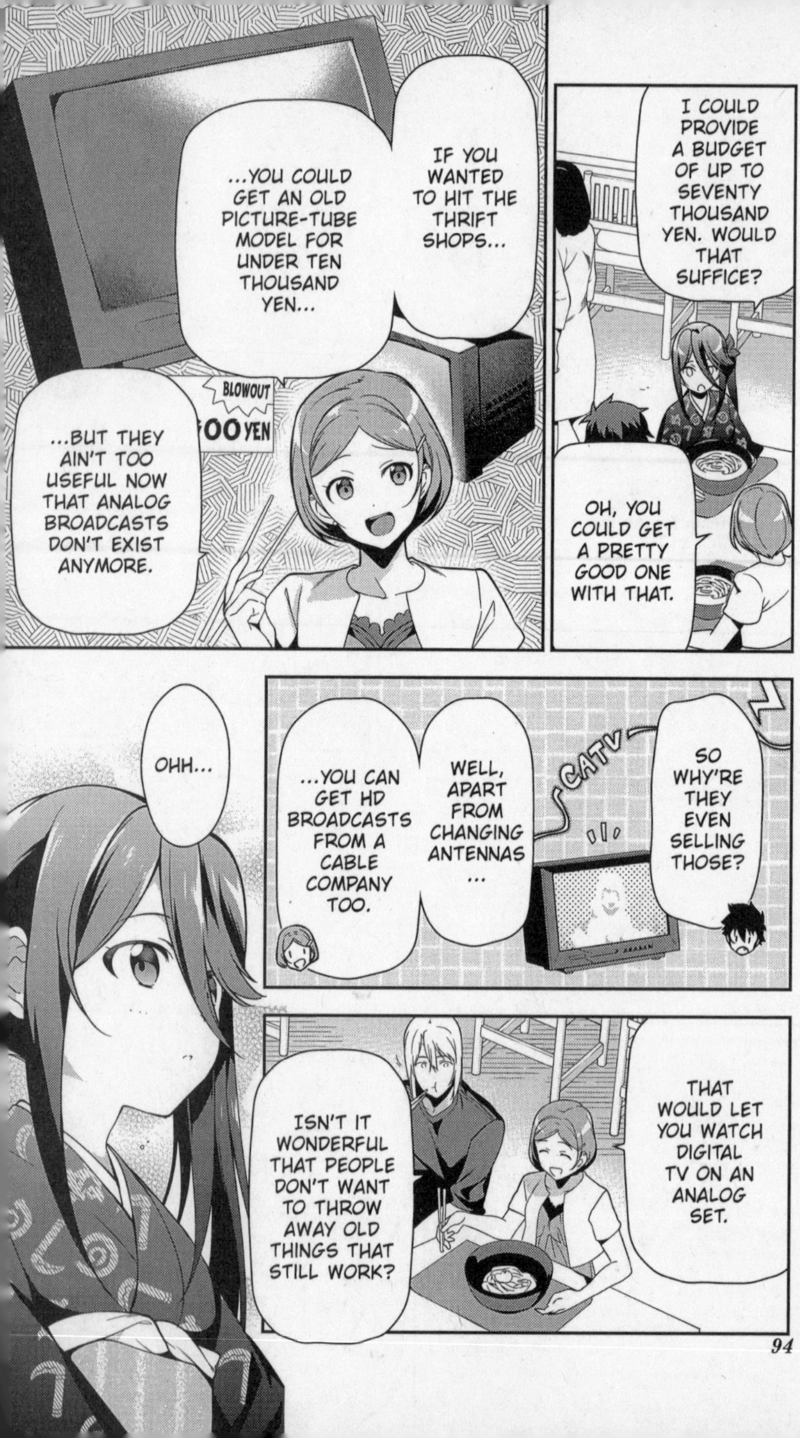
I COULD PROVIDE A BUDGET OF UP TO SEVENTY THOUSAND YEN. WOULD THAT SUFFICE?
OH, YOU COULD GET A PRETTY GOOD ONE WITH THAT.
IF YOU WANTED TO HIT THE THRIFT SHOPS...
...YOU COULD GET AN OLD PICTURE-TUBE MODEL FOR UNDER TEN THOUSAND YEN...
BLOWOUT
...BUT THEY AIN'T TOO USEFUL NOW THAT ANALOG BROADCASTS DON'T EXIST ANYMORE.
SO WHY'RE THEY EVEN SELLING THOSE?
CATV
WELL, APART FROM CHANGING ANTENNAS ...
...YOU CAN GET HD BROADCASTS FROM A CABLE COMPANY TOO.
THAT WOULD LET YOU WATCH DIGITAL TV ON AN ANALOG SET.
ISN'T IT WONDERFUL THAT PEOPLE DON'T WANT TO THROW AWAY OLD THINGS THAT STILL WORK?
OHH...

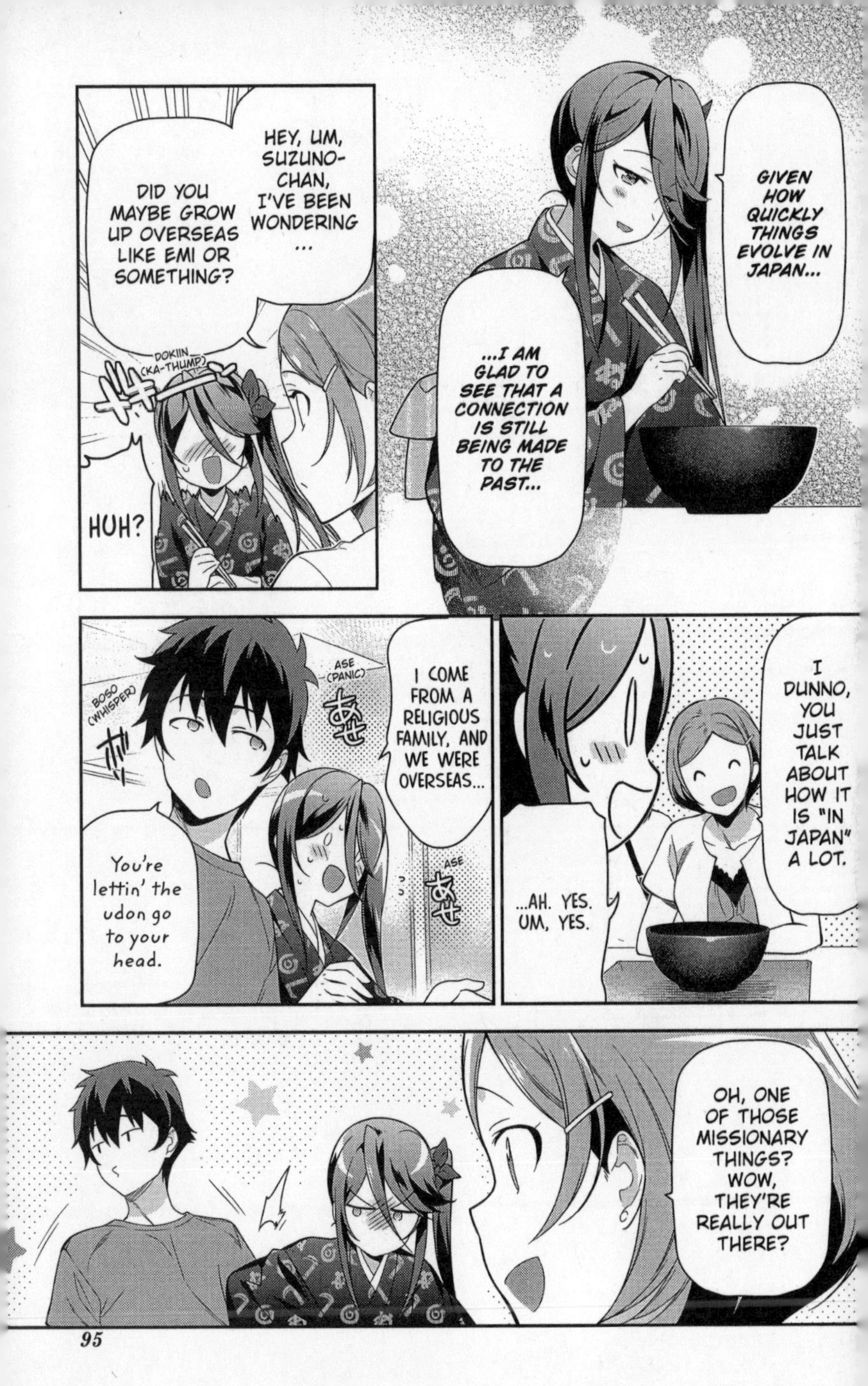
GIVEN HOW QUICKLY THINGS EVOLVE IN JAPAN...
...I AM GLAD TO SEE THAT A CONNECTION IS STILL BEING MADE TO THE PAST...
HEY, UM, SUZUNO-CHAN, I'VE BEEN WONDERING...
DID YOU MAYBE GROW UP OVERSEAS LIKE EMI OR SOMETHING?
DOKIIN (KA-THUMP)
HUH?
I DUNNO, YOU JUST TALK ABOUT HOW IT IS "IN JAPAN" A LOT.
...AH. YES. UM, YES.
ASE (PANIC)
I COME FROM A RELIGIOUS FAMILY, AND WE WERE OVERSEAS...
BOSO (WHISPER)
You're lettin' the udon go to your head.
ASE
OH, ONE OF THOSE MISSIONARY THINGS? WOW, THEY'RE REALLY OUT THERE?

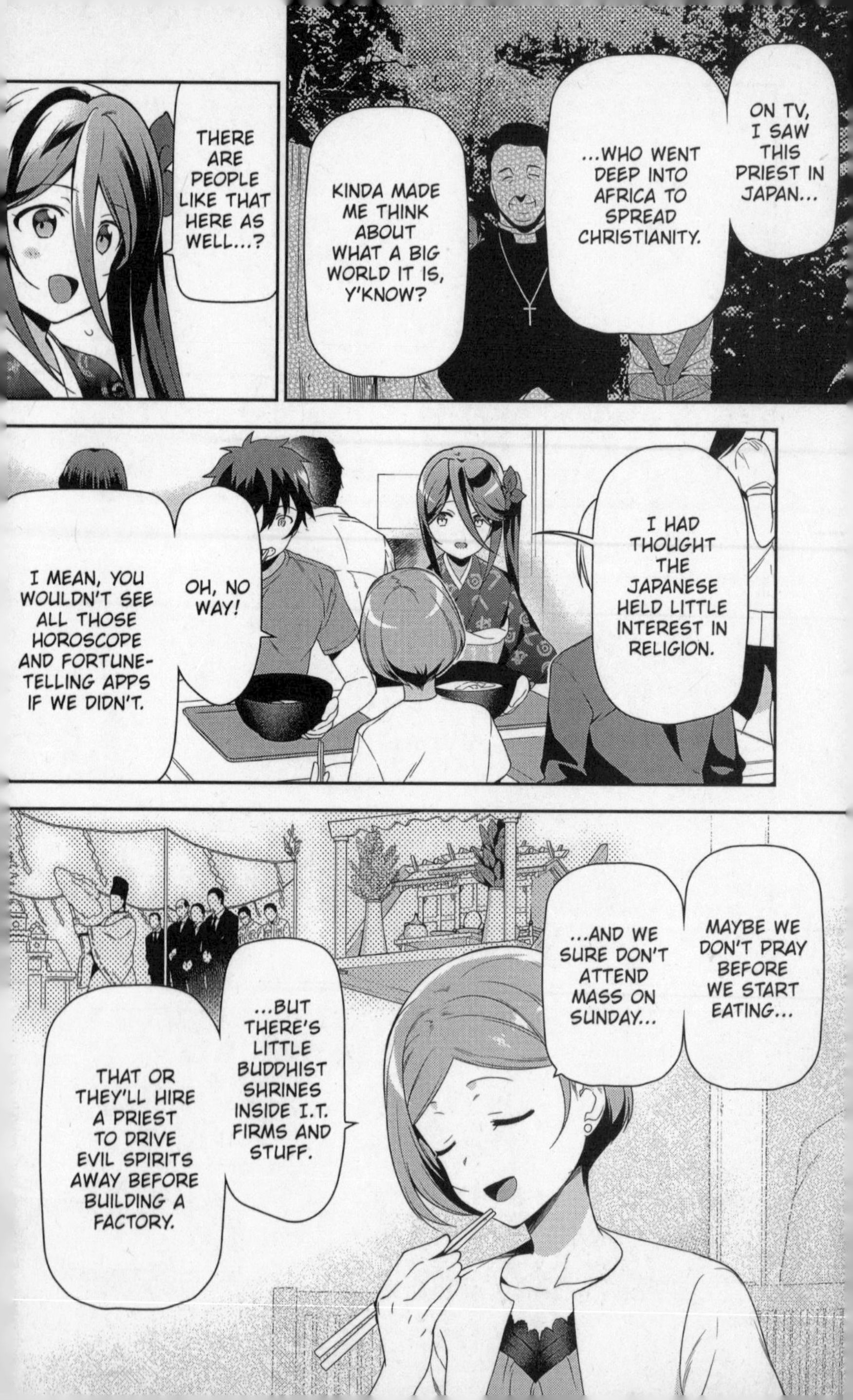
ON TV, I SAW THIS PRIEST IN JAPAN...
...WHO WENT DEEP INTO AFRICA TO SPREAD CHRISTIANITY.
KINDA MADE ME THINK ABOUT WHAT A BIG WORLD IT IS, Y'KNOW?
THERE ARE PEOPLE LIKE THAT HERE AS WELL...?
I HAD THOUGHT THE JAPANESE HELD LITTLE INTEREST IN RELIGION.
OH, NO WAY!
I MEAN, YOU WOULDN'T SEE ALL THOSE HOROSCOPE AND FORTUNE-TELLING APPS IF WE DIDN'T.
MAYBE WE DON'T PRAY BEFORE WE START EATING...
...AND WE SURE DON'T ATTEND MASS ON SUNDAY...
...BUT THERE'S LITTLE BUDDHIST SHRINES INSIDE I.T. FIRMS AND STUFF.
THAT OR THEY'LL HIRE A PRIEST TO DRIVE EVIL SPIRITS AWAY BEFORE BUILDING A FACTORY.

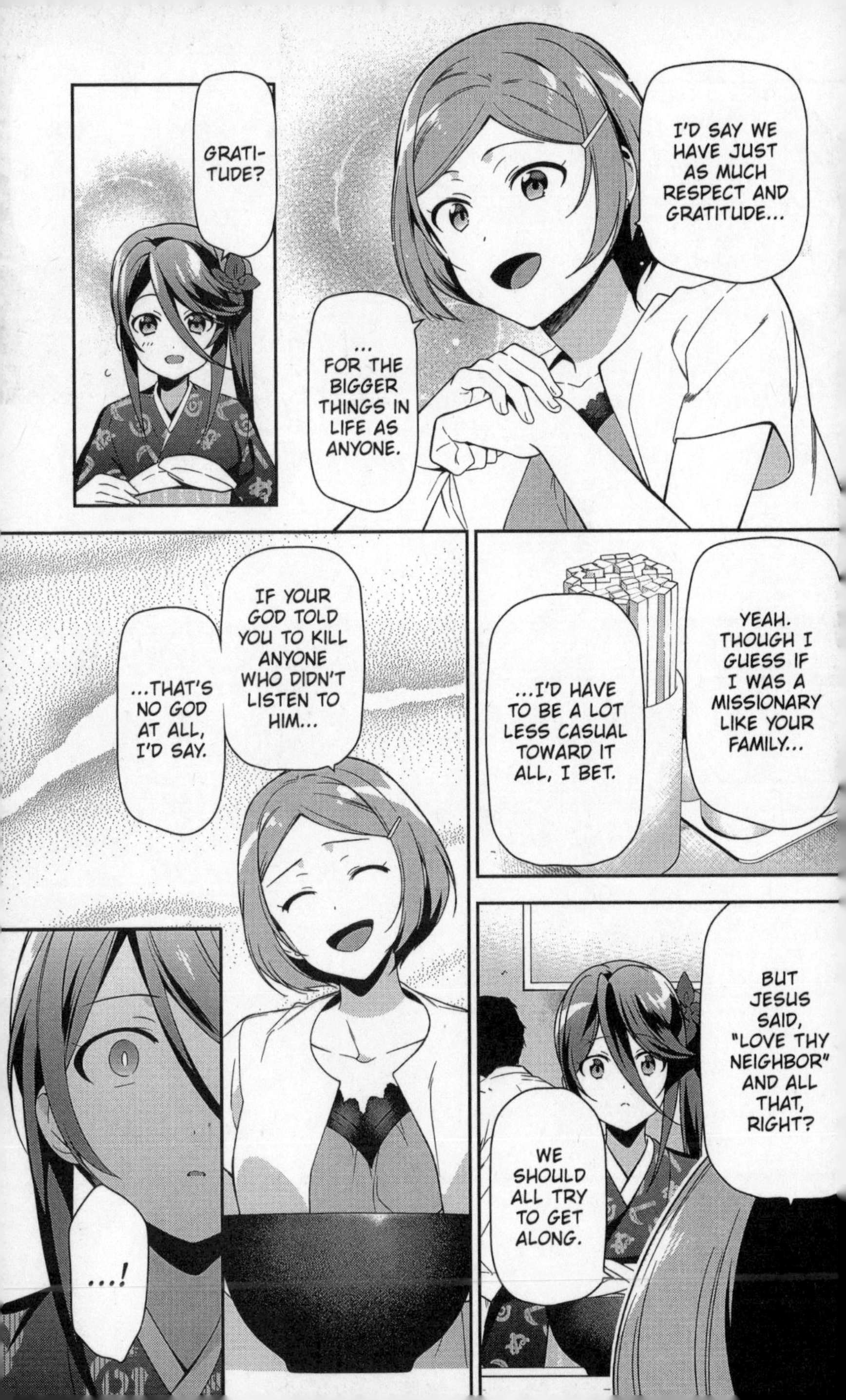
I'D SAY WE HAVE JUST AS MUCH RESPECT AND GRATITUDE...
...FOR THE BIGGER THINGS IN LIFE AS ANYONE.
GRATI-TUDE?
YEAH. THOUGH I GUESS IF I WAS A MISSIONARY LIKE YOUR FAMILY...
...I'D HAVE TO BE A LOT LESS CASUAL TOWARD IT ALL, I BET.
IF YOUR GOD TOLD YOU TO KILL ANYONE WHO DIDN'T LISTEN TO HIM...
...THAT'S NO GOD AT ALL, I'D SAY.
BUT JESUS SAID, "LOVE THY NEIGHBOR" AND ALL THAT, RIGHT?
WE SHOULD ALL TRY TO GET ALONG.
...!

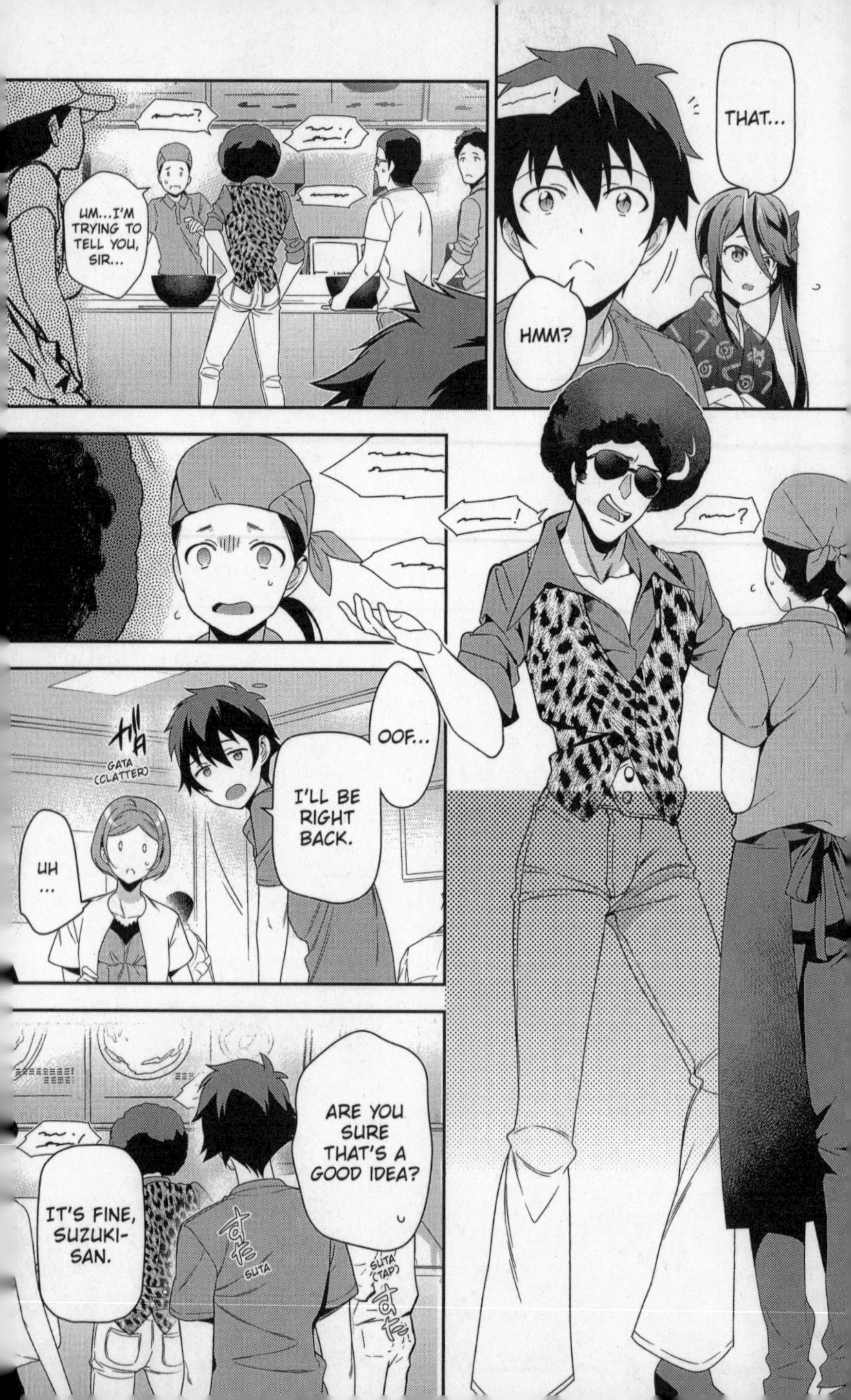
THAT...
HMM?
UM...I'M TRYING TO TELL YOU, SIR...
OOF...
I'LL BE RIGHT BACK.
ガタ
GATA (CLATTER)
UH ...
ARE YOU SURE THAT'S A GOOD IDEA?
すた
SUTA (TAP)
IT'S FINE, SUZUKI-SAN.
すた
SUTA

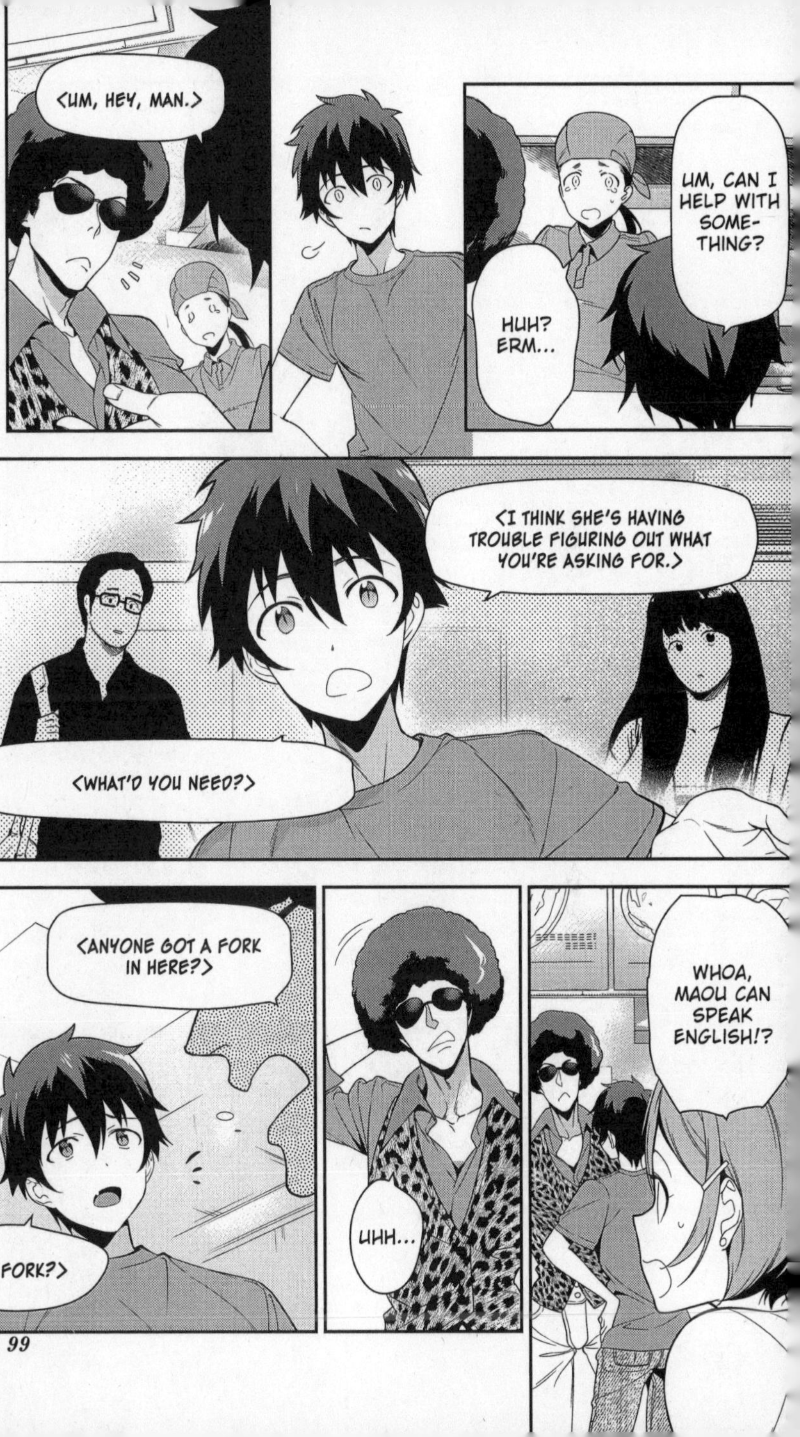
UM, CAN I HELP WITH SOME-THING?
HUH? ERM...
<UM, HEY, MAN.>
<I THINK SHE'S HAVING TROUBLE FIGURING OUT WHAT YOU'RE ASKING FOR.>
<WHAT'D YOU NEED?>
WHOA, MAOU CAN SPEAK ENGLISH!?
UHH...
<ANYONE GOT A FORK IN HERE?>
<A FORK?>

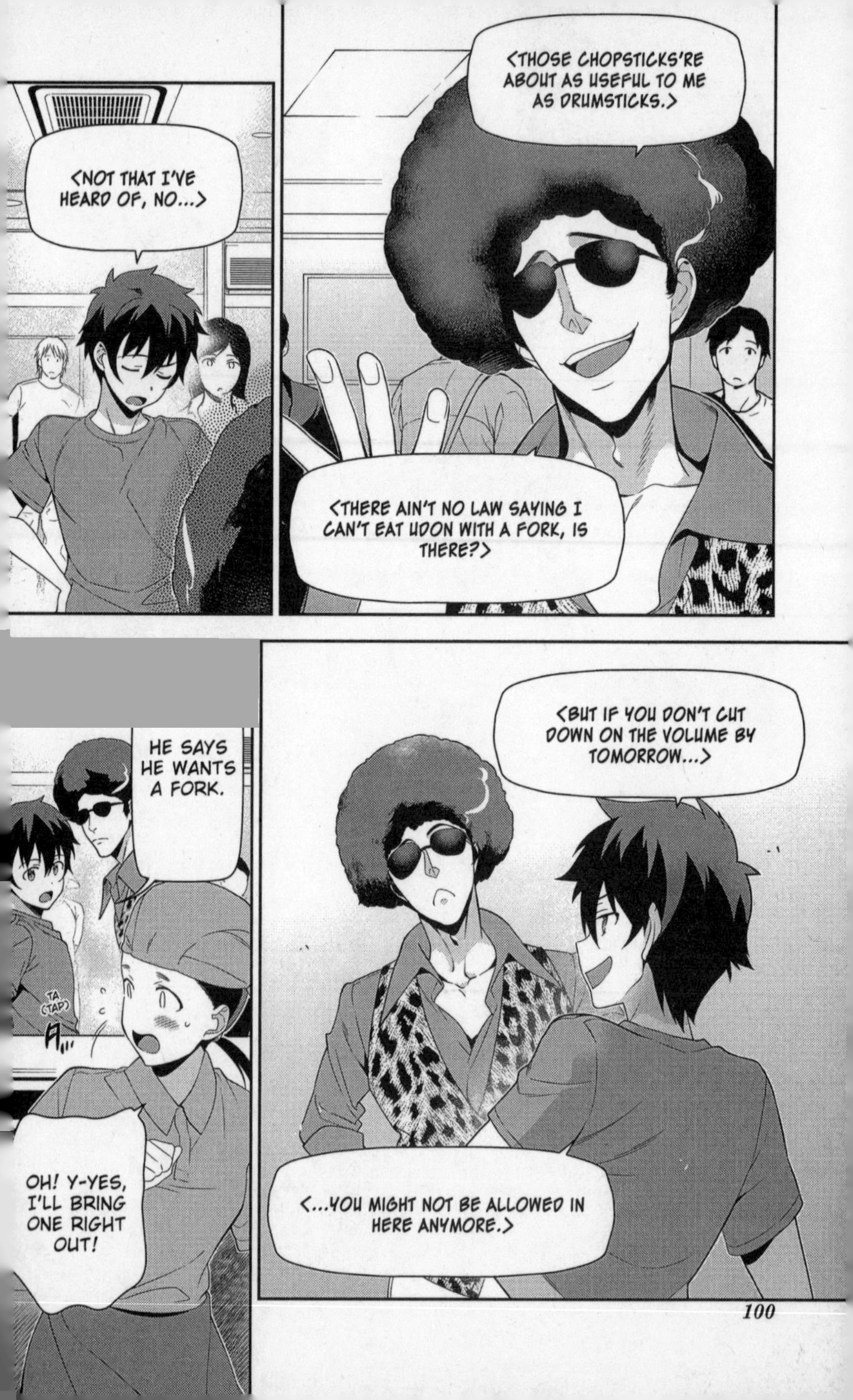
<THOSE CHOPSTICKS'RE ABOUT AS USEFUL TO ME AS DRUMSTICKS.>
<THERE AIN'T NO LAW SAYING I CAN'T EAT UDON WITH A FORK, IS THERE?>
<NOT THAT I'VE HEARD OF, NO...>
<BUT IF YOU DON'T CUT DOWN ON THE VOLUME BY TOMORROW...>
<...YOU MIGHT NOT BE ALLOWED IN HERE ANYMORE.>
HE SAYS HE WANTS A FORK.
TA (TAP)
OH! Y-YES, I'LL BRING ONE RIGHT OUT!

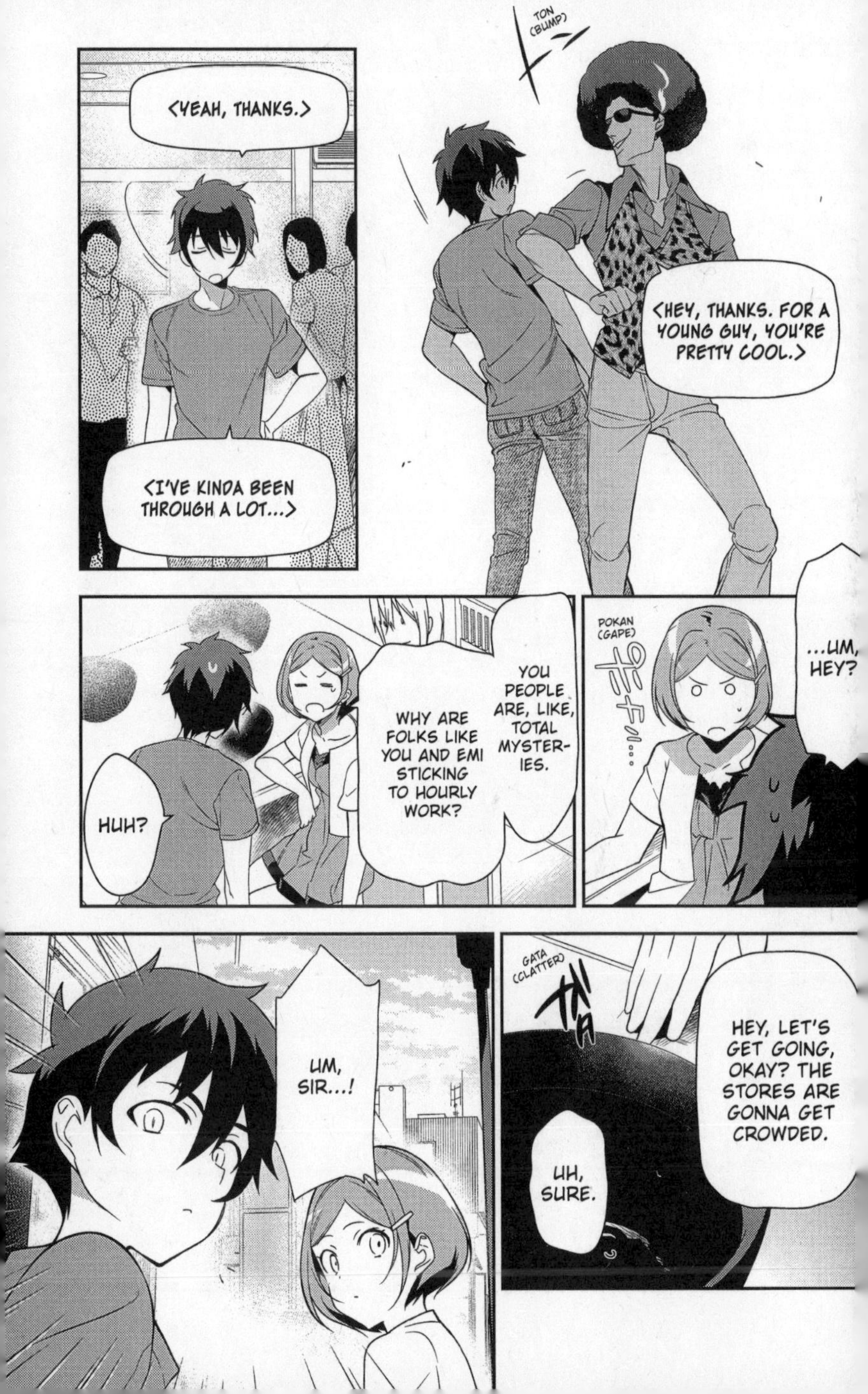
TON (BUMP)
<HEY, THANKS. FOR A YOUNG GUY, YOU'RE PRETTY COOL.>
<YEAH, THANKS.>
<I'VE KINDA BEEN THROUGH A LOT...>
POKAN (GAPE)
...UM, HEY?
YOU PEOPLE ARE, LIKE, TOTAL MYSTERIES.
WHY ARE FOLKS LIKE YOU AND EMI STICKING TO HOURLY WORK?
HUH?
GATA (CLATTER)
HEY, LET'S GET GOING, OKAY? THE STORES ARE GONNA GET CROWDED.
UH, SURE.
UM, SIR...!

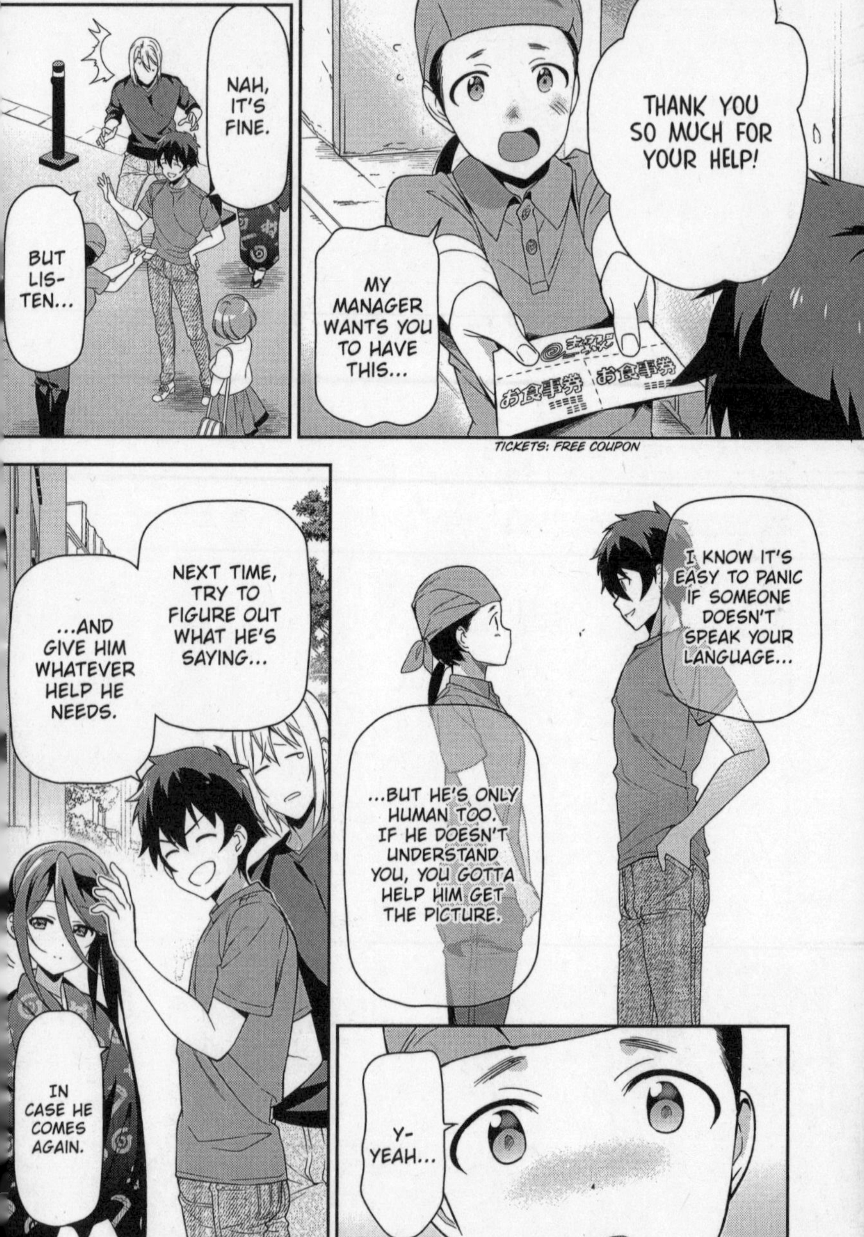
THANK YOU SO MUCH FOR YOUR HELP!
MY MANAGER WANTS YOU TO HAVE THIS...
お食事券
お食事券
NAH, IT'S FINE.
BUT LIS-TEN...
I KNOW IT'S EASY TO PANIC IF SOMEONE DOESN'T SPEAK YOUR LANGUAGE...
...BUT HE'S ONLY HUMAN TOO. IF HE DOESN'T UNDERSTAND YOU, YOU GOTTA HELP HIM GET THE PICTURE.
Y-YEAH...
NEXT TIME, TRY TO FIGURE OUT WHAT HE'S SAYING...
...AND GIVE HIM WHATEVER HELP HE NEEDS.
IN CASE HE COMES AGAIN.

TICKETS: FREE COUPON

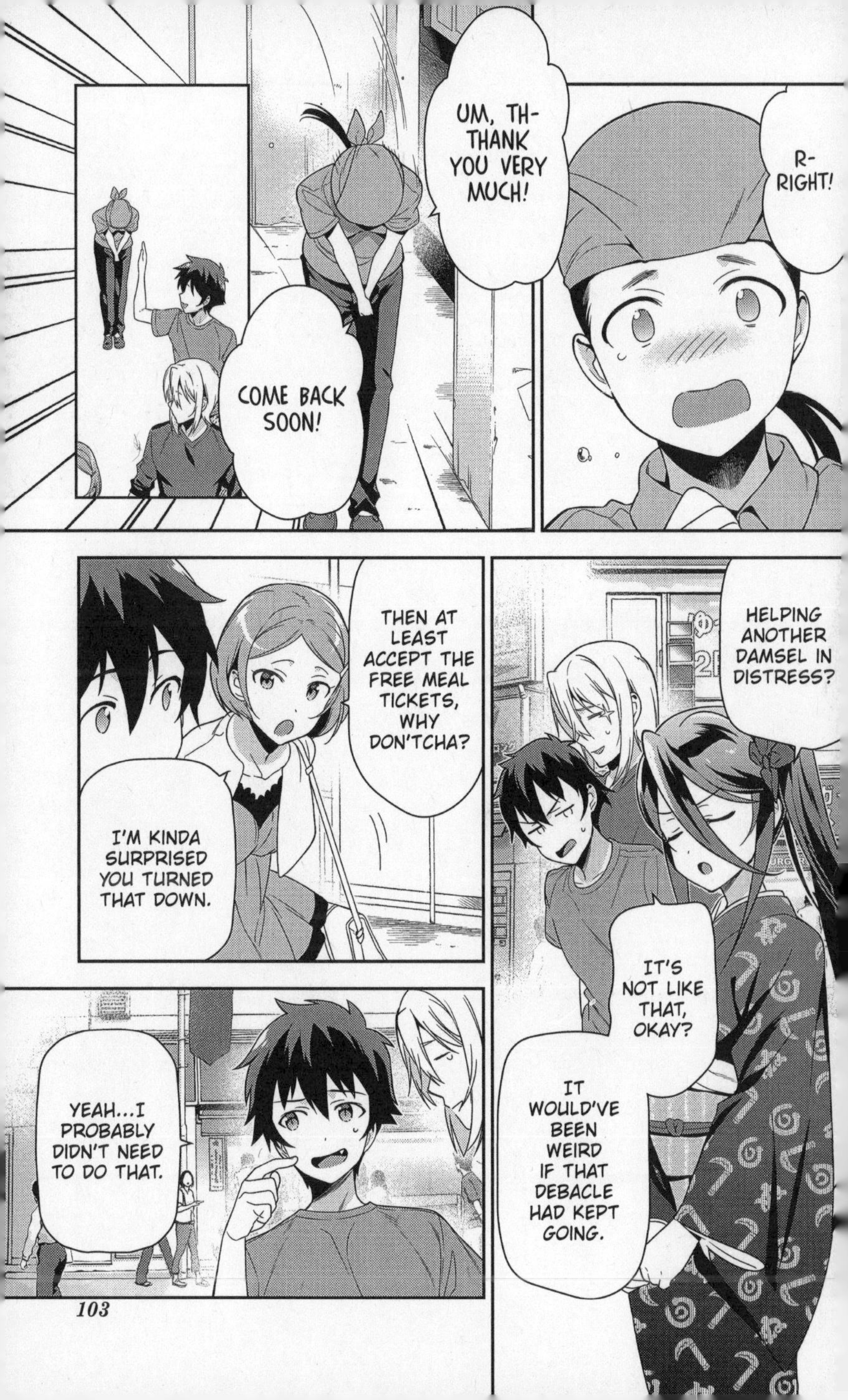
R-RIGHT!
UM, TH-THANK YOU VERY MUCH!
COME BACK SOON!
HELPING ANOTHER DAMSEL IN DISTRESS?
IT'S NOT LIKE THAT, OKAY?
IT WOULD'VE BEEN WEIRD IF THAT DEBACLE HAD KEPT GOING.
THEN AT LEAST ACCEPT THE FREE MEAL TICKETS, WHY DON'TCHA?
I'M KINDA SURPRISED YOU TURNED THAT DOWN.
YEAH...I PROBABLY DIDN'T NEED TO DO THAT.

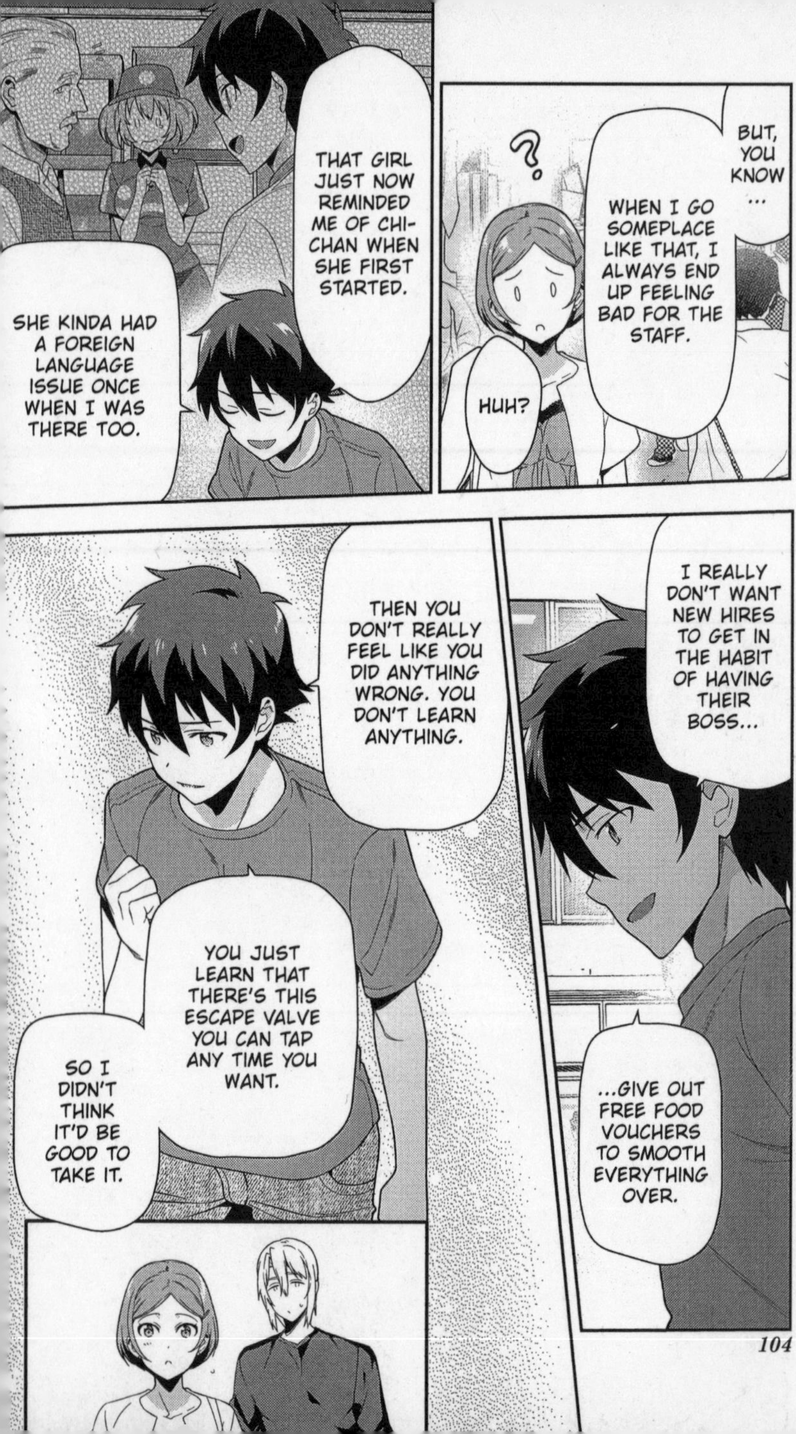
BUT, YOU KNOW ...
WHEN I GO SOMEPLACE LIKE THAT, I ALWAYS END UP FEELING BAD FOR THE STAFF.
HUH?
THAT GIRL JUST NOW REMINDED ME OF CHI-CHAN WHEN SHE FIRST STARTED.
SHE KINDA HAD A FOREIGN LANGUAGE ISSUE ONCE WHEN I WAS THERE TOO.
I REALLY DON'T WANT NEW HIRES TO GET IN THE HABIT OF HAVING THEIR BOSS...
...GIVE OUT FREE FOOD VOUCHERS TO SMOOTH EVERYTHING OVER.
THEN YOU DON'T REALLY FEEL LIKE YOU DID ANYTHING WRONG. YOU DON'T LEARN ANYTHING.
YOU JUST LEARN THAT THERE'S THIS ESCAPE VALVE YOU CAN TAP ANY TIME YOU WANT.
SO I DIDN'T THINK IT'D BE GOOD TO TAKE IT.

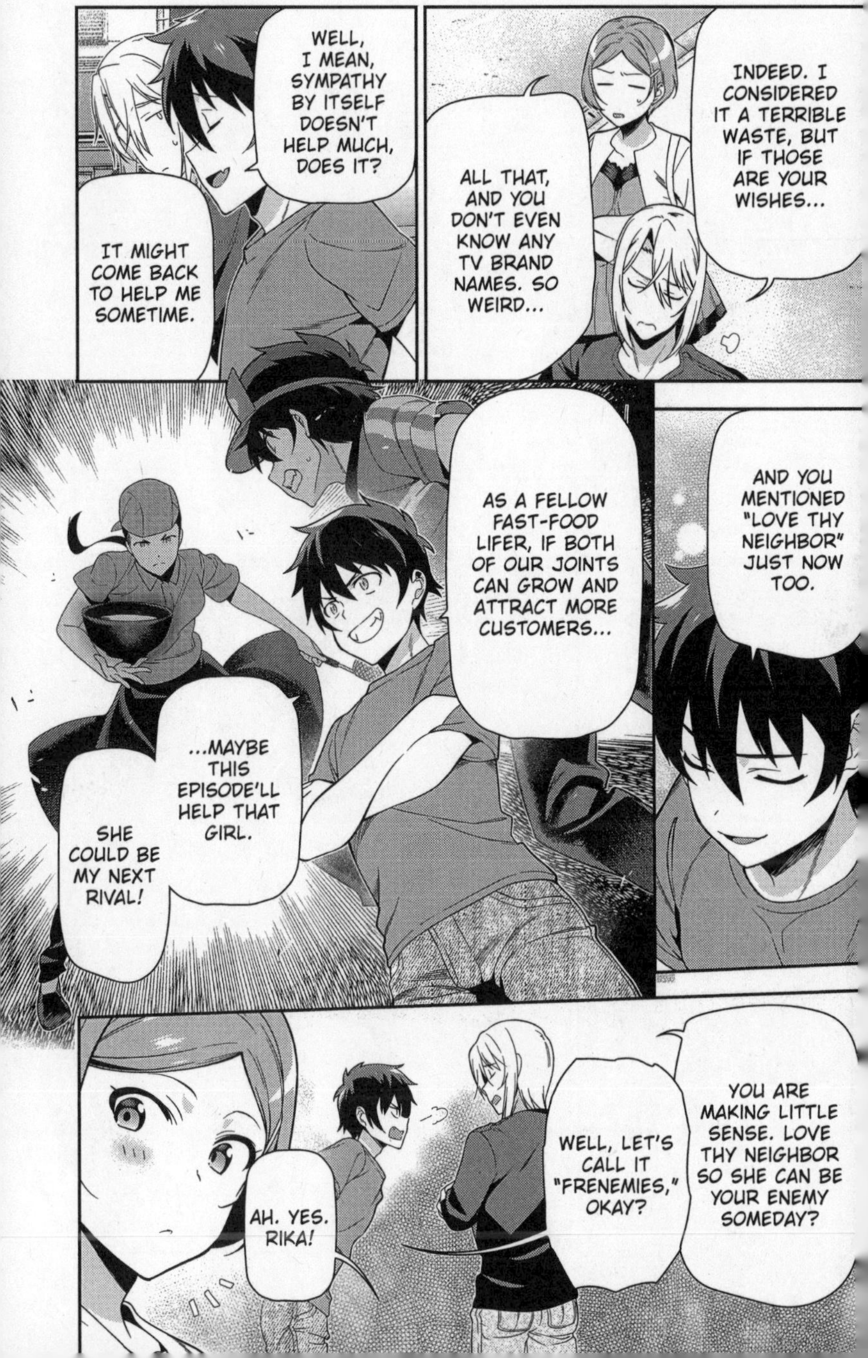
INDEED. I CONSIDERED IT A TERRIBLE WASTE, BUT IF THOSE ARE YOUR WISHES...
ALL THAT, AND YOU DON'T EVEN KNOW ANY TV BRAND NAMES. SO WEIRD...
WELL, I MEAN, SYMPATHY BY ITSELF DOESN'T HELP MUCH, DOES IT?
IT MIGHT COME BACK TO HELP ME SOMETIME.
AND YOU MENTIONED "LOVE THY NEIGHBOR" JUST NOW TOO.
AS A FELLOW FAST-FOOD LIFER, IF BOTH OF OUR JOINTS CAN GROW AND ATTRACT MORE CUSTOMERS...
...MAYBE THIS EPISODE'LL HELP THAT GIRL.
SHE COULD BE MY NEXT RIVAL!
YOU ARE MAKING LITTLE SENSE. LOVE THY NEIGHBOR SO SHE CAN BE YOUR ENEMY SOMEDAY?
WELL, LET'S CALL IT "FRENEMIES," OKAY?
AH. YES. RIKA!

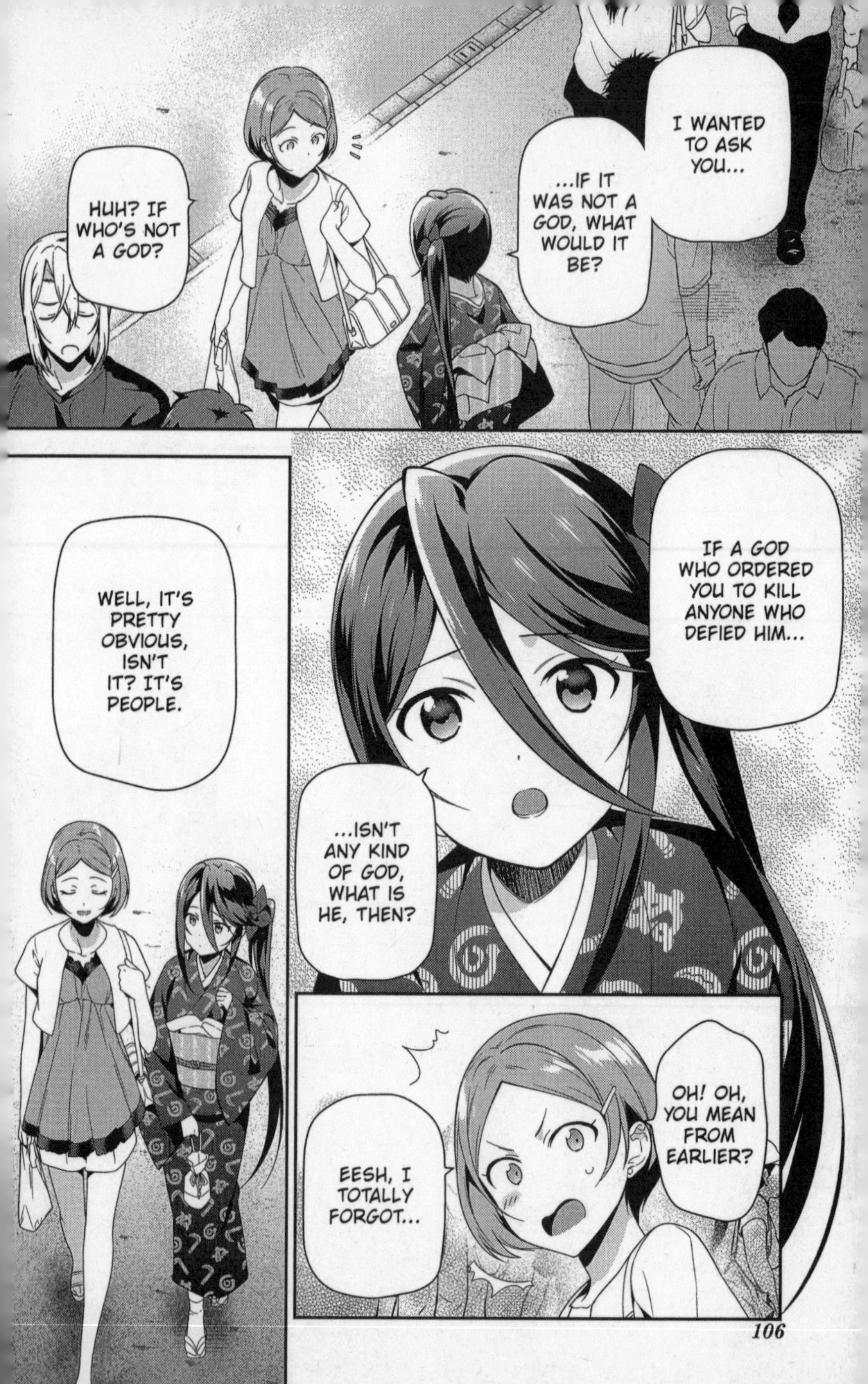
I WANTED TO ASK YOU...
...IF IT WAS NOT A GOD, WHAT WOULD IT BE?
HUH? IF WHO'S NOT A GOD?
IF A GOD WHO ORDERED YOU TO KILL ANYONE WHO DEFIED HIM...
...ISN'T ANY KIND OF GOD, WHAT IS HE, THEN?
OH! OH, YOU MEAN FROM EARLIER?
EESH, I TOTALLY FORGOT...
WELL, IT'S PRETTY OBVIOUS, ISN'T IT? IT'S PEOPLE.

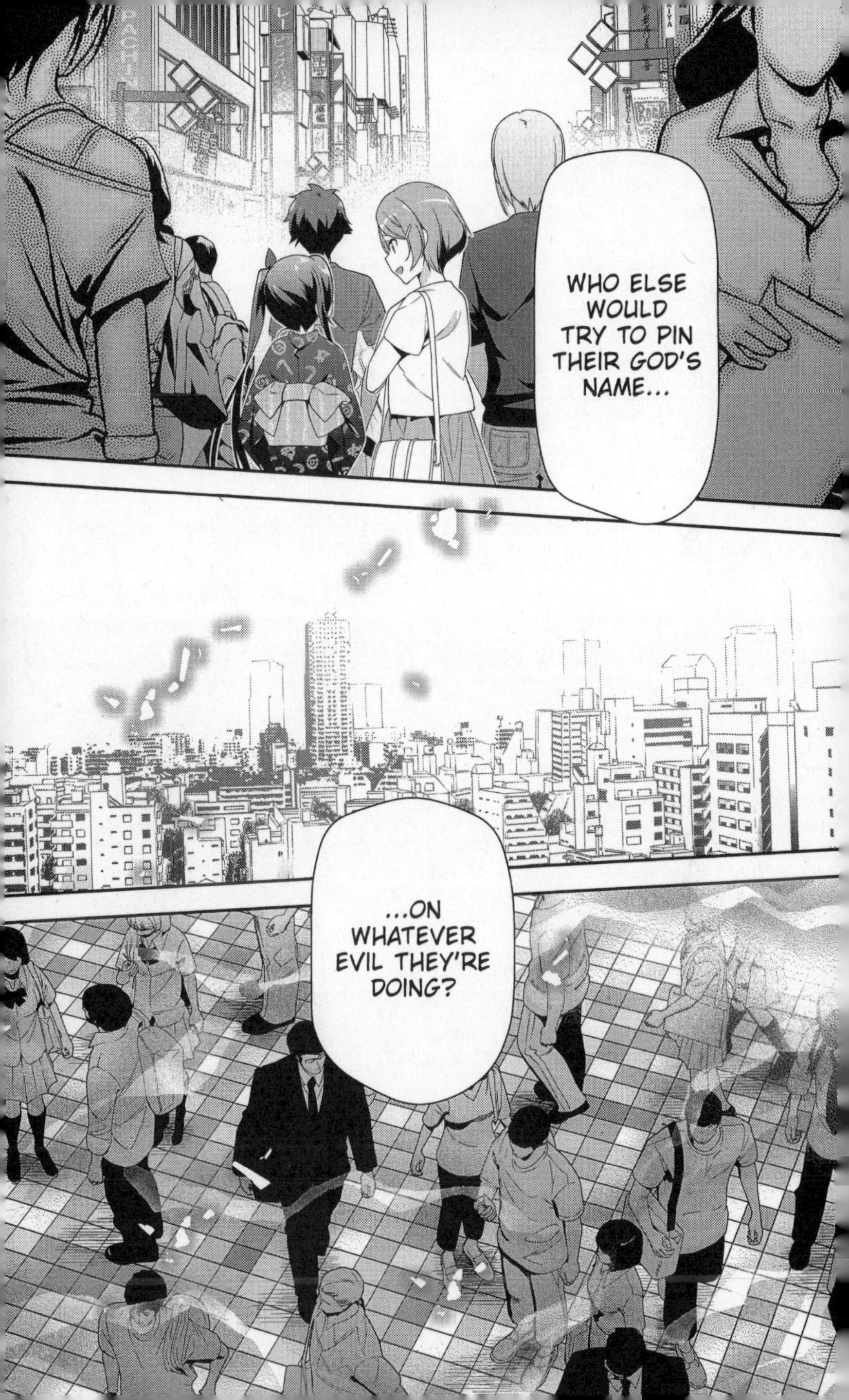
WHO ELSE WOULD TRY TO PIN THEIR GOD'S NAME...
...ON WHATEVER EVIL THEY'RE DOING?

THE DEVIL IS A PART-TIMER! THAT HIIRAGI-SAN DRAWS IS A TREASURE TROVE OF NEW AND ENTICING DISCOVERIES.
THIS COMIC VERSION TAKES THE ASSORTED SCENES THAT GET OVERLOOKED IN THE NOVELS, LOST IN THE GREATER FLOW OF THE STORY, AND MAKES THEM AS CLEAR AS BLACK AND WHITE. A NOVEL PUTS THE SPOTLIGHT ON A SINGLE PERSON AT A TIME AS THEY SPEAK, BUT WITH MANGA, YOU CAN SEE EVERYONE THEY'RE TALKING TO AT THE SAME TIME. YOU CAN SEE THAT, AS THEY'RE ALL WALKING DOWN THE STREET AND TALKING, THEY'RE MAKING THIS KIND OF FACE, THAT KIND OF REACTION.
I REALLY FEEL LIKE A LUCKY MAN SEEING THESE EVERYDAY SCENES HAVE NEW, VIVID LIFE BREATHED INTO THEM BY HIIRAGI-SAN'S ART. AND THAT GOOD FORTUNE HAS NOW TAKEN US ALL THE WAY TO VOLUME 10! CAN YOU BELIEVE IT? THE TENTH VOLUME! THAT'S SIMPLY INCREDIBLE! AND GOING FORWARD, I, WAGAHARA, WILL JOIN ALL OF THE MANGA READERS AS WE MAKE NEW *DEVIL* DISCOVERIES FOR WHAT WILL HOPEFULLY BE A LONG TIME TO COME.
HERE'S TO THE FUTURE—BOTH WITH HIIRAGI-SAN AND WITH ALL OF OUR READERS.

SATOSHI WAGAHARA

THE COMIC VERSION OF *DEVIL* HAS FINALLY HIT THE DOUBLE DIGITS! SEEING THE SERIES CONTINUE FOR THIS LONG FILLS ME BOTH WITH GREAT JOY AND GREAT SURPRISE. IT'S ALL THANKS TO WAGAHARA-SENSEI, ONIKU-SENSEI, EVERYONE ELSE INVOLVED WITH THIS PROJECT, AND ALL THE READERS AS WELL.
THIS VOLUME BRINGS US INTO THE EVENTS OF NOVEL VOLUME 5, AS WELL AS THE FUTON-BUYING SHORT STORY THAT I'VE BEEN DYING TO DRAW. IT'D BE GREAT IF I COULD RENDER SOME OF THE OTHER SIDE STORIES IN MANGA FORMAT...A SECRET LUST OF MINE, IF YOU WILL, HEH.

IF I'M GOING TO MAKE THAT HAPPEN, I'LL NEED MORE SUPPORT THAN EVER FROM ALL OF YOU. HERE'S HOPING!

SPECIAL THANKS!
SHIBA - TAKASHI YAMANO - AND YOU!

AKIO HIIRAGI

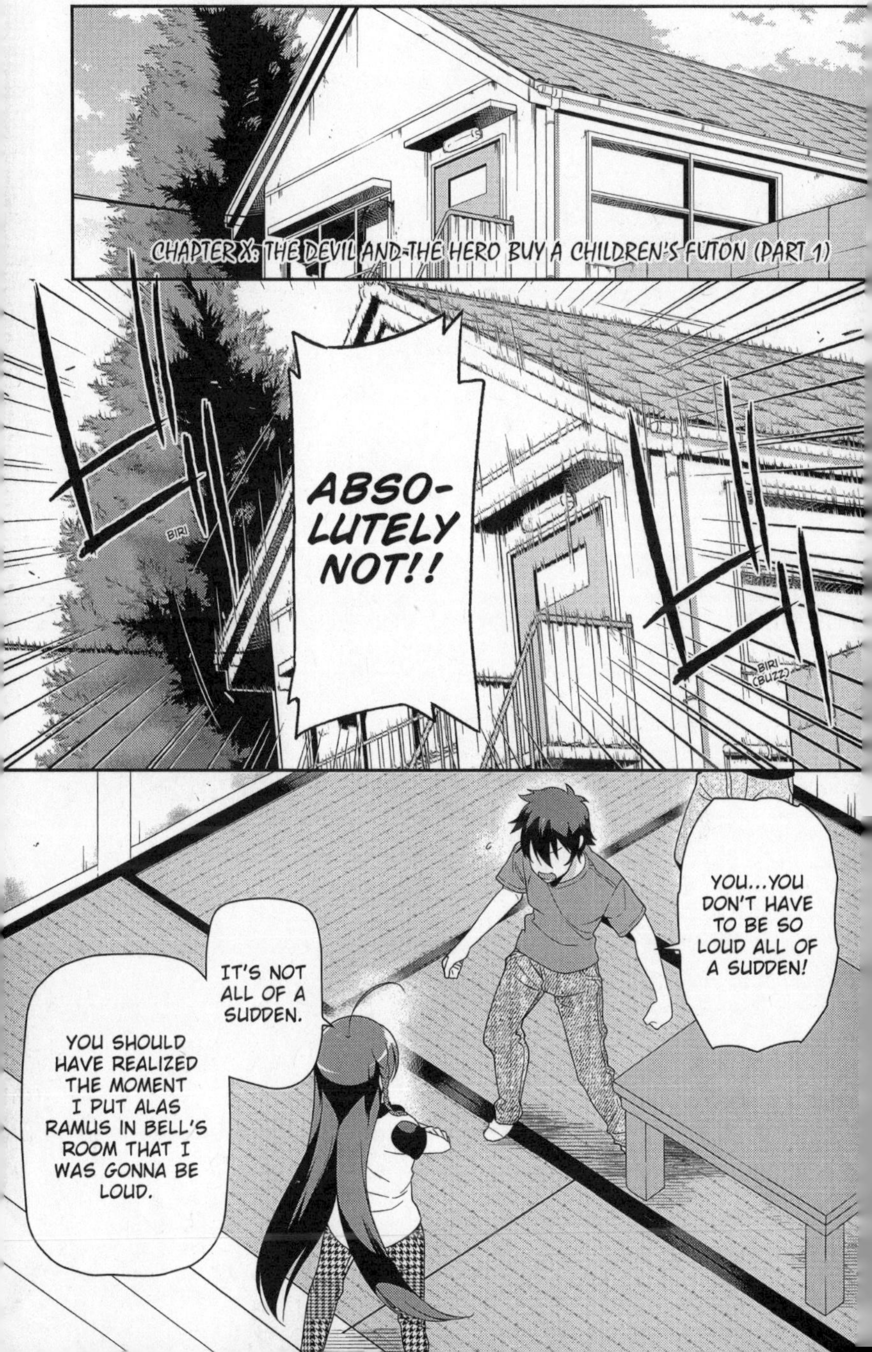
CHAPTER X: THE DEVIL AND THE HERO BUY A CHILDREN'S FUTON (PART 1)
BIRI (BUZZ)
ABSO-LUTELY NOT!!
BIRI
YOU...YOU DON'T HAVE TO BE SO LOUD ALL OF A SUDDEN!
IT'S NOT ALL OF A SUDDEN.
YOU SHOULD HAVE REALIZED THE MOMENT I PUT ALAS RAMUS IN BELL'S ROOM THAT I WAS GONNA BE LOUD.

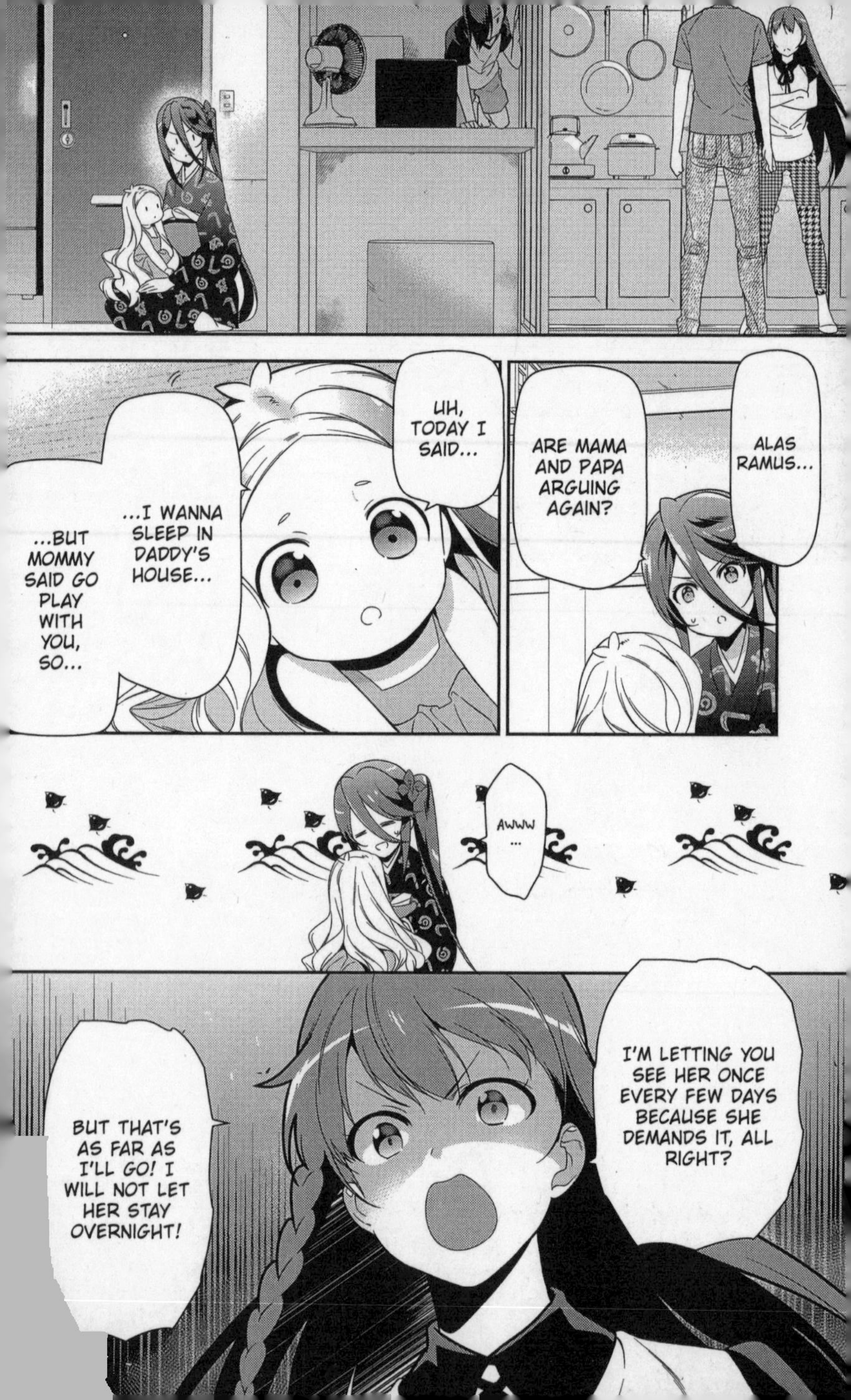
ALAS RAMUS...
ARE MAMA AND PAPA ARGUING AGAIN?
UH, TODAY I SAID...
...I WANNA SLEEP IN DADDY'S HOUSE...
...BUT MOMMY SAID GO PLAY WITH YOU, SO...
AWWW ...
I'M LETTING YOU SEE HER ONCE EVERY FEW DAYS BECAUSE SHE DEMANDS IT, ALL RIGHT?
BUT THAT'S AS FAR AS I'LL GO! I WILL NOT LET HER STAY OVERNIGHT!

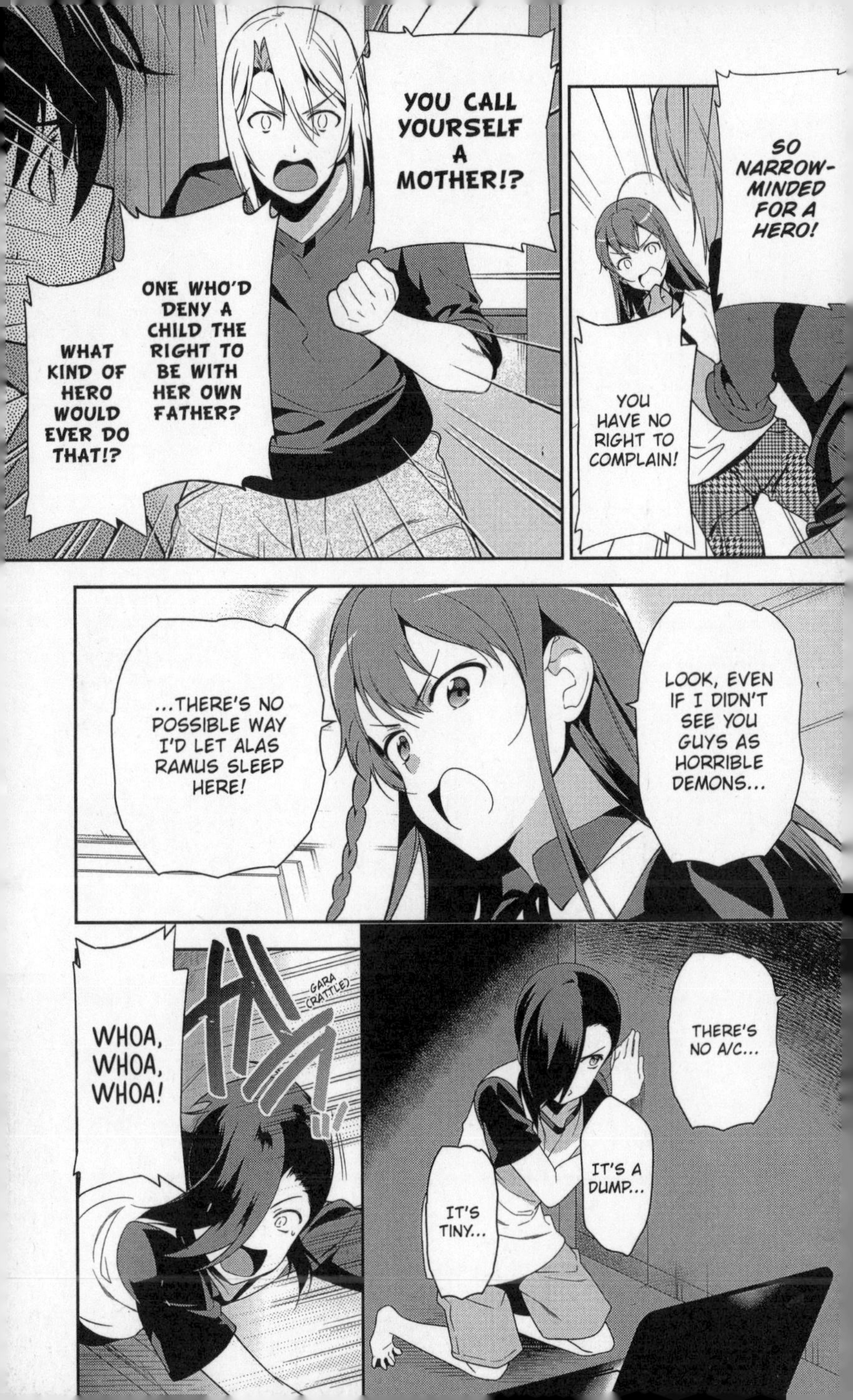
SO NARROW-MINDED FOR A HERO!
YOU HAVE NO RIGHT TO COMPLAIN!
YOU CALL YOURSELF A MOTHER!?
ONE WHO'D DENY A CHILD THE RIGHT TO BE WITH HER OWN FATHER?
WHAT KIND OF HERO WOULD EVER DO THAT!?
LOOK, EVEN IF I DIDN'T SEE YOU GUYS AS HORRIBLE DEMONS...
...THERE'S NO POSSIBLE WAY I'D LET ALAS RAMUS SLEEP HERE!
THERE'S NO A/C...
IT'S A DUMP...
IT'S TINY...
GARA (RATTLE)
WHOA, WHOA, WHOA!

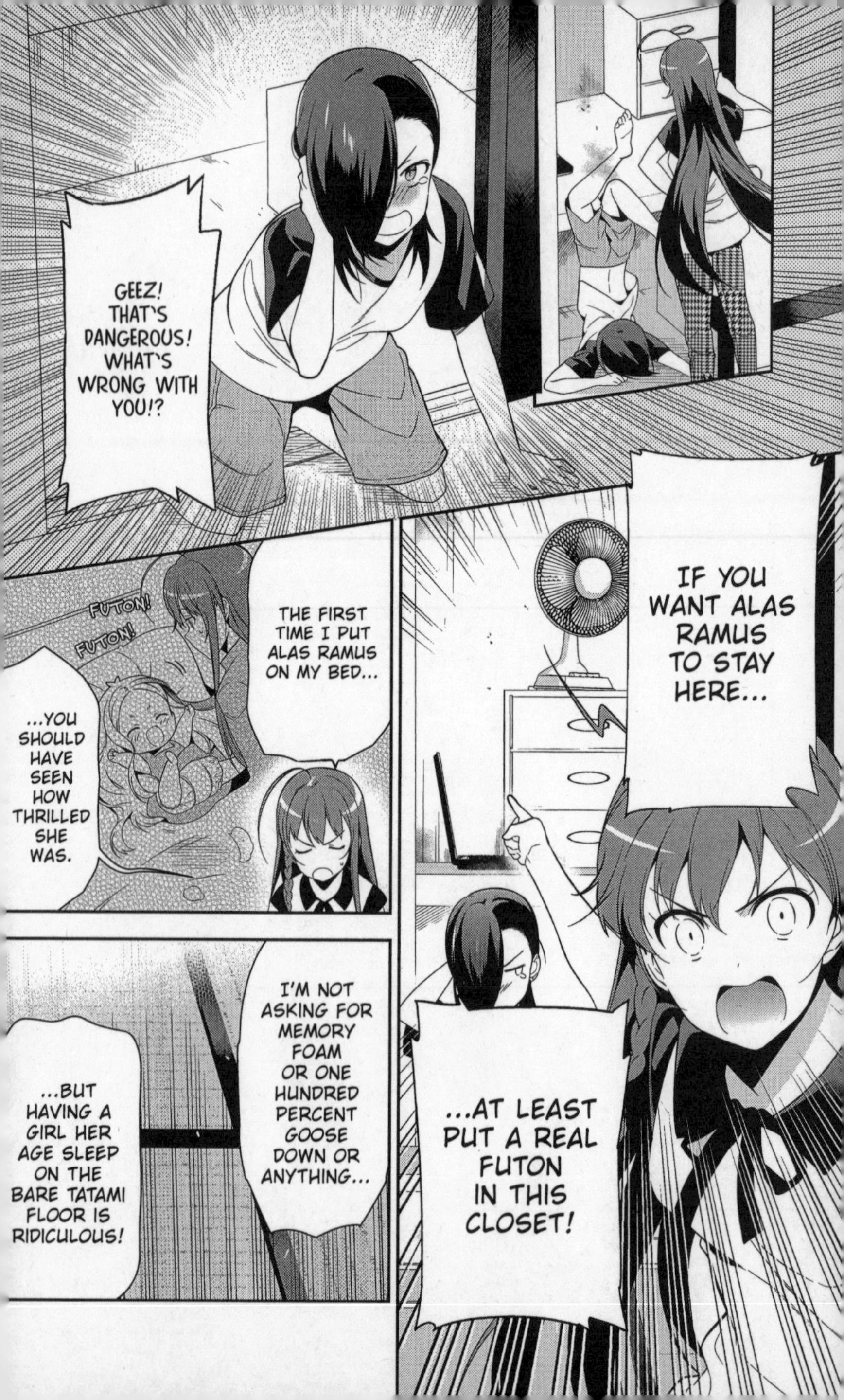
GEEZ! THAT'S DANGEROUS! WHAT'S WRONG WITH YOU!?
IF YOU WANT ALAS RAMUS TO STAY HERE...
...AT LEAST PUT A REAL FUTON IN THIS CLOSET!
THE FIRST TIME I PUT ALAS RAMUS ON MY BED...
FUTON!
FUTON!
...YOU SHOULD HAVE SEEN HOW THRILLED SHE WAS.
I'M NOT ASKING FOR MEMORY FOAM OR ONE HUNDRED PERCENT GOOSE DOWN OR ANYTHING...
...BUT HAVING A GIRL HER AGE SLEEP ON THE BARE TATAMI FLOOR IS RIDICULOUS!

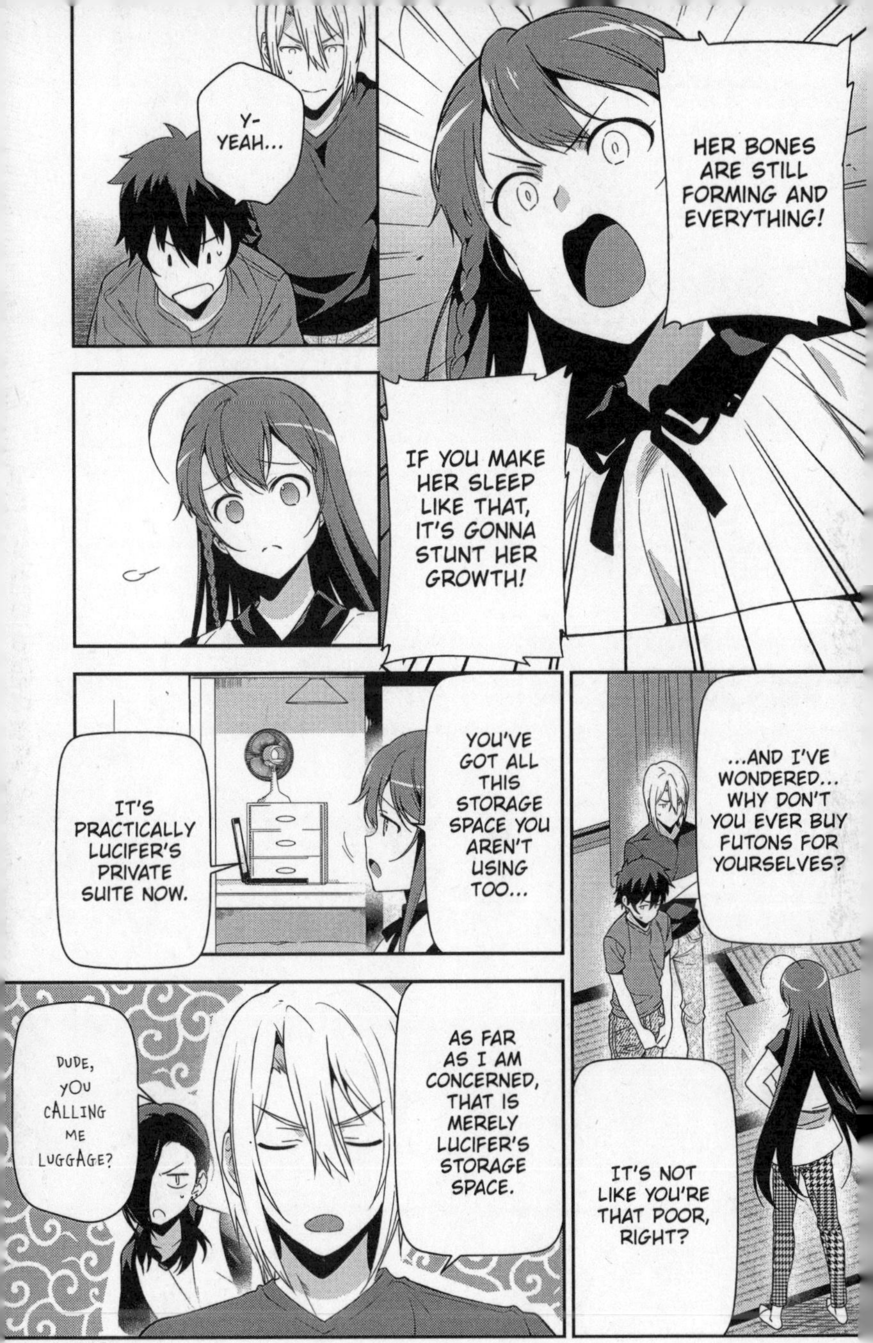
HER BONES ARE STILL FORMING AND EVERYTHING!
IF YOU MAKE HER SLEEP LIKE THAT, IT'S GONNA STUNT HER GROWTH!
Y-YEAH...
...AND I'VE WONDERED... WHY DON'T YOU EVER BUY FUTONS FOR YOURSELVES?
IT'S NOT LIKE YOU'RE THAT POOR, RIGHT?
YOU'VE GOT ALL THIS STORAGE SPACE YOU AREN'T USING TOO...
IT'S PRACTICALLY LUCIFER'S PRIVATE SUITE NOW.
AS FAR AS I AM CONCERNED, THAT IS MERELY LUCIFER'S STORAGE SPACE.
DUDE, YOU CALLING ME LUGGAGE?

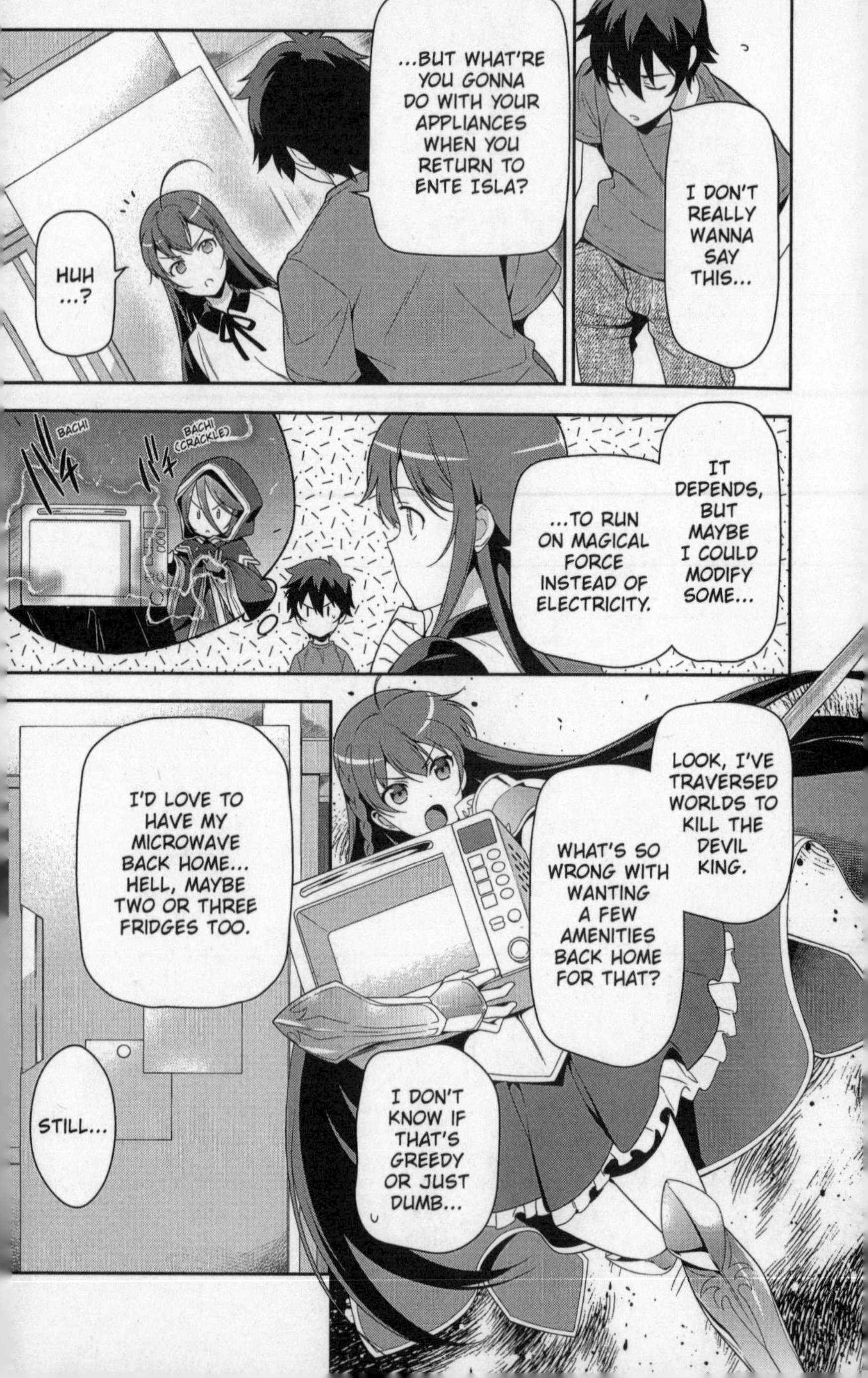
I DON'T REALLY WANNA SAY THIS...
...BUT WHAT'RE YOU GONNA DO WITH YOUR APPLIANCES WHEN YOU RETURN TO ENTE ISLA?
HUH ...?
IT DEPENDS, BUT MAYBE I COULD MODIFY SOME...
...TO RUN ON MAGICAL FORCE INSTEAD OF ELECTRICITY.
BACHI
BACHI (CRACKLE)
LOOK, I'VE TRAVERSED WORLDS TO KILL THE DEVIL KING.
WHAT'S SO WRONG WITH WANTING A FEW AMENITIES BACK HOME FOR THAT?
I'D LOVE TO HAVE MY MICROWAVE BACK HOME... HELL, MAYBE TWO OR THREE FRIDGES TOO.
STILL...
I DON'T KNOW IF THAT'S GREEDY OR JUST DUMB...

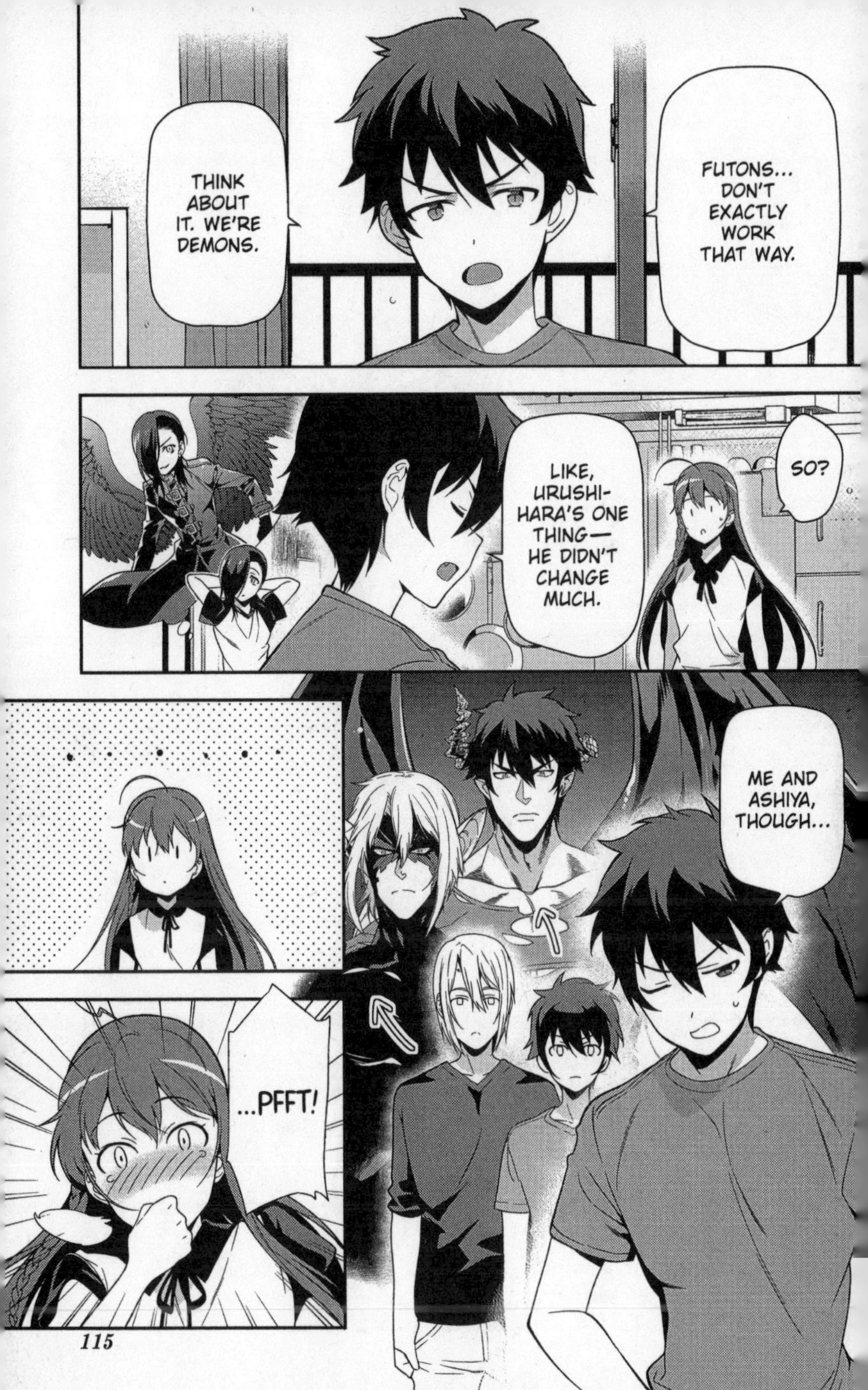
FUTONS... DON'T EXACTLY WORK THAT WAY.
THINK ABOUT IT. WE'RE DEMONS.
SO?
LIKE, URUSHI-HARA'S ONE THING— HE DIDN'T CHANGE MUCH.
ME AND ASHIYA, THOUGH...
. . . . . .
...PFFT!

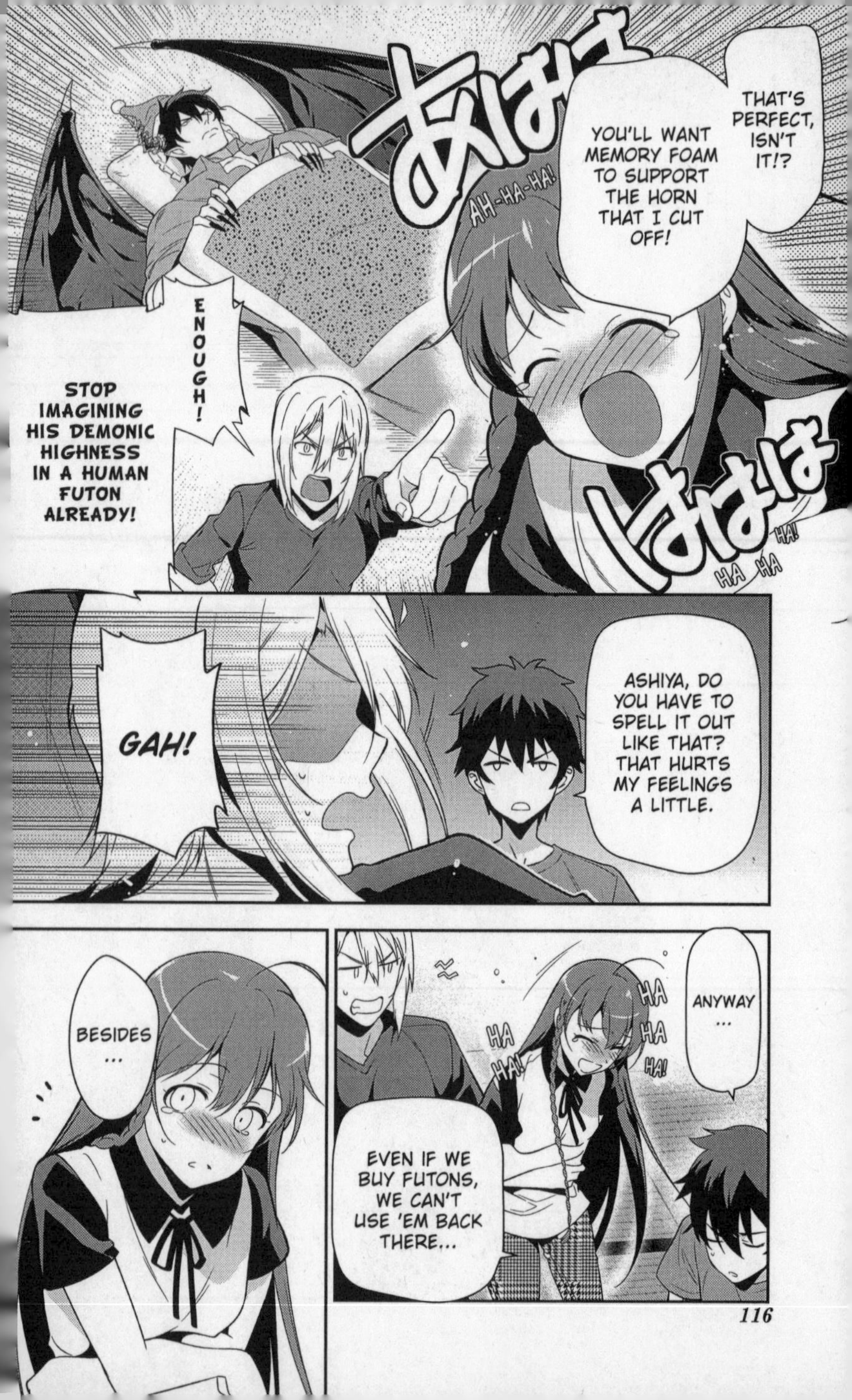

THAT'S PERFECT, ISN'T IT!?
YOU'LL WANT MEMORY FOAM TO SUPPORT THE HORN THAT I CUT OFF!
AH-HA-HA!
ENOUGH!
STOP IMAGINING HIS DEMONIC HIGHNESS IN A HUMAN FUTON ALREADY!
HA HA HA!
ASHIYA, DO YOU HAVE TO SPELL IT OUT LIKE THAT? THAT HURTS MY FEELINGS A LITTLE.
GAH!
ANYWAY...
HA HA HA!
HA HA!
EVEN IF WE BUY FUTONS, WE CAN'T USE 'EM BACK THERE...
BESIDES...

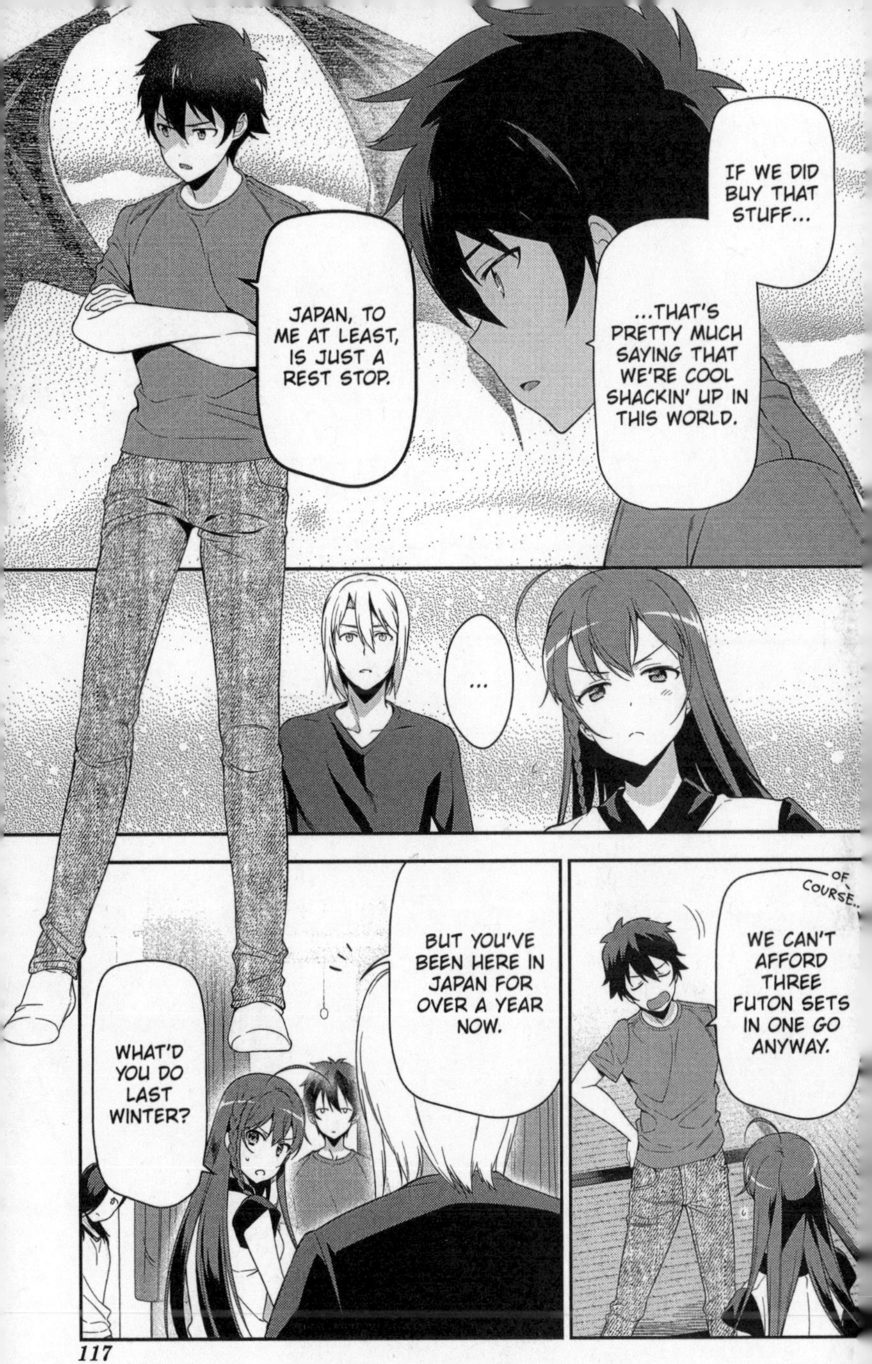
IF WE DID BUY THAT STUFF...
...THAT'S PRETTY MUCH SAYING THAT WE'RE COOL SHACKIN' UP IN THIS WORLD.
JAPAN, TO ME AT LEAST, IS JUST A REST STOP.
...
OF COURSE..
WE CAN'T AFFORD THREE FUTON SETS IN ONE GO ANYWAY.
BUT YOU'VE BEEN HERE IN JAPAN FOR OVER A YEAR NOW.
WHAT'D YOU DO LAST WINTER?

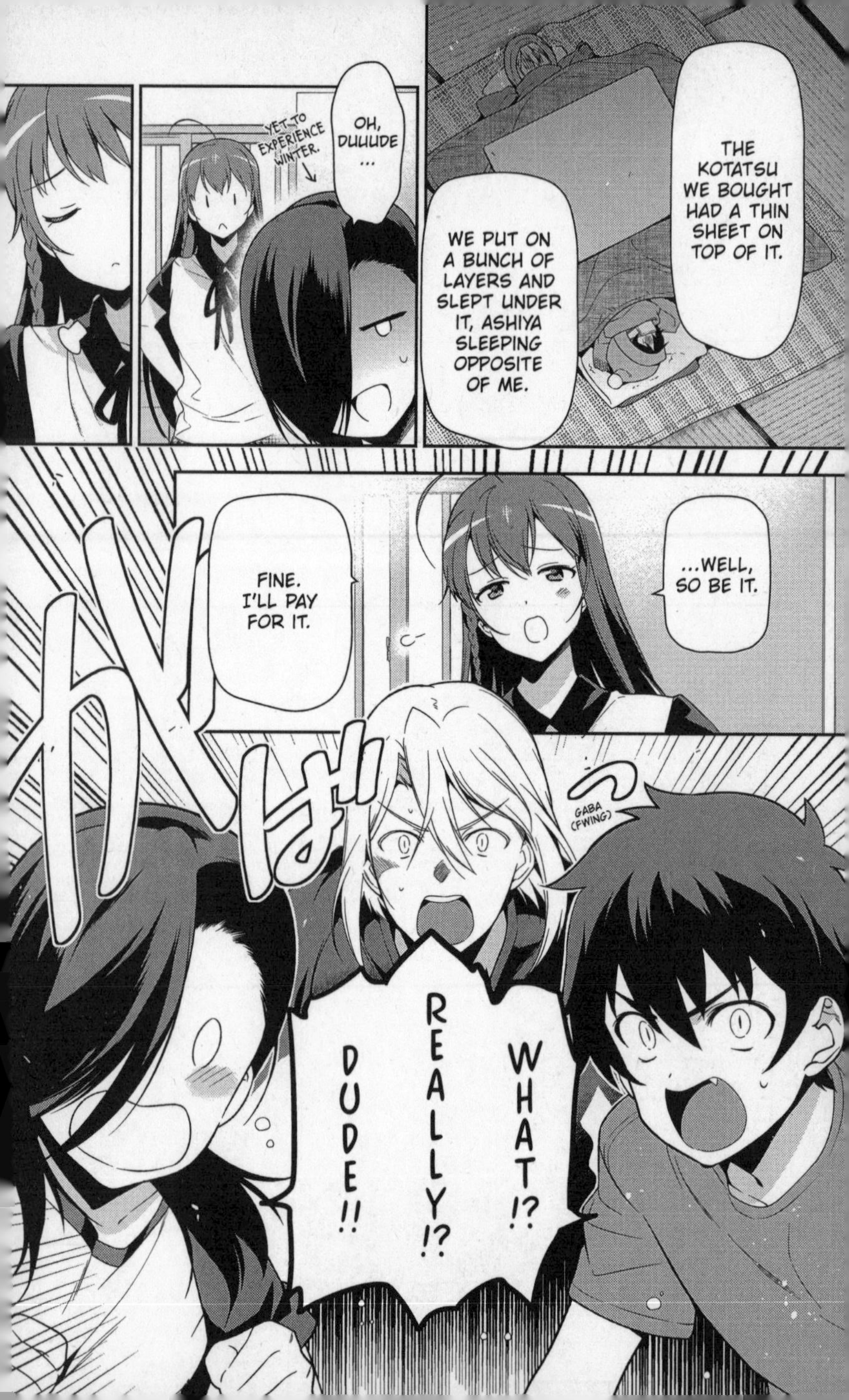
THE KOTATSU WE BOUGHT HAD A THIN SHEET ON TOP OF IT.
WE PUT ON A BUNCH OF LAYERS AND SLEPT UNDER IT, ASHIYA SLEEPING OPPOSITE OF ME.
OH, DUUUDE ...
YET TO EXPERIENCE WINTER.
...WELL, SO BE IT.
FINE. I'LL PAY FOR IT.
GABA (FWING)
がばっ
WHAT!? REALLY!? DUDE!!

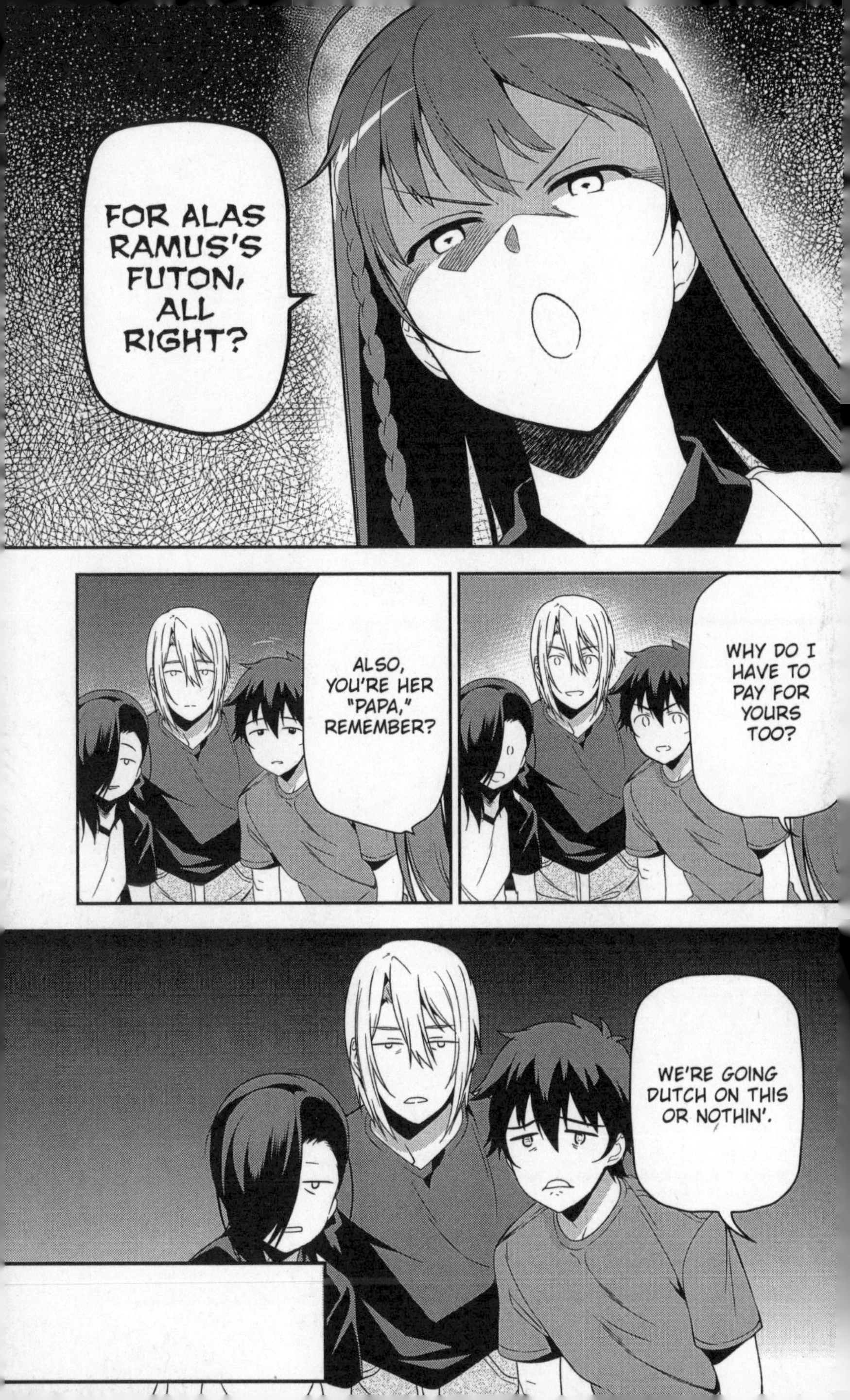
FOR ALAS RAMUS'S FUTON, ALL RIGHT?
WHY DO I HAVE TO PAY FOR YOURS TOO?
ALSO, YOU'RE HER "PAPA," REMEMBER?
WE'RE GOING DUTCH ON THIS OR NOTHIN'.

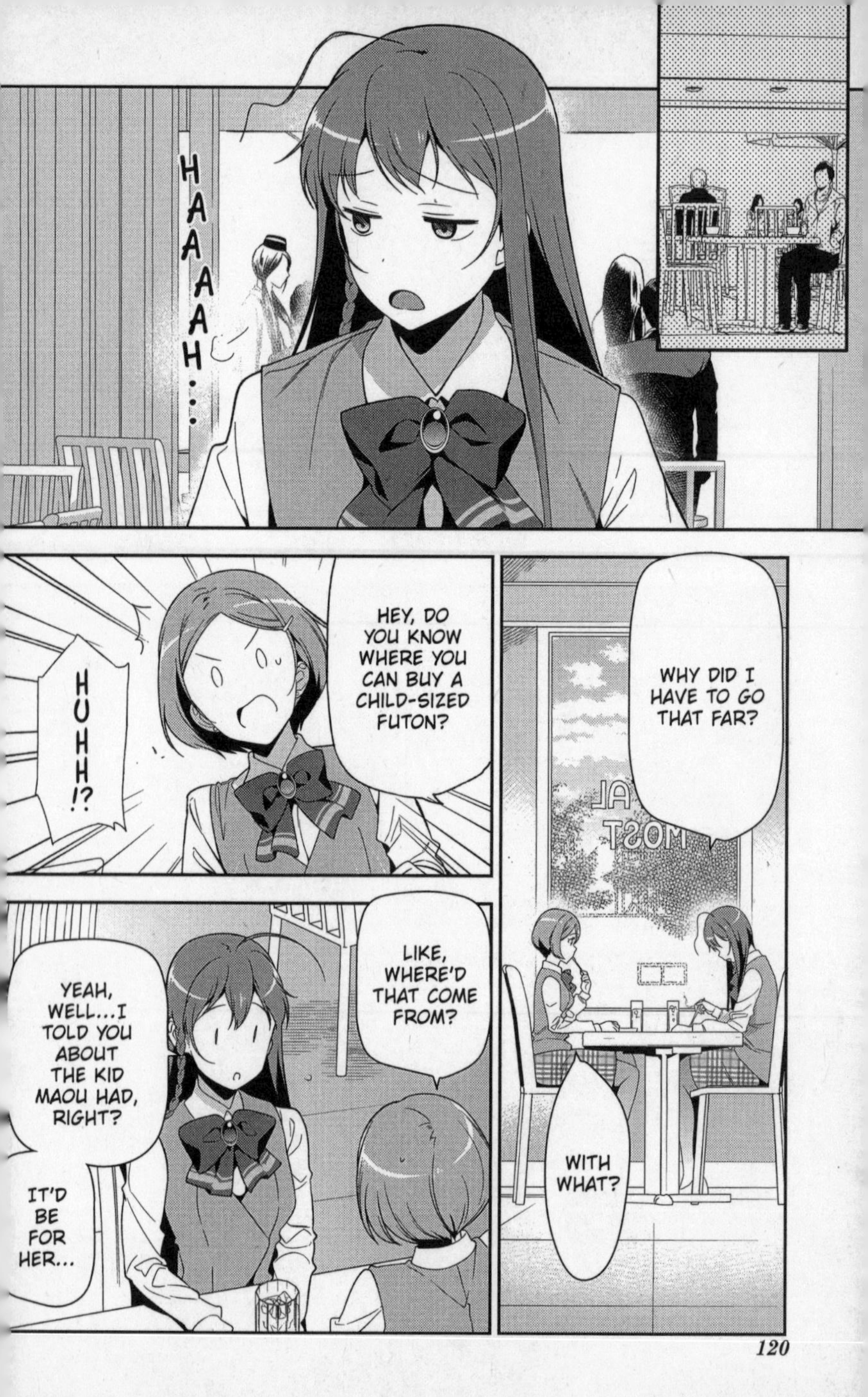
HAAAAAH...
WHY DID I HAVE TO GO THAT FAR?
WITH WHAT?
HEY, DO YOU KNOW WHERE YOU CAN BUY A CHILD-SIZED FUTON?
HUHH!?
LIKE, WHERE'D THAT COME FROM?
YEAH, WELL...I TOLD YOU ABOUT THE KID MAOU HAD, RIGHT?
IT'D BE FOR HER...

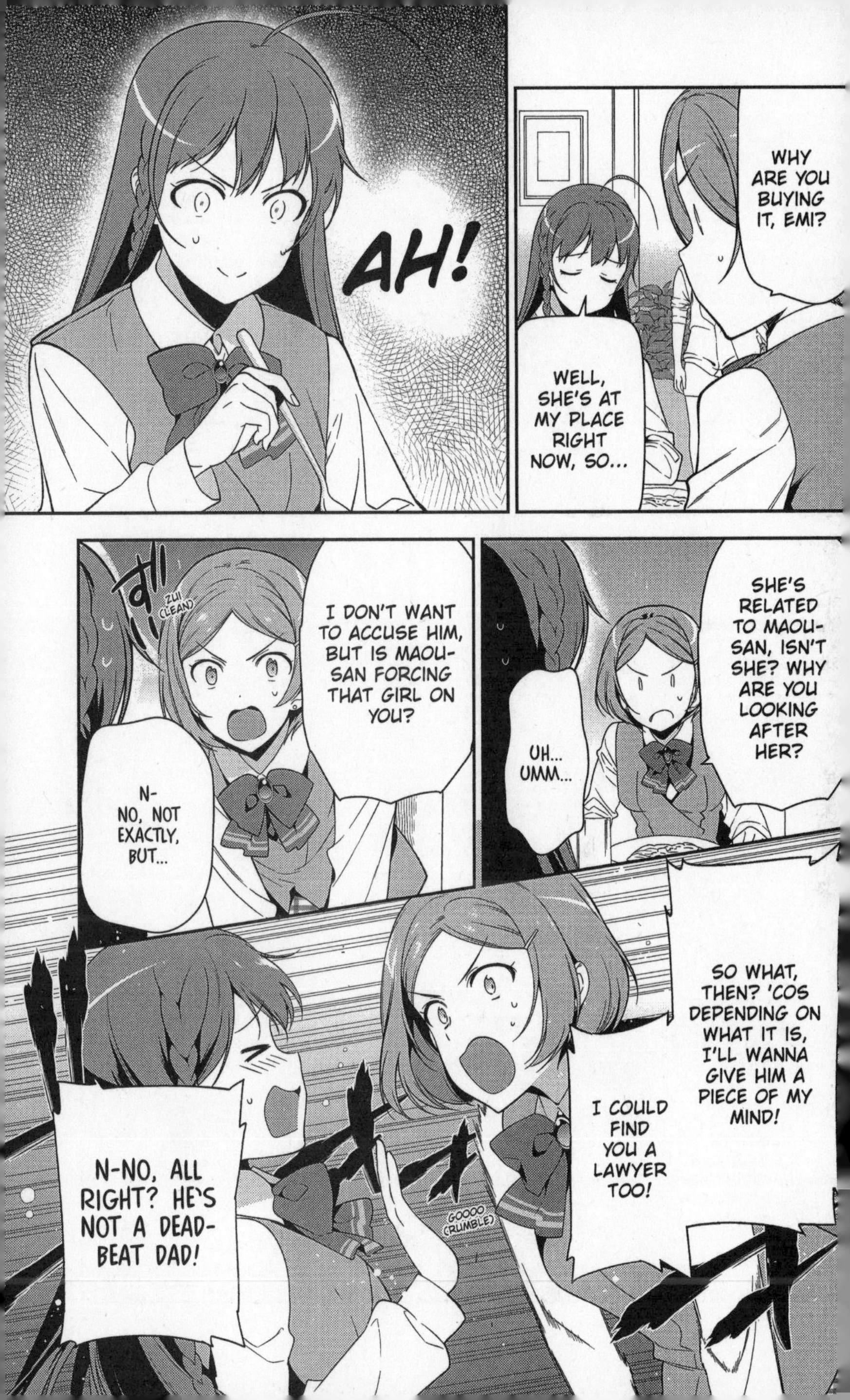
WHY ARE YOU BUYING IT, EMI?
WELL, SHE'S AT MY PLACE RIGHT NOW, SO...
AH!
SHE'S RELATED TO MAOU-SAN, ISN'T SHE? WHY ARE YOU LOOKING AFTER HER?
UH... UMM...
ずい
ZUI (LEAN)
I DON'T WANT TO ACCUSE HIM, BUT IS MAOU-SAN FORCING THAT GIRL ON YOU?
N-NO, NOT EXACTLY, BUT...
SO WHAT, THEN? 'COS DEPENDING ON WHAT IT IS, I'LL WANNA GIVE HIM A PIECE OF MY MIND!
I COULD FIND YOU A LAWYER TOO!
GOOOO (RUMBLE)
N-NO, ALL RIGHT? HE'S NOT A DEAD-BEAT DAD!

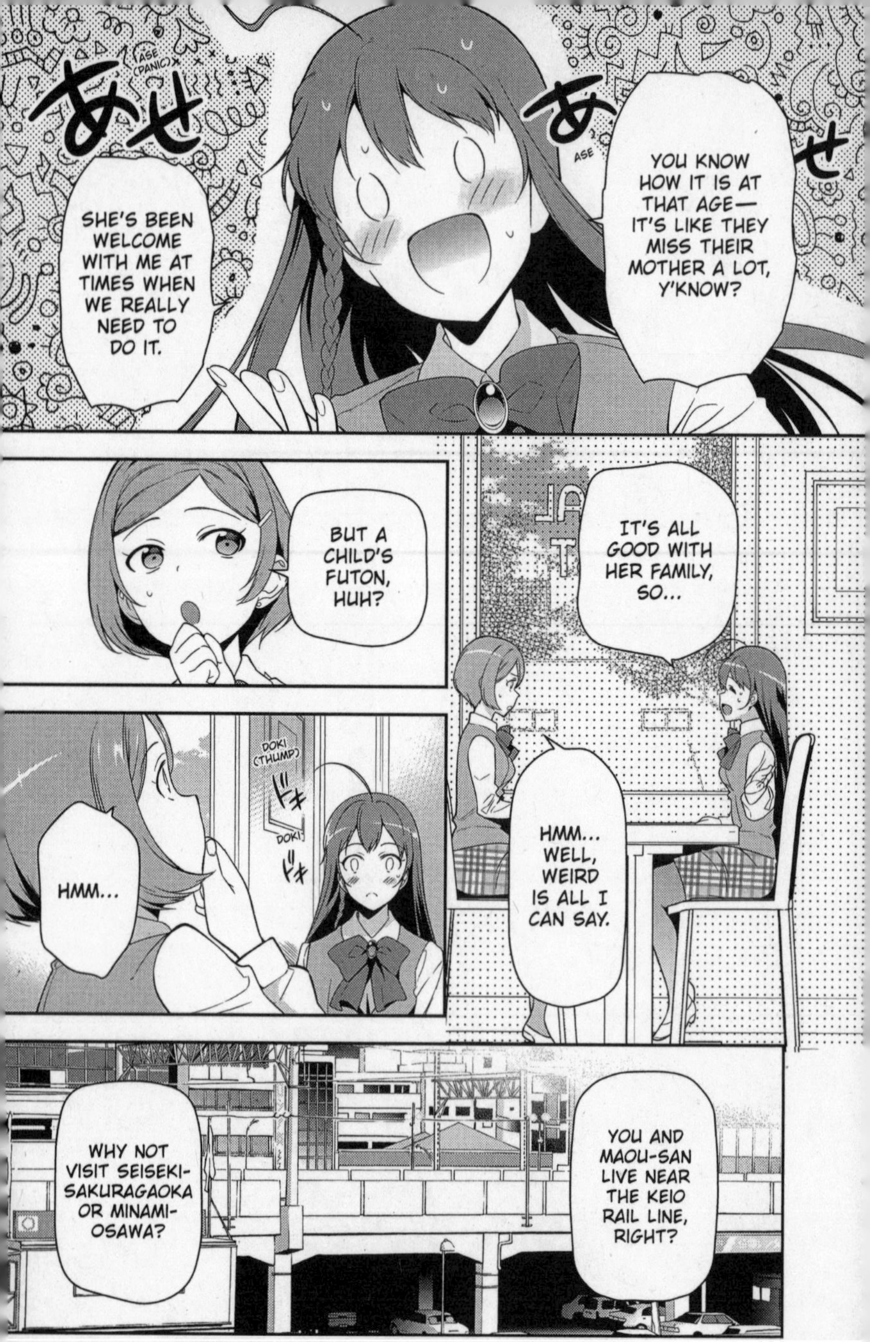
あせ
ASE
YOU KNOW HOW IT IS AT THAT AGE— IT'S LIKE THEY MISS THEIR MOTHER A LOT, Y'KNOW?
あせ
ASE (PANIC)
SHE'S BEEN WELCOME WITH ME AT TIMES WHEN WE REALLY NEED TO DO IT.
IT'S ALL GOOD WITH HER FAMILY, SO...
HMM... WELL, WEIRD IS ALL I CAN SAY.
BUT A CHILD'S FUTON, HUH?
ドキ
DOKI (THUMP)
ドキ
DOKI
HMM...
YOU AND MAOU-SAN LIVE NEAR THE KEIO RAIL LINE, RIGHT?
WHY NOT VISIT SEISEKI-SAKURAGAOKA OR MINAMI-OSAWA?

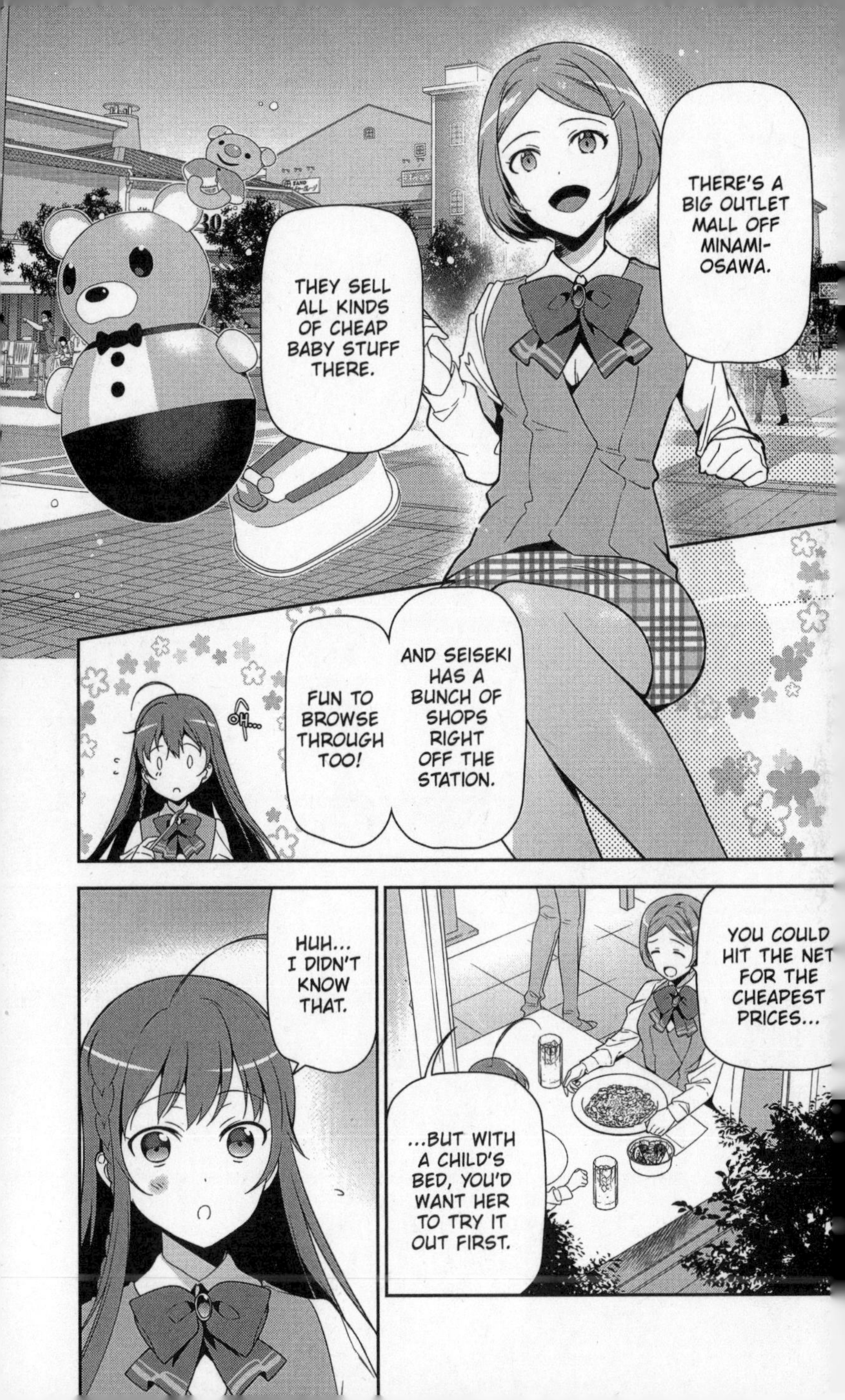
THERE'S A BIG OUTLET MALL OFF MINAMI-OSAWA.
THEY SELL ALL KINDS OF CHEAP BABY STUFF THERE.
AND SEISEKI HAS A BUNCH OF SHOPS RIGHT OFF THE STATION.
FUN TO BROWSE THROUGH TOO!
OH...
YOU COULD HIT THE NET FOR THE CHEAPEST PRICES...
...BUT WITH A CHILD'S BED, YOU'D WANT HER TO TRY IT OUT FIRST.
HUH... I DIDN'T KNOW THAT.

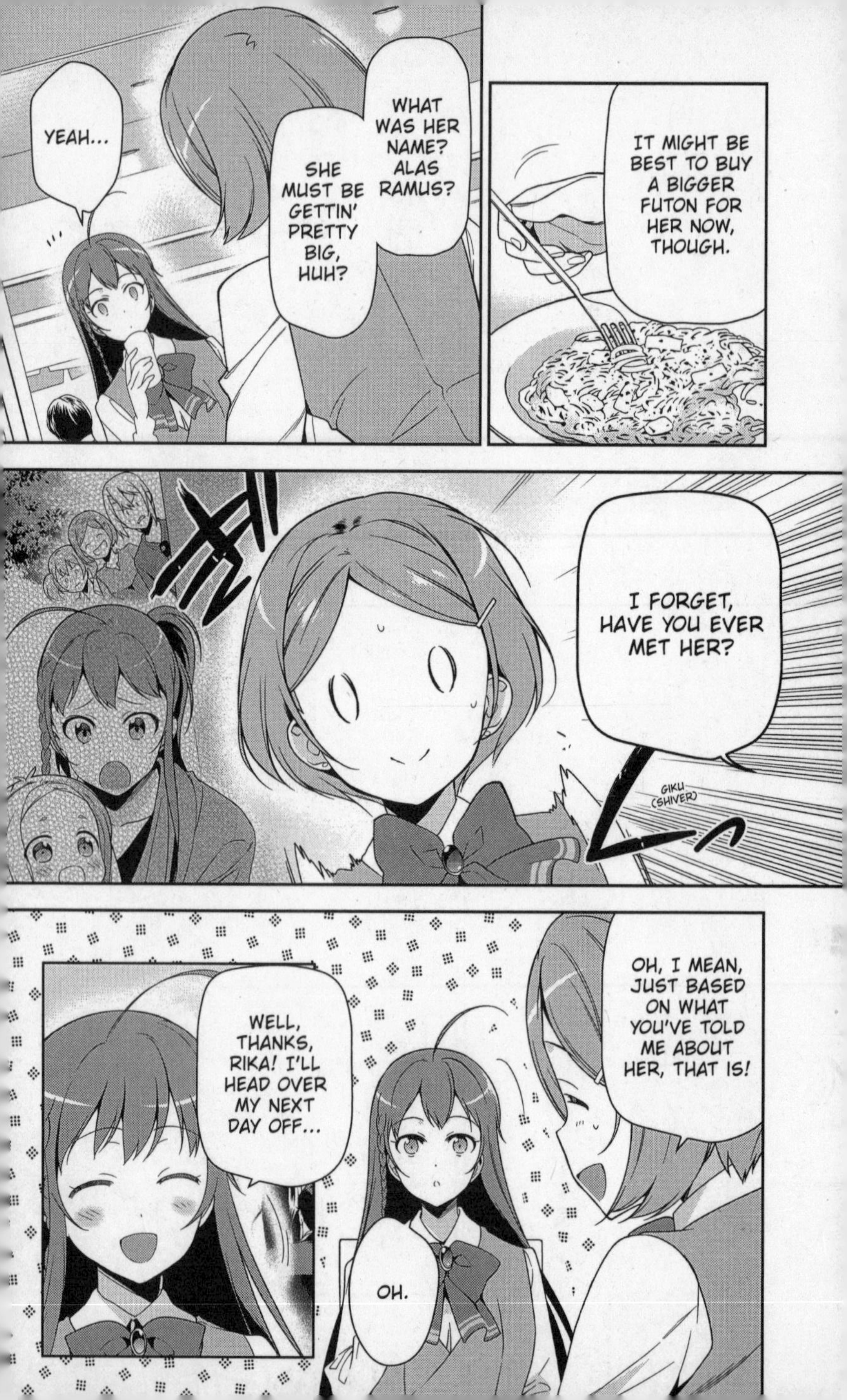
IT MIGHT BE BEST TO BUY A BIGGER FUTON FOR HER NOW, THOUGH.
WHAT WAS HER NAME? ALAS RAMUS?
SHE MUST BE GETTIN' PRETTY BIG, HUH?
YEAH...
I FORGET, HAVE YOU EVER MET HER?
GIKU (SHIVER)
OH, I MEAN, JUST BASED ON WHAT YOU'VE TOLD ME ABOUT HER, THAT IS!
OH.
WELL, THANKS, RIKA! I'LL HEAD OVER MY NEXT DAY OFF...

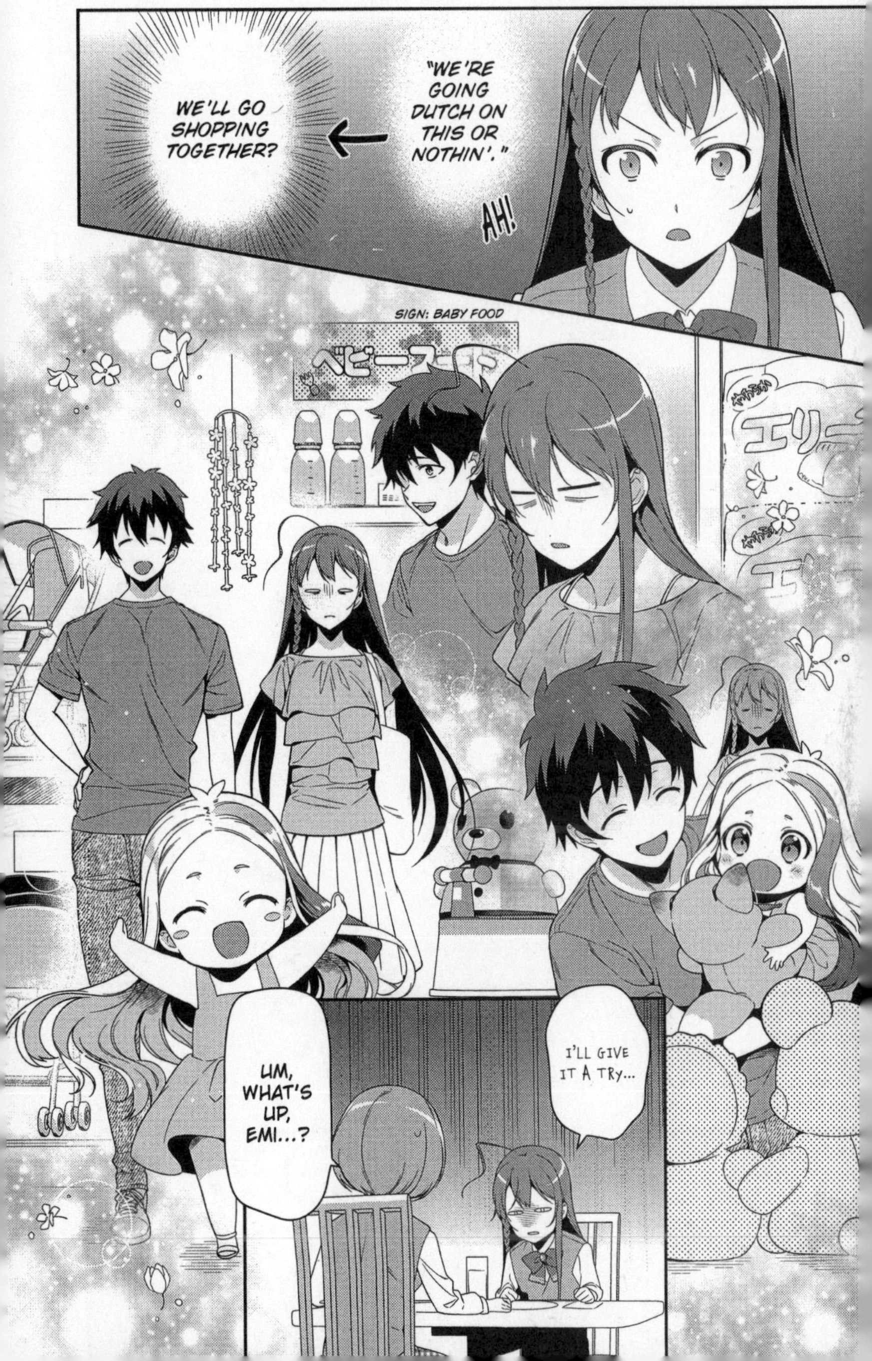
"WE'RE GOING DUTCH ON THIS OR NOTHIN'."
WE'LL GO SHOPPING TOGETHER?
AH!
SIGN: BABY FOOD
I'LL GIVE IT A TRY...
UM, WHAT'S UP, EMI...?

THE DEVIL IS A PART-TIMER!

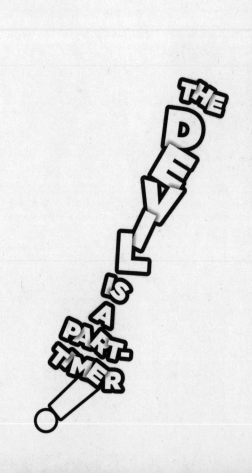

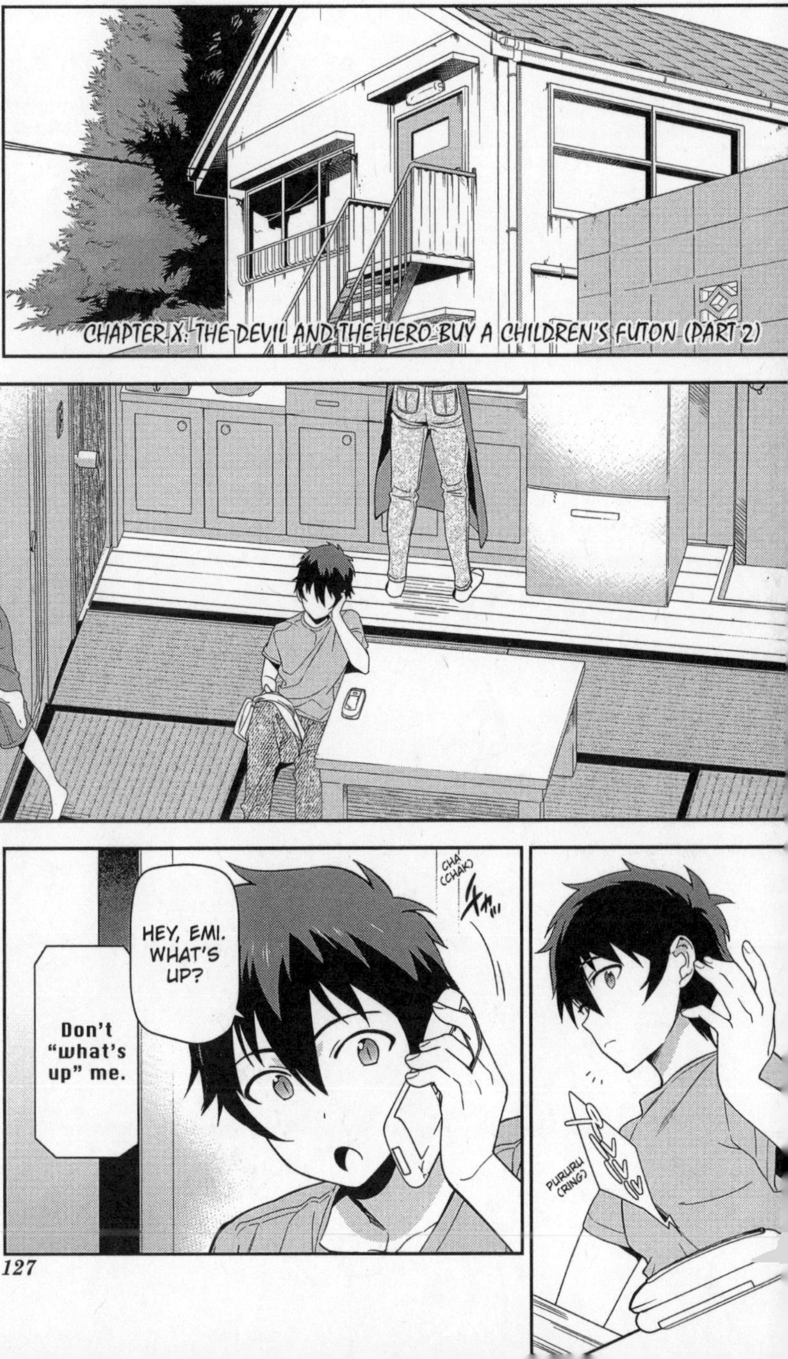
CHAPTER X: THE DEVIL AND THE HERO BUY A CHILDREN'S FUTON (PART 2)
PURURU (RING)
...
CHA (CHAK)
HEY, EMI. WHAT'S UP?
Don't "what's up" me.

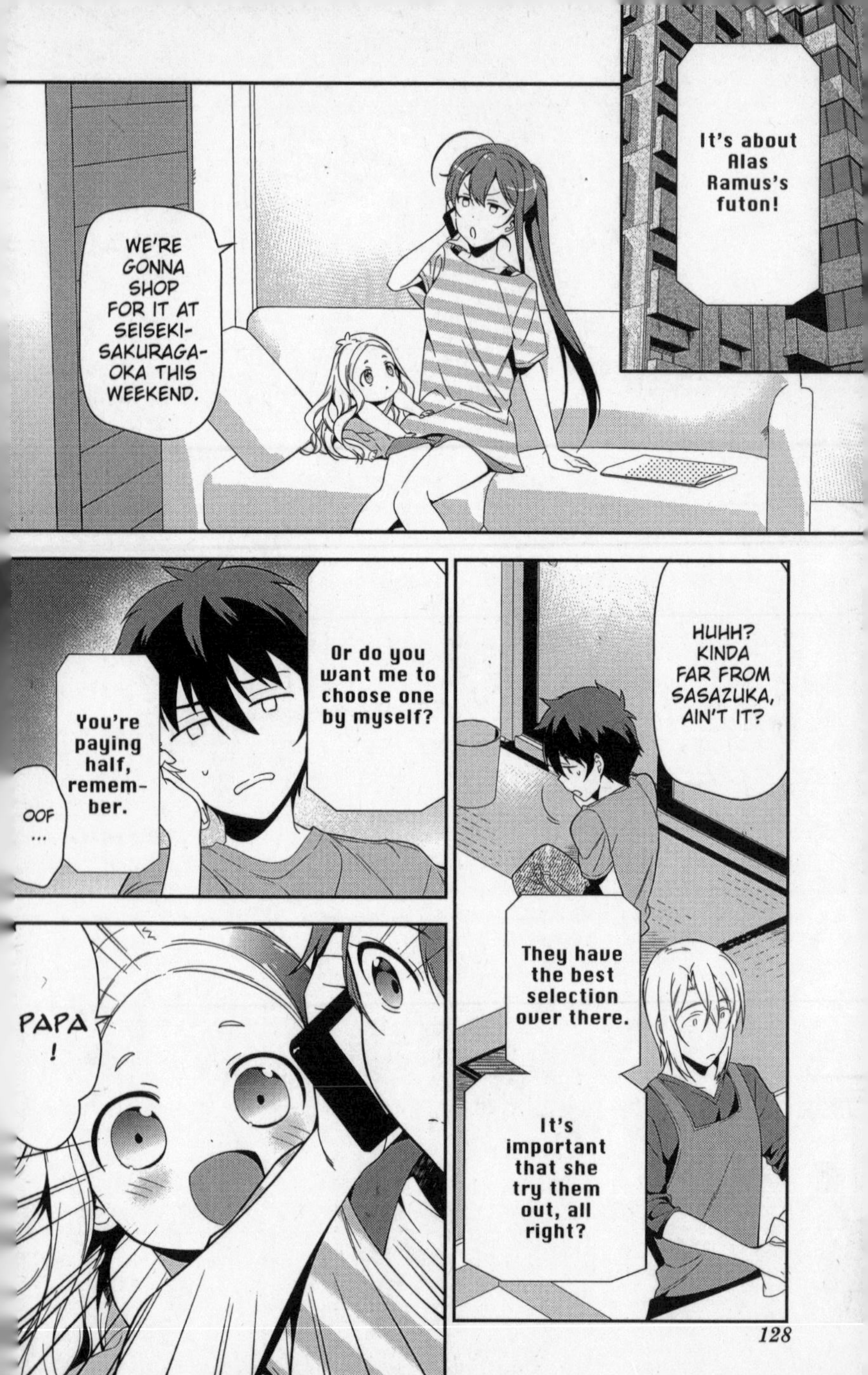
It's about Alas Ramus's futon!
WE'RE GONNA SHOP FOR IT AT SEISEKI-SAKURAGAOKA THIS WEEKEND.
HUHH? KINDA FAR FROM SASAZUKA, AIN'T IT?
They have the best selection over there.
It's important that she try them out, all right?
Or do you want me to choose one by myself?
You're paying half, remember.
OOF...
PAPA!

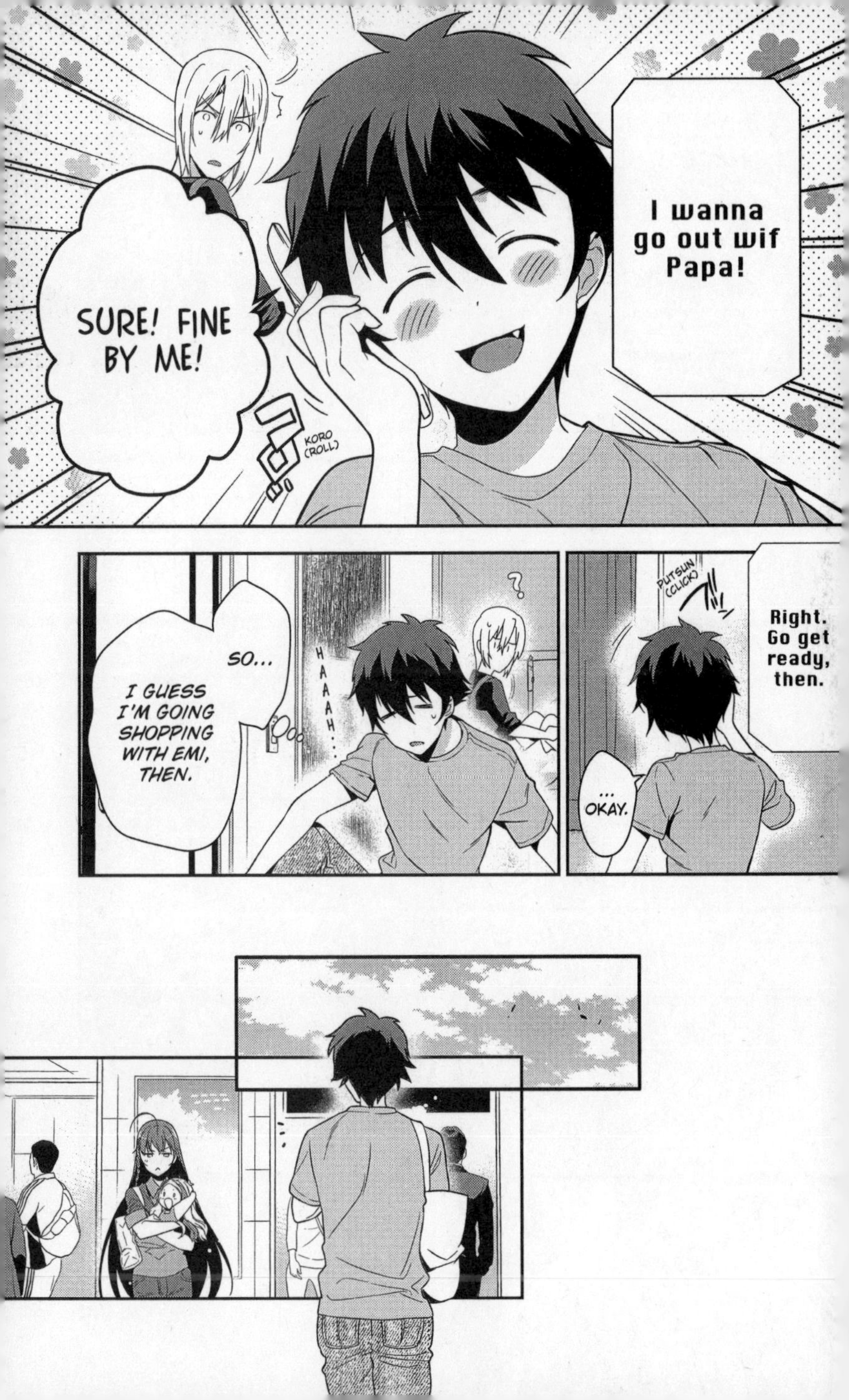
I wanna go out wif Papa!
SURE! FINE BY ME!
KORO (ROLL)
PUTSUN (CLICK)
Right. Go get ready, then.
... OKAY.
SO... I GUESS I'M GOING SHOPPING WITH EMI, THEN.
HAAAH...

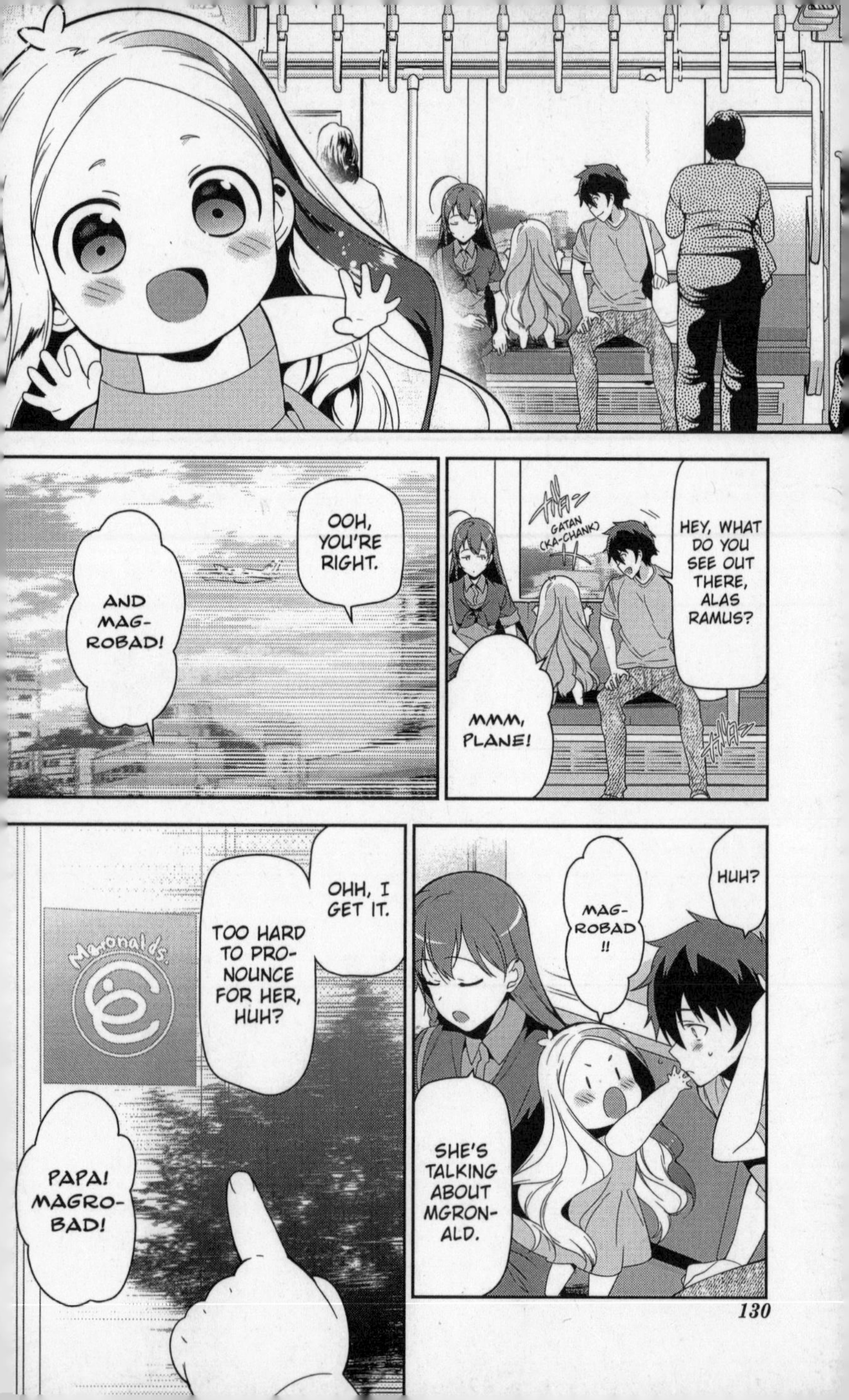
HEY, WHAT DO YOU SEE OUT THERE, ALAS RAMUS?
GATAN (KA-CHANK)
MMM, PLANE!
OOH, YOU'RE RIGHT.
AND MAG-ROBAD!
HUH?
MAG-ROBAD!!
SHE'S TALKING ABOUT MGRON-ALD.
OHH, I GET IT.
TOO HARD TO PRO-NOUNCE FOR HER, HUH?
Mgronalds.
PAPA! MAGRO-BAD!

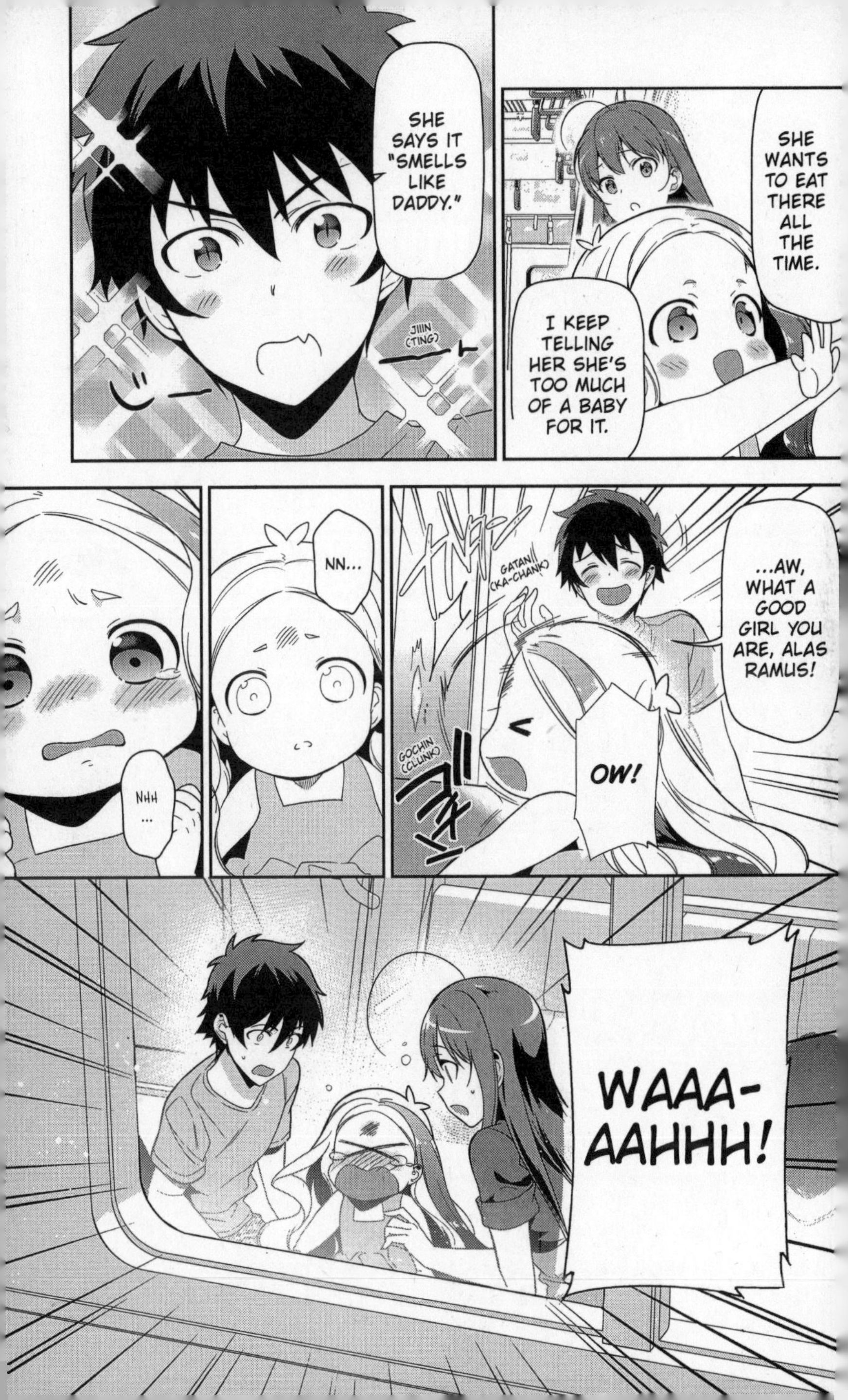
SHE WANTS TO EAT THERE ALL THE TIME.
I KEEP TELLING HER SHE'S TOO MUCH OF A BABY FOR IT.
SHE SAYS IT "SMELLS LIKE DADDY."
JIIN (TING)
...AW, WHAT A GOOD GIRL YOU ARE, ALAS RAMUS!
GATAN (KA-CHANK)
OW!
GOCHIN (CLUNK)
NN...
NHH ...
WAAA-AAHHH!

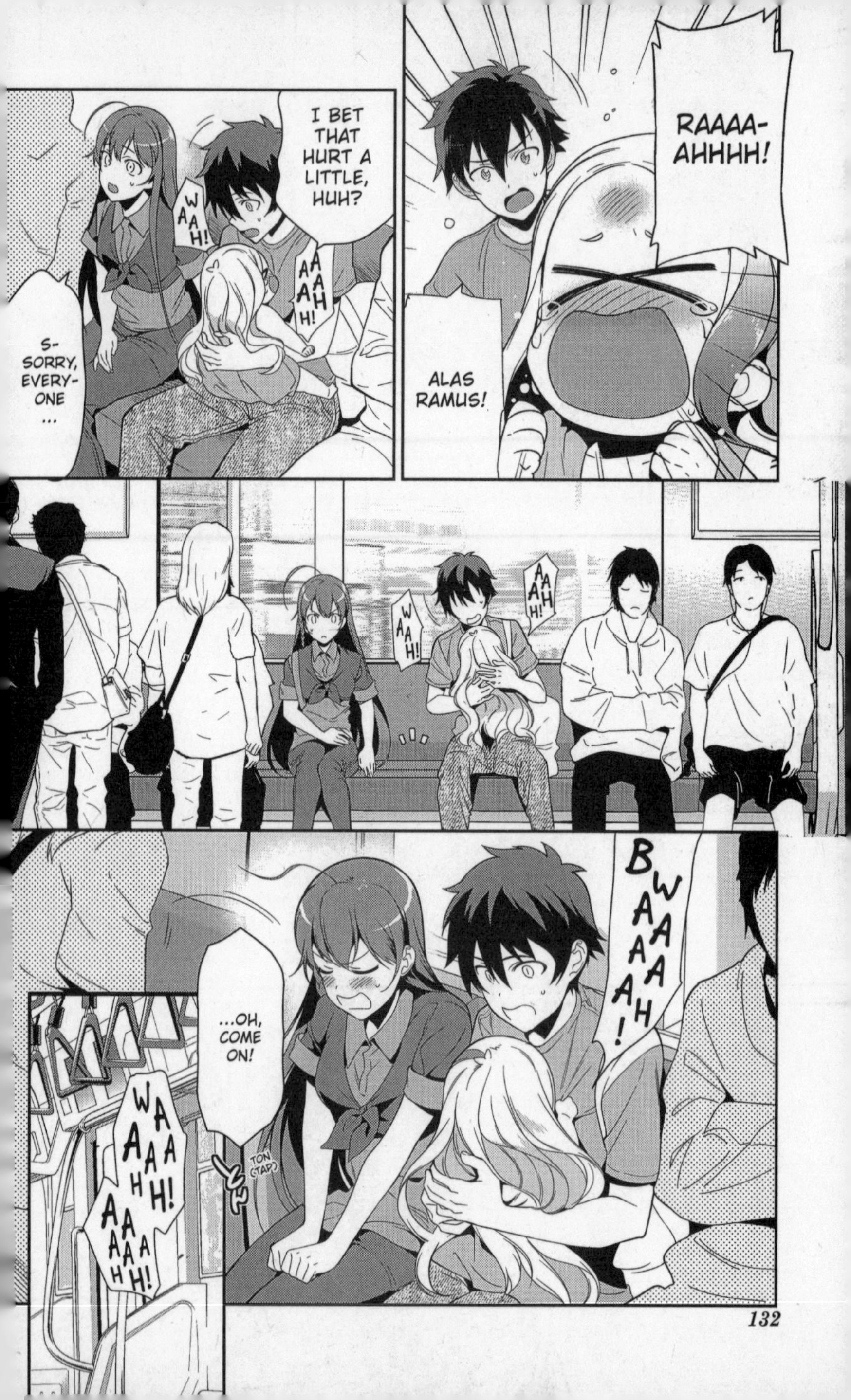
RAAAA-AHHHH!
ALAS RAMUS!
I BET THAT HURT A LITTLE, HUH?
AAAAH!
WAAH!
S-SORRY, EVERY-ONE ...
AAAAH!
WAAAH!
BWAAAAAAH!
...OH, COME ON!
TON (TAP)
WAAAAH! AAAAAAH!

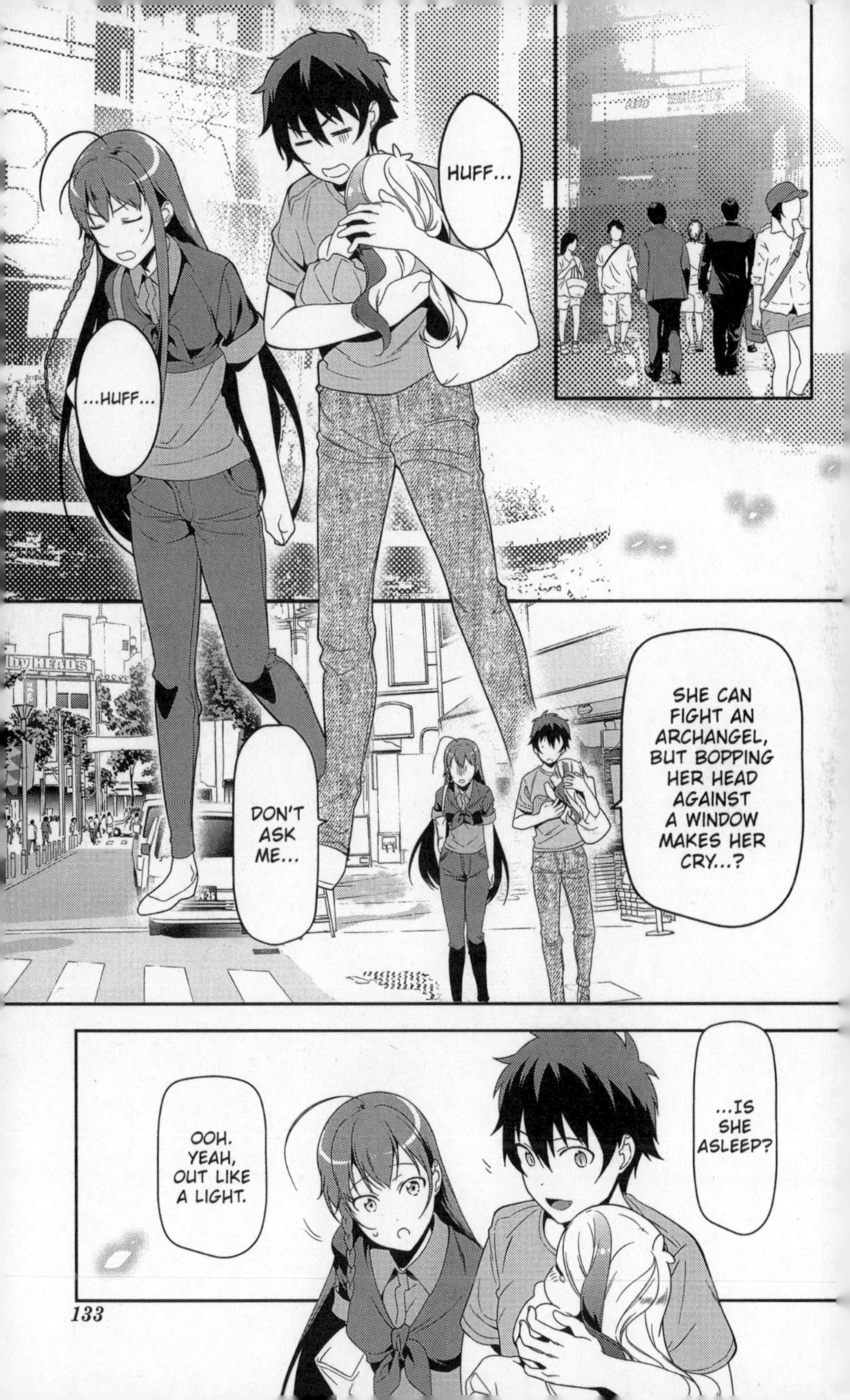
HUFF...
...HUFF...
SHE CAN FIGHT AN ARCHANGEL, BUT BOPPING HER HEAD AGAINST A WINDOW MAKES HER CRY...?
DON'T ASK ME...
...IS SHE ASLEEP?
OOH. YEAH, OUT LIKE A LIGHT.

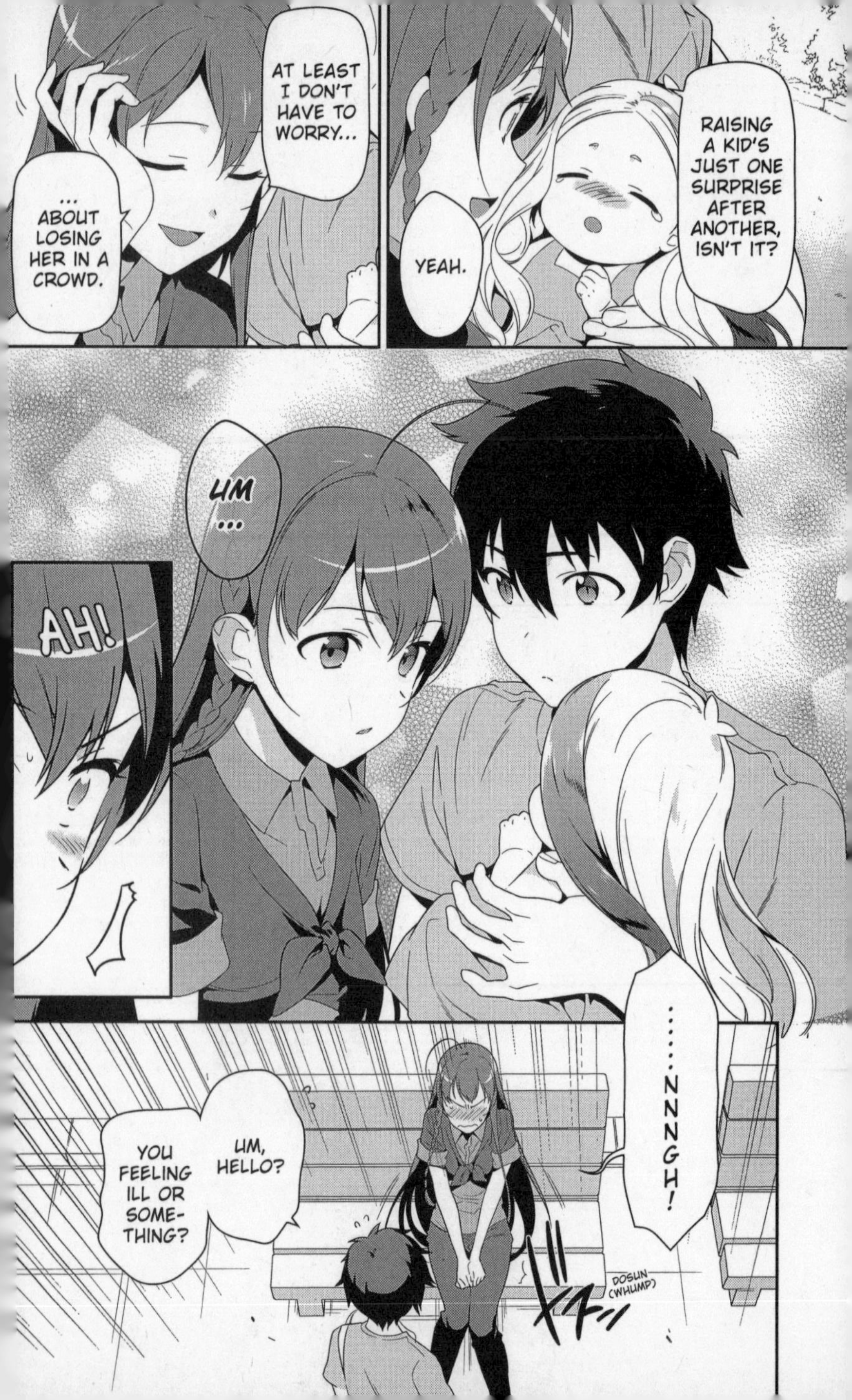
RAISING A KID'S JUST ONE SURPRISE AFTER ANOTHER, ISN'T IT?
YEAH.
AT LEAST I DON'T HAVE TO WORRY...
... ABOUT LOSING HER IN A CROWD.
UM ...
AH!
.....NNNGH!
DOSUN (WHUMP)
UM, HELLO?
YOU FEELING ILL OR SOME-THING?

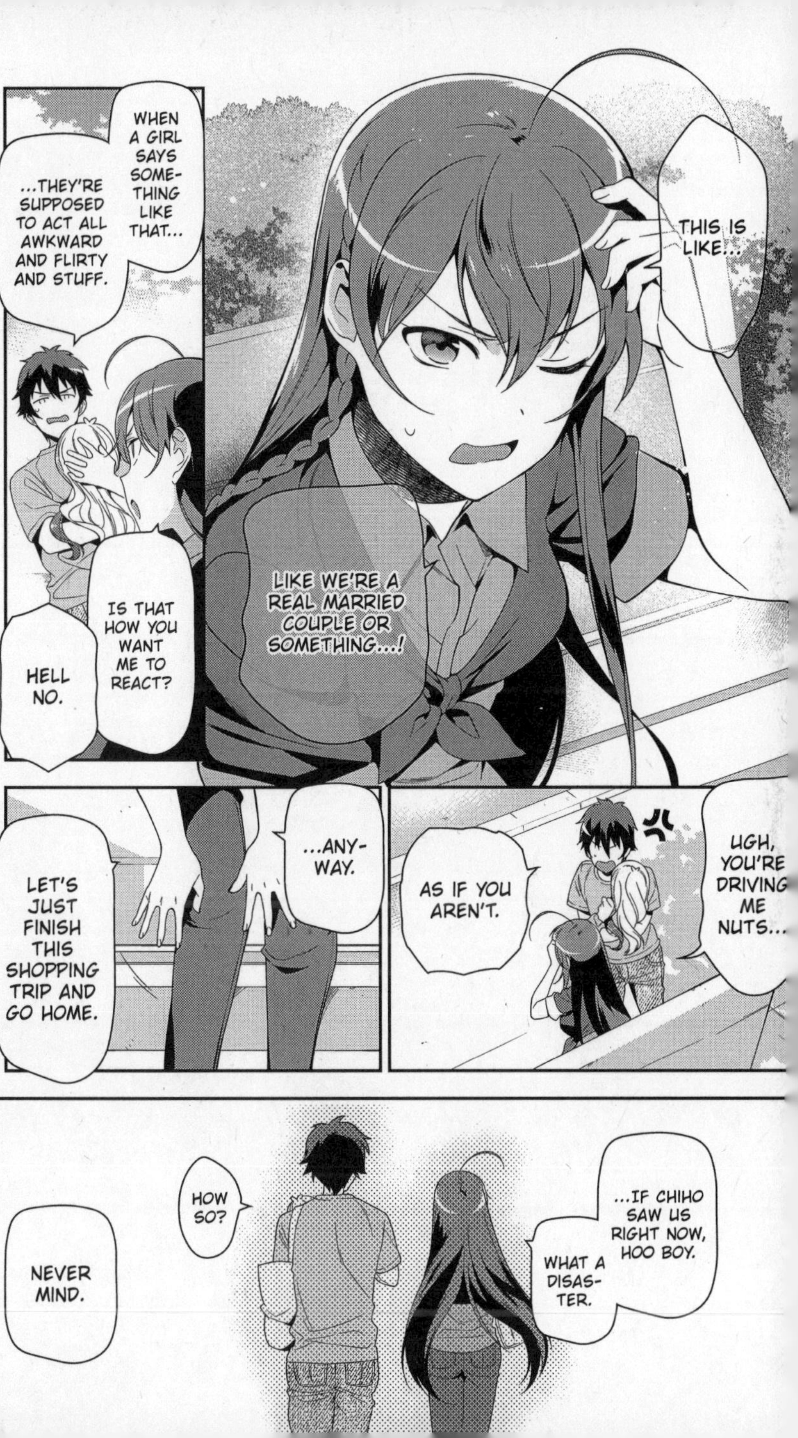
THIS IS LIKE...
LIKE WE'RE A REAL MARRIED COUPLE OR SOMETHING...!
WHEN A GIRL SAYS SOMETHING LIKE THAT...
...THEY'RE SUPPOSED TO ACT ALL AWKWARD AND FLIRTY AND STUFF.
IS THAT HOW YOU WANT ME TO REACT?
HELL NO.
UGH, YOU'RE DRIVING ME NUTS...
AS IF YOU AREN'T.
...ANYWAY.
LET'S JUST FINISH THIS SHOPPING TRIP AND GO HOME.
...IF CHIHO SAW US RIGHT NOW, HOO BOY.
WHAT A DISASTER.
HOW SO?
NEVER MIND.

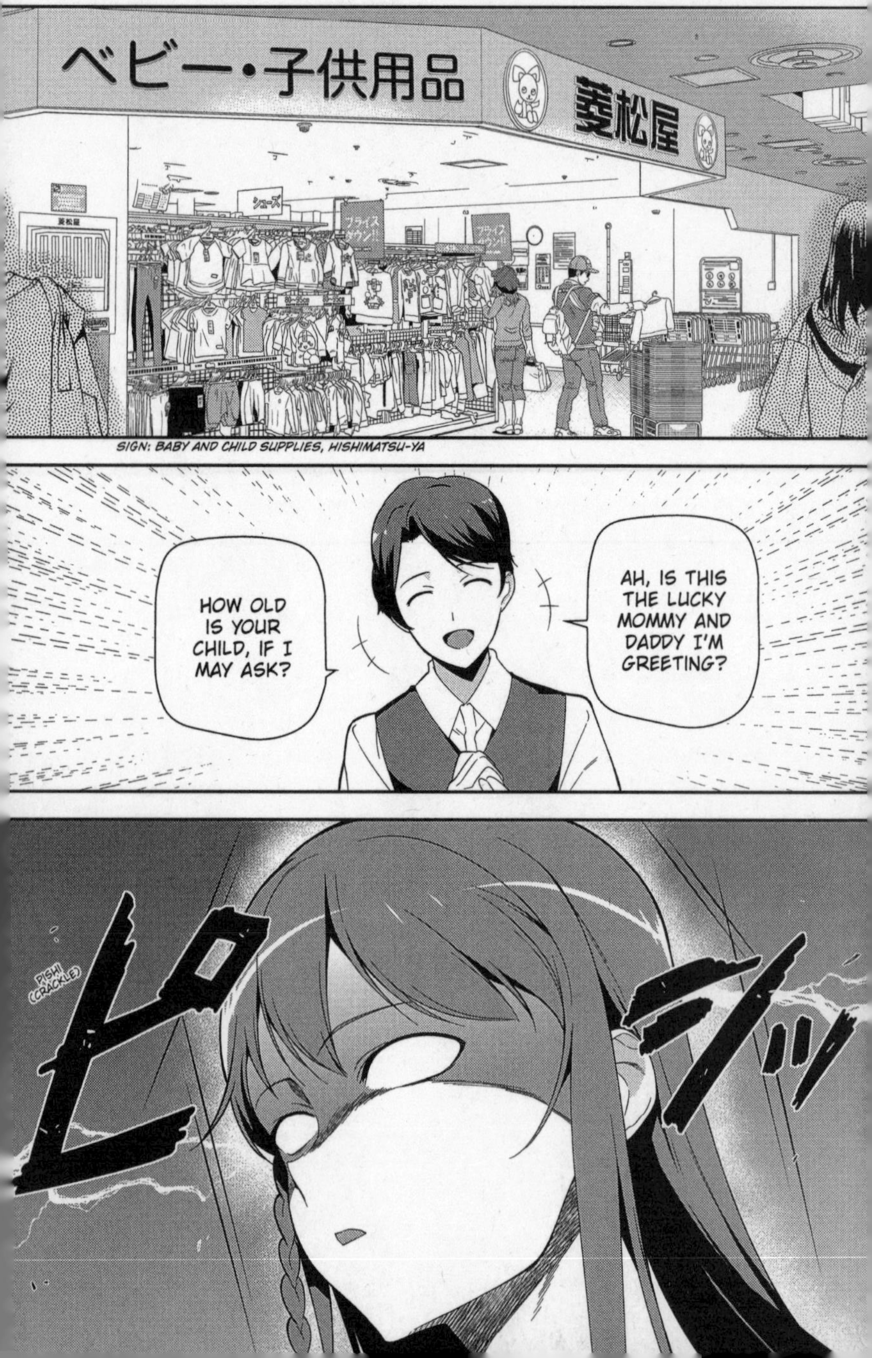
ベビー•子供用品
菱松屋
シューズ
SIGN: BABY AND CHILD SUPPLIES, HISHIMATSU-YA
AH, IS THIS THE LUCKY MOMMY AND DADDY I'M GREETING?
HOW OLD IS YOUR CHILD, IF I MAY ASK?
ピシッ
PISHI (CRACKLE)

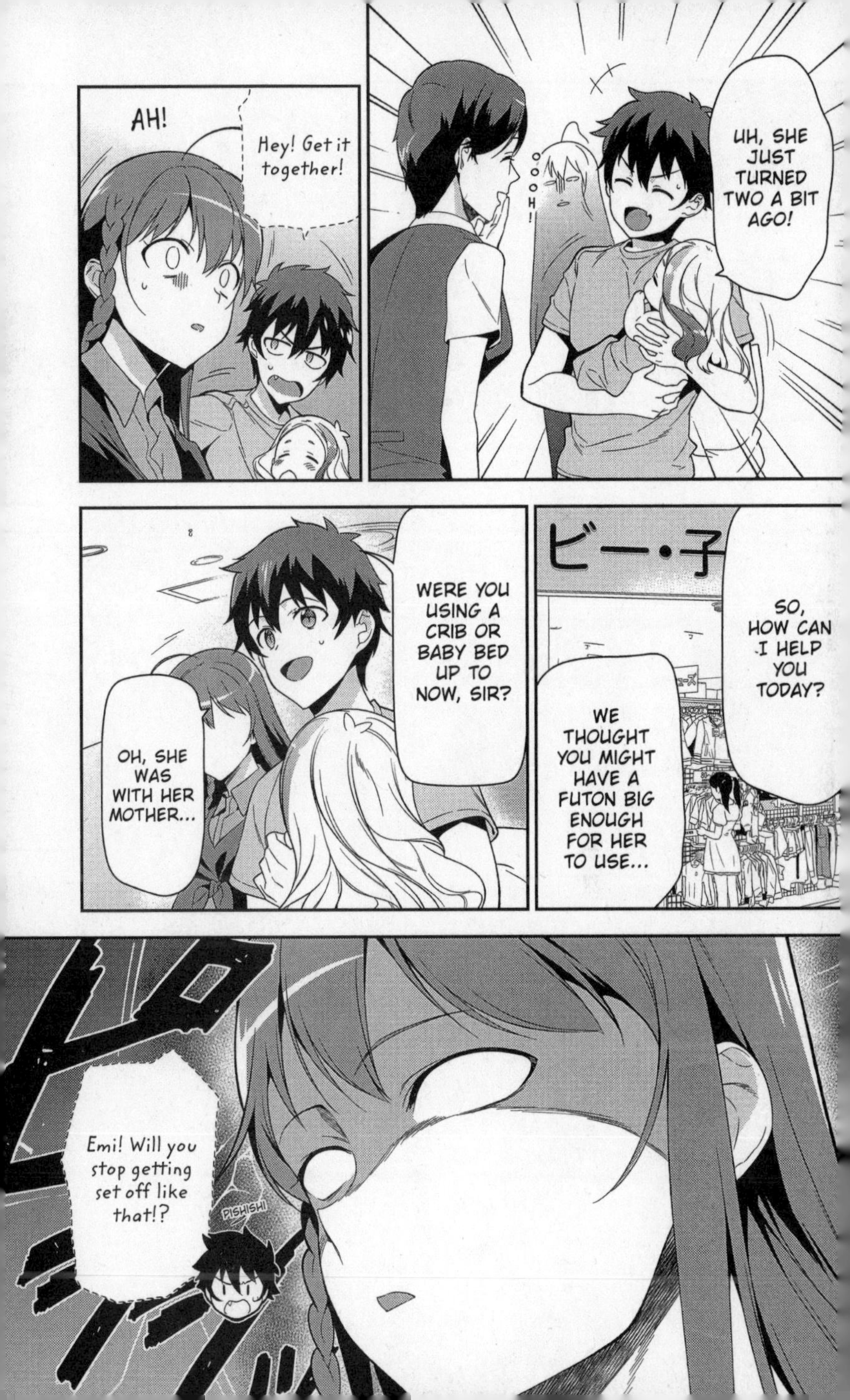
UH, SHE JUST TURNED TWO A BIT AGO!
O-O-O-H!
AH!
Hey! Get it together!
ビー・子
SO, HOW CAN I HELP YOU TODAY?
WE THOUGHT YOU MIGHT HAVE A FUTON BIG ENOUGH FOR HER TO USE...
WERE YOU USING A CRIB OR BABY BED UP TO NOW, SIR?
OH, SHE WAS WITH HER MOTHER...
Emi! Will you stop getting set off like that!?
PISHISHI

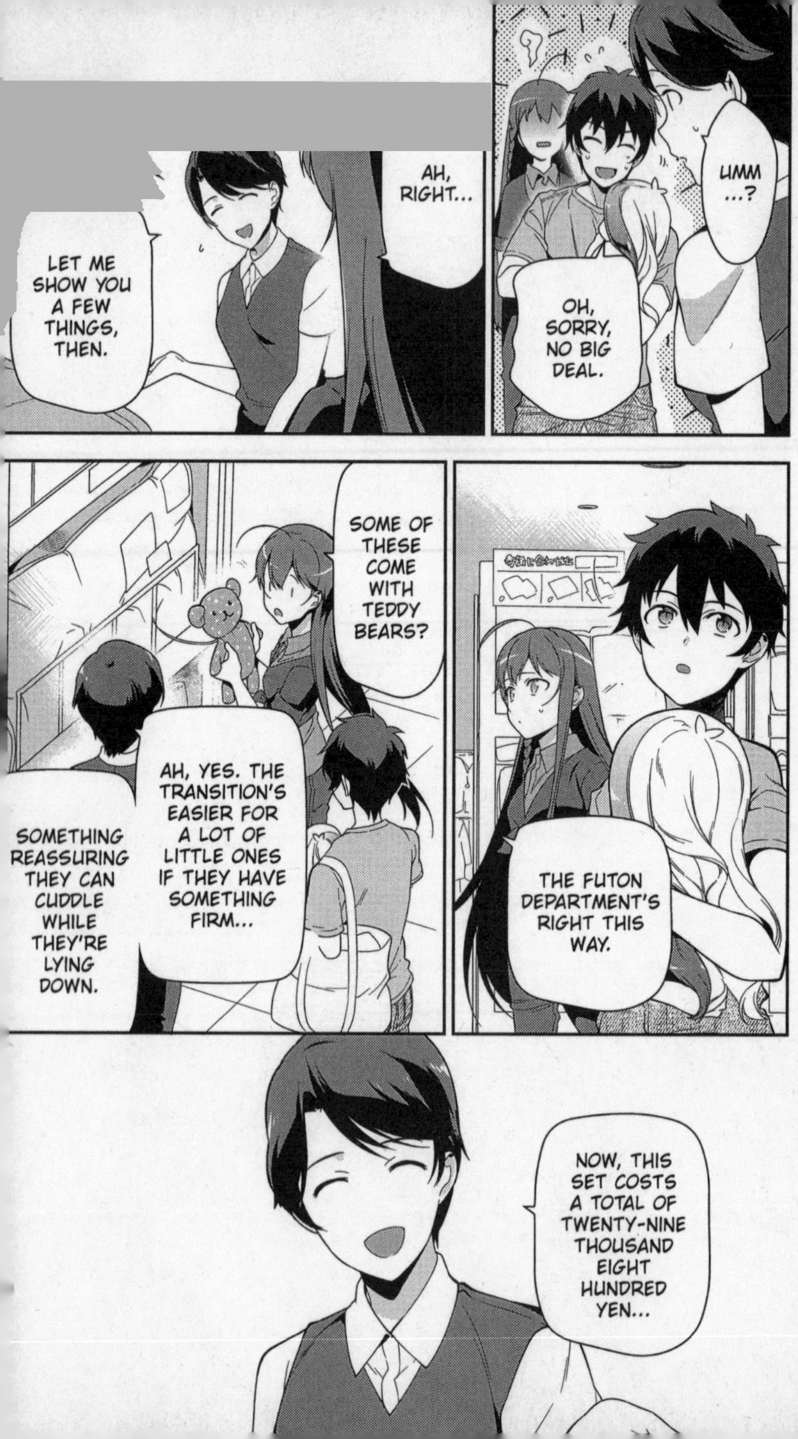
UMM ...?
OH, SORRY, NO BIG DEAL.
AH, RIGHT...
LET ME SHOW YOU A FEW THINGS, THEN.
THE FUTON DEPARTMENT'S RIGHT THIS WAY.
SOME OF THESE COME WITH TEDDY BEARS?
AH, YES. THE TRANSITION'S EASIER FOR A LOT OF LITTLE ONES IF THEY HAVE SOMETHING FIRM...
SOMETHING REASSURING THEY CAN CUDDLE WHILE THEY'RE LYING DOWN.
NOW, THIS SET COSTS A TOTAL OF TWENTY-NINE THOUSAND EIGHT HUNDRED YEN...

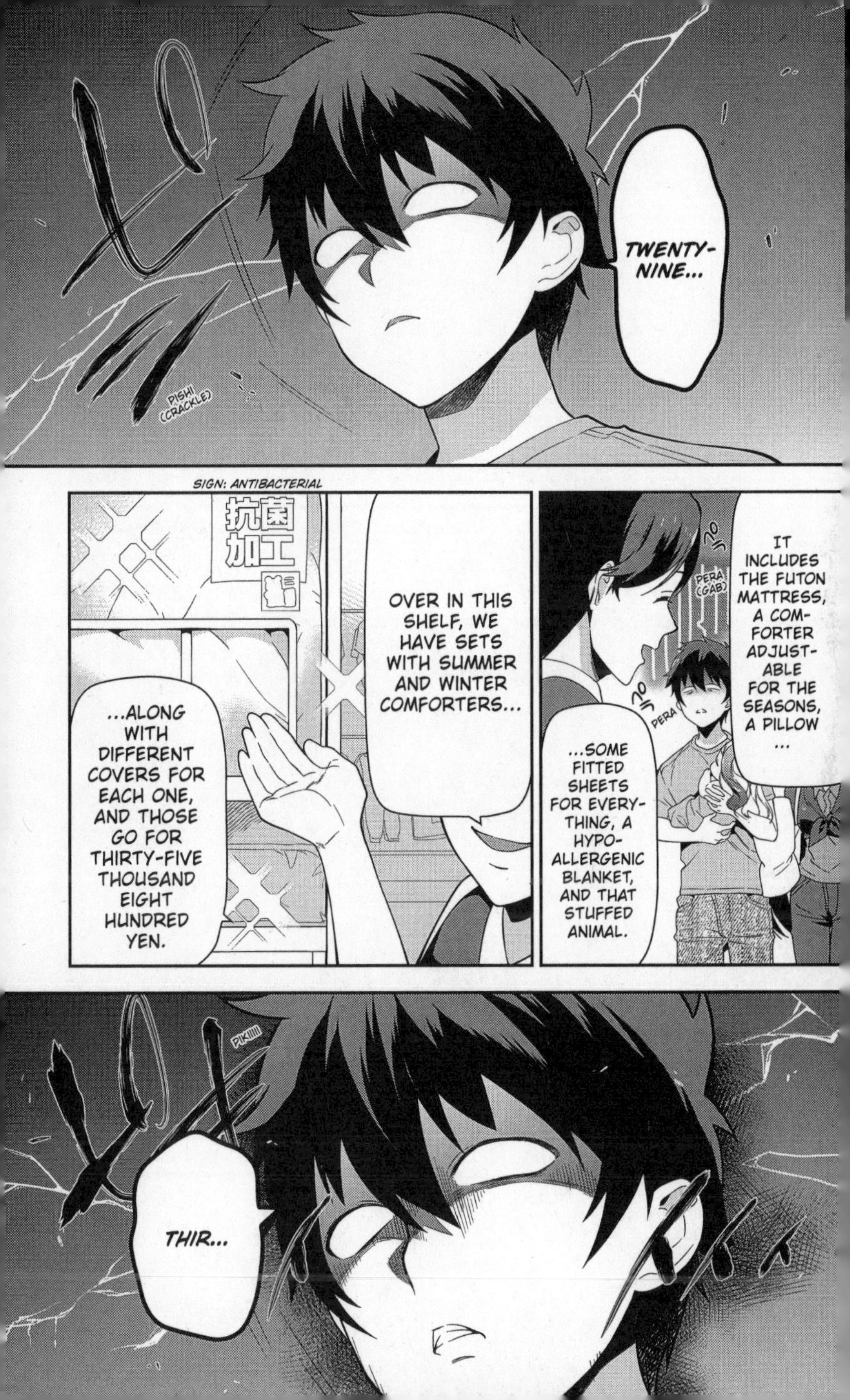
TWENTY-NINE...
PISHI (CRACKLE)
SIGN: ANTIBACTERIAL
PERA (GAB)
IT INCLUDES THE FUTON MATTRESS, A COMFORTER ADJUSTABLE FOR THE SEASONS, A PILLOW ...
PERA
...SOME FITTED SHEETS FOR EVERYTHING, A HYPOALLERGENIC BLANKET, AND THAT STUFFED ANIMAL.
抗菌加工
OVER IN THIS SHELF, WE HAVE SETS WITH SUMMER AND WINTER COMFORTERS...
...ALONG WITH DIFFERENT COVERS FOR EACH ONE, AND THOSE GO FOR THIRTY-FIVE THOUSAND EIGHT HUNDRED YEN.
PIKIIII
THIR...

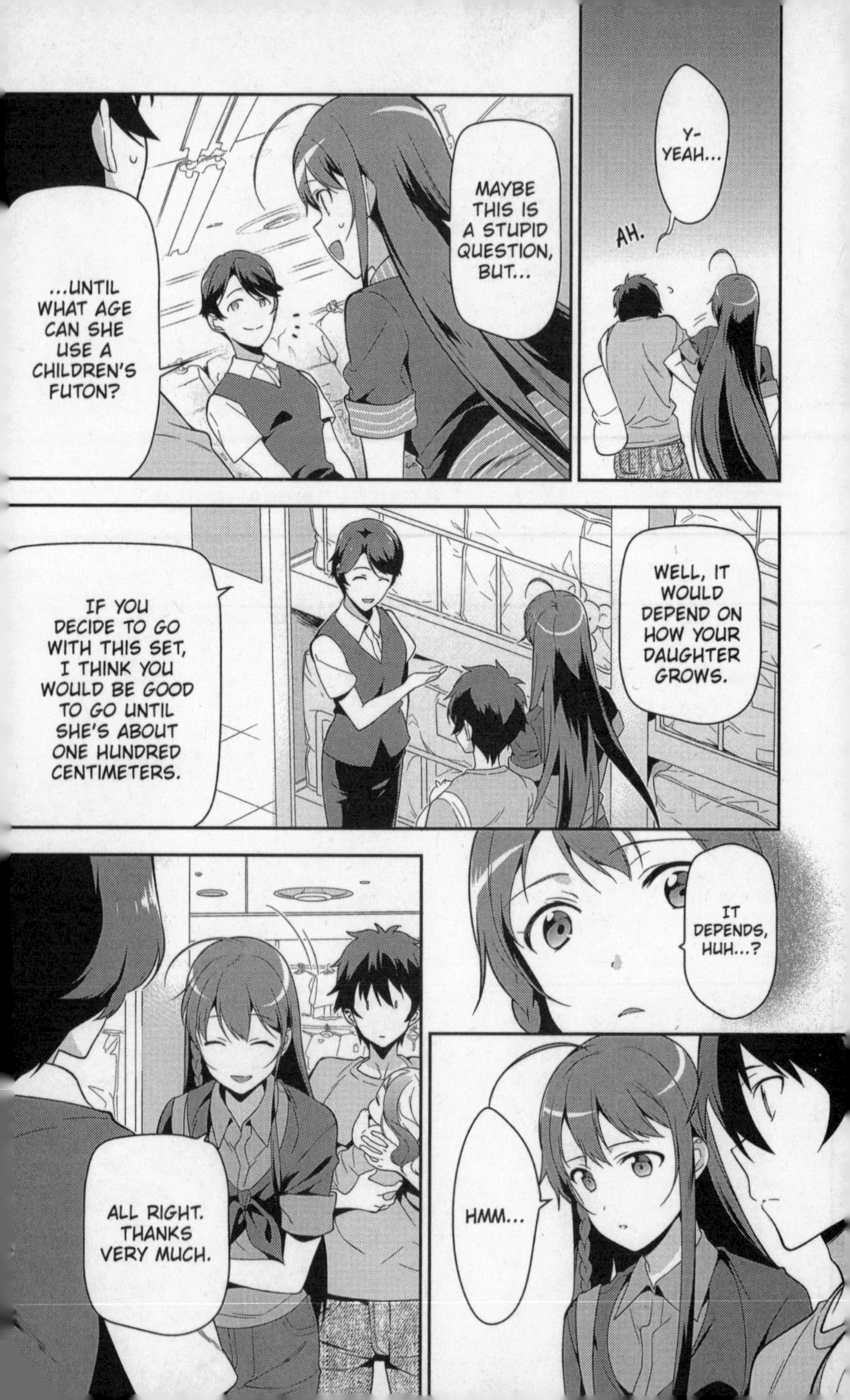
Y-YEAH...
AH.
MAYBE THIS IS A STUPID QUESTION, BUT...
...UNTIL WHAT AGE CAN SHE USE A CHILDREN'S FUTON?
WELL, IT WOULD DEPEND ON HOW YOUR DAUGHTER GROWS.
IF YOU DECIDE TO GO WITH THIS SET, I THINK YOU WOULD BE GOOD TO GO UNTIL SHE'S ABOUT ONE HUNDRED CENTIMETERS.
IT DEPENDS, HUH...?
HMM...
ALL RIGHT. THANKS VERY MUCH.

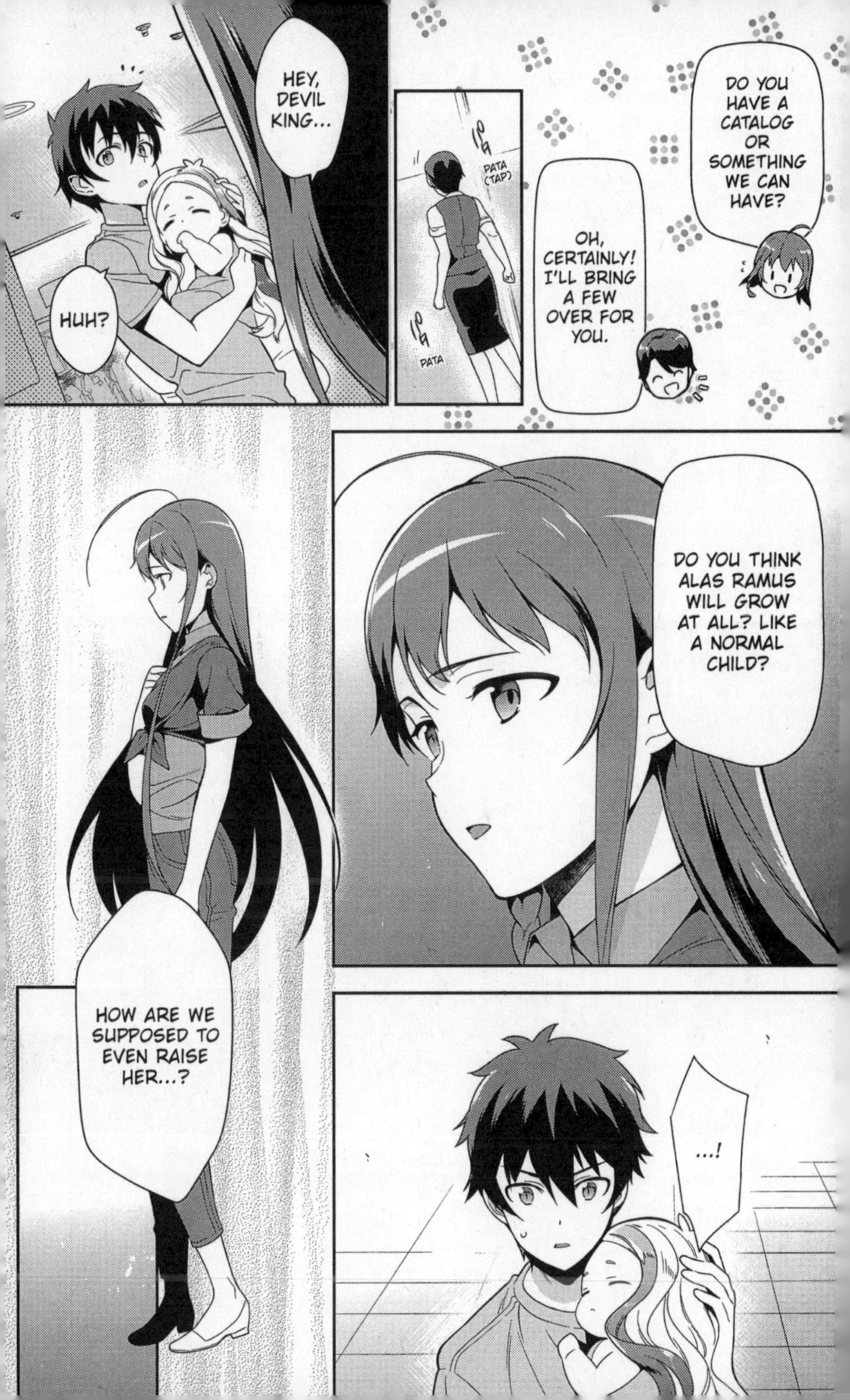
DO YOU HAVE A CATALOG OR SOMETHING WE CAN HAVE?
OH, CERTAINLY! I'LL BRING A FEW OVER FOR YOU.
PATA (TAP)
PATA
HEY, DEVIL KING...
HUH?
DO YOU THINK ALAS RAMUS WILL GROW AT ALL? LIKE A NORMAL CHILD?
...!
HOW ARE WE SUPPOSED TO EVEN RAISE HER...?

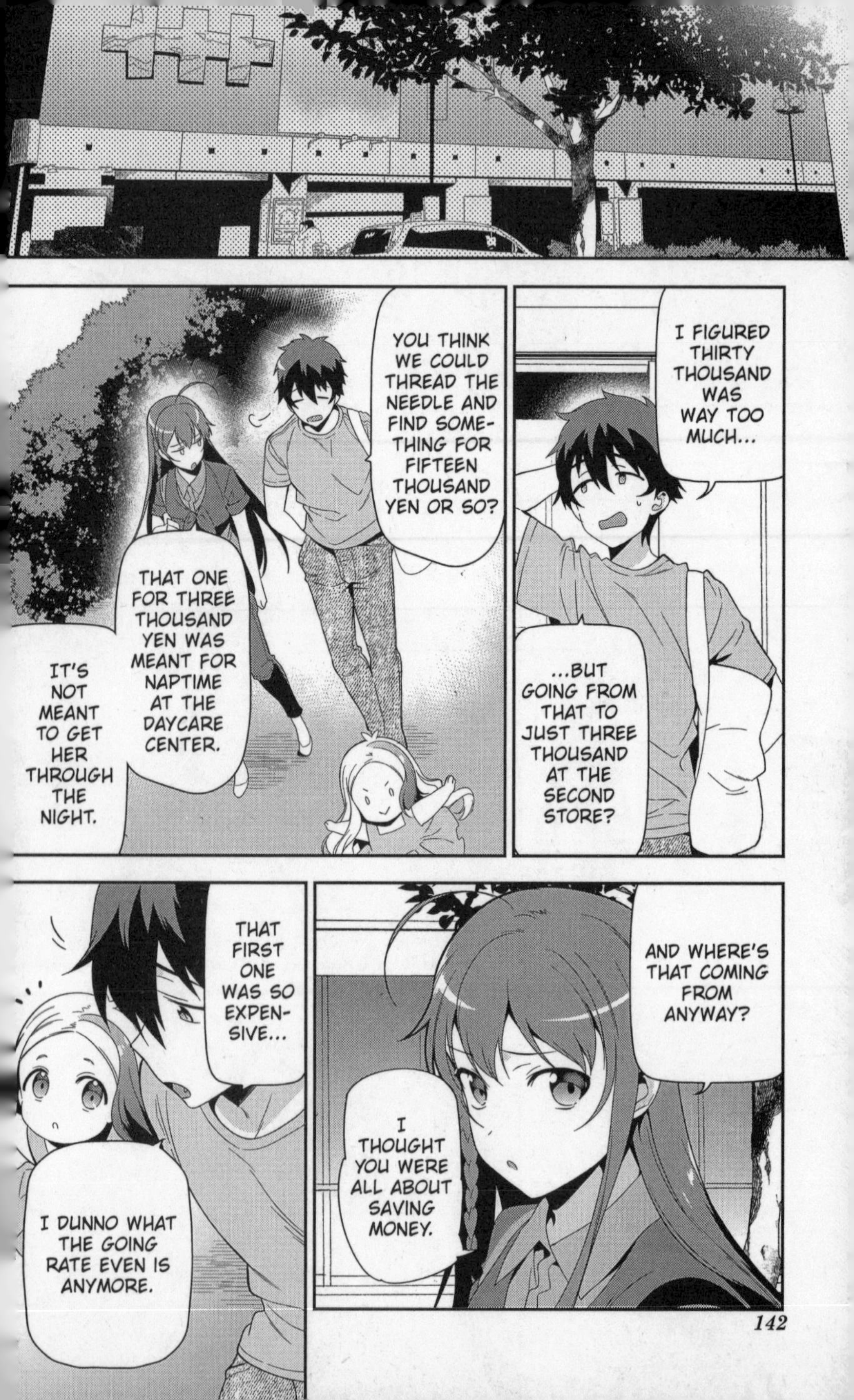
I FIGURED THIRTY THOUSAND WAS WAY TOO MUCH...
...BUT GOING FROM THAT TO JUST THREE THOUSAND AT THE SECOND STORE?
YOU THINK WE COULD THREAD THE NEEDLE AND FIND SOME-THING FOR FIFTEEN THOUSAND YEN OR SO?
THAT ONE FOR THREE THOUSAND YEN WAS MEANT FOR NAPTIME AT THE DAYCARE CENTER.
IT'S NOT MEANT TO GET HER THROUGH THE NIGHT.
AND WHERE'S THAT COMING FROM ANYWAY?
I THOUGHT YOU WERE ALL ABOUT SAVING MONEY.
THAT FIRST ONE WAS SO EXPEN-SIVE...
I DUNNO WHAT THE GOING RATE EVEN IS ANYMORE.

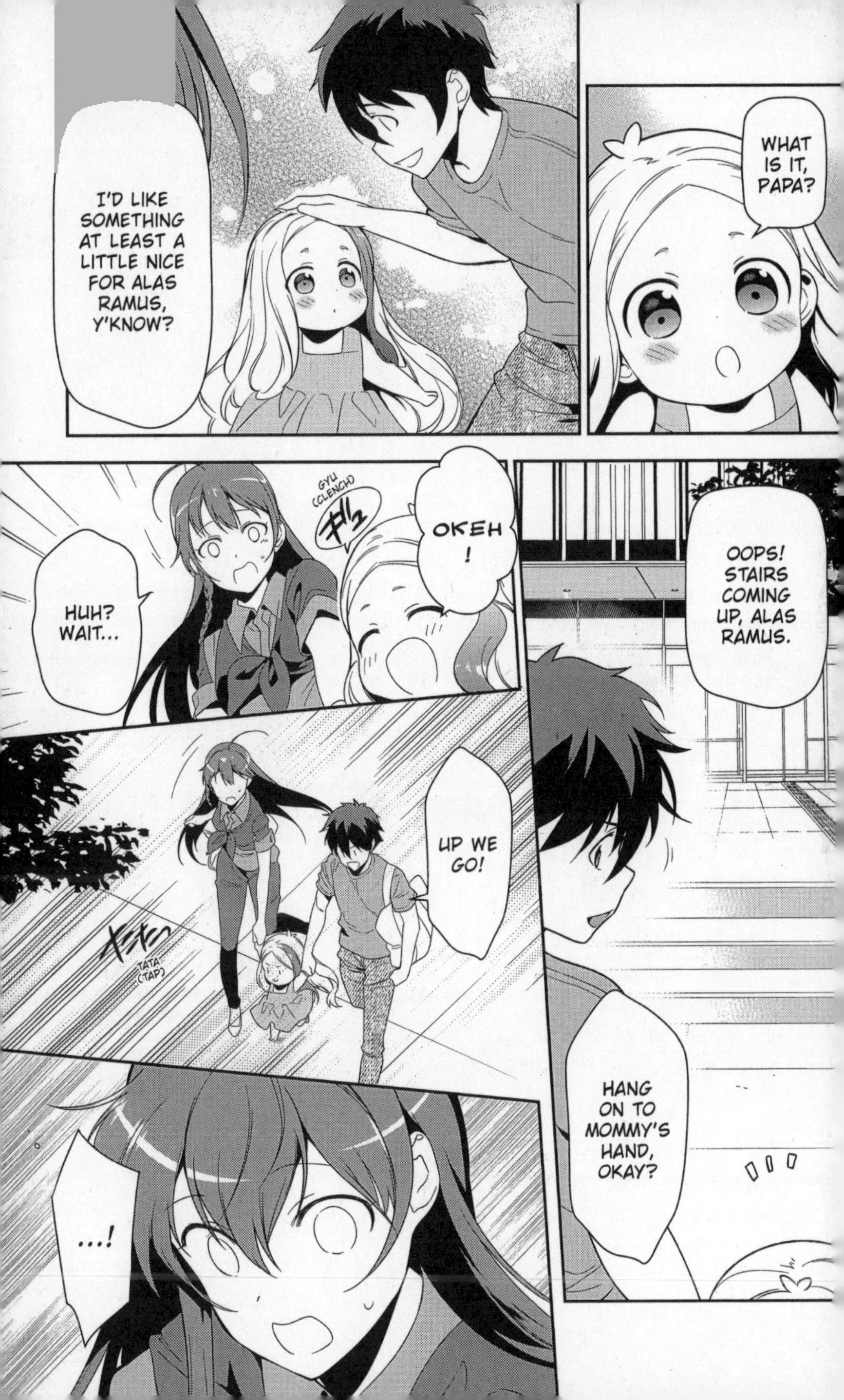
WHAT IS IT, PAPA?
I'D LIKE SOMETHING AT LEAST A LITTLE NICE FOR ALAS RAMUS, Y'KNOW?
OOPS! STAIRS COMING UP, ALAS RAMUS.
HANG ON TO MOMMY'S HAND, OKAY?
OKEH!
GYU (CLENCH)
HUH? WAIT...
UP WE GO!
TATA (TAP)
...!

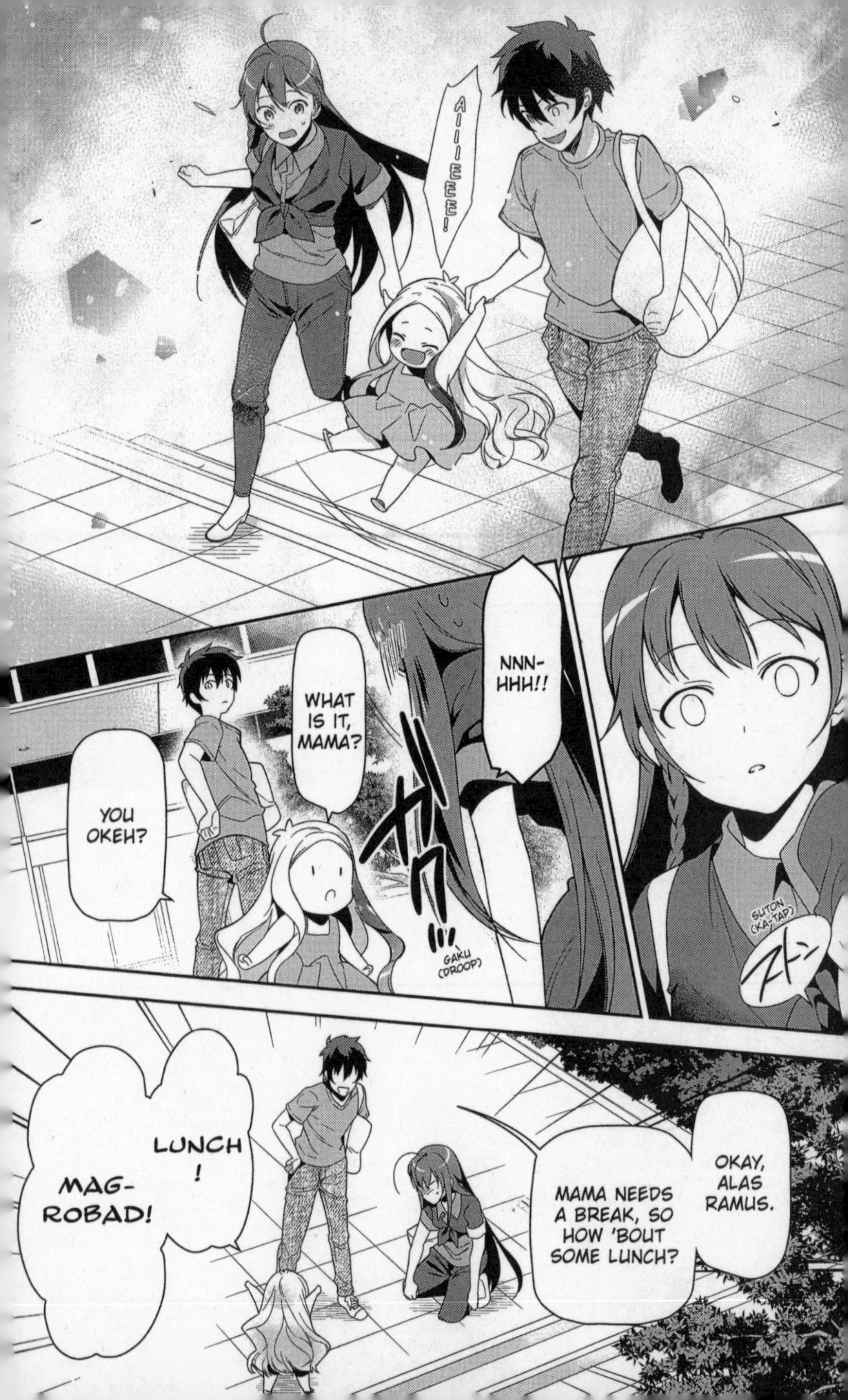
AIIIEEEE!
SUTON (KA-TAP)
NNN-HHH!!
GAKU (DROOP)
WHAT IS IT, MAMA?
YOU OKEH?
OKAY, ALAS RAMUS.
MAMA NEEDS A BREAK, SO HOW 'BOUT SOME LUNCH?
LUNCH!
MAG-ROBAD!

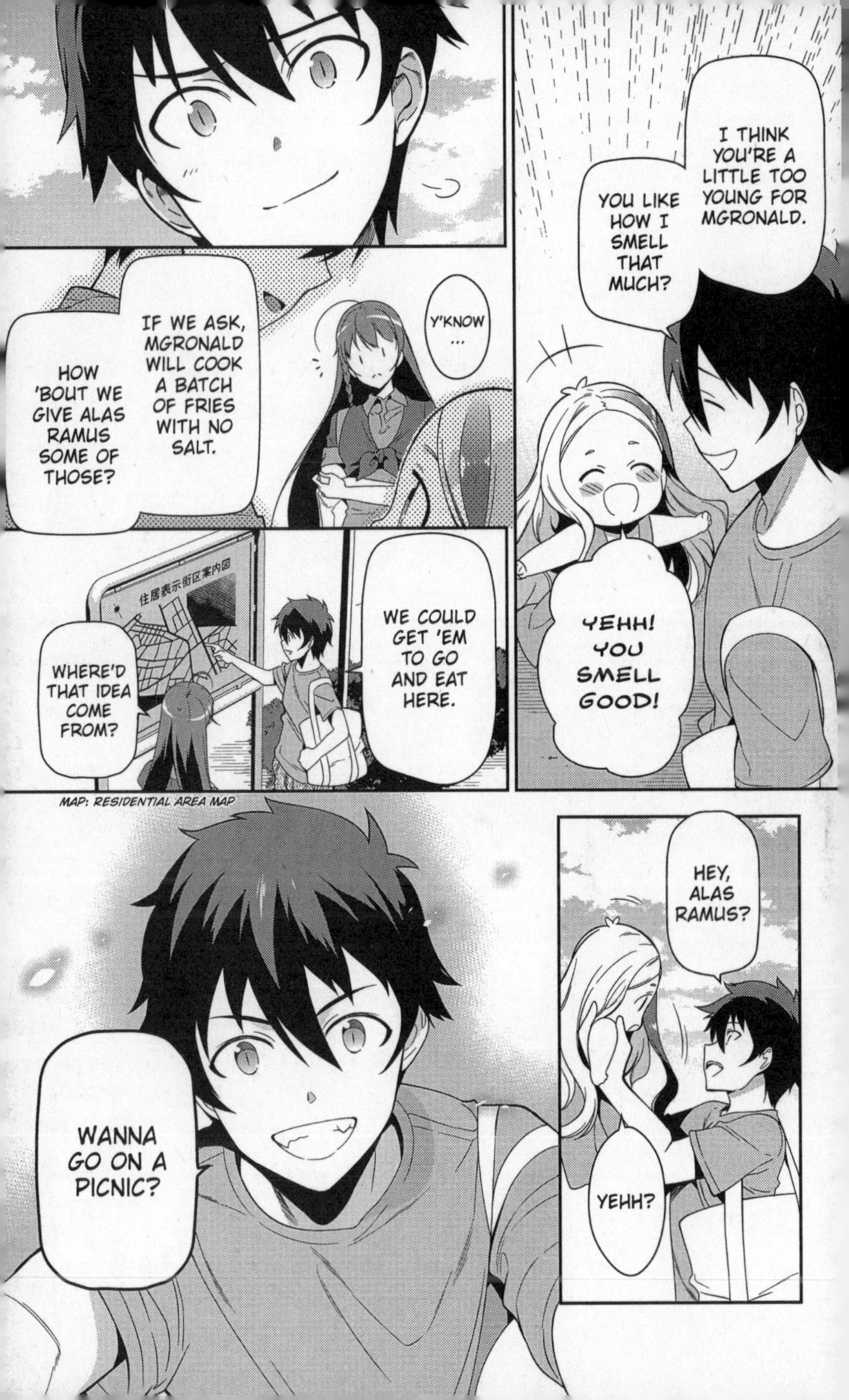
I THINK YOU'RE A LITTLE TOO YOUNG FOR MGRONALD.
YOU LIKE HOW I SMELL THAT MUCH?
YEHH! YOU SMELL GOOD!
Y'KNOW ...
IF WE ASK, MGRONALD WILL COOK A BATCH OF FRIES WITH NO SALT.
HOW 'BOUT WE GIVE ALAS RAMUS SOME OF THOSE?
住居表示街区案内図
WE COULD GET 'EM TO GO AND EAT HERE.
WHERE'D THAT IDEA COME FROM?
MAP: RESIDENTIAL AREA MAP
HEY, ALAS RAMUS?
YEHH?
WANNA GO ON A PICNIC?

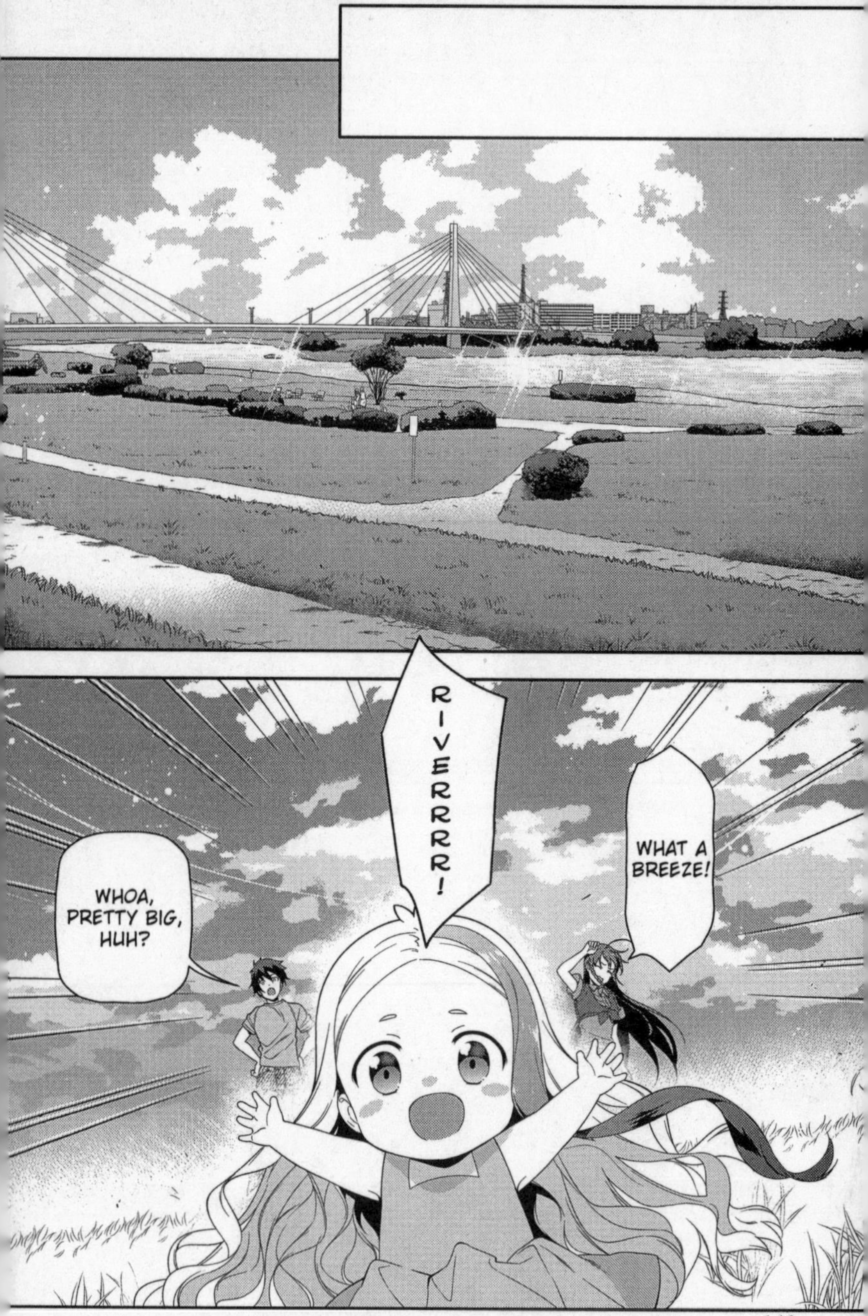
WHAT A BREEZE!
RIVERRRR!
WHOA, PRETTY BIG, HUH?

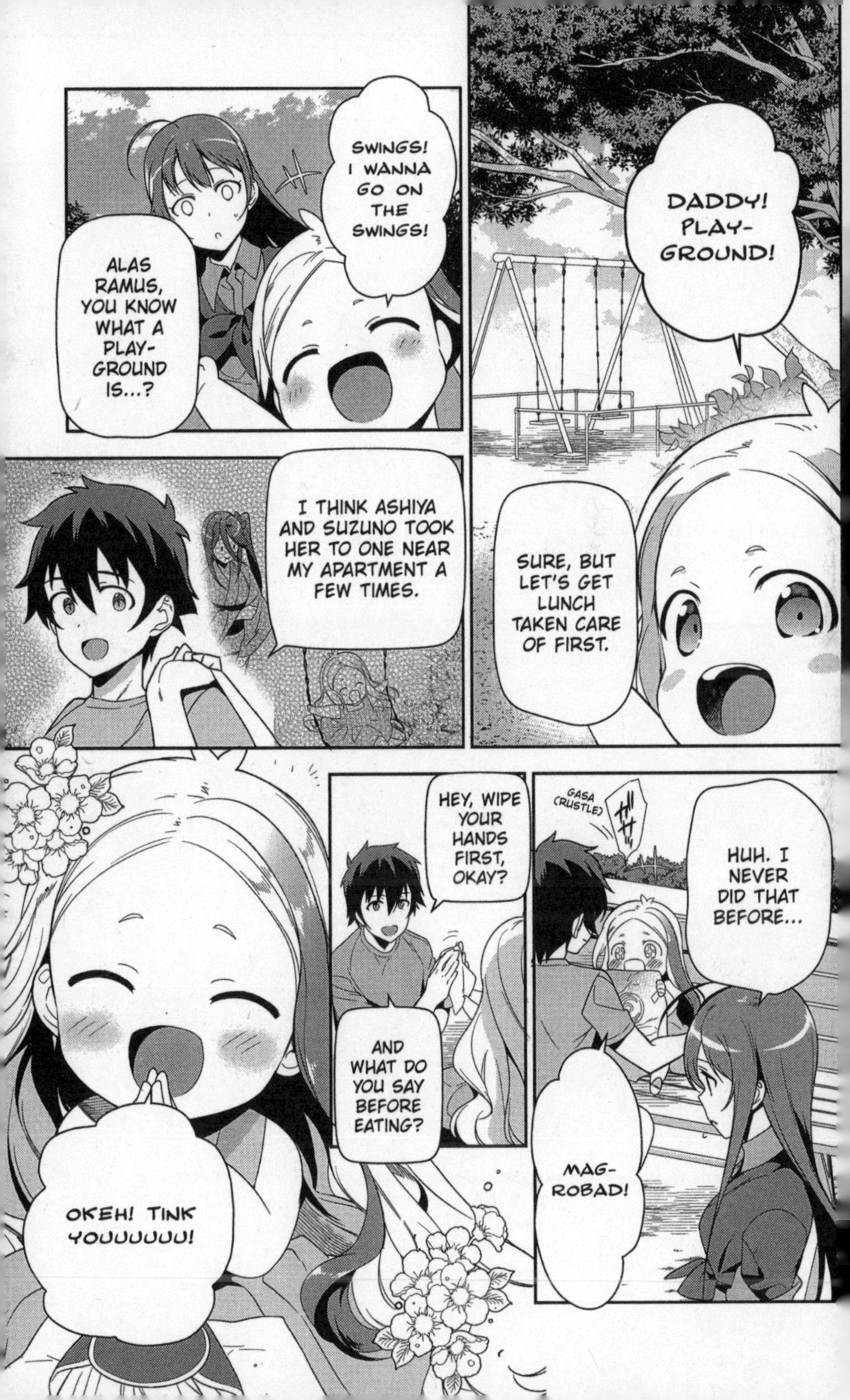
DADDY! PLAY-GROUND!
SURE, BUT LET'S GET LUNCH TAKEN CARE OF FIRST.
SWINGS! I WANNA GO ON THE SWINGS!
ALAS RAMUS, YOU KNOW WHAT A PLAY-GROUND IS...?
I THINK ASHIYA AND SUZUNO TOOK HER TO ONE NEAR MY APARTMENT A FEW TIMES.
HUH. I NEVER DID THAT BEFORE...
GASA (RUSTLE)
MAG-ROBAD!
HEY, WIPE YOUR HANDS FIRST, OKAY?
AND WHAT DO YOU SAY BEFORE EATING?
OKEH! TINK YOUUUUUU!

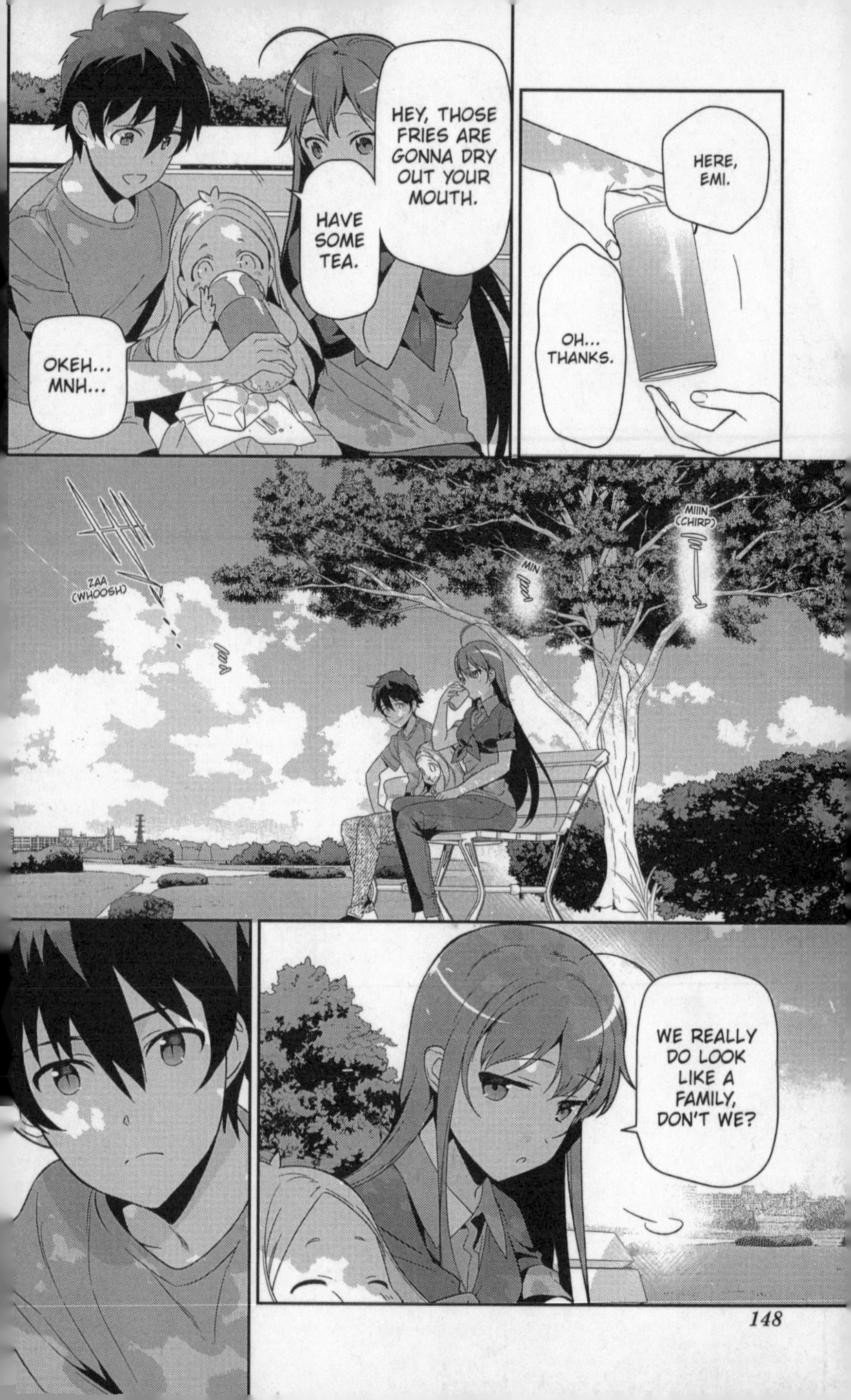
HERE, EMI.
OH... THANKS.
HEY, THOSE FRIES ARE GONNA DRY OUT YOUR MOUTH.
HAVE SOME TEA.
OKEH... MNH...
MIIN (CHIRP)
MIN
ZAA (WHOOSH)
WE REALLY DO LOOK LIKE A FAMILY, DON'T WE?

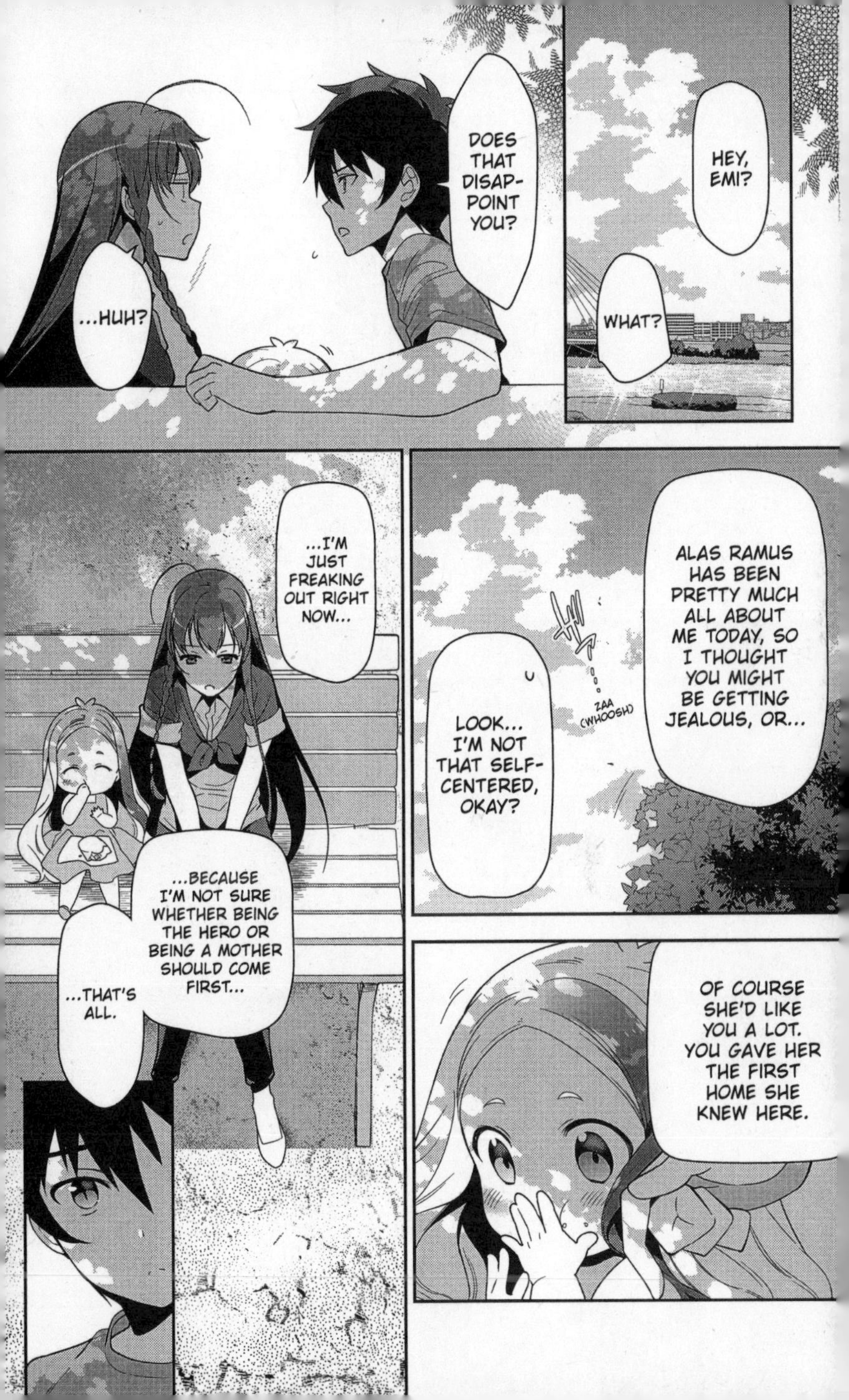
HEY, EMI?
WHAT?
DOES THAT DISAP-POINT YOU?
...HUH?
ALAS RAMUS HAS BEEN PRETTY MUCH ALL ABOUT ME TODAY, SO I THOUGHT YOU MIGHT BE GETTING JEALOUS, OR...
ZAA (WHOOSH)
LOOK... I'M NOT THAT SELF-CENTERED, OKAY?
OF COURSE SHE'D LIKE YOU A LOT. YOU GAVE HER THE FIRST HOME SHE KNEW HERE.
...I'M JUST FREAKING OUT RIGHT NOW...
...BECAUSE I'M NOT SURE WHETHER BEING THE HERO OR BEING A MOTHER SHOULD COME FIRST...
...THAT'S ALL.

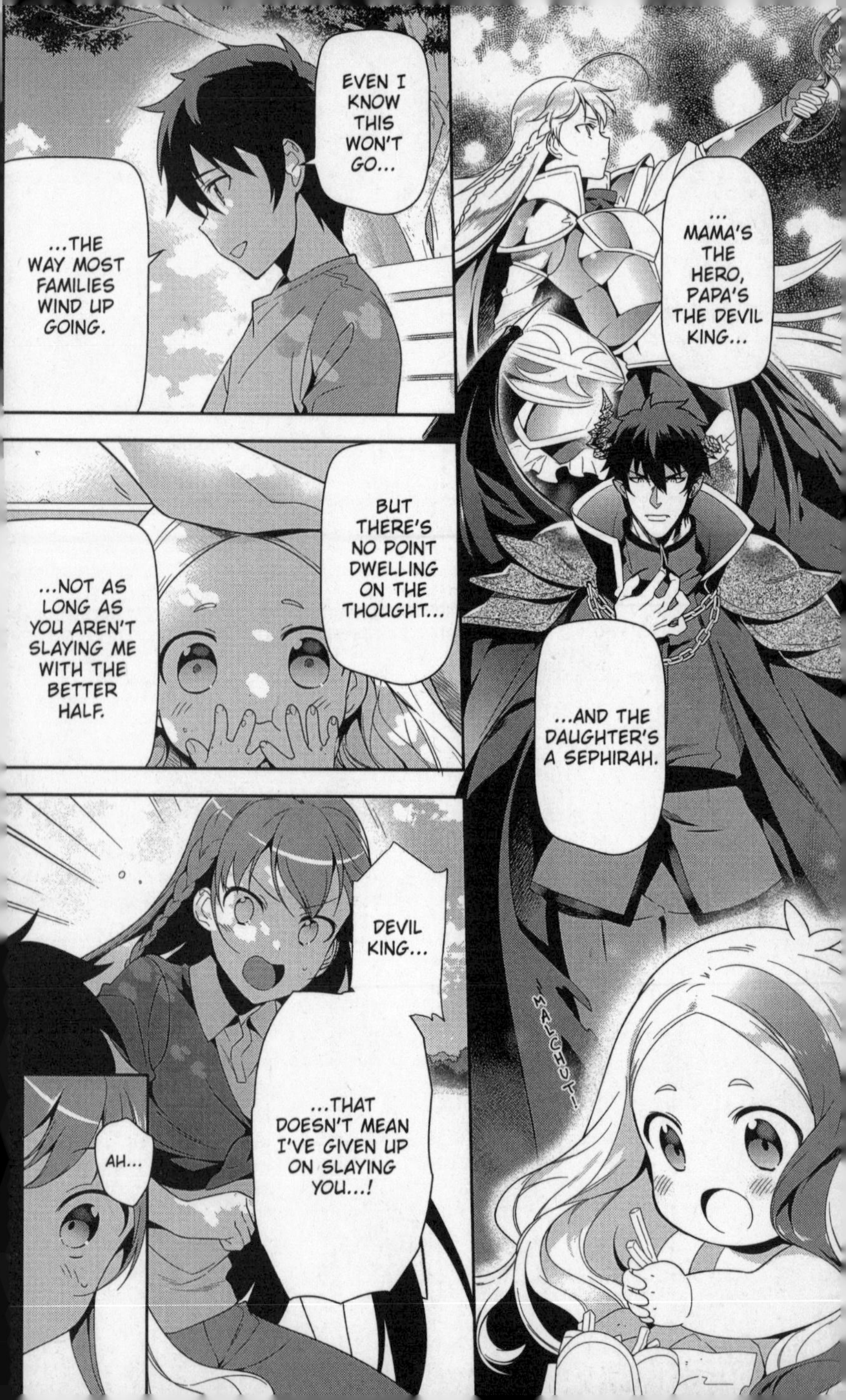
... MAMA'S THE HERO, PAPA'S THE DEVIL KING...
...AND THE DAUGHTER'S A SEPHIRAH.
MALCHUT!
EVEN I KNOW THIS WON'T GO...
...THE WAY MOST FAMILIES WIND UP GOING.
BUT THERE'S NO POINT DWELLING ON THE THOUGHT...
...NOT AS LONG AS YOU AREN'T SLAYING ME WITH THE BETTER HALF.
DEVIL KING...
...THAT DOESN'T MEAN I'VE GIVEN UP ON SLAYING YOU...!
AH...

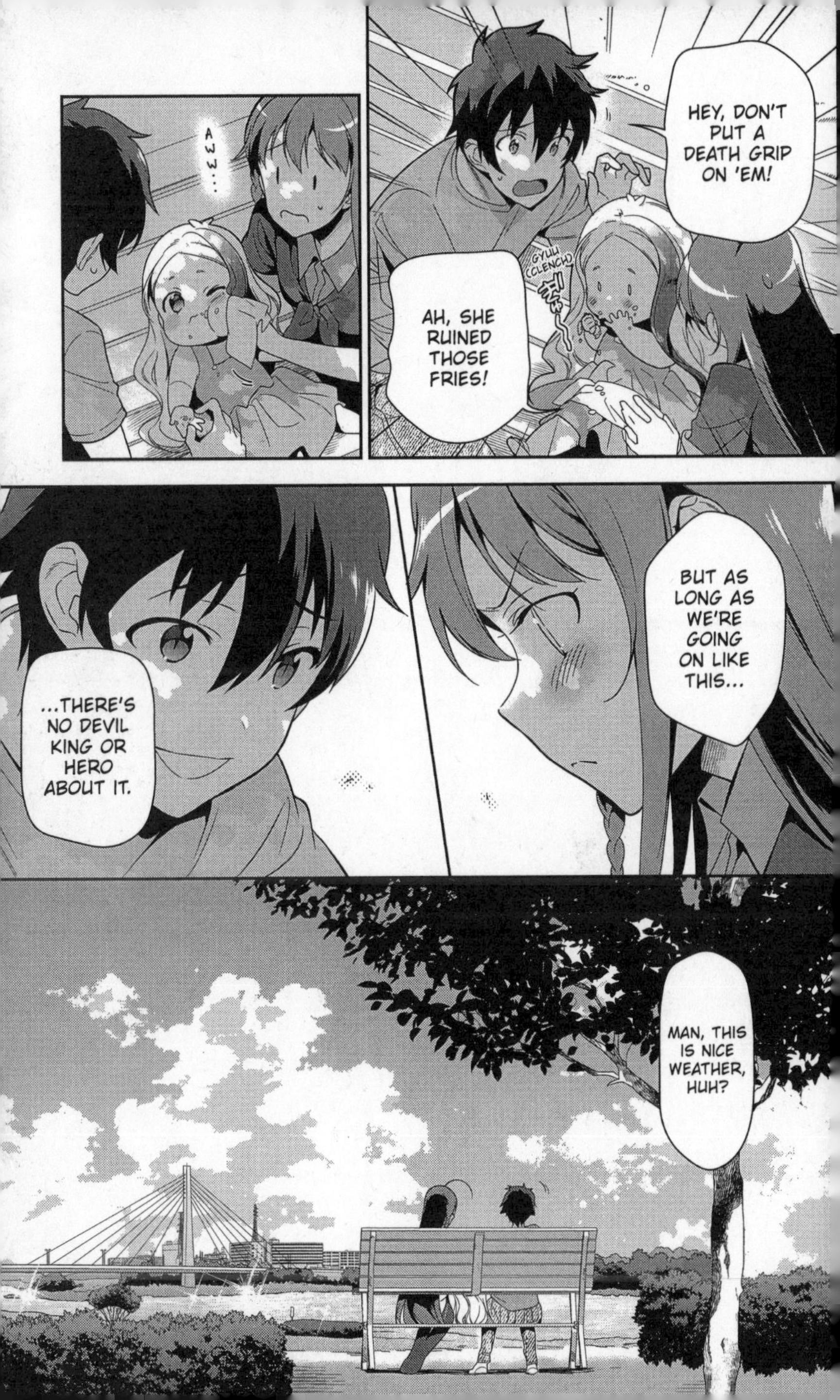
HEY, DON'T PUT A DEATH GRIP ON 'EM!
GYUU (CLENCH)
AH, SHE RUINED THOSE FRIES!
AWW...
BUT AS LONG AS WE'RE GOING ON LIKE THIS...
...THERE'S NO DEVIL KING OR HERO ABOUT IT.
MAN, THIS IS NICE WEATHER, HUH?

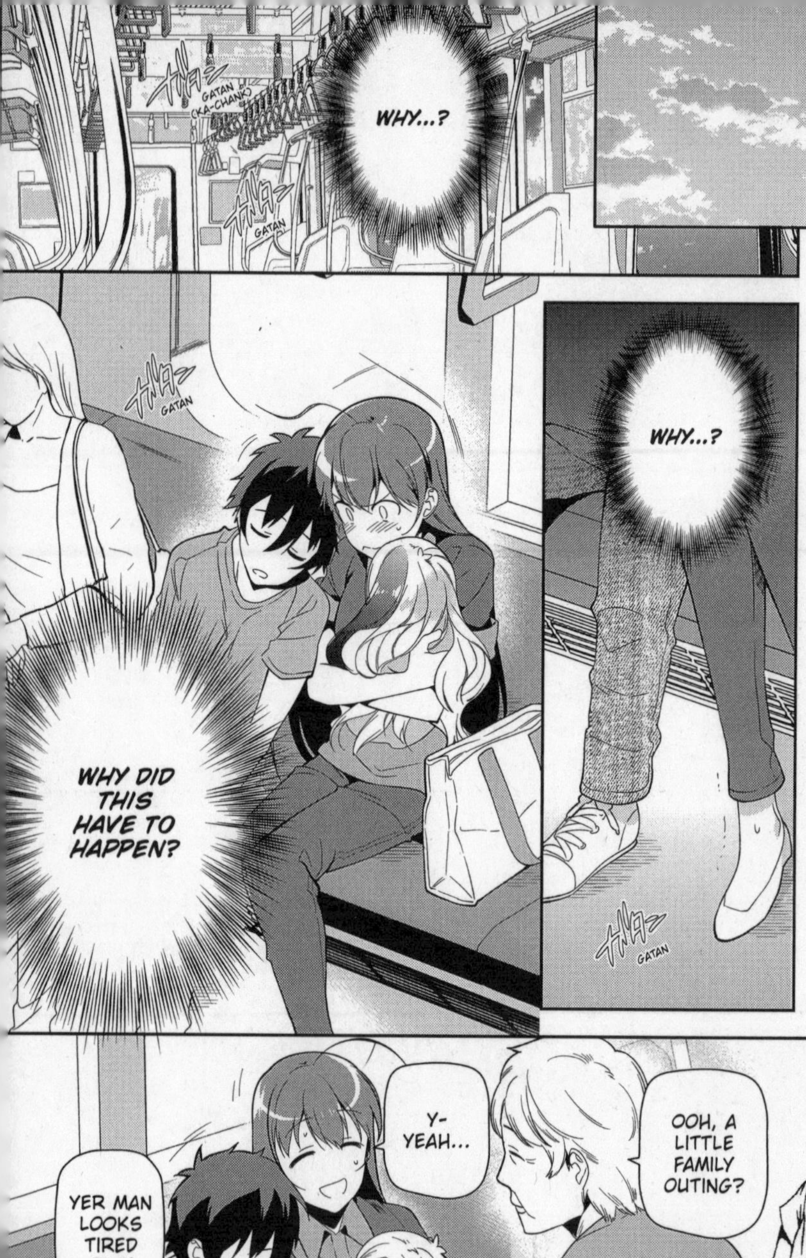
WHY...?
GATAN (KA-CHANK)
GATAN
WHY...?
GATAN
GATAN
WHY DID THIS HAVE TO HAPPEN?
OOH, A LITTLE FAMILY OUTING?
Y-YEAH...
YER MAN LOOKS TIRED OUT!

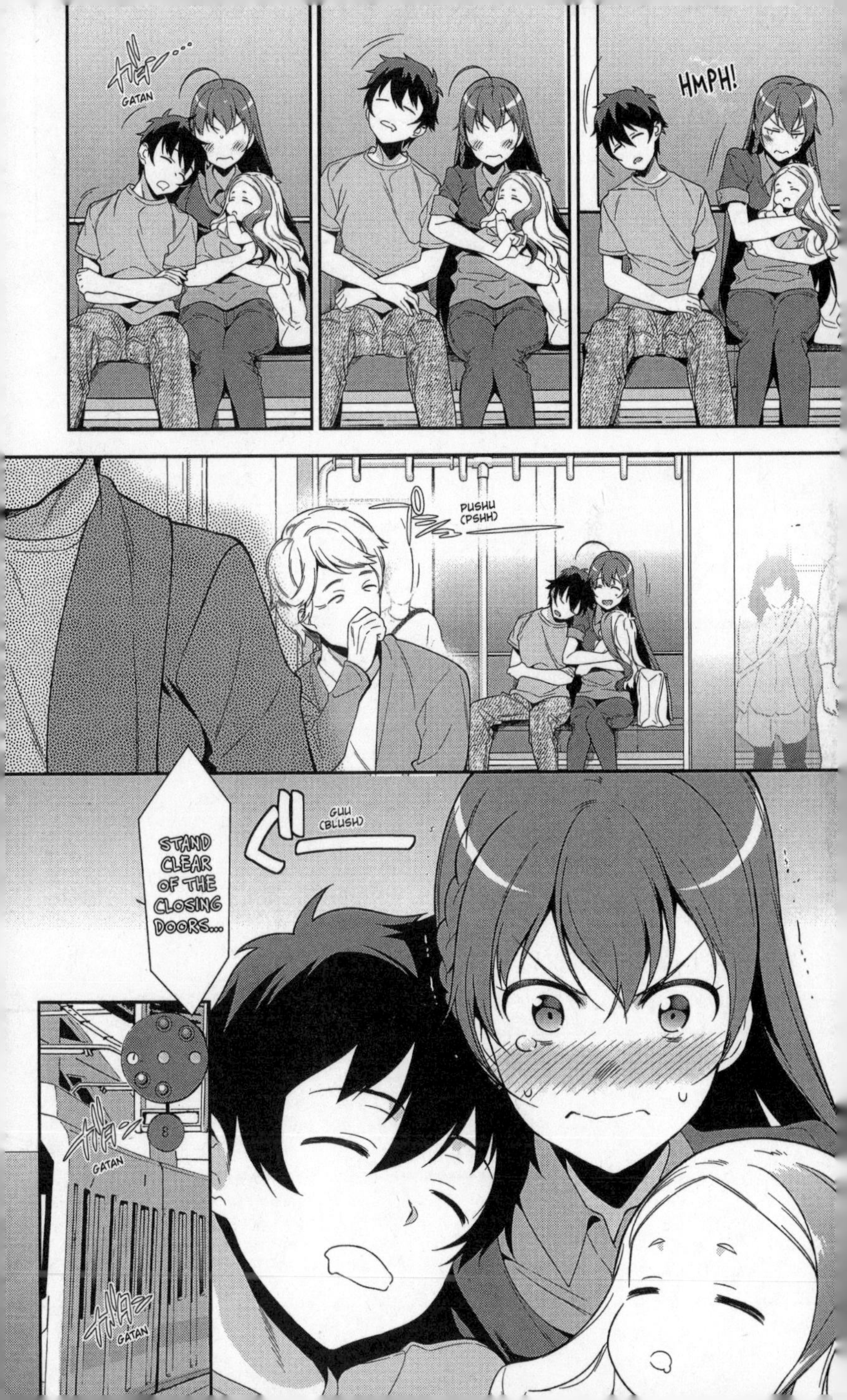
HMPH!
GATAN
PUSHU (PSHH)
GUU (BLUSH)
STAND CLEAR OF THE CLOSING DOORS...
GATAN
GATAN

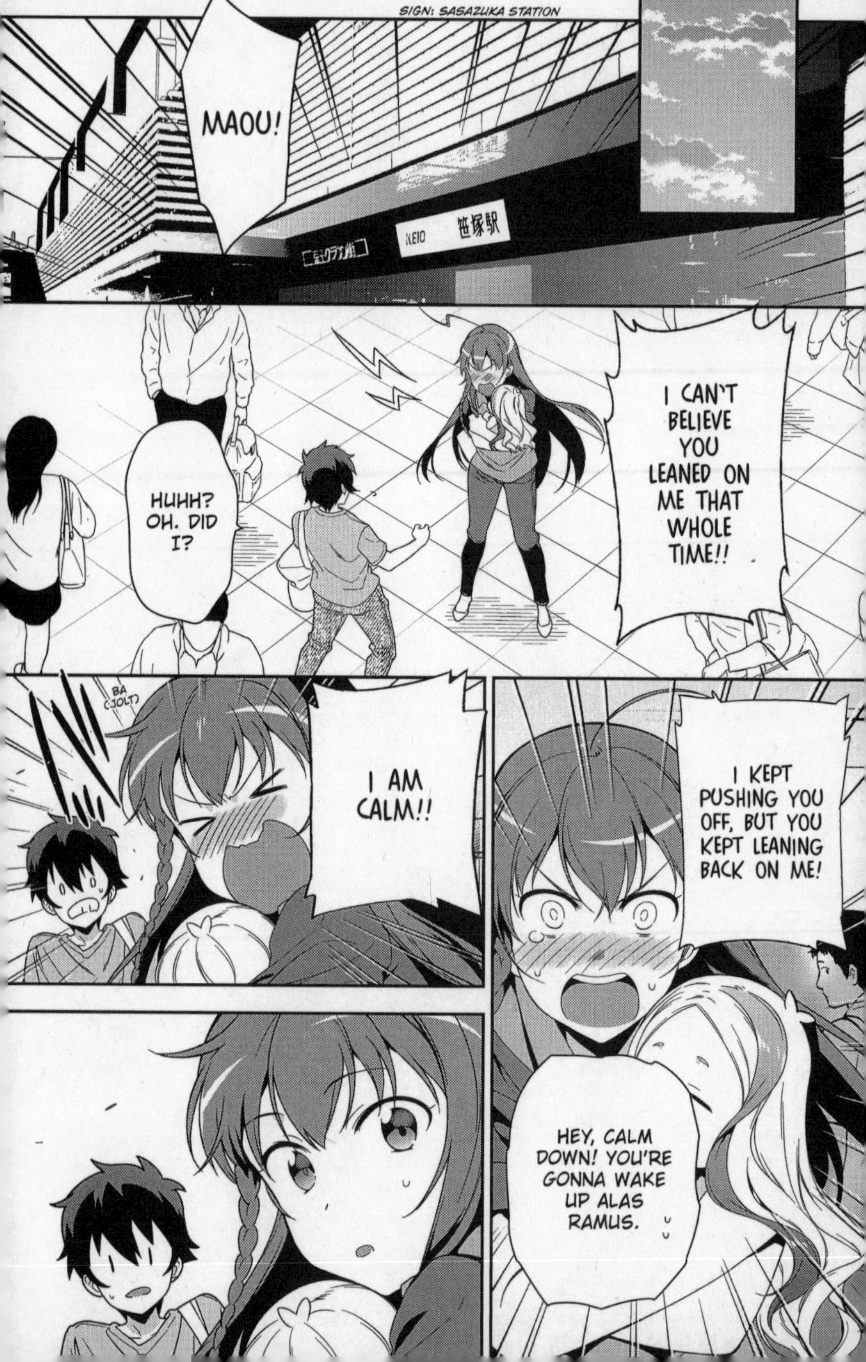
SIGN: SASAZUKA STATION
MAOU!
KEIO 笹塚駅
I CAN'T BELIEVE YOU LEANED ON ME THAT WHOLE TIME!!
HUHH? OH. DID I?
I KEPT PUSHING YOU OFF, BUT YOU KEPT LEANING BACK ON ME!
HEY, CALM DOWN! YOU'RE GONNA WAKE UP ALAS RAMUS.
BA (JOLT)
I AM CALM!!

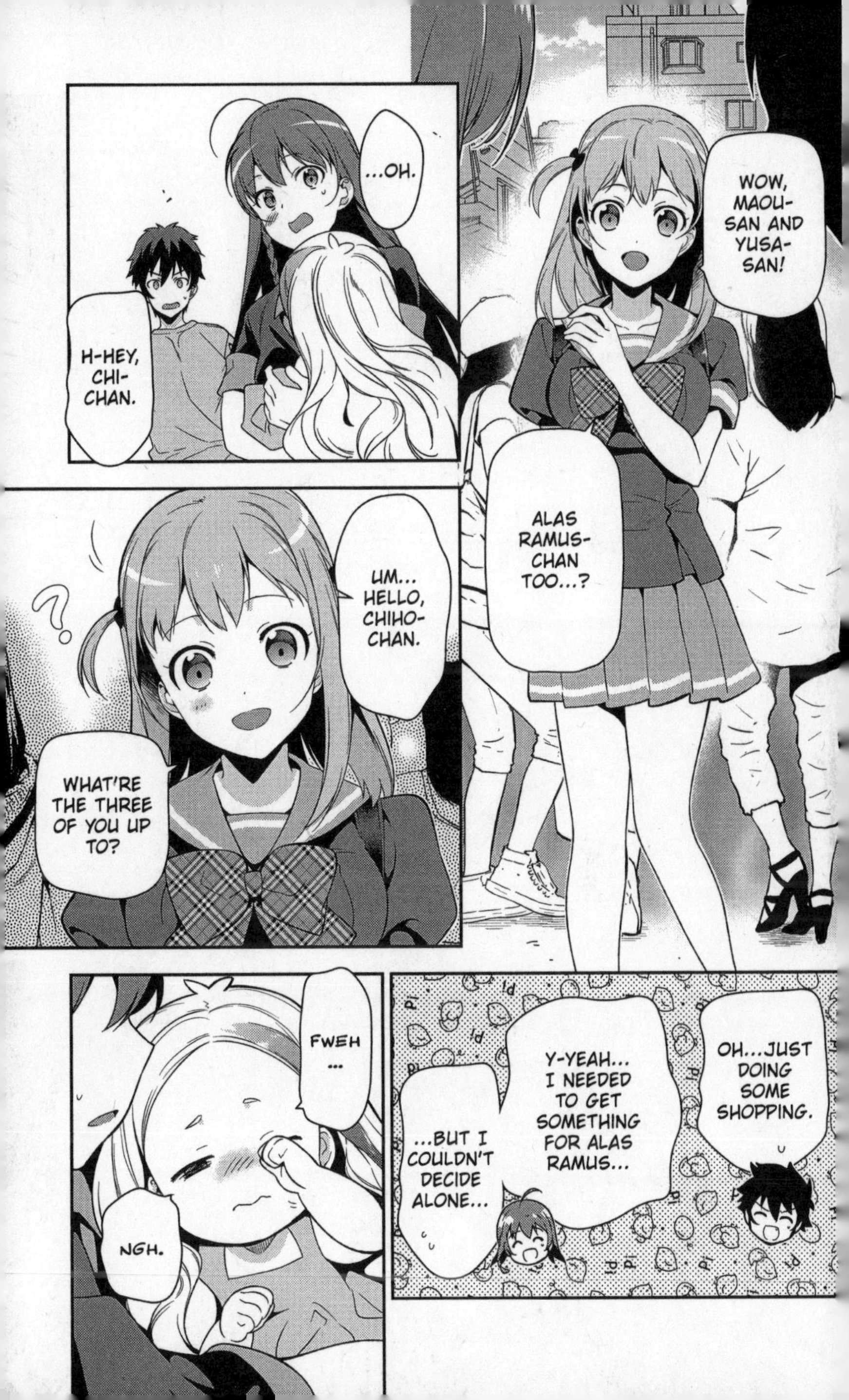
WOW, MAOU-SAN AND YUSA-SAN!
ALAS RAMUS-CHAN TOO...?
...OH.
H-HEY, CHI-CHAN.
UM... HELLO, CHIHO-CHAN.
WHAT'RE THE THREE OF YOU UP TO?
OH...JUST DOING SOME SHOPPING.
Y-YEAH... I NEEDED TO GET SOMETHING FOR ALAS RAMUS...
...BUT I COULDN'T DECIDE ALONE...
FWEH ...
NGH.

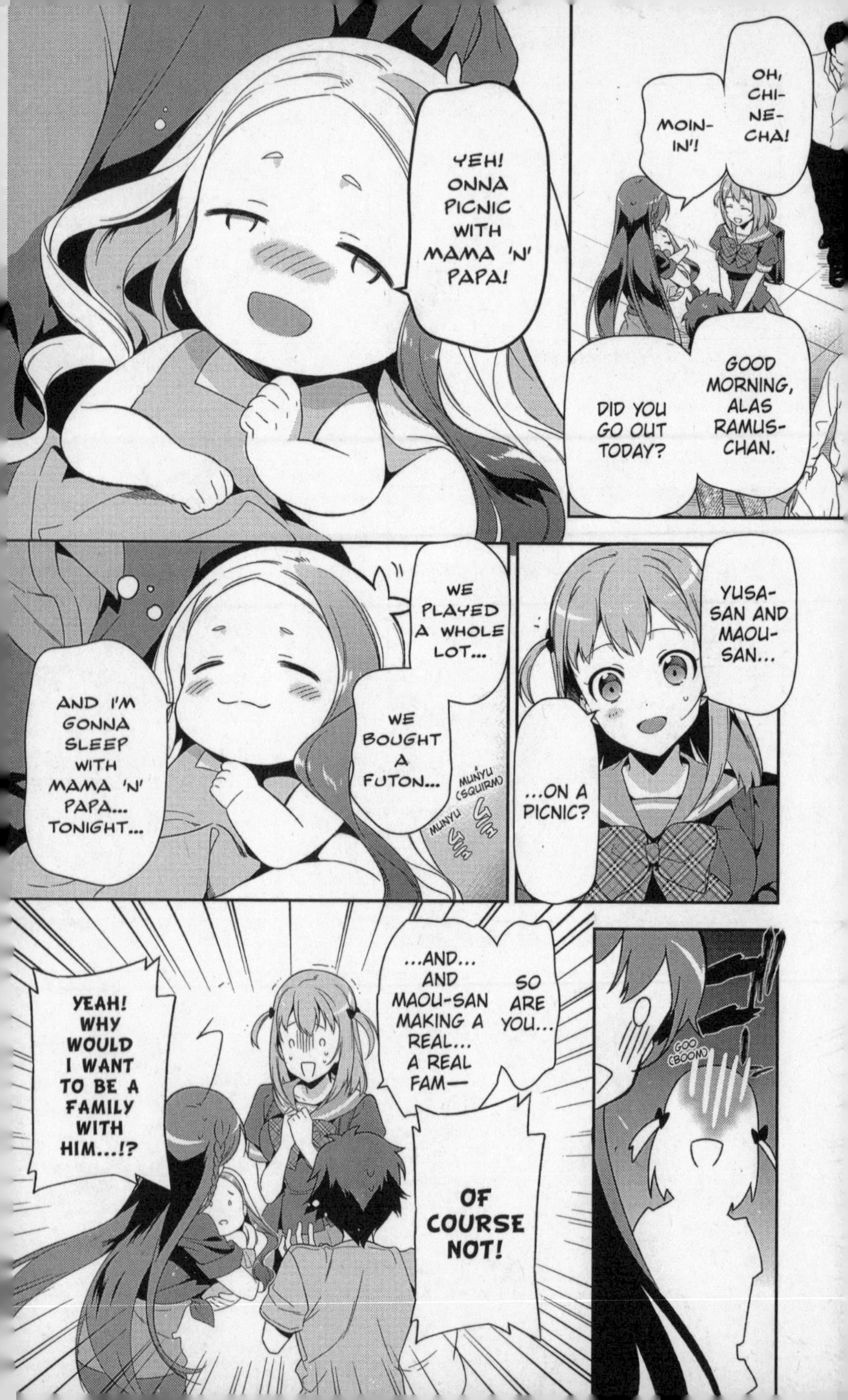
OH, CHI-NE-CHA!
MOIN-IN'!
GOOD MORNING, ALAS RAMUS-CHAN.
DID YOU GO OUT TODAY?
YEH! ONNA PICNIC WITH MAMA 'N' PAPA!
YUSA-SAN AND MAOU-SAN...
...ON A PICNIC?
WE PLAYED A WHOLE LOT...
WE BOUGHT A FUTON...
MUNYU (SQUIRM)
MUNYU
AND I'M GONNA SLEEP WITH MAMA 'N' PAPA... TONIGHT...
GOO (BOOM)
SO ARE YOU...
...AND... AND MAOU-SAN MAKING A REAL... A REAL FAM—
OF COURSE NOT!
YEAH! WHY WOULD I WANT TO BE A FAMILY WITH HIM...!?

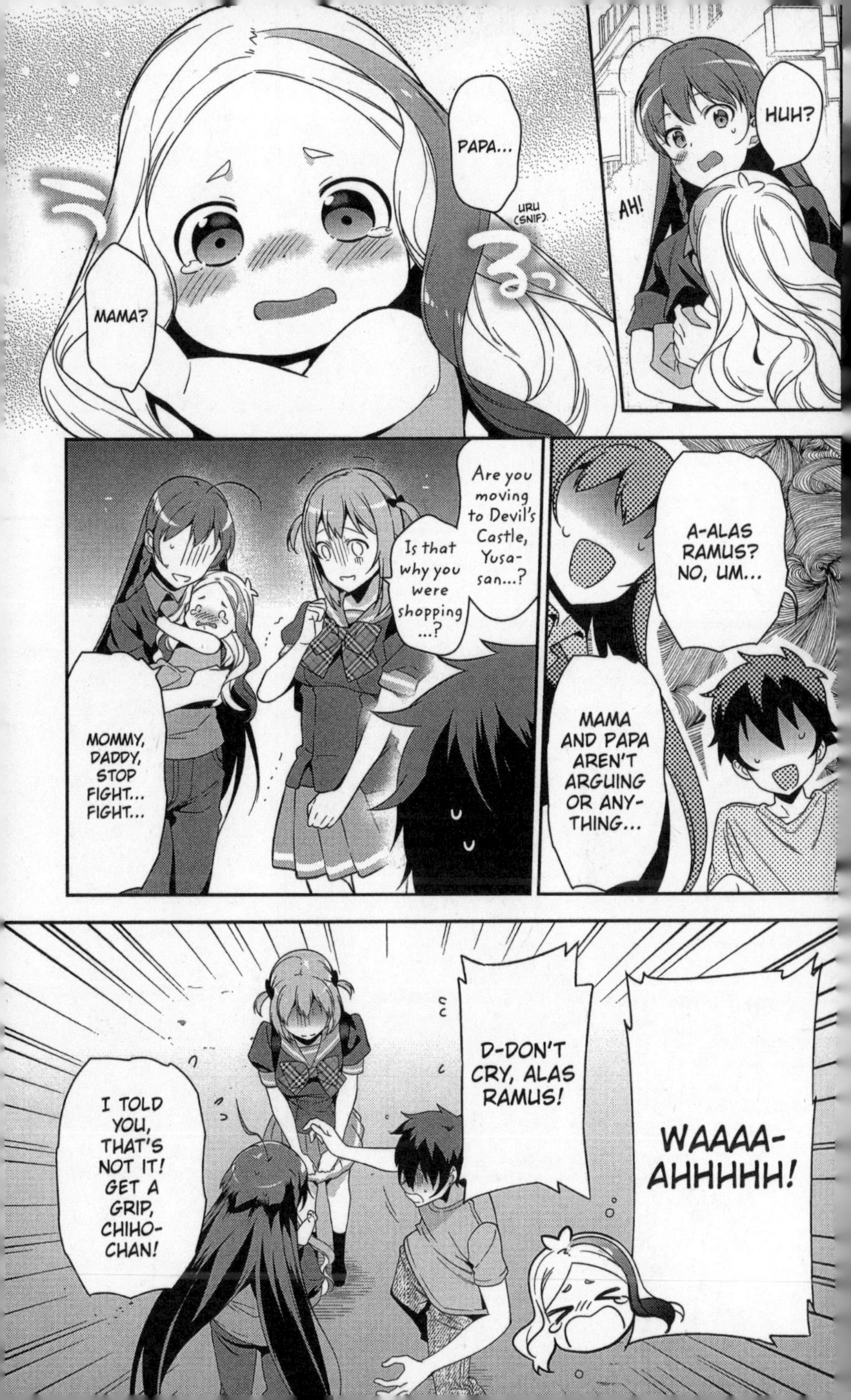
HUH?
AH!
PAPA...
URU (SNIF)
MAMA?
A-ALAS RAMUS? NO, UM...
MAMA AND PAPA AREN'T ARGUING OR ANY-THING...
Are you moving to Devil's Castle, Yusa-san...?
Is that why you were shopping ...?
MOMMY, DADDY, STOP FIGHT... FIGHT...
WAAAA-AHHHHH!
D-DON'T CRY, ALAS RAMUS!
I TOLD YOU, THAT'S NOT IT! GET A GRIP, CHIHO-CHAN!

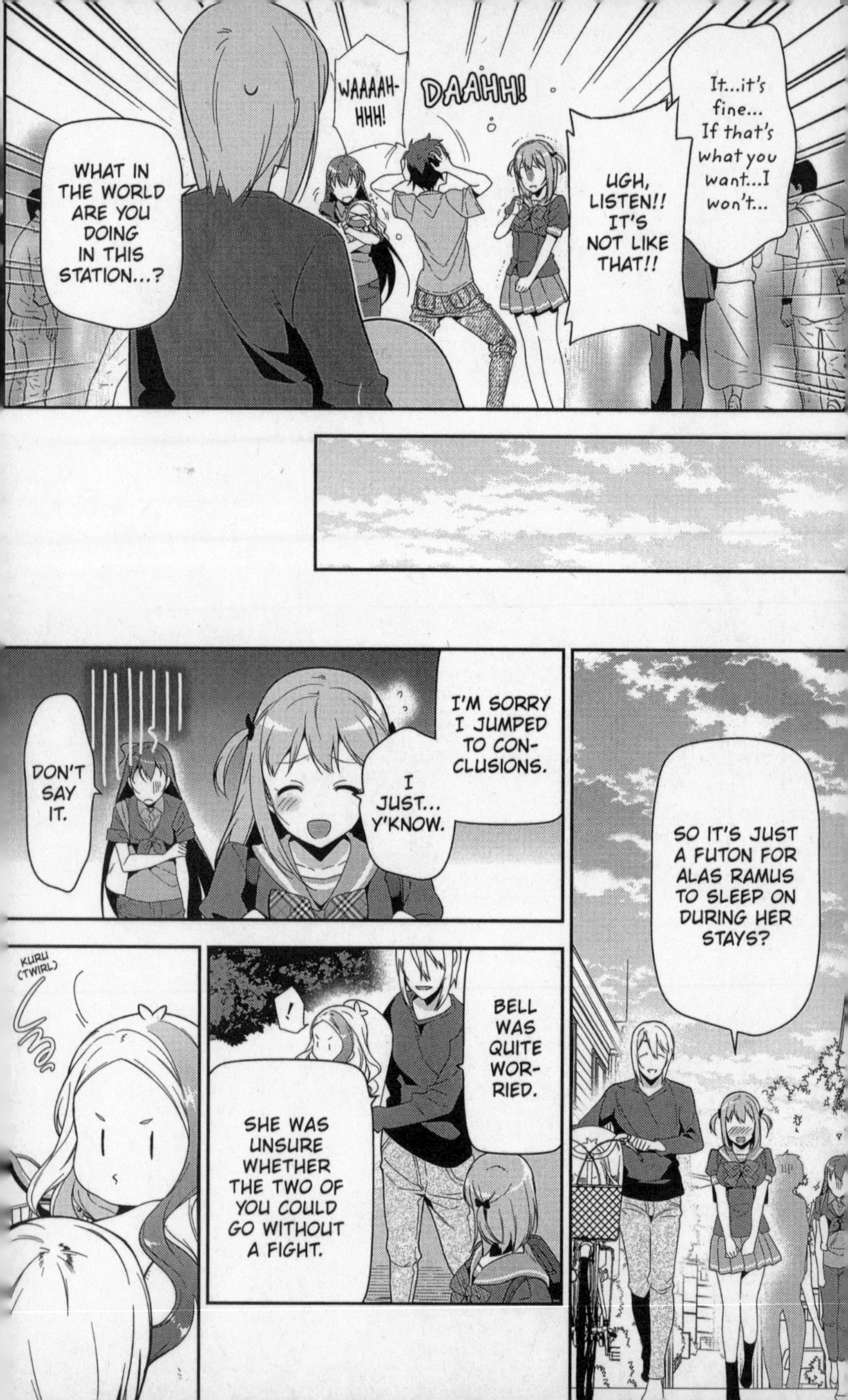
It...it's fine... If that's what you want...I won't...
UGH, LISTEN!! IT'S NOT LIKE THAT!!
DAAHH!
WAAAAH-HHH!
WHAT IN THE WORLD ARE YOU DOING IN THIS STATION...?
SO IT'S JUST A FUTON FOR ALAS RAMUS TO SLEEP ON DURING HER STAYS?
I'M SORRY I JUMPED TO CON-CLUSIONS.
I JUST... Y'KNOW.
DON'T SAY IT.
BELL WAS QUITE WOR-RIED.
!
SHE WAS UNSURE WHETHER THE TWO OF YOU COULD GO WITHOUT A FIGHT.
KURU (TWIRL)

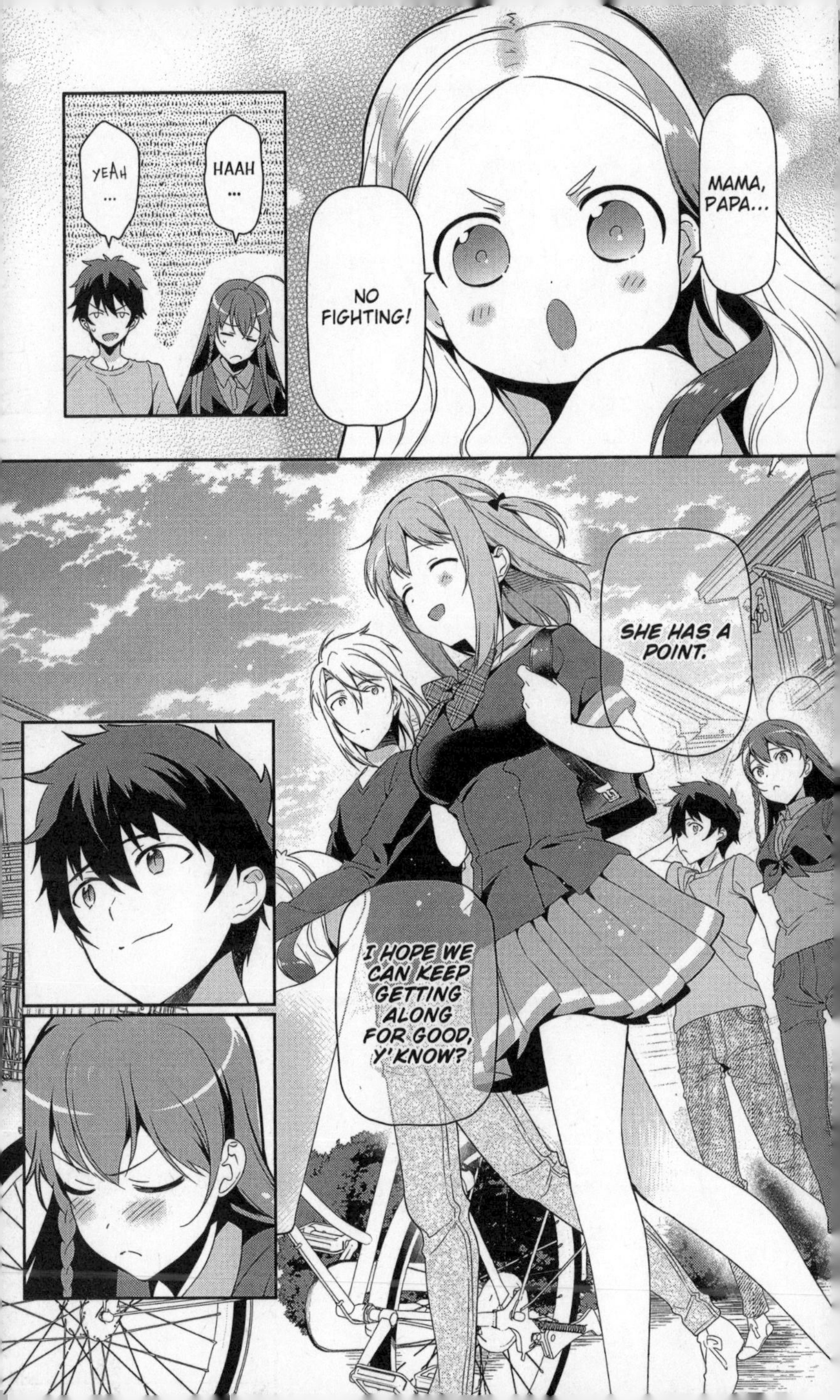
MAMA, PAPA...
NO FIGHTING!
HAAH ...
YEAH ...
SHE HAS A POINT.
I HOPE WE CAN KEEP GETTING ALONG FOR GOOD, Y'KNOW?

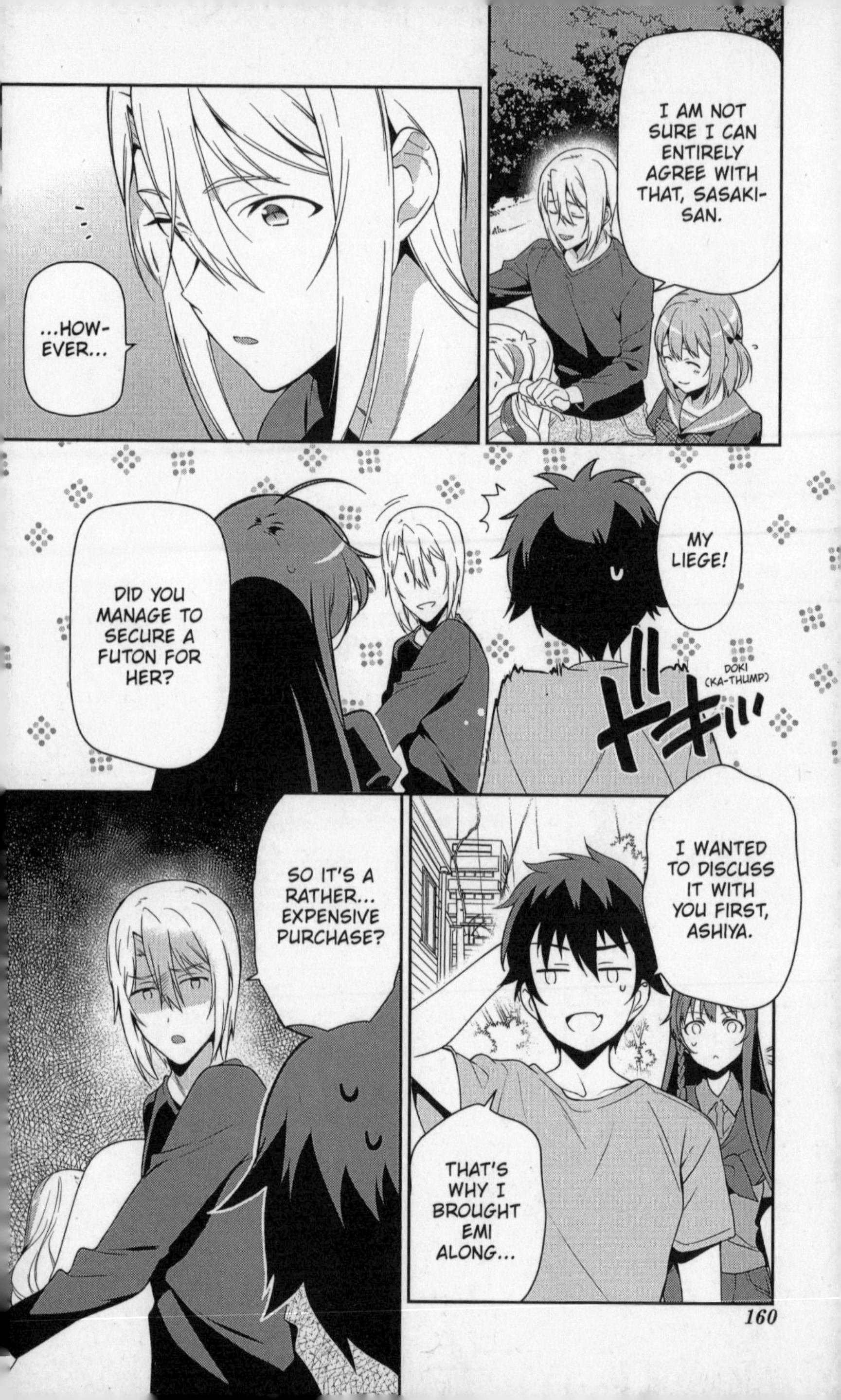

I AM NOT SURE I CAN ENTIRELY AGREE WITH THAT, SASAKI-SAN.
...HOW-EVER...
MY LIEGE!
DOKI (KA-THUMP)
DID YOU MANAGE TO SECURE A FUTON FOR HER?
I WANTED TO DISCUSS IT WITH YOU FIRST, ASHIYA.
THAT'S WHY I BROUGHT EMI ALONG...
SO IT'S A RATHER... EXPENSIVE PURCHASE?

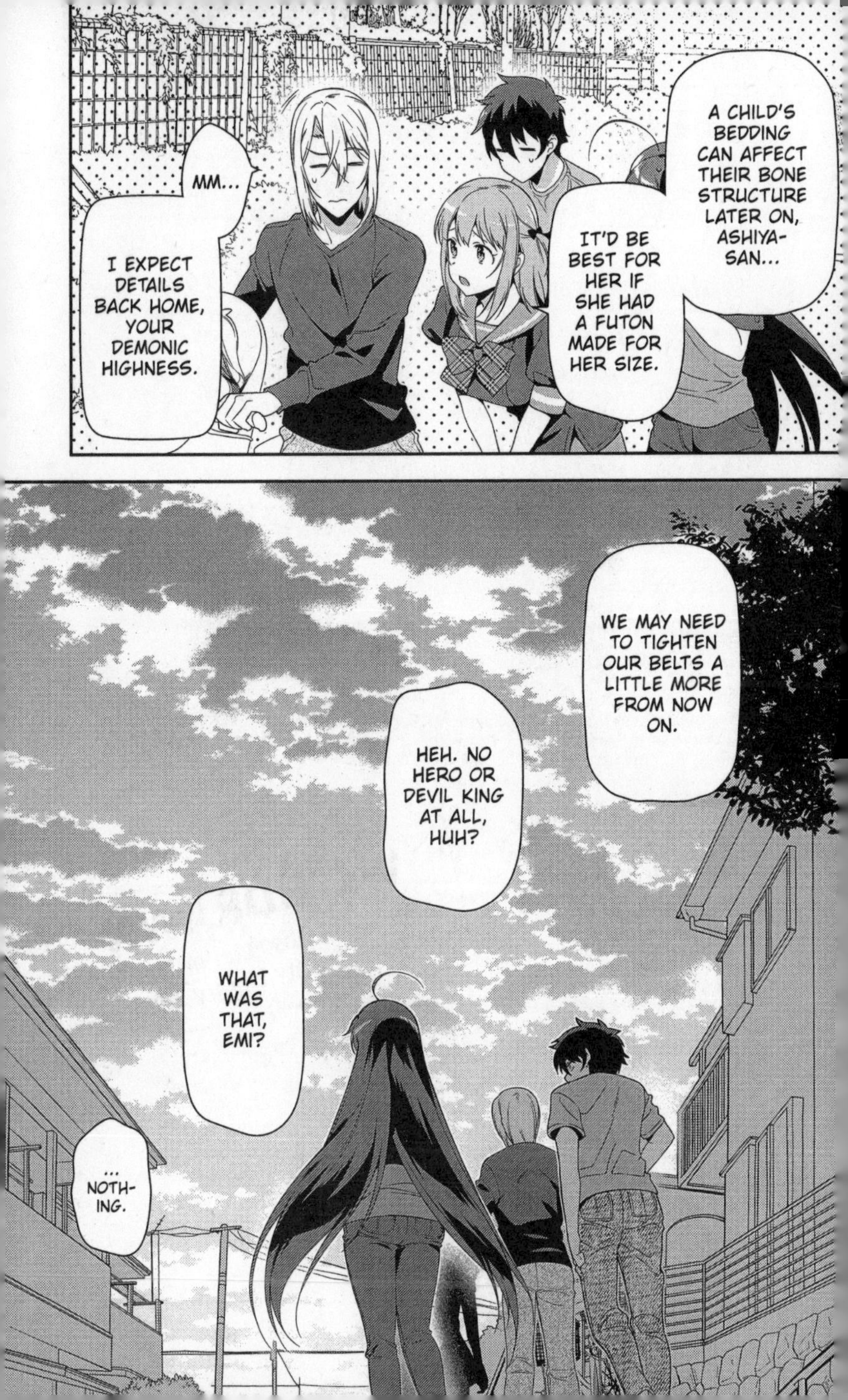
A CHILD'S BEDDING CAN AFFECT THEIR BONE STRUCTURE LATER ON, ASHIYA-SAN...
IT'D BE BEST FOR HER IF SHE HAD A FUTON MADE FOR HER SIZE.
MM...
I EXPECT DETAILS BACK HOME, YOUR DEMONIC HIGHNESS.
WE MAY NEED TO TIGHTEN OUR BELTS A LITTLE MORE FROM NOW ON.
HEH. NO HERO OR DEVIL KING AT ALL, HUH?
WHAT WAS THAT, EMI?
...NOTH-ING.

THE DEVIL IS A PART-TIMER! ⑩

ART: AKIO HIIRAGI
ORIGINAL STORY: SATOSHI WAGAHARA
CHARACTER DESIGN: 029 (ONIKU)

Translation: Kevin Gifford

Lettering: Brndn Blakeslee

HATARAKU MAOUSAMA! Vol. 10
© SATOSHI WAGAHARA / AKIO HIIRAGI 2016
Edited by ASCII MEDIA WORKS
First published in Japan in 2016 by KADOKAWA CORPORATION, Tokyo.
English translation rights arranged with KADOKAWA CORPORATION, Tokyo, through Tuttle-Mori Agency, Inc., Tokyo.

English translation © 2017 by Yen Press, LLC

Yen Press
1290 Avenue of the Americas
New York, NY 10104

Visit us at yenpress.com
facebook.com/yenpress
twitter.com/yenpress
yenpress.tumblr.com
instagram.com/yenpress

First Yen Press Edition: September 2017

Yen Press is an imprint of Yen Press, LLC.
The Yen Press name and logo are trademarks of Yen Press, LLC.

The publisher is not responsible for websites (or their content) that are not owned by the publisher.

Library of Congress Control Number: 2014504637

ISBNs: 978-0-316-56267-6 (paperback)
978-0-316-44223-7 (ebook)

10 9 8 7 6 5 4 3 2 1

BVG

Printed in the United States of America